Unjust Restitution

The publisher and the University of California Press Foundation gratefully acknowledge the generous support of the Peter Booth Wiley Endowment Fund in History.

Unjust Restitution

A CENTURY OF BLACK STRUGGLE FOR EQUALITY

Michael K. Brown

UNIVERSITY OF CALIFORNIA PRESS

University of California Press
Oakland, California

© 2025 by Michael K. Brown

Library of Congress Cataloging-in-Publication Data

Names: Brown, Michael K., author.
Title: Unjust restitution : a century of black struggle for equality / Michael K. Brown.
Description: Oakland, California : University of California Press, [2024] | Includes bibliographical references and index.
Identifiers: LCCN 2024016856 (print) | LCCN 2024016857 (ebook) | ISBN 9780520410107 (hardcover) | ISBN 9780520410114 (paperback) | ISBN 9780520410121 (ebook)
Subjects: LCSH: African Americans—Civil rights—United States. | Equality—United States—History. | Racial justice—United States—History. | United States—Race relations—History.
Classification: LCC E185.61 .B879 2024 (print) | LCC E185.61 (ebook) | DDC 323.1196/07309—dc23/eng/20240823
LC record available at https://lccn.loc.gov/2024016856
LC ebook record available at https://lccn.loc.gov/2024016857

31 32 31 30 29 28 27 26 25
10 9 8 7 6 5 4 3 2 1

CONTENTS

List of Tables and Figures vii
Preface ix

Introduction: Race, Liberalism, and Equality of Opportunity 1

1 · The Political Invention of Equality of Opportunity, 1830–1860 25

2 · "What Shall We Do with the Negro?" Race and Liberalism in the Freedmen's Bureau, 1865–1872 57

3 · Saving Sharecroppers? Black Tenant Farmers and the Southern Enclosure, 1934–1943 101

4 · Black Enclaves and the African American Quest for Land, 1880–1950 142

5 · The Revolution Stalled: The Southern War on Poverty and the Civil Rights Movement, 1964–1972 180

6 · What Does Racial Justice Require? 231

Appendix 245
Notes 253
Select Bibliography 305
Index 311

TABLES AND FIGURES

TABLES

1. Democrat and Whig conceptions of equality of opportunity in the 1830s *34*
2. Union troops and US Army outposts, May–December 1865 *71*
3. Military vs. civilian status of Freedmen's Bureau agents by state and region, 1865–72 *73*
4. Displacement of tenants in the Deep South, 1930–45 *119*
5. Percentage of tenants on single-unit farms, by State, 1945 *120*
6. FSA loans and grants, FY1935–FY1941 *127*
7. FSA loans and grants in Deep South states by county, FY1935–FY1939 *127*
8. Purpose and distribution of FSA rural rehabilitation loans, 1936–44 *133*
9. AAA crop subsidy payments to tenants and planters by agricultural region *134*
10. Southern farm owners by race and farm region typology, 1920 *154*
11. Farm value and size by farm region typology and race of owner, 1925 *161*
12. Resettlement Administration loan amounts, farm areas, and costs for Deep South projects, 1935–43 *170*
13. Summary data for Deep South Resettlement Administration projects *172*

14. Resettlement Administration farm loans, increase in farm ownership, and land values by counties with RA projects, 1935–43 *175*
15. Community action agencies (CAAs) and Black representation in Deep South states *204*
16. Total OEO expenditures in Deep South states, FY1965–FY1971 *214*
17. Comparison of federal grants in rural counties by CAA type, FY1968 *217*
18. Representation, control, and resource allocation of CAAs in Deep South states *219*
A.1. Allocation of Farm Security Administration loans and grants, FY1935–FY1939 *245*
A.2. Change in number of full farm owners by race and type of loan *246*
A.3. Per capita OEO dollars by type of CAA *247*

FIGURES

1. Deployment of Union troops in plantation regions, 1865–66 *72*
2. The tenancy color line in Deep South states, 1920–40 *112*
3. Distribution of FSA loans and grants to Black farmers *138*

PREFACE

In *Unjust Restitution*, I ask whether equality of opportunity was a viable path to racial justice for African Americans after slavery and Jim Crow, and whether it is the means to racial equality today. Equality of opportunity, a widely shared aspiration in America, has been a focal point of political conflict and argument about racial justice since the nineteenth century. African Americans and national political leaders considered it to be the touchstone for economic justice during Reconstruction, the New Deal, and the Great Society. This is hardly surprising given the broad support for the idea in the United States from the American Revolution to the present. But what exactly does equality of opportunity mean? Is it even relevant in a society that still treats every Black child as a potential criminal and tolerates a maternal death rate for Black women that is three times higher than for any other group of women? To many, equality of opportunity connotes a color-blind society, and any policy that takes race into account is seen as unconstitutional and unjust. For others, the reality of deeply embedded racial inequality continues to haunt America sixty years after the civil rights revolution and requires restitution and the provision of genuine opportunities.

My premise in this book is that Americans' contemporary understanding of the concept of equality of opportunity is discordant with the realities of durable racial inequality and needs to be revised. The idea of systemic or structural racism is often construed as either an empty ideological slogan or a discredited theory. Yet structural racism is neither an ideological trope for racial inequality nor an empirically weak idea. This book has grown out of my research on the question of racial inequality over the last thirty-five years. The predicate for this book is the research and writing I and my six coauthors did in *Whitewashing Race: The Myth of a Color-Blind Society*. We developed a conception of structural racism based on the idea of racial accumulation and disaccumulation, and supplied the evidence for it. We concluded that individual choice in the form of intentional racism had little to do with the persistence of racial inequality. *Unjust Restitution* is my effort to reconcile the widespread support for equality of opportunity with the deeply embedded structural racism of today.

We can unravel the meaning and implications of equality of opportunity only by examining how it has been understood and used in the past, examining the policies and practices African Americans, politicians, and reformers thought were necessary to achieve meaningful equality of opportunity. I begin my argument and analysis in the 1830s, when the idea divided Andrew Jackson's Democrats and Daniel Webster's Whigs. The Democrats' vision of equality of opportunity was based on the idea of *antiprivilege egalitarianism*. This is, I admit, an ungainly phrase, but it deftly captures what they were up to. Jacksonian Democrats believed inequality stemmed from unjust political and legal privileges, such as monopoly charters given to private firms, and that equality of opportunity could be achieved only by abolishing them. It was a question of using political power to open opportunities for citizens.

The Whigs invented the canonical idea of equality of opportunity. This is the doctrine that citizens have equal rights to develop their talents and capacities as far as they can and reap the rewards for their efforts based on their performance. For the Whigs, equality of opportunity entailed equipping individuals with the skills and capacities to move up the ladder of success. To open opportunities for formerly subjugated individuals, Whigs devised policies to rehabilitate them by developing their capacities for economic self-sufficiency and discipline and their mastery of the skills necessary for political and civic participation.

These rival conceptions formed the basis for conflict over racial justice during the periods of Reconstruction, the New Deal, and the Great Society. Political leaders from the 1860s through the twentieth century believed slavery and Jim Crow degraded Black people, and they created policies to rehabilitate them. African Americans challenged these policies, asserting claims to economic autonomy and restitution. Blacks' vision of economic justice was based on the idea that a just restitution for their oppression required abolishing the political and legal privileges used by whites and creating viable economic opportunities. To this demand, Black people added claims to education and other elements of equality of opportunity.

We have a lot to learn from African Americans' conception of equality of opportunity. Black abolitionists, freed people, Black landowners and tenants, and civil rights activists in the Deep South had their own ideas of what would secure their future aspirations. African Americans did not always agree about what was needed to secure their future, but there is a historical continuity that is important to understand. The voices of Henry Highland Garnet, the editors of the *Colored American* (a Black abolitionist newspaper), Frederick Douglass, Martin Delany, Tunis Campbell, Isaiah Montgomery, Nate Shaw, the Black tenants who joined the Southern Tenant Farmers Union, Stokely Carmichael, Thelma Barnes and the Black women who created the Child Development Group of Mississippi, A. Philip Randolph, and Martin Luther King Jr., among many others, are vital to the long argument over a just restitution for the oppression of African Americans.

I could not have written this book but for my participation in the collective research and writing that culminated in *Whitewashing Race*. The two years I spent in a seminar room at the University of California, Berkeley, absorbing the knowledge and insights of David Wellman, Troy Duster, Elliott Currie, Martin Carnoy, Marjorie M. Shultz, and David B. Oppenheimer was one of the truly memorable experiences of my academic career. David Wellman always thought that the innumerable trips I made from Santa Cruz to Berkeley were a burden for me. I appreciated his concern, but it was a very small price to pay for the education and intellectual stimulation I received. My one regret is that David, a dear friend, colleague, and collaborator for forty years, passed away before I finished. He would no doubt have had many criticisms that would have improved the book. I miss David's fierce fight for racial justice, his insights, and his friendship.

I first presented some of these ideas to the Workshop on American Political Development at Ohio University, Athens, on May 20 and 21, 2011. I thank the participants, in particular Kimberly Johnson, Desmond King, Naomi Murakowa, Julie Novkov, Gretchen Ritter, and Rogers Smith for their helpful and critical suggestions.

I am indebted to both the readers Niels Hooper, my editor, recruited to read my manuscript. They gave me detailed suggestions for revisions and alerted me to some omissions. In particular, Kimberly Johnson honored me with her deep insights and critical perspectives on the manuscript that led to crucial revisions. I cannot thank her enough for her contribution to this book.

A number of colleagues read all or part of my manuscript and helped make it better. Richard Bensel contributed interesting and useful comments about my account of Reconstruction. Eva Bertram and Dan Wirls, colleagues in the Politics Department at the University of California, Santa Cruz, gave the entire manuscript a close reading. Julie Novkov has been a steady source of support, inspiration, and vital suggestions from the beginning. Peter Agree, who gave the manuscript a careful and thorough reading, was of enormous help. He offered critical suggestions, sage advice, and gave me confidence in what I had written. Paul Frymer contributed critical and critically important comments and suggestions from the very beginning. He was always there, and he was always willing to give me the benefit of his insights and knowledge. And more than once he rescued me from sloppy writing, wrong turns, misguided conceptions, and a lot else. My friend and colleague Wendy Sarvasy was a source of incisive questions and support through the many years I worked on this book.

The UCSC Committee on Research provided a timely grant that enabled me to complete the statistical work of this project. Hamidreza Habibi helped me refine the statistical models that are part of this research. Niels Hooper and Nora Becker of the University of California Press provided the necessary guidance and help I needed to bring *Unjust Restitution* to publication.

Portions of the introduction are drawn from my article "Race and Equality of Opportunity in American Political Development," in *Politics, Groups, and Identities*, 1, no. (2013): 232–36, reprinted by permission.

Michael K. Brown
San Francisco

Introduction

RACE, LIBERALISM, AND EQUALITY OF OPPORTUNITY

> Negroes have proceeded from a premise that equality means what it says and have taken white Americans at their word when they talked of it as an objective. But most whites in America in 1967, including many persons of good will, proceed from a premise that equality is a loose expression for improvement.
>
> MARTIN LUTHER KING JR., *Where Do We Go from Here?*

IN HIS LAST BOOK, *Where Do We Go from Here?*, written under enormous pressure and at a moment of profound disillusionment, Martin Luther King Jr. asked, "Why is equality so assiduously avoided? Why does white America delude itself, and how does it rationalize the evil it retains?" King believed the struggle to overturn Jim Crow had proved less difficult than the quest for "genuine equality;" white outrage toward Bull Connor (the segregationist commissioner of public safety in Birmingham, Alabama) or the murder of four Black girls attending church services evaporated when anything other than symbolic equality was at stake. White Americans simply refused to pay the price to overturn racial inequality, King wrote, a price that was not just monetary but required the overturning of an "ontological affirmation ... that the very being of a people is inferior." King may have been disillusioned, but he was not surprised that a virulent white backlash to Blacks' demand for equality and to "basic constitutional rights and God-given rights for Negroes" had emerged in the wake of the passage of the civil rights and voting rights laws. White backlash had been going on for over three hundred years.[1]

Today, America is at another crossroads. The murder of George Floyd in May 2020 provoked widespread outrage and massive protests across the country, led by the Black Lives Matter movement. They succeeded, for the first time, in persuading many white people of the idea that durable racial inequality is grounded in structural racism rather than individual racial prejudice and the cultural pathologies of low-income Black Americans. Many people took this idea as a call to action and proclaimed that the time had come for an attack on racial injustices.[2] Yet more than four years after Floyd's murder, the country is embroiled in disputes over the teaching of critical race theory and any suggestion that legacies of slavery and Jim Crow persist. Police reforms to reduce violence against Blacks have been stalled, and the Supreme Court recently declared that the use of race as a criterion in college admissions is unconstitutional. The court seems intent on reading any mention of race out of the Constitution. The Biden administration's modest attempt to compensate Black farmers for historical discrimination was struck down by two different federal judges on the grounds that the policy amounted to reverse discrimination. The government, one of the judges wrote, must "heed its obligation to do away with governmentally imposed discrimination based on race."[3]

Americans think of themselves as a nation that eschews group identities in favor of universal beliefs, defined as individual liberty, equality before the law, and limited government—the principles enshrined in the Declaration of Independence and the Constitution. Yet Americans have lived with an extreme contradiction for most of their history by being dedicated not only to political equality but also to its complete rejection. A long time ago Judith Shklar asked what explained the history of political and economic exclusion of Blacks, Latinos, and Asian Americans in a nation ostensibly dedicated to equality and fairness.[4] Shklar's question has prompted many different answers; indeed, historians and social scientists have long been preoccupied with the history of racial and gender exclusion, and rightly so.[5]

Martin Luther King's reflections prompt another question: what do racial equality and freedom come to mean after the liberation of a subjugated people? The history of African American demands for inclusion and opposition to white supremacy is often framed as a succession of political coalitions fighting for racial equality against coalitions striving to sustain white privileges and racial hierarchies. This story, as Dr. King suggested, is incomplete, if not misleading. It assumes a shared understanding between Black and white advocates of racial equality of what a racially equal society might look like. But this is exactly what we cannot assume. Racial conflict is not only at the center of the question of whether to redeem the promise of the Declaration of

Independence: it is also at the center of how to redeem that promise. There is no unitary tradition or conception of liberal equality and equality of opportunity that both Blacks and whites accept—notwithstanding Jennifer Hochschild's argument that "Black and white Americans occupy the same moral domain when they think about the American Dream as an ethical imperative." Dr. King was explicit about the divide between Blacks and whites. "There is not even a common language when the term 'equality' is used," he wrote. "Negro and white have a fundamentally different definition."[6]

Instead of a singular antiracist political ideology, multiple overlapping cultural and ideological precepts structure the content and meaning of national political agendas for racial equality. And these agendas are always politically contested. What did freedom require after the end of slavery? Was it merely the opposite of slavery? Many abolitionists and Republicans advocated civil rights, equality before the law, and eventually voting rights, but they believed the freed people were on their own. James McPherson called these beliefs "egalitarian laissez-faire." Horace Greeley, editor of the *New-York Tribune*, wrote that the now-freed slaves needed to "root, hog, or die." "Give everyone a chance," Greeley editorialized, "and let his behavior control his fate. If negroes will not work, they must starve or steal; and if they steal, they must be shut up like other thieves." Speaking for many Republicans and abolitionists, Senator Charles Sumner of Massachusetts advocated guardianship, believing "the curse of slavery is still upon [the freedmen]. Somebody must take them by the hand; not to support them but simply to help them to that work which will support them." The freed people, reveling in their new freedoms, had other ideas. They demanded land as restitution for their unrequited labor and asserted their "divine right to land," because, in the words of Bayley Wyat, a Virginia freedman, "Our wives, our children, our husbands, has been sold over and over again to purchase the lands we now locate upon."[7]

Does the aftermath of Jim Crow require color-blind policies and laws, or a regime of restitution and compensation? What would constitute a just restitution? Many people believed that the civil rights and voting rights laws enacted in the 1960s ushered in opportunities for Black Americans to chart their own paths in an integrated society. Many whites understand integration, usually taken to be the chief end of civil rights struggles, as only the dismantling of legal segregation, the prohibition of racial discrimination, and the advent of a color-blind society. Yet the enduring existence, in both Northern cities and the rural South, of racially segregated "opportunity deserts"—"places of tremendous hardship, joblessness, and ... permanent marginalization [that] lack the resources and give those who live there a chance to reach beyond their current lives"—calls into question this limited understanding of the goals of the civil rights movement.[8] Robert L. Carter, who argued *Brown v. Board of Education* alongside Thurgood Marshall, recalled, "It was not until Brown I was decided that Blacks were able to understand that the fundamental vice was not legally enforced *racial segregation* itself; [it] was a mere by-product, a symptom of the greater and more pernicious disease—white supremacy." Today many Blacks not only reject a color-blind conception of freedom and equality but consider the meliorative policies of the last sixty years inadequate to undo the legacy of slavery and Jim Crow. They favor a liberalism predicated on what Michael Dawson refers to as the "moral autonomy of free black communities" and a radical egalitarianism that is state centered, preferring a redistributive welfare state but emphasizing the mutual obligations all citizens, Black and white, have to one another.[9]

If anything, Dr. King's pointed question is more salient today. The political and legal rights gained in the civil rights era are threatened, but so far most remain intact. The question of economic justice for Black Americans remains open and the subject of bitter conflict and competing conceptions. While the Supreme Court has overturned the use of race as a criterion in college and university admissions, there are vigorous debates over reparations for slavery. It is not enough to oppose conservatives and white racists who would roll back the gains of the 1960s. We should ask, What constitutes economic justice for Blacks in the twenty-first century? Today deeply embedded racial inequality does not stem from individual racial prejudice; nor is it a consequence of a dysfunctional Black culture, as all too many whites believe. It is the consequence of a long history of discrimination and exclusion.[10]

A rich contemporary literature addresses the question of racial justice, encompassing theoretical studies, justifications for reparations, and policy proposals.[11] I approach the question of racial justice by asking how Dr. King's question has been answered in the past, at those historical junctures when it mattered. Desmond King and Rogers Smith address this question by describing the history of racial policy alliances of social movements, interest group organizations, political parties, and public officials who were "united by their agreement on how the central racial policy issues of their eras—slavery, segregation, race conscious policymaking—should be resolved."[12] This is an inadequate approach to unraveling how freedom and equality were understood after the two Reconstructions. The differences between the freedmen and Republicans in the 1860s, or civil rights activists and Great Society liberals in the 1960s, were not just about specific policies but about what freedom, equality and economic justice required. My alternative approach examines these rival conceptions of economic justice and the ways those conceptions were translated into public policies.

In *Unjust Restitution*, I investigate the politics of inclusion and economic justice for African Americans during Reconstruction, the New Deal, and the Great Society. These were unique periods of conflict and innovation when significant change appeared to be a real possibility to Blacks, their white allies, and their white opponents. It is only by focusing on political conflict over racial justice at pivotal moments like these that we can decipher the underlying conceptions of equality and equality of opportunity that quotidian political conflict obscures. Historically, political leaders and reformers have answered Dr. King's question by assuming that equal protection under the laws and voting rights, coupled with equality of economic opportunity, would rectify America's tortured history of racial oppression and discrimination, providing the necessary economic foundation for the transition to freedom and independence and restitution for the brutal legacies of slavery and Jim Crow. But what exactly did their commitment to equality of opportunity entail? And what did African Americans think was a just restitution for their exploitation?

RACIAL JUSTICE IN HISTORICAL PERSPECTIVE

Both Abraham Lincoln and Lyndon B. Johnson put equality of opportunity at the center of their visions for the aftermath of slavery and Jim Crow. Lincoln justified the Civil War explicitly as a fight to preserve equality of opportunity, a war to maintain a government "whose leading object is, to elevate the condition of men—to lift artificial weights from all soldiers—to clear paths of laudable pursuit for all—to afford all, an unfettered start, and a fair chance, in the race of life." He appealed to this justification throughout the Civil War, notably when he addressed Union soldiers about to depart for the battlefront: they were fighting, Lincoln told the 166th Ohio Regiment, so that "you may all have equal privileges in the race of life, with all its desirable human aspirations. It is for this the struggle should be maintained."[13]

Lincoln believed equality of opportunity was part of the liberty enshrined in the Declaration of Independence, and he denied that America was a nation riven by conflict between labor and capital or based on the idea that the "free hired laborer [is] fixed to that condition for life." And despite his well-known racism, Lincoln did say Blacks were entitled to civil rights, the fruits of their labor, and equality of opportunity, even though one could construe his reflections on the war and equality of opportunity as a manifesto for the rights of free white labor. In a March 1860 speech, Lincoln said, "I want every man to have the chance—and I believe a black man is entitled to it—in which he can better his condition—when he may look forward and hope to be a hired laborer this year and the next, work for himself afterward, and finally hire men to work for him!" Yet Lincoln, like most Republicans, drew the line at social equality, and he was ambivalent if not evasive about voting rights.[14]

Like Lincoln, Lyndon B. Johnson believed that equality of opportunity is "the bedrock ideal of our society and of our system." The freedoms established by the 1964 Civil Rights Act and the 1965 Voting Rights Act were fundamental to racial equality, but "the plight of the Negro American can never be solved just by laws alone," Johnson told a White House conference. The legal freedoms from segregation and discrimination established by the new laws were not enough, Johnson proclaimed in his 1965 Howard University speech. "You do not wipe away the scars of centuries by saying: now you are free to go where you want," he passionately declared. "You do not take a person who for years has been hobbled by chains and liberate him . . . and then say, 'You are free to compete with all the others.'" True opportunity necessitated more than opening the "gates of opportunity. All our citizens must have the ability to walk through those gates." In the best-known part of that speech, Johnson called for "not just equality as a right and a theory but equality as a fact and equality as a result." Although many conservatives believe that Johnson's speech exceeded what equality of opportunity demands, he did not offer African Americans a modern version of forty acres and a mule; instead, the path out of exploitation and oppression was education, job training, and a plea to confront the "collapse" of the Black family.[15]

A commitment to equality of opportunity inspired the creation of three federal agencies dedicated to establishing a path to economic independence for formerly subjugated people: the Freedmen's Bureau; the Farm Security Administration (FSA); and the Office of Economic Opportunity (OEO). The histories of these three agencies trace the arc of Black lives from the short-lived freedom of Reconstruction to the depths of Jim Crow to their liberation by the civil rights movement. This book is an account of events in the South, in particular the five states of the Deep South— Alabama, Georgia, Louisiana, Mississippi, and South Carolina—where antebellum slavery and the plantation system were etched deeply into the political economy. Created during times of national crisis, these agencies are a window into pivotal moments of political conflict and upheaval in which equality of opportunity was the chosen instrument to redress Black subjugation. I use an analytical history of these three agencies and their policies, similar in significant ways but acting under three different political regimes and at very different historical moments, to address Martin Luther King's question about the meaning of racial equality and white resistance to it.

Established in the waning days of the Civil War to aid the freed people, the Freedmen's Bureau was not just a relief agency but the fulcrum of Republican plans to reconstruct the South on a foundation of free labor. Based on the idea that hard work, frugality, and access to farmland through wage-labor contracts would open up economic doors and banish the evils of slavery, the agency embodied Republicans' belief in equality of opportunity.

Franklin D. Roosevelt launched an agricultural revolution in the South that destroyed the Southern tenant economy. It ushered in large farms dependent on investment in tractors and mechanical cotton pickers, shoving Black and white tenants off the land. New Dealers believed the only way to alleviate the traumatic poverty and destitution of displaced sharecroppers in the rural South was by providing federal loans for seed and feed, and credit that would reestablish them on government-supervised farms. The New Deal's farm security policies, the historian Paul Conklin wrote, were "directed, realistically or not, at the old Jeffersonian idea of true property and true enterprise, at restored opportunity in the most sweeping sense."[16] The Resettlement Administration (RA), succeeded by the Farm Security Administration (FSA), was the one New Deal agency that could be said to have had African Americans as constituents—as much by default as anything else. Almost 80 percent of Blacks still lived in the South in 1940, and one-third were farmers, compared to one-sixth of Southern whites.

Lyndon Johnson's Office of Economic Opportunity (OEO), the centerpiece of a vast array of job training and educational programs, was the Great Society's effort to end the legacy of racial oppression and poverty in Northern cities and the rural South. Great Society liberals understood the administration's antipoverty programs to be the necessary foundation for tax policies that would create private-sector jobs and laws prohibiting labor market discrimination, notably Title VII of the Civil Rights Act. They were responding to the rising unemployment and deep poverty of African American migrants to Northern cities and the desperation of impoverished Southern Blacks. Johnson's War on Poverty set out to give these formerly subjugated individuals the capacity and habits to claim their rightful place in American society. "Let us equip the poor and the oppressed—let us equip them for the long march to dignity and to well-being," Johnson told a White House conference.[17]

Both the RA and the OEO were presidential agencies under the authority of two of the most aggressive and successful twentieth-century presidents—Franklin D. Roosevelt and Lyndon B. Johnson. Of the two, only OEO was initially invested with statutory authority; the RA was created out of the massive 1935 Emergency Relief Appropriation Act and acquired statutory authority only when Congress enacted the 1937 Farm Security Act. By contrast, the Freedmen's Bureau, created by Congress, encountered opposition from President Andrew Johnson to its very existence. Yet the Freedmen's Bureau was the arm of an occupying army in the South and had powerful supporters among Republicans in Congress who were able to defeat Johnson's attempt to scuttle the agency.

All three agencies were established with sweeping powers to intervene directly in Southern counties, operating independently of state and local authorities, though obviously administrators had to deal with local officials. Structurally, all three agencies were based on direct agency-client relationships. Freedmen's Bureau agents acted as mediators between landowners and freedmen while establishing contracts for wage labor. The agency had relief responsibilities at the outset of Reconstruction, but this was not its mission. In fact, relief was subordinated to the larger mission of establishing norms for free labor markets and restarting the Southern cotton economy. Among its staff, from Commissioner Oliver Otis Howard to local agents, relief was understood as a barrier to forcing freedmen to work in the fields. OEO was in the business of distributing money through federal grants-in-aid, but not to local governments. It was a direct pipeline for distributing money from the Executive Office of the President to nonprofit community action agencies. Unlike the other two agencies, the RA operated under Jim Crow rules of engagement. Rexford Tugwell, Roosevelt's appointee to run the agency, centralized authority, enabling RA administrators to limit the influence of local governments and bypass county agricultural committees that in the 1930s were dominated by Southern planters and their allies, county extension agents.

These three agencies were an integral part of national movements of liberal reform and liberation, aligned with hitherto subjugated people, and engaged in nation building in the South. Republicans during Reconstruction, New Deal Democrats, and Great Society liberals launched campaigns to integrate the South into the nation, but on Northern terms—free labor in the 1860s, capital-intensive agriculture that would pave the way for Southern industrialization in the 1930s, and civil rights and dismantling Jim Crow in the 1960s. Each of these national movements sought to undo the economic and racial consequences of slavery and Jim Crow and integrate Blacks into a "new, reordered" Southern economy. Policies for economic opportunity were cast in the mold of plans for the economic reconstruction of the South.

Yet in each historical moment, Blacks challenged the assumptions of federal policy. Their vision of their future was not chained to a narrow conception of equality of opportunity. Instead it was grounded in the idea of autonomy, of their capacity for independence and self-determination. For Black people freedom was not an abstraction; it meant overturning the political and social relations of slavery and Jim Crow by establishing not just voting rights but also economic independence. From Reconstruction to the civil rights era, Southern Blacks believed their independence required access to land. Imani Perry vividly captures the historical and cultural meaning of land for African Americans: "Property, land, and freedom are all intertwined for us." Nothing else would constitute a just restitution for their oppression and a guarantee for their future security. Malcolm X made this clear in his 1963 speech "Message to the Grass Roots," delivered in Detroit. "Land," he asserted, "is the basis of all independence. Land is the basis of freedom, justice, and equality."[18]

Black leaders have denounced Lincoln's and Lyndon Johnson's conceptions of equality of opportunity as a "sense of injustice," a denial of what Blacks were due.[19] W. E. B. Du Bois ridiculed what he called the "American assumption"—Lincoln's idea that anyone could become a person of wealth through hard work. To the question of what freedom really meant to the freed people after the civil war, he gave a caustic answer: "Not a cent of money, not an inch of land, not a mouth of victuals—not even ownership of the rags on his back. Free."[20] Martin Luther King Jr. regarded Johnson's efforts as inadequate, denouncing a society that told African Americans that equality of opportunity required them to lift themselves by their "own bootstraps, advice which does not take into account that [they are] barefoot."

Whites, Dr. King said, seemed to think that equality of opportunity was just another name for personal improvement.[21]

Conflict between federal policy makers and Southern Blacks occurred when virulent white opposition arose, dedicated to maintaining white supremacy and suppressing Black aspirations. White planters and their political allies sought to reestablish the economic relations of slavery using the Black codes— labor laws Southern legislatures enacted after the end of the civil war. Planters also routinely cheated freedmen and fostered violent terrorist movements. Rexford Tugwell faced emboldened Southern politicians and planters who wielded extensive power within the New Deal coalition and sought to emasculate the RA. Sargent Shriver, director of the OEO, confronted hostile Southern governors and local officials maneuvering to siphon off federal money and divert it to political cronies while roving bands of white thugs fire-bombed Head Start centers.

At stake in the political debate and conflict between African American freedom fighters, leaders of national political regimes, and intransigent defenders of white supremacy was the meaning of freedom and economic justice, specifically equality of opportunity, and the terms that would govern Blacks' entry into a reordered Southern economy. Conflict turned not just on Southern white opposition to federal remedies but also on African Americans' judgments of their adequacy and justice. What exactly did the politicians and administrators in charge of the Freedmen's Bureau, the Resettlement Administration, and the War on Poverty mean by equality of opportunity? What policies and practices did the idea entail? Did cultural and racial beliefs and ideologies influence their conception of equality of opportunity—its meaning, scope, and implications?

Most Blacks had an expansive view of the policies necessary to ensure their freedoms. During Reconstruction, members of Black conventions believed land ownership was necessary to protect their civil and political rights, and that without such economic power their "political privileges [would] become ... the source of personal peril." During the 1930s, Black farmers and tenants, along with radical reformers in the Southern Tenant Farmers Union, championed land reform that went beyond the loan and grant policies of the Resettlement Administration. The Black leaders and organizations who devised the Freedom Budget in the 1960s in response to Johnson's antipoverty policies insisted that massive federal investment in Black communities was essential for Black economic progress and autonomy. They believed that federal antidiscrimination policies would fail without it.[22]

In the pages that follow, I analyze the gestation and implementation of the policies of these three federal agencies and their relationship to the African Americans who were the object of federal campaigns to undo the ravages of slavery and Jim Crow. Using data drawn from archival research and quantitative analysis, I examine the effects of agency policies and Black challenges to each agency's conception of economic justice. The conflict between agency administrators and Blacks turned on two very different conceptions of equality of opportunity. At each historical rupture, federal officials understood it to require the *rehabilitation* of victims of oppression and exploitation through the growth of their capacities for independence and self-development. African Americans rejected this conception in favor of a vision of *antiprivilege egalitarianism,* a doctrine centered on questions of power and freedom that called for the abolition of illegitimate legal and political barriers to economic opportunity. Both conceptions derive from America's liberal political culture, and both originated in the political conflicts and racism of the White Republic of the 1830s.

Although all three agencies are often considered failures, I think this view misunderstands what these agencies represented at the time and the significance for enduring questions about restitution for African Americans.[23] My detailed account of the struggle in the Deep South between African American freedom fighters, national political leaders, and intransigent defenders of white supremacy reveals the significance of these conflicting visions for economic justice and their consequences for any contemporary analysis of racial justice.

RACE, POLITICAL CULTURE AND EQUALITY OF OPPORTUNITY

Although the idea of equality of opportunity commands broad support in the United States, there is no consistent or enduring meaning of the concept. It is always contested. When asked about how to ensure equality of opportunity, Americans usually mention access to education as their preferred policy and reject the idea of equality of results. Yet the conventional distinction between equality of opportunity and of results is highly misleading. If we assume that an appropriate policy should enable people to start in (more or less) the same place, such a policy would require a massive infusion of resources and redistribution from some groups of citizens to others thereby erasing the distinction between opportunity and results. Leslie McCall's analysis of public opinion shows that individual citizens judge the fairness of economic opportunities by judging outcomes.[24] Therefore the meaning and justification of equality of opportunity vary depending on how politicians and the public define the term, what kind of resources they are willing to commit, and who the putative beneficiaries are.

What Friedrich Nietzsche said about the idea of punishment could also be said of equality of opportunity. One could not say, he observed, why people are punished, because any concept "in which an entire process is semiotically concentrated eludes definition; only that which has no history is definable."[25] Similarly, political movements and leaders have struggled to put their own stamp on the idea of equality of opportunity, but its meaning can be untangled only through a historical analysis of how it has been interpreted and used. My approach to this question draws on Pierre Rosanvallon's argument that concepts like equality and equality of opportunity must be understood in relation to their social and political contexts and the ways and circumstances in which they have been contested. *The Society of Equals*, Rosanvallon's study of the idea of equality from the French and American Revolutions to the present, maps, as Nick Bromell points out, the "relation between equality as a political principle and equality as a social aspiration.... We must look to the moment when equality was 'invented' and recover how it was first understood ... and justified, tracing its history forward to our own time."[26] But we cannot treat analysis of equality of opportunity simply as an exercise in intellectual history. We must also examine how the idea was used at specific moments and for what purposes.

I analyze the political invention of the idea of equality of opportunity in the turmoil between Jacksonian Democrats, their Whig opponents, and the abolitionist movement, and then trace how the three agencies, and the Blacks challenging them, understood and used the idea. To do this, I have adopted Richard Ashcraft's idea of analyzing the struggle to define the "meaning in use" of *equality, freedom*, and *inequality* during moments of social conflict when the constituent elements of opposing moral views surface. In an exemplary study of the ideology of nineteenth-century British working-class radicals, Ashcraft shows how working-class writers used the language of liberalism to counterpose "the pursuit of happiness to the pursuit of wealth, the rights of labor to the tyranny of capital, the claims of equality and popular sovereignty to the privileges of class rule."[27] Similarly, I use meaning in use to understand how cultural and ideological assumptions about economic justice and race influenced agency agendas, the design and implementation of agency policies, and the responses of African Americans. The assumptions and discourse of Freedmen's Bureau agents and the freedmen during the first few years of Reconstruction, for example, reveal how each group understood the meaning of wage-labor contracts and access to land, and what this understanding meant for their conceptions of economic justice.

There are multiple meanings of *liberalism* in the American political lexicon, and they cannot easily be divorced from racial ideologies. Carol Horton argues that the liberal tradition in America has been molded as much by the language of race as by a European tradition of political thought. Social Darwinism, she points out, flourished after the failure of Reconstruction: it was a thoroughly liberal doctrine, anchored in ruthless economic competition, that assumed the existence and desirability of racial hierarchies.[28] Cultural and ideological beliefs about race—about African Americans and their place in American society—influenced the agencies and the institutionally based policies dedicated to fostering some measure of equal opportunity. As a constituent element of civic nationalism, equality of opportunity has been punctuated historically by a racist particularism that has distorted its claim to be the embodiment of a universal right. We can say that racist beliefs have colonized the concept of equality of opportunity just as they colonize the idea of "dependence" or even "economic rationality." So-called race-neutral policies are rarely like that. The 1996 welfare reform law, for example, was putatively neutral, but as Sanford Schram observes, it was "part of a vicious cycle of race bias [in which] ... neutral, euphemistic discourse masks the fact that it perpetuates racial disadvantage in society."[29] Black challenges to federal policies justified in the name of economic opportunity were predicated on unveiling the racial particularism embedded in a policy. An important example of this phenomenon is the conflict between OEO's understanding of integration of community action boards and that of Southern Blacks who challenged it.

Two Concepts of Equality of Opportunity

The two different meanings and practices associated with equality of opportunity—the rehabilitation of subjugated populations through the development of their human faculties and antiprivilege egalitarianism—derive from two distinct strands of liberalism that J. David Greenstone sees as endemic to American political culture. These are a liberalism of possessive individualism that is instrumental, and a reform liberalism that springs from normative assumptions about positive liberty and requires an individual's adherence to common moral precepts. Possessive individualism assumes the ethical priority of individual preferences. Individuals are the best judges of their own goals and aspirations, and freedom is attained only when they can achieve their chosen ends unimpeded by unjust privileges or barriers to opportunity imposed by others. Undergirding reform liberalism are normative assumptions about positive liberty, which is usually defined as self-mastery or overcoming personal impediments to achieving an individual's goals. It invokes the use of government authority to equip individuals to realize their goals and live up to their intellectual and moral capacities. Reform liberalism entails the obligation, indeed the duty, of individuals to help their fellow citizens meet these community standards and by so doing develop fully their faculties for freedom and democratic citizenship. This requires that individuals meet or exceed communal standards of excellence.[30]

These two strands of liberalism underpin antiprivilege egalitarianism and rehabilitation, respectively. They are a manifestation of United States political culture—"practices of meaning making" that produce political effects. Greenstone defines culture as a "social state—the total complex of beliefs and actions, of values and institutions" in which words and deeds are mutually constitutive.[31] Because words and actions are intertwined, change comes only when beliefs and actions change. Rehabilitation and antiprivilege egalitarianism as cultural manifestations of equality of opportunity can be reformulated as the political and social context of action changes. A significant example is the shift of antiprivilege egalitarianism from an antistate doctrine in the 1830s to a justification for state intervention into the economy after the Civil War. These two cultural templates are not policies but rather cultural maps that define different approaches to equality of opportunity. But since both are elements of American political culture, there is an enduring coherence in these two concepts.

Rehabilitation is a constituent part of reform liberalism, and it is based on the cultivation of the human abilities necessary for self-development and self-understanding through education or social and occupational programs. This vision of equality of opportunity derives in part, Greenstone argues, from a "New England Puritan tradition ... according to which individuals have an obligation—not just the option—to cultivate and develop their physical, intellectual, aesthetic, and moral faculties."[32] One reason abolitionists hated slavery was that it precluded the development of an individual's human abilities. William Lloyd Garrison excoriated his adversaries, declaring that slavery carried the "awful guilt of debasing the physical and defiling the moral workmanship of the great God—creatures made little lower than the angels, and capable of the highest intellectual attainments."[33] Liberation meant that the now-freed slaves could fully develop their ability to flourish as economically independent democratic citizens. This idea spread from evangelical denominations to the Whig Party and became the engine for moral-reform movements in the 1830s and beyond.

Since the 1830s, rehabilitation has had a common meaning of lifting up a formerly excluded or subjugated people and inculcating values necessary for individual improvement and integration into the norms of the culture. Abolitionists saw these practices as a step toward the "preparation for freedom." As a constituent part of reform liberalism, rehabilitation lies behind many of the most significant reform movements in American history. These reformers have sought to inculcate the values deemed necessary for citizenship and success in American society—values such as self-reliance, discipline, and mastery of the skills needed for economic self-sufficiency and political and civic participation. In the nineteenth century, this goal underpinned the development of the asylum—in the form of prisons, poorhouses, and orphanages—as well as the temperance movement. Welfare policy—from the creation of mothers' pensions to the welfare-reform policies of the 1990s—occupational training programs, and many other initiatives has been based on the principle of rehabilitation.

Reform liberalism, Greenstone suggests, has powerfully influenced American political development precisely because it contains an immanent critique of America. But in its dedication to the development of human faculties as a path to equality of opportunity, it insists on conformity to centrally held cultural values and "obedience to moral norms." Greenstone insists that reform liberalism does not entail illicit forms of domination, because it views development of human capacities as a matter of individual choice. "There is no question of some individuals subjugating others," Greenstone argues, since the values, as part of political culture, have been tacitly and "universally" accepted and embraced by the individuals. But this assertion evades the question of coercion, and Greenstone admits as much. Reform liberalism, he writes, is not "neutral with respect to preferences or desires but ranks them in terms of intrinsic worth." What are the communal values that reform liberalism demands? Greenstone does not answer this question. Does reform liberalism open the door to a racial hierarchy of values and preferences?[34] It smacks of paternalism, which can "arouse a sense of injustice" because it presumes that those slated to benefit from the policies of rehabilitation are simply incapable of understanding what is best for their future lives.[35]

Antiprivilege egalitarianism, by comparison, rests on the idea that privileges, unlike rights, are exclusive and granted to the holder and made available only to a small group, thus denying opportunity to others. Antiprivilege egalitarianism opens opportunities by abolishing illegitimate legal and political privileges.[36] It surfaced in the 1830s as the justification for Jacksonian Democrats' campaign to abolish monopoly charters and other economic privileges granted by states. It underpinned the producer ideology of the populists and the Knights of Labor in the late nineteenth century, again by linking antiprivilege egalitarianism to antimonopoly campaigns.

At the outset, antiprivilege egalitarianism was an antistate doctrine, but this changed with the Homestead Acts and the rise of the modern corporation in the nineteenth century. The Jacksonians' assumption that antiprivilege egalitarianism entailed a minimal state lost its relevance in an age of industrial capitalism, Henry George contended, because it assumed "each should sink or swim for himself in crossing a river, ignoring the fact that some had been artificially supplied with corks and others artificially with lead."[37] It was now government's responsibility to lighten the load of those swimming with lead on their backs. More than anyone else, the Progressive Era reformer Herbert Croly exposed the Jacksonian idea of equality of opportunity as an empty formula. Any American who believes in equality of opportunity, Croly wrote in the early twentieth century, is "wholly blind to the fact that under a legal system which holds private property sacred there may be equal rights, but there cannot possibly be any equal opportunities for exercising such rights." Croly turned the Jacksonian formula on its head: with the rise of corporations and concentrated economic power, "the exercise of certain legal rights became substantially equivalent to the exercise of a privilege." Equality of opportunity could not be saved by laissez-faire policies or noninterference in the economy.[38]

For New Dealers, antiprivilege egalitarianism was one element of a political formula for equality of opportunity. (The other, as we will see, was rehabilitation of downtrodden tenants.) Beginning with Roosevelt's attacks on "economic autocrats," New Dealers justified their policies as an assault on privilege and a move toward social justice. Secretary of Agriculture Henry Wallace said the New Deal would make it "less possible for the powerful ones, whether they be in business, agriculture, or labor, to profiteer in terms of wages or prices at the expense of those at the bottom of the heap."[39] Equality of opportunity depended on redistributing political power in order to create a level playing field for contending social groups, such as workers and capitalists. One can construe affirmative action policies as a form of antiprivilege egalitarianism. These policies regulate labor markets in order to diminish white control of access to jobs. Similarly, Leslie McCall finds that many Americans favor regulations that would constrain corporate pay practices and regulate labor-market inequalities—policies, in other words, that would undo the labor-market privileges of corporate executives.[40]

If rehabilitation inspires programs geared toward individual uplift, antiprivilege egalitarianism points toward structural changes in the economy and polity. Rights are meaningless without the capacity to exercise them. Acquisition of land for the freed people was never just a matter of compensation for their unpaid slave labor but a necessary foundation for their freedom after the end of slavery. Individuals or members of social groups confront not only the question of what they are entitled to do by virtue of their rights, but also that of what they are able to do.

Amartya Sen's idea of the capability approach to justice underlies my concept of antiprivilege egalitarianism. Sen argues that opportunity is not just a matter of pursuing one's goals but a process by which individuals or groups make relevant choices. Capability, Sen writes, is a "departure from concentrating on the means of living to the actual opportunities of living."[41] What matters is not only the resources that individuals have access to but also their ability to use those resources to improve their lives. Consider, for example, cash payments to low-income Black or Latino families in economically depressed communities. Those resources, while they help ensure survival, do not necessarily open opportunities. That requires enlarging the realm of freedom, the choices available to people to improve their lives. That in turn entails public investments in high-quality schools and health-care facilities, providing access to affordable housing and, importantly, providing access to jobs.

The capability framework replaces formal or technical justifications for equality of opportunity—are resources distributed to compensate for circumstances beyond an individual's control, without negating opportunities due to individual effort?—with a comprehensive understanding of the "exact processes through which the eventual states of affairs [or outcomes] emerge."

Poverty, Sen argues, should not be seen as a lack of money but as "capability deprivation." The relationship between poverty and resources is "both variable and deeply contingent on the characteristics of the respective people and the environment in which they live."[42] Families and individuals living in opportunity deserts—segregated neighborhoods and towns devoid of resources—are unable to make the choices that would allow them to flourish.

Antiprivilege egalitarianism is an attack on a rigged economy and society. That is how Jacksonian Democrats, the freed people during Reconstruction, nineteenth-century populists, Black landowners and tenants, New Dealers, and Southern civil rights activists understood their versions of the idea. It opens doors to economic opportunity for individuals, whether they are farmers no longer victimized by monopoly pricing, workers facing unrestricted corporate power, or Blacks subject to an exploitative economic system. No one expressed this idea better than Roosevelt when he accepted the Democratic Party nomination for president at the 1936 convention. Americans, he proclaimed, were being crushed by "privileged enterprise.... Opportunity was limited by monopoly[, and] individual initiative was crushed in the cogs of a great machine."[43]

Capability, and thus antiprivilege egalitarianism, cannot be reduced to a version of methodological individualism. Sen makes clear that the capability framework applies to groups as well as individuals, precisely because of the "value that members of that group (or for that matter, other people) place on the proficiency of that group."[44] What Sen means is that people's beliefs, their consciousness of their capacity to be free, are a product of the social and political realities they experience both as individuals and as members of a social class or racial group. The language of antiprivilege egalitarianism was a political cudgel wielded by social classes, economic groups (farmers), and women in national reform movements for equality from the end of Reconstruction to the New Deal. These movements sought "equal rights for all and special privileges for none"—but only for white people. As Charles Postel shows, late-nineteenth-century movements for regulation of monopolies, temperance, women's rights, and labor rights were based on equality and white supremacy.[45]

From the 1830s to the civil rights era, Blacks appropriated the language of antiprivilege egalitarianism to fuel demands for land, education, and economic autonomy and to challenge the doctrine of rehabilitation. Ironically, African Americans took a doctrine invented by white racists and used it to advance their own aims for freedom and equality.

Race and Rehabilitation in the Deep South

During each historical rupture, federal officials understood equality of opportunity to require the rehabilitation of victims of oppression and exploitation. Rehabilitation defined what E. E. Schattschneider refers to as the "mobilization of bias" in the policy agendas and decisions of all three agencies I examine.[46] In the ensuing chapters, I explain how a cultural conception of equality of opportunity hatched in the political conflict of the 1830s became the vehicle for the inclusion of a subjugated people. I examine the consequences for the freed people, farm tenants, and impoverished Blacks in the civil rights era. Although each agency confronted different circumstances, officials had a common conception of the people they served: damaged individuals degraded by slavery, Jim Crow, and abject poverty, and unable to function in a modern market economy. Rehabilitation would restore them to a semblance of normalcy and inculcate the habits and values they needed to move up the economic ladder.

That rehabilitation was the basis of these agencies' policies and practices raises two related questions. First, to what extent does rehabilitation evade fundamental questions of power and conflicts of interest? Equality of opportunity is about power, about the relationships between contending groups, not just about the resources and capacities of individuals. By embracing the rehabilitation of formerly subjugated people, federal officials sought to legitimize their agencies. They invoked the verities of American political culture: uplift, self-reliance, independence. But their policies provoked opposition from Blacks who charged that rehabilitation was inadequate to secure their freedom, as well as whites opposed to the very idea of aiding Blacks. Southern white fury hurled at the Freedmen's Bureau and the War on Poverty stemmed from what Jefferson Cowie calls "racialized antistatism." Beginning during Reconstruction, an insidious narrative emerged that tied federal authority to Black rights, which are always seen as illegitimate and a threat to Southern racial hierarchies. White opposition to these agencies was never just a matter of preserving class privileges. How, if at all, did agency agendas and policies change as a result of these challenges, and what were the consequences for the people these agencies served?[47]

Second, what is the relationship between race and rehabilitation? Was racial particularism embedded in doctrine of rehabilitation, and if so, how? As a formula for uplift, rehabilitation has been directed not only toward Blacks but also toward working- and lower-class people. Vagrancy laws, which James Schmidt calls "class-based paternalist reformation," are a classic example.[48] Yet we cannot collapse the idea of rehabilitation into a class framework and assume that it was race-neutral.

Rehabilitation is double-edged. Federal officials believed it was necessary in order to provide equality of opportunity, but it was stamped with cultural and racial assumptions. In the Freedmen's Bureau and the War on Poverty, rehabilitation incorporated assumptions about the inadequacies of Blacks' capacity to become independent farmers and workers and meet the requirements for democratic citizenship. Although the Farm Security Administration evaded the question of racial oppression in favor of social class, New Deal tenant policies were influenced by the assumption that Black tenants and sharecroppers (who far outnumbered whites) were incapable of becoming independent farmers without rehabilitation.

To understand the relationship between race and rehabilitation, and its relevance to the ways an agency's mobilization of bias structured its policies and practices, we can draw on Reva Siegel's idea that the destruction of one system of oppression entails the simultaneous protection of the preexisting status hierarchies. She calls this phenomenon "preservation through transformation." For example, the Fourteenth and Fifteenth Amendments established a commitment to civil and political rights for Blacks, but not social rights. Supreme Court decisions culminating in *Plessy v. Ferguson* accepted formal equality before the law for Blacks and whites but preserved status or social distinctions between the races. By constructing a realm of social relations outside the Fourteenth Amendment, Siegel argues, the legal discourse of the post-Reconstruction court preserved the subordinate social and economic status of Blacks.[49]

In the post–civil rights era, the color-blind discourse of antidiscrimination law has done the same thing. The restriction of any race-conscious policy in the name of color-blind constitutionalism, Siegel writes, "construes the constitution to protect the existing racial order." In *Hopwood v. Texas* (1996), a case that challenged the University of Texas's affirmative action policies, the Fifth Circuit Court of Appeals struck down a race-conscious remedy on grounds that it amounted to discrimination, but "other modes of state action that sustain racial stratification of American society" were ruled to be "presumptively race neutral."[50] The appellate court in this case, Siegel argues, had a particular view of equality of opportunity. Since the court understood race after the civil rights revolution to lack any social relevance, it eschewed the idea that race matters at all and is seen as divisive. Consequently, the court reverted to judging the distributive consequences of laws in terms of a person's individual characteristics—their achievements, such as grade-point average, or other meritocratic criteria—instead of their experiences as a member of an exploited group. Equality of opportunity was construed as a matter of individual success or failure, in which markets are "race-neutral mechanism(s) of distribution" to the extent that they are color-blind. The market is assumed to institutionalize racial justice.[51] This formulation of the relationship between economic markets and equality of opportunity goes back to the Whig conception of the 1830s.

Rehabilitation may be construed as a racially neutral or color-blind conception of equality of opportunity. It presumes that once an individual is rehabilitated, the market will determine whether an individual achieves economic success. Like antiprivilege egalitarianism, it has both individual and group aspects. Rehabilitation is presumed to remedy those attributes that make an individual or a group unfit, without necessarily changing the social practices and institutions that have subordinated them, let alone admitting grounds for restitution for prior subjugation. This idea was one root of the free-labor ideology and abolitionists' insistence that Black labor would be treated like any other workers, and of the Freedmen's Bureau's view of contracts. Agents strove for a version of formal equality in constructing a contract regime and assumed that the market for labor in the South would allow the freed people to prosper.

Nonetheless, racial stereotypes penetrated rehabilitation, and agency clients were treated accordingly. For example, some historians argue that the Freedmen's Bureau and white abolitionists promoted the "moral regeneration" of the freed people as a substitute for land reform. A more accurate explanation is the belief among white abolitionists and Northerners that Blacks were fitted only for manual labor. As a cultural practice, rehabilitative policies are filtered through the lens of racist beliefs and stereotypes that are then amplified. People holding to a belief in color-blind laws and policies, Siegel points out, "also hold beliefs about the nature of race as a social formation" that determine "to what extent claims about color blindness tend to undermine or legitimate social stratification." In other words, prior beliefs about racial inferiority cannot be ignored and will shape the requirements of rehabilitation policies.[52] Thus rehabilitation preserves preexisting power relationships. The Freedmen's Bureau's contract regime did little to alter the imbalance of power between planters and freedmen. Similarly, the insistence of the OEO that Southern community action agencies be formally integrated perpetuated the imbalance of power between Blacks and Southern whites.

African Americans and Antiprivilege Egalitarianism in the Deep South

In this account of the Black struggle for equality of opportunity in the Deep South, I juxtapose agency histories with an analysis of Black aspirations and the challenge they posed to federal policies of rehabilitation. Blacks rejected the idea that they had been damaged by slavery and Jim Crow and insisted that any program for economic justice must establish their independence and freedom.

This opposition began in the 1840s, when Black abolitionists recast the idea of rehabilitation into a scathing denunciation of white racism. White abolitionists fused rehabilitation with free labor as a template for the transition from slavery to freedom. Black abolitionists rejected this conception and turned the antebellum understanding of equality of opportunity into a weapon for liberation. They were reform liberals in their acceptance of positive liberty and their belief in the necessity of self-discipline and uplift, but this view was always construed in opposition to white racism and slavery. Black abolitionists, in other words, used the Jacksonian rhetoric of unjust and unearned privileges to attack the white republic of the 1830s and 1840s. The freed people who demanded land as restitution and as a bulwark against exploitation, the Black tenants who energized farm tenants' unions in the 1930s, and the local civil rights activists in the 1960s who fought to control community action agencies all cast their opposition to federal policies and their vision of their future in the language of antiprivilege egalitarianism.

The most important manifestation of this position prior to the civil rights movement was African Americans' ambitions and actions to acquire and hold on to land. Land signified what they had lost after the failure of Reconstruction; it was the means to secure their freedom and prosperity and a just restitution for their enslavement. It was their counterpoint to the very idea of rehabilitation. Agents of the Freedmen's Bureau did not see the freedmen as former slaves who had been exploited but as poor Blacks, an underclass in need of guidance and uplift. The bureau assumed that land ownership had to be earned through wage labor. But the freed people rejected demands that they sign labor contracts and give up any claim to land. White terror and Northern capitulation ended Reconstruction, leaving Blacks entrapped in tenancy, debt peonage, and apartheid. But African Americans' quest for land ownership and the autonomy it might grant never died.

Negro agrarianism, the freed people's term for antiprivilege egalitarianism, emerged full-blown during Reconstruction. It fueled rural Black mobilization and a surge in landowning beginning in the 1880s. It was the alternative to tenancy. By 1920 there were over two hundred thousand Black landowners in the South, representing the backbone of a rural Black middle class. Over half of them were in the five Deep South states. Rural enclaves of Black landowning households emerged across the South, islands of relative autonomy in a sea of white oppression. Paradoxically, many Black farmers acquired land just as the curtain of Jim Crow descended. I develop a typology of geographical patterns of Black landownership that challenges conventional interpretations. My analysis demonstrates the importance of antiprivilege egalitarianism for Black aspirations and agency.

The New Deal marked the end of land as a tangible goal for Black freedom. The story of Black landowning in the twentieth century is a story both of gains and of dispossession and loss. The New Deal's agricultural revolution destroyed the Southern system of tenancy, driving both Black and white tenants off the land. The Farm Security Administration propped up displaced tenants with loans and farm management plans, but this was less a path forward than a policy intended to keep tenants from migrating to cities during the Great Depression. The Southern Tenant Farmers Union, a mostly Black union with white leadership, challenged the FSA's policies of rehabilitation but failed to bring about land reform that would have helped tenants.

New Deal agricultural policies contributed to substantial gains in white farm ownership in the years 1935–45 but did nothing for Black land ownership, which had increased significantly by 1945 and declined rapidly thereafter. Southern Democrats captured the Farmers Home Administration, the agency that replaced the FSA in 1946, and transformed it into a tool to drive Black farmers off their land. The massive decline in the number of Black landowners occurred after the New Deal and, ironically, at the hands of the New Deal agency created to rescue Southern tenants.

The New Deal transformed the Southern economy, integrating it into the national economy and setting the stage for the civil rights movement. But it also left the enemies of Black aspirations in control of the South. White Southerners availed themselves of New Deal grants-in-aid to build a Jim Crow welfare state, embedding discrimination in social policies. The civil rights movement and federal policies ended Jim Crow and began to unravel the segregated Southern welfare state. But the revolution stalled with the failure of the War on Poverty in the South, a failure rooted in the antinomy between the deeply racist culture and practices of white Southerners and the idea that policies of rehabilitation and integrated community action agencies would lead to individual economic progress and racial harmony.

My account of the rise and decline of Black landowners underscores the futility of any policy of equality of opportunity based on rehabilitation, and the enduring and pervasive effects of structural racism. Equality of opportunity has been seen as the path to racial justice and social equality. But the history of these three agencies and the experience of African Americans suggests otherwise. Yet if rehabilitation or any ameliorative version of equality of opportunity is discredited, what might it take to undo structural racism, the legacies of slavery and Jim Crow? Is a modern version of antiprivilege egalitarianism an alternative to contemporary doctrines of equality of opportunity? I consider these questions in the conclusion.

ONE

The Political Invention of Equality of Opportunity, 1830–1860

> Today it is difficult to comprehend that courageous radicalism was once thoroughly compatible with calls for moral discipline as defined by a self-appointed elite. This fusion of protest and self-help was as characteristic of the [Black] emigrationists as it was of the so-called [Black] assimilationists.
>
> DAVID BRION DAVIS,
> *The Problem of Slavery in the Age of Emancipation*, 2014

THE CONCEPT OF EQUALITY of opportunity has its political origins in the tumultuous and deeply rooted conflicts of the 1830s. Fueled by the evangelical fervor unleashed by the Second Great Awakening and the revolution in transportation and communication that heralded America's industrial age, this decade witnessed the democratization of white men and the birth of mass political parties. Economic divisions between Jacksonian Democrats and Whigs overlapped cultural and religious divides shattering the republican vision that united the nation's founders. Partisan conflict over the national bank, monopoly charters, federal support for building roads and canals to undergird economic growth and expansion, banning mail delivery on Sundays, the question of public education, Indian removal, and the disposition of unsettled lands were all matters that turned on radically different visions of America's future.

Both the Democratic and the Whig visions were liberal and capitalist. Neither favored an equal distribution of wealth or the abolition of private property. "Democrats," writes Sean Wilentz, "favored a more secure and egalitarian commercialism ... which they believed would distribute wealth more evenly while keeping political power in the hands of the majority of the citizenry."[1] Whigs championed a modernizing economy but believed, in the words of Lee J. Benson, that government should "promote the general welfare, raise the level of opportunity for all men and aid all individuals to develop their full potentialities."² Democrats decried the conflict between those who produced the wealth of the country and those who leeched off the profits of producers. The key to Jacksonian politics, Wilentz writes, was "a belief that relatively small groups of self-interested men were out to destroy majority rule and, with it, the Constitution." Whigs sought to dampen conflict and promote economic development; they championed a society of interdependent citizens who labored in harmony.³

At stake for each was the meaning of equality. The founding generation of the United States defined the idea of equality in opposition to British subjugation. The American Revolution was driven by a demand for equal recognition and a rejection of deference and social distinctions. The most common meaning of equality was the idea that everyone was on the same footing, that the opinions and ideas of one man were equal to those of any other man. "Ordinary Americans," Gordon Wood observed, "came to believe that no one in a basic down-to-earth and day-in-and-day-out manner was really better than anyone else." Pierre Rosanvallon has referred to this belief, which was characteristic of both the French and American Revolutions, as *similarity*. It was an attack on the privileged status of the French aristocracy and British colonialists.⁴ Yet by the 1830s the idea of similarity was unraveling under the pressure of industrial capitalism and manufacturing in both societies. This was one of Alexis de Tocqueville's insights. Americans, he wrote, "have abolished the troublesome privileges of some of their fellows, but they come up against the competition of all. . . . This constant strife between the desires inspired by equality and the means it supplies to satisfy them harasses and wearies the mind. . . . No matter how a people strives for it, all the conditions of life can never be perfectly equal."⁵

In response, two versions of the idea of equality of opportunity emerged, grounded in different strands of liberalism. Jacksonian Democrats promoted an antistate conception of equality of opportunity that I call antiprivilege egalitarianism. Whigs fashioned a program of moral improvement based on uplift and rehabilitation. Many writers acknowledge that the meaning of equality changed in the 1830s, but they ascribe that change in meaning to one conception or the other. John Schaar thinks the Whigs invented a rhetoric of equality of opportunity "that could accommodate the impulses of equality and individualism, while still defending inequality of income, wealth, and status." This, Schaar argues, is the canonical conception of equality of opportunity, the idea that each individual should be free to use their talents to achieve the ends they desire. Yet this formulation tells us very little about what the Whigs really thought.[6] Richard Ellis argues that the equality of opportunity, defined as the abolition of privilege, came into its own only with the Jacksonians, who "fused a strong egalitarian impulse with an equally fervent commitment to the unregulated marketplace."[7] In fact, these were competing conceptions of equality of opportunity that derived from different philosophical and political interpretations of the founding liberal values of the country. Members of both parties thought they were reclaiming the republican ideals that had guided the founders. But they were reclaiming these ideals only for white Americans. Whigs and Democrats may have disagreed about the meaning of equality, but partisans in both parties were deeply committed to the idea that America was conceived as, and should remain, a white nation.

Elites of both parties ruled any discussion of slavery off the table. Imbued with newly fashionable doctrines of racial inferiority, citizens of the emergent white republic denied that similarity applied to African Americans. Other than as slaves, who were commodities bought and sold in the domestic slave market, Black people had no place in America. Free Blacks were stateless, in effect, regardless of any rights they were presumed to have. Hosea Easton, a Black abolitionist, understood this better than most. Blacks were "literally stolen from their native country," he wrote in 1837, and lost any legal status they had, but even when freed they were denied any rights or acknowledgement as citizens. Blacks were "accounted as aliens and outcasts ... identified as belonging to no country—denied birthright in one, and had it stolen from them in another.... [T]hey had lost title to both worlds."[8]

Free Blacks' status before the Civil War is analogous to that of stateless Jews during the 1930s and 1940s. As stateless people, Jewish refugees had no rights and no clear way of obtaining any rights or any of the civil protections accorded citizens of the countries to which they fled. Because of the Jews' "abstract nakedness of being nothing but human[,] ... their greatest danger," Hannah Arendt wrote, was that "they were regarded as savages."[9] Likewise, for African Americans living in the "free" North, there was no distinction between abolishing slavery and gaining their own freedom; it was all the same struggle. In a speech to the seventh anniversary meeting of the American Anti-slavery Society, Henry Highland Garnet, a fiery Black abolitionist, proclaimed, "I am not, nay, cannot be entirely free. I feel for my brethren as a man—I am bound with them as a brother. Nothing but emancipating my brethren can set me at liberty."[10]

Long before the Dred Scott decision, most whites believed the Constitution applied only to them. The 1830s marked the emergence of a rock-solid belief that America was a white nation and that citizenship was explicitly tied to skin color. Two developments, underpinned by doctrines of biological racism, paved the way for this shift in consciousness and identity, both of which repudiated any of the lingering racial egalitarianism and gradual emancipation that flourished in the North immediately after the revolution. One was the founding in 1816 of the American Colonization Society, an elite campaign based on the fantastical idea that the salvation of the country depended on removing Blacks from American soil. Often traced to Jefferson's fears of a race war should the slaves be emancipated, this notion appealed to whites, mostly in the Northern states, who were troubled by slavery but feared racial amalgamation and the slave revolts that they saw as the inevitable consequence of a growing population of free Blacks. Writing in 1823 that slavery was abhorrent and immoral, Leonard Bacon, a prominent New England clergyman and advocate of colonization, nevertheless denied that slaves could be emancipated: "You may call him free, but you cannot bleach him into the enjoyment of freedom.... [Free Blacks are] as a body, ignorant and vicious."[11] Bacon's attitude was fairly typical among New Englanders, but colonization also attracted some Southern slaveholders, Henry Clay and some antislavery Virginians among them.

For most white Americans, however, the shift in consciousness came as skin color replaced property ownership as a requirement for voting. For many white men, voting rights were a source of leverage against hated property-owning elites, a recognition of their membership in the polity, and a validation of their standing.[12] As states dropped property requirements for the franchise, they added provisions restricting it to white men. By 1837, twenty-one of the twenty-six states in the Union had no property requirement for white male voters. None of the thirteen of the states admitted to the Union after ratification of the Constitution required that voters own property, and eight of the original thirteen states rescinded previous property requirements. But as the new states enfranchised white men, they denied the franchise to Blacks, and eight states changed their voting requirements to exclude Black men. Only five states allowed free African Americans to vote, and New York State permitted it only if they owned property. The laws did not really matter, though, as Tocqueville pointed out, since white majorities could override them whenever they pleased, through intimidation or violence.[13]

In the white republic, party conflict usually turned on class resentment and religious beliefs. Jacksonian Democrats regarded Whigs and their sympathizers as arrogant elites bent on subverting democracy and imposing alien religious or moral doctrines and mandates on citizens. The Whigs thought the Jacksonians were uncouth, resentful, and given to mob rule because they were unable to accept the modern world. Nevertheless, the two parties were in accord on the matters of race and slavery. Abolitionists upset this accord, and by the end of the decade they had inflamed Southern anger, provoking strident defenses of slavery, and Northern racial hostility.

Although David Walker's jeremiad against slavery was the spark that aroused Black aspirations and white fear, it was the mobilization of Black opposition to the colonization movement that marked the start of the second wave of the abolition movement. Black abolitionists, namely Walker and Samuel Cornish, influenced William Lloyd Garrison's conversion to abolition, and his newspaper, the *Liberator*, would not have survived but for Black subscriptions. By the end of the 1830s, the abolitionist movement numbered almost three hundred thousand adherents in two thousand chapters across the North.[14]

The abolitionist challenge not only set the antislavery movement in motion; it gave African Americans in the North the opportunity to challenge their exclusion from voting booths, discriminatory laws that excluded them from occupations, and their day-to-day treatment by whites, particularly in churches, where they were forced to sit in segregated pews. Out of this struggle, northern Blacks forged a conscious identity as an oppressed nation within the white republic. Black political action after 1840 was by turns nationalist and assimilationist. But despite different assessments of whether African Americans could obtain freedom and on what terms, leaders as different as Martin Delany, Henry Highland Garnet, Frederick Douglass, and Samuel Cornish articulated a common belief in the necessity of economic mobility and opportunity.

The political and racial conflict leading up to the Civil War entwined abolition with the status of African Americans in the North, and as a result, conceptions of equality of opportunity were stamped by skin color. By the time it became apparent to most white Northerners and white abolitionists in 1863 and 1864 that slaves would be emancipated, equality of opportunity meant one thing for the freed people and something altogether different for white men on the make. Antiprivilege egalitarianism, always at the cutting edge of class resentment and conflict, became synonymous with white men demanding free land; rehabilitation became the badge of Black citizenship. Black abolitionists rejected this dichotomy and fused the two conceptions of equality of opportunity into a manifesto for freedom and independence and an attack on white racism. To understand how and why this shift occurred, we need to look more closely at the intersection between racial identity and equality of opportunity in antebellum America.

THE ANTINOMIES OF POLITICAL IDEOLOGY AND EQUALITY IN JACKSONIAN AMERICA

Jacksonian Democrats summed up the ills of their age in one word: *privilege*. Everything wrong with America could be attributed to the illegitimate acquisition of privileges through law or custom. Andrew Jackson articulated the Democrats' chief complaint when he vetoed the US Bank charter, a law he considered a form of privilege, in 1832. "Every man is equally entitled to protection by the law," Jackson said, "but when the laws undertake to add to these natural and just advantages *artificial distinctions,* to grant titles, gratuities, and exclusive privileges... the humble members of society—the farmers, mechanics, and laborers—who have neither the time nor the means of securing like favors to themselves, have a right to complain of the injustice of their Government."[15] The game was rigged. An editorial in the *Democratic Review,* a Jacksonian political journal, succinctly defined the Jacksonian idea of antiprivilege egalitarianism:

> As far as superior knowledge and talent confer on their possessor a natural charter of privilege to control his associates and exert an influence on the direction of the general affairs of the community, the free and natural action of that privilege is best secured by a perfectly free democratic system which will abolish all artificial distinctions, and preventing *the accumulation of any social obstacles to advancement,* will permit the free development of every germ of talent, wherever it may chance to exist, whether on the proud mountain summit, in the humble valley, or by the wayside of common life.[16]

Social or economic privilege is often but not always underpinned by law. Similarity is the opposite of privilege, and as such repudiates deference or any acknowledgment of social distinctions. Opposition to privilege was a weapon in both the American and French Revolutions. The Abbé Emmanuel Joseph Sieyes, a leader of the French Revolution, said, "The privileged individual considers himself, along with his colleagues, as constituting a distinct order, a nation of the select within the nation."[17] As a leveling ideology, antiprivilege egalitarianism fueled Democratic opposition to Whigs in the 1830s. Privileges gained through government were the source of class divisions in society. William Leggett, a radical Democrat, declared that "a class continually gaining ground in the community who desire to monopolize the advantage of Government to hedge themselves [would] elevate themselves at the expense of the great body of people." Government-derived privileges denied the similarity of men and fueled class resentment.[18]

Jackson's political opponents, the Whig party, championed a very different conception of economic opportunity. *Improvement* is the key term in the Whig lexicon, linking moral and economic concerns. It is the counterpart to the Jacksonian obsession with privilege. Just as one could improve the national economy by building roads and canals, individuals could improve themselves through education, abstaining from alcohol, and religious worship. Whig culture, Daniel Howe argues, was based on "a conception of progress that was the collective form of redemption: like the individual, society as a whole was capable of self-improvement through conscious effort.... [It] demanded the moral regeneration of society, not simply of the individuals within it."[19] To Whig reformers, morality and material progress were inseparable. For Henry Clay and Lyman Beecher, both prominent Whigs, equality of opportunity required moral reform and the rehabilitation of fallen individuals, especially people on the frontier. The theologian William Ellery Channing, a leader in the moral reform movement of the early nineteenth century, described himself as a "leveler" but said, "I would accomplish my object by elevating the low, by raising from a degrading indigence and brutal ignorance the laboring multitude."[20] For Whigs, religious beliefs such as the idea of benevolent action translated into support for economic policies, notably the tariff and the national bank.

The religious revivals of the early nineteenth century, the Second Great Awakening, shaped both antiprivilege egalitarianism and rehabilitation. American culture in the age of Jackson was, in many ways, an evangelical culture; by 1840 about 40 percent of the population were either evangelicals or sympathized with them.[21] The religious movements of this period were not only pervasive but national in scope. But they embodied two separate strands of religiously inspired activism. One was a profound religious populism, driven by the spreading democratic ethos after 1800—itself a consequence of the Revolution and the nation's founding—that spurred the Jacksonian revolt against elites. The other strand grew out of the new Calvinism that flourished in the 1820s and inspired evangelicals to launch campaigns for individual moral reform.

Nineteenth-century religious populism was all about equality. "The democratic Arminianism of the Methodists," Richard Carwardine writes, "the most potent and pervasive doctrinal force of the Awakening, proffered a theology of human equality and opportunity." Religious populism leveled the relationship between clergy and parishioners; it was obsessively antiauthoritarian. The idea of a bishop conjured up monarchism in the minds of rural Methodists. Populist preachers exalted an "empire of [individual] conscience." Faith was construed as a matter of individual belief and acknowledgment of God's presence, and as such it denied that the established clergy were set apart from and over members of the congregation. This movement had its greatest impact on the frontier, where itinerant preachers like Lorenzo Dow could assume the mantle of both holy man and Jeffersonian Democrat, and John Leland preached a message that "combined [the] ideological leverage of evangelical urgency and Jeffersonian promise."[22] In this way, the populist side of the Second Great Awakening fed into the Jacksonian revolt against elites. Just as Jackson railed against the privileged elites running the United States Bank, frontier preachers taught that "divine insight was reserved for the poor and humble rather than the proud and learned."[23]

Unlike the premillennialist religious populists who gravitated to the Democratic Party, the evangelicals drawn to the Whig Party were both postmillennialist and reform-minded. They believed that the second coming of Christ would be preceded by a thousand years of peace and could be hastened by good works. These reformers created benevolent societies and voluntary associations (mainly in Northern states), championed temperance, promoted prison reform, created schools for the blind and institutions for the mentally ill, advocated vagrancy laws and poorhouses, opposed corporal punishment, and above all sought the moral reformation of society. The abolitionist movement grew out of the seeds planted by evangelical moral reform.

These Christian reformers were inspired by the New School Calvinism, a religious movement led by Charles Finney, a charismatic, influential preacher. Finney taught that anyone, not just the elect, could receive God's grace. Sin was a matter not of predestination but of individual moral choice. Every human had the capacity to shape their life according to the scriptures. As Finney explained in his autobiography, "Instead of telling sinners to use the means of grace and pray for a new heart, we called on them to make themselves a new heart."[24] Finney's accomplishment was to merge New School Calvinism with evangelical revivalism and encourage the spread of religiously inspired social reform. Although these evangelicals pioneered voluntary societies, one might call them state-centered Calvinists who linked God and politics in the service of the Christian nation they were intent on creating. Finney said that "politics are a part of religion in such a country as this." They were drawn to political action as a matter of duty. These evangelicals became a core constituency of the Whig party.[25]

If the postmillennial Whigs could justify support for the tariff on religious grounds, Jacksonian Democrats' religious beliefs inclined toward limited government. Democrats resented the Whig program of moral reform as an effort by hated elites to impose an alien set of moral values upon them, whether it was temperance or breaking down the wall between church and state by banning mail delivery on the Sabbath. Because individuals' religious and political-economic stands were not typically at odds in the 1830s, those who identified as Democrat or Whig were predisposed toward very different, and conflicting, values and policies. The difference was a matter of religious doctrine rather than of denomination. New England Congregationalists were committed Whigs, but Presbyterians were found on both sides of the partisan divide.[26]

Underlying these differences in religious and economic beliefs was a more fundamental ideological and cultural divide over liberalism. Louis Hartz famously described America as a liberal society, one in which liberalism was bound up with national identity. To be an American was to be liberal. Hartz depicted Jacksonian-era politics as a form of shadow boxing, phony conflicts that concealed an underlying consensus on values. In one respect he was dead right: both Whigs and Democrats were committed to republican political institutions, liberty, and private property—what Hartz called "democratic capitalism." J. David Greenstone calls this underlying agreement the boundary condition of liberalism "because it embodies certain norms of speech and action that preclude non-liberal politics." But Greenstone's point is that agreement on the boundary conditions does not mean the absence of conflict over the meaning of liberty, equality, the scope of government action, or, in antebellum America, the relationship between the Union and slavery. The two strands of liberalism in American political culture that he identifies—possessive individualism and a reform liberalism based on adherence to common moral traditions—underpin the conflict between Jacksonian Democrats' commitment to antiprivilege egalitarianism and Whigs' belief in moral reform and rehabilitation.[27]

Greenstone seeks to explain the onset of conflict in a society that agreed on the basic tenets of liberalism. My concern is understanding the

TABLE 1 Democrat and Whig conceptions of equality of opportunity in the 1830s

	Democrat	Whig
Origins of inequality	Political privileges	Individual talents and effort
Visions of equality	Antiprivilege egalitarianism	Rehabilitation
Conception of liberty	Negative	Positive
Basis of equality	Natural equality of men	Upward and downward mobility
Conception of labor	Independent producer-owner	Self-ownership
Self-interest	Self-regulation	Discipline, self-control
Cultural values	Diversity	Uniformity
Political program	Abolish political privileges	Moral and social reform

relationship of these two philosophical and ideological traditions to ideas about race and equality of opportunity. Table 1 summarizes the fundamental differences in the two conceptions of equality of opportunity that derive from the two strands of American liberalism and in the 1830s and 1840s were core parts of Whig and Democratic party agendas. Not every Whig or every Democrat accepted or believed in every element of these agendas, but the table does capture the animating beliefs of party elites, activists, and ideologues. And, inevitably, there was slippage between their ideological commitments and the policies party elites supported and defended. To understand the connection to race, we need to explore each conception in more detail.

Privilege and Inequality

Jacksonian Democrats located the origins of inequality not in society but in politics. Absent political privileges, they thought a natural equality would prevail among men. Twenty-first-century discussions of inequality begin with the economy; Jacksonian discussions began with the government. William Leggett wrote that government usurped the rights of citizens by exercising "the right of dispensing favours to one or another class of citizens at will[,] ... of investing wealth with new and exclusive privileges." Leggett, like many Jacksonians, assumed that government favors were the source of conflict in society, as public policies "may at pleasure elevate one class and depress another." Citizens "become mere puppets of legislative cobbling and tinkering.... [Government] assumes the functions which belong alone to an overruling Providence, and affects to become the universal dispenser of good and evil." The inevitable result would be the spread of selfish feelings that would "overpower the social feeling."[28] Jacksonian ire was directed, in particular, at monopoly charters for commercial activity to small numbers of people. These charters were like vested rights, and once institutionalized, either by law or practice, were difficult to remove and a source of resentment.

Government-granted privileges were a form of theft, as they denied individual men the right to the fruits of their labor. Jacksonians subscribed to a producer ethic derived loosely from the labor theory of value, the idea that an individual producer should receive the full benefit of their labor. Deeply embedded in Jacksonian rhetoric, the producer ethic was wielded not only to discredit monopoly charters but also to oppose government policies. In justifying his opposition to Henry Clay's plan to raise revenue for federally sponsored improvements from land sales, Jackson said that not only did landholders pay for the land they tilled, but "it is their labor alone which gives real value to the lands, and that the proceeds arising from their sale are distributed among States which had not originally any claim to them."[29] Jackson believed that states' continuing to tax the land would prevent men from acquiring an independent freehold. Radicals like Leggett agitated for an extreme version of laissez-faire, believing, for instance, that public ferries subsidized users at the expense of nonusers. He even railed against tax-supported asylums for the insane. Leggett was no doubt extreme, but he accurately reflected the desire of Jacksonian Democrats for limited government and a free economy.

The independent-producer was the bedrock of Jacksonian democracy. The producing classes worked for themselves, at their own speed and on their own land or in their own shops, and their earnings were "regulated by the wants of the community at large, not by the discretion of a pernicious master."[30] They included farmers, mechanics, workers, and many small proprietors. What mattered was their independence. Jackson described them as the "bone and sinew of the country [who] hold the great mass of our national wealth, although it is distributed in moderate amounts among the millions of freemen who possess it." Producers did not sell their labor: they owned the products of their labor, and the role of government was to protect their ownership of those products. The Jacksonians drew a clear distinction between privileges, which were restricted to a few, and rights, which all white men possessed. Protecting the fruits of producers' labor depended on the principle of equal rights, Leggett wrote. This protection would "safeguard against oppression" and leave to all men "the free exercise of their talents and industry within the limits of the GENERAL LAW." To political and civil rights, Leggett added economic rights.[31]

These economic rights guaranteed only opportunity. Jacksonian Democrats went out of their way to insist that they did not oppose the acquisition of property or promote equality of wealth. Stephen Simpson, author of *The Workingman's Manual*, wrote, "It is a perversion of the aims of the enlightened advocates of labor to represent that they are contending for an equality of wealth or a community of property.... Equality of rights to what we produce is not equality of possession, for some will produce more than others."[32] Even though Jacksonian Democrats lambasted aristocratic Whigs for their elitism, it is misleading to characterize them as defending a working-class agenda; they were not opposed to the market and clearly valued individual opportunities. But neither would it be correct to reduce them to bourgeois men on the make (though many were certainly acquisitive). They remained levelers, presuming that the absence of government interference in economic relations would produce a natural equality among men.

But why would Jacksonian Democrats assume that unleashing individuals to pursue their self-interested economic aims would result in equality instead of inequality? Here antiprivilege egalitarianism depended on the assumption of similarity, men's common characteristics and their equality of condition. As John Ashworth points out, the Jacksonians "emphasized self-interest as the basis of liberty and democracy," believing that so long as men received the full value of the contribution of their labor, wide disparities in income and wealth could be avoided. Self-interest was self-regulating precisely because men were similar; it was only because of government-sanctioned privileges that economic inequality existed. "The natural equality" of men, Ashworth writes, "was the link between equality of opportunity and equality of condition. It was a leveling equality."[33]

One explanation of why the idea of a natural equality among men under laissez-faire was widespread at a time of growth in manufacturing and transportation was the low level of deskilling of labor as the economy developed horizontally through the expansion of small agricultural and commercial enterprises and white men's ability to acquire land. Outside the South, economic inequality was rather low. The reason was the low price of land, which enabled most people to become landowners.[34] The availability of land, however, depended on white settlers expropriating it from Native Americans. The Jacksonian vision of an egalitarian agricultural utopia was contingent on Jackson's Indian removal legislation. Over the twelve years that Democrats were in the White House, Presidents Jackson and Martin Van Buren forced over ninety thousand Cherokees, Choctaws, Creeks, and Chickasaws from their native lands, opening over one hundred million acres of land in Alabama and Mississippi to settlement. Jackson claimed his policies were voluntary, but they entailed various means of coercion, fraud, and bribery, and a failure to honor the terms of treaties. Jackson's Indian removal policies were pivotal to the gestation of mass political parties in the 1830s. In fact, according to Fred S. Rolater, "Indian voting became the most consistent predictor of whether a congressman or a senator was a Whig or a Democrat."[35] It also prompted many who opposed Indian removal to abandon their support for colonization, which they believed was no different from Jackson's removal policies. From there, for Garrison, Theodore Weld, and Lydia Maria Child, among others, it was a short step to demands for the immediate abolition of slavery.[36]

Jackson was explicit about who would benefit from Indian removal: white settlers. In his fourth annual message to Congress, he said "It cannot be doubted that the speedy settlement of these lands constitutes the true interest of the Republic.... Independent farmers are everywhere the basis of society and the true friends of liberty."[37] Yet the white yeoman farmers whose virtues Jackson extolled lost out to speculators and planters who took advantage of preemption, a law that allowed buyers to settle on land and then buy it at very low prices, so long as they improved it.[38] Jackson's policies further entrenched slavery in the Black Belt of Alabama and Mississippi. Between 1830 and 1840 the number of slaves in Alabama increased by 135,893; in Mississippi the slave population increased by 129,552. Of this total increase, 43 percent was in new counties created out of lands formerly occupied by Native Americans.[39] Jackson's action fueled the expansion of slavery and mocked his excoriation of privilege.

Uplifting the Nation

Whigs rejected similarity and the idea of natural equality. Instead, they asserted that inequality among men was due to primarily to individual differences in motivation and talent. Inequality was not a reason for despair; on the contrary it was an engine of progress, as it allowed men of different talents to emerge, prosper, and climb the social and economic ladder. This strongly meritocratic ideology was not antidemocratic, but there is no doubt that Whigs disdained the common man and longed for the rule of better men. Yet neither Whigs nor Democrats objected to inequality of outcomes; both assumed that it did not matter. The Whig alternative to Democrats' doctrine of natural inequality was the idea of the circulation of differences. Daniel Webster stated the doctrine in an 1838 speech on the Senate floor: "Property," he said, "is everywhere distributed as fast as it is accumulated, and not in more than one case out of a hundred is there an accumulation beyond the earnings of one or two generations." For Webster it was "no matter of regret or sorrow that few are very rich; but it is our pride and glory that few are very poor." What mattered was upward mobility, the idea that inequalities would not congeal into class or status differences. The Whig idea of equality was anchored by the belief that there would be both upward and downward mobility in a growing economy and a fluid society.[40]

Daniel Howe argues that the Whigs were the harbingers of modernity, or rather a modern conception of a market society. Elites in both parties accepted elements of the labor theory of value, as both believed that reaping the rewards of one's labor was just. But whereas Democrats believed in preserving a society of small-scale agricultural producers and artisans, Whigs advocated an economically diverse society based on market transactions. For most Whigs (and abolitionists), wage labor was a constituent part of a modern economy, as it afforded people choice. Again Webster stated the Whig belief with precision: "I know of no country far advanced in civilization and happiness, whose people are confined to one single pursuit, and I regard a nation much happier, much better refined, much more moral, in proportion as its avenues of industry are multiplied and the modes of its labor varied."[41]

The Whigs believed that an individual's worth was determined by their labor and their ability to exchange that labor, at least initially, for wages. People were not producers but workers who owned nothing but their labor. This did not mean everyone would remain in the same occupation or in the same place on the economic ladder for life. A diverse economy would open doors for the poorest of citizens, who might start out as manual workers but in time could become employers. Many Whigs denied any difference between workers (employees) and owners; all were laborers, and at any time one could replace the other. Whigs' conception of equal opportunity denied that unequal outcomes would lead to class stratification. They based their belief on precisely the same assumption as the Jacksonians: American exceptionalism. Because the United States lacked the hard class lines of Europe—according to one Whig, "among our native population, laborers for hire do not exist as a class"—a diverse, growing economy opened opportunities for everyone.[42] In other words, the market revolution of the 1830s would provide sufficient opportunities to prevent the emergence of a sharp class divide.

To their conception of opportunity and mobility, the Whigs added a belief in the necessity of discipline and self-control. Whigs elevated reason over emotion, spoke of duty, and, as Howe puts it, assumed that "the good life entailed continual self-discipline, as one sought to 'suppress his passions or cultivate and improve his virtues.'"[43] If Jacksonian Democrats valued diversity, Whigs promoted conformity in the service of the values they saw as necessary for a market society. Economic prosperity depended on moral conformity and the cultivation of those values we associate with the Protestant ethic: frugality, deferred gratification, sobriety, self-discipline, and self-improvement. Howe characterizes the Whig attitude as "a conjunction of ancient Christianity with the cognitive expansion and disciplinary needs of the modern market society."[44] There were good reasons Democrats loathed Whig schemes for moral improvement and saw the party as a bunch of patronizing, oppressive elitists. But whereas Democrats saw their conflict with Whigs as rooted in a clash between opposing classes and social groups, Whigs believed that the harmonious, interdependent society they envisioned required sober, responsible citizens.

Evangelicals conceived their moral reforms as redemptive. This is one reason they embraced temperance. Their net included the insane, criminals, vagrants, poor people, children (of course), lazy workers, and, importantly, slaves. Evangelicals passed out Bibles, preached the virtues of Sunday schools, and sent missionaries into the homes of the urban poor, the working class, and Native Americans in order to show them "the true origins of their suffering [and offer] encouragement and counsel on the path to rehabilitation." Observance of the Sabbath, they thought, "gives seriousness and poise to character [and] . . . teaches self-control, self-knowledge, and self-respect." But as Steven Mintz points out in his history of antebellum reform, religious proselytizing often turned into campaigns for social reform that led to the establishment of orphanages, poorhouses, institutions for the blind, insane asylums, industrial training, and public charities.[45]

Many reformers thought institutionalization of the poor and of criminals would instill moral character. Samuel Gridley Howe, who founded schools for the blind and was instrumental in the creation of the Freedmen's Bureau, believed in "human perfection through social reform." Although Howe despised evangelicals and attributed many of the ills of the age—infidelity, moral laxness, class animosities, alcohol consumption—to Jacksonian politics, he nonetheless believed that class inequality could be ameliorated only through social reforms promoting rehabilitation, self-sufficiency, and education.[46] He was cut from the same cloth as the evangelical reformers.

It is easy to see the Whigs as narrow-minded paternalists and defenders of class privileges. But they believed that a market society based on avarice and self-interest could function only if it was grounded by values that promoted cooperation, trust, and honesty. This is a recurring theme in histories of capitalism from Adam Smith to Daniel Bell: a market society, paradoxically, depends on the inculcation of religious values, which provide the social foundation for a hedonistic, individualistic, calculating market system. Whig evangelicals sought to promote internal discipline in place of external methods of social control and discipline. They saw moral reform as the necessary foundation for economic reform. Howe describes evangelical identity as "both follower of Christ and rational, autonomous individual"—a paradox.[47] These attitudes influenced abolitionists and were important to their conception of Reconstruction.

The difference in the two conceptions of equality of opportunity is evident in their attitudes toward public education. Both Whigs and Democrats valued public education and advocated policies to expand educational opportunities. But they valued it for very different reasons. Whigs saw education as a tool to mold citizens who could fulfill their roles as economic agents in the emerging market society and counter the "mob rule" they foresaw in Democratic ascendancy. Democrats thought public education served their conception of equality of opportunity by removing barriers to mobility and allowed greater participation in public affairs. It ensured an equal society and enabled individuals to pursue their own ends. The Philadelphia Working Men's Party believed that "the original element of despotism is monopoly of talent[,] which consigns the multitude to comparative ignorance and secures the balance of knowledge on the side of the rich and the rulers." And Democrats preferred schools that eschewed attempts to impose moral uniformity.

These philosophical differences did not always lead to conflict. Horace Mann, the leading antebellum education reformer and a prominent Whig, was able to implement a centralized curriculum based on moral presuppositions in Boston because he appealed to Democrats' desire for an education that would both expand economic opportunities *and* instill a common Protestant religious identity.[48]

BLACK NATIONALISM IN THE WHITE REPUBLIC

By 1840 a rock-solid consensus on white supremacy "pervaded nearly every element of northern society," James Stewart writes. For Jacksonian Democrats, white identity was tied to territorial expansion and based on the moral equality of white producers. Their disparate coalition of urban workers, yeoman farmers, and slaveholders was glued together with an ideology that "asserted the political, civil, and moral equality of white male citizens." For Whigs, white identity grew out of the fear of amalgamation of the races. Colonization, a British observer traveling the United States in 1835 pointed out, amounted to a "salutary preventative of that amalgamation that would confound the two races and obliterate their distinction." Adopting the mantle of whiteness also made the Whigs competitive in elections. Both parties played the race card. Underlying Jacksonian politics, then, was the establishment of a white identity that straddled class divisions and sought to exorcise Blacks from American society. In response, northern Blacks forged an independent Black identity. According to Stewart, the 1830s saw the beginnings of modern racial stratification and the identities and ideological baggage underpinning it.[49]

White identity took hold partly because "scientific" racial doctrines asserting the biological supremacy of whites replaced the vague racial environmentalism that characterized late eighteenth-century writing on race. But the catalyst that congealed widespread racial prejudice into a hard white identity was the abolitionist movement, which attacked not just slavery but racial oppression and exclusion in the North. Black abolitionists convinced William Lloyd Garrison that colonization was misguided and morally wrong, and that racial equality was imperative. Black abolitionism started in opposition to colonization, but by the late 1820s, Black writers and activists were focused on challenging both slavery and white racism in the North. David Walker delivered a scalding indictment of slavery and racism in his *Appeal to the Colored Citizens of the World*: "White Americans . . . treat us in that condition more cruel (they being an enlightened and Christian people), than any heathen nation did any people whom it had reduced to our condition." This sounded the tocsin for Black militancy and abolition and was echoed in the fledgling Black press in Philadelphia and Boston.[50] James Forten, a wealthy Black merchant from Philadelphia, bankrolled Garrison's newspaper, the *Liberator*, for years, and in its early days Black subscriptions and writers sustained it.[51] Black abolitionists set the terms for the nascent abolition movement and were staunch supporters of Garrison's Anti-slavery

Society—at least until 1840, when many Black abolitionists joined the antislavery Liberty Party, and the Black convention movement embraced Black nationalism. A distinctive Black identity and discourse of equality and opportunity emerged out of this struggle, one that incorporated elements of both rehabilitation and antiprivilege egalitarianism.

From Moral Suasion to Black Nationalism

From the beginning, Garrison and the members of the Anti-slavery Society linked the immediate abolition of slavery with racial equality and the rehabilitation of a people degraded by slavery. The society's constitution declared that its mission was "to improve the character and condition of the free people of color, to inform and correct public opinion in relation to their situation and rights and obtain for them equal civil and political rights and privileges with the whites." Lydia Maria Child denounced white Northerners in her 1833 abolitionist tract, *An Appeal in Favor of That Class of Americans Called Africans*:

> While we bestow our earnest disapprobation on the system of slavery, let us not flatter ourselves that we are in reality any better than our brethren of the South.... [T]he *form* of slavery does not exist among us; but the *spirit* of the hateful and mischievous thing is here in all its strength.... Our prejudice against colored people is even more inveterate than it is at the South. The planter is often attached to his negroes, and lavishes caresses and kind words upon them, as he would on a favorite hound: but our cold-hearted, ignoble prejudice admits of no exception—no intermission.

She admonished whites for laws prohibiting interracial marriages (which she thought unlikely anyway), opposition to educating Blacks, segregated pews in churches, and public hostility to Blacks.[52]

White abolitionists believed that slavery and white racism were moral transgressions. Slavery annihilated "the individual worth and responsibility conferred upon man by his Creator [and deprived] him of the power of self-improvement, to which he is bound by the unchangeable law of his Maker." Racism violated God's law, as he had "created of ONE BLOOD all the nations to dwell on all the face of the earth, and whoever interposes a barrier to their living as brethren breaks the harmony which He has established."[53] In this respect, the abolitionists manifested the religious upheavals in antebellum America. They were postmillennialist Calvinists who believed they were duty bound to oppose slavery and racism. These practices offered clear evidence of the moral degradation and rot of American society. They were morally wrong because they denied to slaves and free Blacks the God-given right to develop and perfect their human faculties. These deeply religious radicals turned evangelicalism against Christians: "Will you look your Maker in the face," they demanded, "and tell him you find a natural 'instinct' in your bosom, which He has implanted there—and which forbids you to love any of his equal children, except the *white* man?"[54]

Garrison and his fellow abolitionists eschewed political action in favor of moral suasion, demanding the immediate abolition of slavery as a moral imperative. But invoking the moral principle of immediatism was also a political tactic. Abolitionists used it to challenge white preachers and evangelicals. They brought the issue of slavery into Northern churches, exposing their hypocrisy and demanding that Christians live up to their beliefs. One could not be a good churchgoing American and still believe that slavery was either justified (by scripture) or tolerated. In this approach, abolitionists echoed David Walker: "Can anything be a greater mockery of religion than the way it is conducted by the Americans?.... [T]hey chain and handcuff us and our children and drive us around the country like brutes and go into the house of God of justice to return him thanks for having aided them in their infernal cruelties inflicted upon us." For abolitionists, however, antislavery was only one part (albeit the most important part) of the campaign for moral reform in America. Asked why slavery was not put on the same plane as temperance and moral reform, Amos Phelps replied that the "doctrine of immediate emancipation is nothing more or less than that of immediate repentance, applied to this particular sin."[55]

Abolitionists combined moral suasion with rehabilitation. They believed that white prejudice was largely a consequence of ignorance and could be dispelled by pointing out white culpability in racism and the consequences for Black behavior. In her appeal to white people, Child accepted that "negroes, with many honorable exceptions, are ignorant, and show little disposition to be otherwise," but she argued that this was due to discrimination. Black ignorance, she wrote, would cease "just in proportion as [Negroes] are free. The fault is in their unnatural situation, not in themselves. Tyranny always dwarfs the intellect." But abolitionists called on Blacks to change their behavior as well. "Nothing will contribute more to break the bondman's fetters," the abolitionist authors of the *Address to Free Colored Americans* enjoined free Blacks, "than an example of high moral worth, intellectual culture and religious attainments." The women abolitionists who wrote this pamphlet denied that Black Americans were inferior to whites and explicitly invoked the mantra of rehabilitation: "Under favorable circumstances [former slaves] would rise again to the rank they formerly held." Believing that changes in Black behaviors were necessary to assuage white anxieties and garner support for abolition, white abolitionists threw themselves into promoting Black schools and Black temperance. They also believed that rehabilitation or uplift was the prerequisite for citizenship of former slaves.[56]

White abolitionists forged the connection between rehabilitation and citizenship in the 1790s. These early white abolitionists coupled uplift with gradual abolition, believing that slavery had rendered Blacks unfit for citizenship. Benjamin Rush, president of the Pennsylvania Society for the Abolition of Slavery, wrote, "When we have broken his chains and restored to the African his rights, the work of justice and benevolence is not done, newborn citizens must receive instruction, educate him in the highest branches of sciences and learning, prove to the enemies of truth that despite the degrading influence of slavery they are in no wise inferior to the more fortunate inhabitants of Europe and America." The habits of servitude and dependence induced by slavery were just the opposite of those attributes necessary for citizenship in a republic. Rehabilitating freed slaves would enable them to become independent property owners and thus voters. Manisha Sinha points out that most abolitionists did not expect free Blacks to remain menial laborers; they envisioned free Blacks becoming farmers, artisans, or business operators. Nonetheless, a paternalism and racist logic underpinned their belief in the necessity of rehabilitation of former slaves.[57]

Abolitionists applied the principles of moral suasion and rehabilitation to Native Americans. Resolution of the "Indian question" required the same "civilizing" process that applied to free Blacks and emancipated slaves. "Both," Linda Kerber writes, "were perceived as basically lazy people who needed to be taught 'respect for labor' and to scorn dependence on charity." In other words, abolitionists undertook to rehabilitate Blacks and Native Americans in order to assimilate them into white society and make them fit for citizenship. Racial equality for both groups entailed acceptance of white cultural values, which white abolitionists assumed would diminish white prejudice.[58]

In pursuing this political strategy, abolitionists were in agreement with those Black abolitionists and activists who linked antislavery with moral improvement, education, and discipline. Long before white abolitionists joined the crusade, Northern African American reformers had assumed that efforts to uplift their people would assuage white anxieties and diminish white racism. By the 1830s an extensive network of Black benevolent societies and churches was engaged in promoting education, temperance, self-discipline, and moral reform. Black elites threw themselves into the temperance campaign, believing that abstention was "the principal test of morality" and would demonstrate the upstanding character of Black people.[59] The First National Black Convention in Philadelphia endorsed moral suasion in 1831, and the American Moral Reform Society, founded in 1835 and led by William Whipper, became the main Black organization promoting it. A Philadelphia Black abolitionist spoke for many when he said, "The colored man who, by dint of perseverance and industry, educates himself and elevates himself, prepares the ways for others, gives character to the race, and hastens the day of general emancipation."[60] He could not have been more wrong.

Black elites assumed that moral reform and uplift could counter white prejudice. Moral suasion was partly a strategy adopted by Black leaders to counter the racism of the American Colonization Society. They believed they could call white people to account and change white opinions. Like Garrison, Lydia Maria Child, the Grimke sisters, and other prominent abolitionists, Whipper and members of his society understood slavery and racism as a sin that could be expiated by confronting white Americans with their sinfulness and Blacks with demands for industriousness and moral rectitude. Whipper thought racism was a matter of "situational deficiencies" that could be overcome through behavioral changes that would compel white Americans to recognize the humanity and worth of colored people.

This logic is similar to that underpinning Gunnar Myrdal's idea of the vicious cycle of racism, propounded more than a century later: white racism produces Black degradation and poverty, which in turn confirms white prejudices and belief in the inferiority of African Americans. Black uplift would diminish white prejudice. Like Myrdal, Whipper assumed that racism was predicated on a conflict between personal values—for Whipper, "God's moral ethics," for Myrdal, the American creed—and prejudiced attitudes and behavior. White racism in the 1830s was bolstered by pseudoscientific doctrines that allegedly "proved" the inferiority of Blacks but had been discredited by the time Myrdal wrote *An American Dilemma*. Yet Whipper's belief that whites would accept Blacks as equals once they recognized Black efforts at uplift led not to equality but instead to violence.[61]

Anti-abolition riots were, in effect, race riots. Many Northern cities experienced violent white riots in the 1830s—including Cincinnati in 1829, New

York in 1834, and Philadelphia in 1834, 1835, 1838, 1842—that destroyed Black property and churches, rendered many Black families homeless and injured, and ended many Black lives. In the 1834 Philadelphia riot, white homeowners in the riot-torn neighborhoods left lights in the windows of their homes. The rioters bypassed these homes but aimed their venom at Black homes and churches, destroying thirty-seven of them.[62]

The perpetrators of this violence were white upper- and middle-class citizens and angry white workers fearing Black competition for jobs. The pervasive violence in Northern cities was invariably precipitated, in Stewart's words, "by some highly visible incident that abolitionists regarded as evidence of 'respectable uplift' but that whites of all classes interpreted as 'amalgamationism.'"[63] Joint efforts by Black and white abolitionists to establish schools for Blacks, racial mixing, fear of interracial marriage, the establishment of Black churches and benevolent societies—all signified to whites the possible erasure of the color line and dilution of the white nation. Whites of all social classes acted to suppress this possibility by attacking symbols of Black organizational strength (churches) and institutions dedicated to uplift (schools and training programs).

White rioters in Philadelphia singled out the very small Black middle class for their wrath. Their success, Emma Lapsansky points out, was seen as an injury to Philadelphia whites. Whig and Democratic newspapers and politicians alike advocated resistance to Black uplift and possible integration in the name of white supremacy and all but encouraged mob action.[64] As abolitionist chapters proliferated and abolitionists launched a petition drive to overturn the gag rule Southerners had imposed to prevent Congress from debating slavery, the abolitionists found themselves on the defensive, their dream of an interracial society disappearing in a fog of violence. Many backtracked and asserted their opposition to interracial marriages and amalgamation. Even Lydia Maria Child tempered her advocacy of interracial relationships; abolitionists, she wrote, "have not the slightest wish to do violence to the distinctions of society by forcing the rude and illiterate into the presence of learned and the refined."[65]

White violence contributed to the solidification of white identity, but, combined with the failure of moral suasion and the breakup of the abolitionist movement into competing factions in the 1840s, it also opened the door to Black nationalism. In his *Appeal* of 1830, David Walker articulated the elements of antebellum Black nationalism that had been more or less moribund, advocating militancy, Black pride, and solidarity in the face of white racism and hypocrisy. "[Whites] think because they hold us in their infernal chains of slavery," he wrote, "that we wish to be white, or of their color—but they are dreadfully deceived—we wish to be just as it pleased our Creator to have made us."[66] Samuel Cornish, Henry Highland Garnet, Samuel Ringgold Ward, David Ruggles, and the anonymous authors writing in the *Colored American,* a Black newspaper, revived Walker's nationalism. They eschewed the colorless language of moral suasion and demanded a race-conscious approach to the exploitation and oppression facing Black Americans, whether slave or free. Ruggles, a radical abolitionist who was instrumental in founding the New York Committee on Vigilance, told an abolitionist convention in 1841: "We have no right to hope to be emancipated from thralldom until we honestly resolve to be free. We must remember that while our fellow countrymen of the south are slaves to individuals, we of the north are slaves to the community, and ever will be so, until we rise, and by the help of HIM who governs the destiny of nations, go forward, and like the reformed inebriates, ourselves strike for reform—individual, general, and radical reform, in every ramification of society."[67]

Nurtured in antebellum Black churches, this language provided Blacks with the capacity for organization and mobilization, but the events of the late 1830s led to a divide within the Black community and between the Garrisonite faction of the abolitionist movement and militant Blacks. Many Blacks rebelled at the paternalism of white abolitionists. Samuel Ward accused them of failing to defend the rights of Blacks, and articles in the *Colored American* decried white abolitionist manipulation of antislavery conventions. Writing under the pseudonym "A," a Black militant wrote, "As long as we attend the Conventions called by our white friends we will be looked upon as playing second fiddle to them. They will always form the majority of such Conventions, and the sentiments and opinions thus promulgated will go forth as the sentiments and opinions of white men."[68] Black militants promoted conventions that were controlled and dominated by African Americans, and after 1840 the Black convention movement was dominated by militant nationalists who rejected Garrisonite moral suasion in favor of political action. Led by Garnet and Ward, many of these militants were drawn to the Liberty Party because of its opposition to slavery and discriminatory legislation. The Ohio Liberty Party demanded repeal of "the oppressive laws which degrade the Black man without benefitting the white" and proclaimed that both state and federal laws throughout the country should be based on the same principle: "that all men are created equal."[69]

These agitators and writers developed a language and a discourse of racial inequality grounded in Black solidarity and racial uplift, at the time a radical combination. Radical Black abolitionists forged a Black identity in the face of white violence and white paternalism.

The Egalitarian Language of Black Nationalists and Abolitionists

Northern Black abolitionists, white abolitionists, and Whig reformers all subscribed to rehabilitation, and all can be called reform liberals. The idea of Black uplift is notoriously controversial in the early twenty-first century because it denotes a preoccupation with "Black pathology" and the fear among middle-class African Americans that the behavior of the Black poor diminishes their status. Yet the antebellum Black convention movement was anything but a middle-class project. Patrick Rael's data on Black conventions indicates that they were not dominated by the middle class, property-owning Black elites who usually occupied the leadership positions: if anything, Southern-born Blacks who had escaped slavery were often prominent. Organizers took steps to ensure that the conventions were representative, and robust debate and conflict were characteristic of meetings.[70] The political discourse of Black abolitionists went beyond opposition to slavery and racial discrimination to challenge the racist science then emerging and to champion universal democratic reforms. A Black abolitionist newspaper, the *Weekly Advocate*, editorialized in 1837, "We shall oppose all Monopolies, which oppress the Poor and laboring classes of society."[71]

Antebellum Black abolitionists' ideology of racial equality fused Black nationalism with the politics of respectability, but, as Eddie Glaude Jr. argues, Black ideas of uplift had two very different faces in antebellum America. One was the "privatization of racial discrimination," the idea that if Blacks changed their attitudes and behavior to conform to bourgeois norms, respect would follow, thereby diminishing prejudice. This was the view of Whipper and members of the American Moral Reform Society. Believing that racism was a problem of evil, not of social and political practice, they eschewed racial language and assumed, as we have seen, that respectable behavior would break the cycle of Black degradation and white prejudice. The other meaning of *uplift* was an "immanent conversation about racial discrimination and its effects," which, Glaude argues, pointed to Black agency as the remedy. This form of the politics of respectability "constituted a call of sorts for solidaristic efforts to reject white paternalism and to alleviate the condition of Black people in general." Both interpretations of uplift assumed the need for self-discipline, morally upright behavior, and education, but the latter pointed to self-help as a weapon against racism and racial science, while the former assumed that Blacks were incapable of liberating themselves, a precept fundamental to the Whig idea of rehabilitation. Glaude's interpretation, then, assumes that the politics of respectability was grounded in a politics of solidarity and nation building; it was not just a mask for the Black middle class. He calls it a "common sense" strategy, a form of "cultural politics that assumes the importance of self-determination." In this respect, antebellum Black nationalists' politics of respectability was a politics of Black agency and what Nell Painter calls "collective self-respect."[72]

This understanding is the common thread among Black abolitionists after 1840, despite their profound disagreements over emigration and whether Blacks should resort to violence. Frederick Douglass, Martin Delany, Henry Highland Garnet, and many other Black abolitionists accepted the idea that a politics of respectability was integral to abolition and Black liberation. It was not a politics of separatism, even though Garnet and Delany advocated emigration throughout the 1850s. Emigration, in fact, was understood as an avenue for the politics of respectability, as it would allow Blacks to demonstrate their capacity for self-improvement and industriousness. Philip A. Bell, a Black abolitionist who was instrumental in the campaign to remove suffrage restrictions in New York, wrote, "We hold it important that we should, generally, being possessed of power and faculties equal to other men, look out for every chance of enterprise—every door of emigration, where we can, build individually, better our condition and build up our character."[73] The political discourse of Black abolitionists in the 1840s and 1850s centered on Black self-determination and autonomy—acquiring the power and respect to overcome the dehumanization and oppression that was the lot of all Black Americans.

How did this immanent understanding of Black uplift differ from the evangelical and Whig idea of rehabilitation? Or to put it another way, where did rehabilitation fit into Black abolitionist discourse in the two decades before the Civil War? Black abolitionists were reform liberals in their acceptance of positive liberty and the necessity of self-discipline and improvement, but this necessity was always framed in opposition to white racism and slavery. When David Walker admonished Blacks to "higher attainments than *wielding the razor* and *cleaning boots and shoes*," and Martin Delany told Frederick Douglass, "We *must* become mechanics—we must become tradesmen—we must become farmers—we must be educated if we ever expect to become elevated," they were challenging Black people's dehumanization and asserting an equal right to economic opportunity. When Elder John W. Lewis wrote, "There cannot be any conceivable right under any circumstances in life for one to prevent another from improving his moral, mental, or physical condition by the exercise of the faculties which God his Maker has given him," he was echoing a fundamental precept of abolitionist ideology.[74] The difference was that Black abolitionists embedded their conception of uplift or rehabilitation in a scathing denunciation of white privilege and used the rhetoric of antiprivilege egalitarianism to do so.

Invoking the language of betrayal and hypocrisy, the leading Black abolitionists turned America's professed republican beliefs against slaveholders and the white republic. Douglass's Fourth of July address is the best-known example. Independence Day for the slave, Douglass admonished his audience, "reveals ... more than all other days in the year, the gross injustice and cruelty to which he is the constant victim.... [F]or revolting barbarity and shameless hypocrisy, America reigns without a rival."[75] In an 1840 speech, Garnet praised the principles of the Declaration of Independence but complained of the "base conduct" of the "degenerate sons" of the founders who denied basic rights to "millions of American citizens." Garnet implicated both Southern slaveholders and Northern manufacturers in this crime, asking, "If the privilege of American citizenship is granted in return for services done in contributing to the agricultural prosperity of the country, what class of Americans stands above the colored inhabitants of the soil?" If Garnet exempted Thomas Jefferson from the sins of slavery and racism, the editors of the *Colored American* did not. Appropriating the language of Jacksonian Democrats, they accused Jefferson of championing "the perfect equality of all the members of the privileged order ... for equality among the aristocrats, and laboring to forget that of the unprivileged class,—some of whom, to believe the voice of common report, were his own children,—had any greater capacities or rights than beasts of burden, he curtailed the expansive and universal clauses of his political creed, till the mantle of liberty, which should have extended its protection to every citizen, embraced within its torn and mutilated folds only the privileged order."[76]

Black abolitionists repeatedly used Jackson's doctrine of unjust and unearned privileges to hammer the white republic. In Douglass's speeches and essays, the language of antiprivilege egalitarianism is always linked to his belief in uplift and rehabilitation. At the same time that he engaged Harriet Beecher Stowe to help start an industrial school to train Black mechanics, he was demanding that Congress give Black settlers the right of preemption, which was then legally restricted to whites, and remove the word *white* from the 1854 Homestead Bill. In a fiery article in the *North Star,* Delany proclaimed that "the most prominent feature of the American policy is, to preserve inviolate the liberty of WHITES in this country; and to attempt to deny or disguise this, is both unjust and dishonest."[77]

In the Black abolitionist lexicon, uplift meant independence and was understood as a necessary condition for recognition as citizens and for racial equality. But Black abolitionists did not construe independence as embracing possessive individualism or simply assimilating bourgeois norms. Although they accepted that individuals might rise or fall in the economic hierarchy through their own efforts—Douglass was famous for extolling the virtues of self-made men—they denied that individual success depended solely on individual effort. Moral uprightness, striving, self-improvement, and hard work were necessary but insufficient: "All had begged, borrowed, or stolen from somebody or somewhere," Douglass wrote in 1860, criticizing "self-made men" for failing to acknowledge they were the product of a community. Douglass, Delany, Garnet, and others understood that African Americans could not survive unless they were integrated into the emerging market economy, and this would be impossible if they were confined to two or three occupations. In the political divide over the antebellum market revolution, Black abolitionists came down on the side of engagement and were drawn to Whig economic programs.[78]

Black independence rejected white paternalism and asserted Black solidarity. As Douglass pointed out, white racism overshadowed any Black accomplishment: "As appendages to white men," he said, "we are universally esteemed; as independent and responsible men we are universally despised."[79] Douglass had personal experience of this double standard at the hands of white abolitionists who thought that they were in charge and Blacks should accept their appointed role as subservient actors in the abolition movement. This conflict led to Douglass's break with Garrison and his followers when he set out to start his own newspaper. White abolitionists had "little sense that the oppressed Black people could be agents of their own destiny."[80] But it was Garnet, more than any other Black abolitionist, who put white abolitionists on notice and asserted Black independence.

Garnet's fiery 1843 speech calling for slave insurrections fused the politics of respectability with Black militancy and solidarity. For him the sinfulness of slavery was eclipsed by the sinfulness of submission to slavery. "God will not receive slavery, nor ignorance, nor any other state of mind, for love and obedience to him," Garnet thundered. "Your condition does not absolve you from your moral obligation." Nor did it absolve Northern Blacks, who "must feel for the slaves as bound with them." Yet Garnet also preached that militancy required self-help, which he believed was an invincible principle ordained by God. Independence was not an individual matter; it was collective. "We are," Douglass argued, "as a people, chained together. We are one people—one in general complexion, one in a common degradation, one in popular estimation. As one rises, all must rise, and as one falls all must fall." If Black abolitionists embraced uplift, they did so as part of militant attack on slavery and Northern racism.[81]

After 1840, rehabilitation and Black nationalism were two sides of the same struggle. Delany and Douglass parted ways in the 1850s after Delany came to believe that the Fugitive Slave Act rendered Black life in America impossible and that the only future for free African Americans was emigration. Although he never abandoned his belief in uplift, Delany was skeptical that it would make any difference to the lives of Black people in a country dominated by the slave power and antislavery racists in the Free Soil Party who demanded that the territories acquired after the Mexican War must be free of slavery and reserved for white people.[82]

THE COLOR OF FREE LABOR AND FREE SOIL BEFORE THE CIVIL WAR

Free labor, the ideological pillar of the Republican Party's antislavery credo, became the rallying cry for opposition to the expansion of slavery in the territories in the 1840s and 1850s. Antislavery Whigs and Democrats aligned themselves with abolitionists in the Liberty Party to form the Free Soil Party in 1848. Its platform pledged "to maintain the rights of free labor against the aggressions of the slave power, and to secure free soil for a free people." For Abraham Lincoln and Republicans, free labor and free soil meant equality of opportunity and upward mobility. They affirmed the dignity of labor and the availability of economic opportunities for any man willing to take advantage of them. Preventing slavery's expansion to the Western territories meant that the opportunity to acquire land would be there for those men willing to pursue it.[83]

Republicans justified free wage labor as necessary and socially virtuous. Some Republicans, like Senator Charles Sumner, went so far as to argue that labor without wages was tantamount to evil. Republicans envisioned a free-labor utopia in the South in which Black workers were equal to whites and able to avail themselves of the economic opportunities that would materialize after the end of slavery. Many Republicans, at great political risk, did stand for legal and political equality for Blacks, and some Free Soil Party members were committed to a measure of racial equality. Yet free-labor ideology offered little to African Americans. Land policy was yoked to the aspirations, ambitions and rapacious demands of white men, and the ambiguities of free labor, as it was understood in the 1850s, conformed to Northern white racist assumptions about the viability of Black labor in a free market.[84]

Free-labor ideology appropriated the language of antiprivilege egalitarianism. It grew out of the spread of wage labor in the twenty years before the Civil War, replacing an economy based on farmers, artisans, and small producers. Labor leaders and radicals decried wage labor as a form of wage slavery that annihilated workers' independence and put them under the thumb of the boss. Led by George Henry Evans, a radical agrarian, they argued that the path to economic independence for white men was land reform, not wage labor. Evans helped forge the free-soil vision of antislavery politics and the claim that slavery in the territories would threaten the livelihoods of farmers and workers.[85] Antislavery racists who flocked to the Free Soil Party under the banner of antiprivilege egalitarianism believed that the West was a place "where the sons of toil of my own race and own color," as David Wilmot told members of Congress, "can live without the disgrace which association with negro slavery brings upon free labor." Or, as B. Gratz Brown, a Missouri free-soiler, proclaimed, the free-soil movement would emancipate "the white man from the yoke of competition with the Negro."[86]

The land reform and homestead plans of the 1840 and 1850s were the first instances of politicians and reformers advocating government policies that would promote equality of opportunity, severing the Jacksonian link between antiprivilege egalitarianism and antistate ideology. Antebellum land reform movements and Homestead plans created the template for the post–Civil War reform movements for equality that combined a version of antiprivilege egalitarianism with white supremacy.[87] Beginning with the first Homestead Act, introduced in Congress in 1846, which proposed to give "every white man one hundred and sixty acres of ground 'provided he would work it,'" all the homestead bills introduced in Congress presumed that the land would be open only to white settlers. This was certainly Stephen Douglas's intention when he submitted a bill in 1849, and in 1854 when a

Pennsylvania congressman proposed that the word *white* be added to pending legislation—something many politicians assumed was unnecessary. Douglas clearly understood that the white settlers who would take advantage of homestead legislation were antislavery racists who were fiercely opposed to opening land in the territories to Blacks. The amendment to restrict the 1854 homestead bill to whites passed the House of Representatives by a vote of 101–78, and it was congressmen from abolitionist states who cast 80 percent of the no votes.[88]

Restricting land bills to white farmers put Black abolitionists in a bind. They gravitated to the Liberty Party because of its stand on racial equality and opposition to discriminatory state laws. Liberty Party activists understood that Northern racial discrimination was a prop for slavery. Prominent Black abolitionists—Garnet, Samuel Ward, Henry Bibby, and Martin Delany —actively supported the Liberty Party. The Free Soil Party was another matter. Black abolitionists were staunch advocates of land reform. Garrit Smith, who donated three thousand acres of his land to set up Black farmers, believed land reform was one of the keys to abolishing slavery. Other Black abolitionists shared this view, notably Garnet, who wrote in the *North Star* that even "where there is no chattel slavery, there do the iron heels of Land Monopolists grind out the life of the suffering poor." Garnet was referring to Ireland, but he thought emancipation would be a hollow achievement if emancipated slaves ended up laboring under land monopolists. Many Blacks reluctantly supported the Free Soil Party despite its lack of any commitment to Black civil and political rights and its adherence to a platform of "freedom national," the idea that slavery was constitutionally protected in the states but should not be permitted in the territories. Frederick Douglass argued that the Liberty Party was the only true abolitionist party, quipping that the Free Soil platform was "slavery local, liberty national, not really emancipation." But he and others voted for Free Soil candidates. Delany was the exception. After attending the 1848 Free Soil convention, Delany concluded that the Free Soil Party stood "not for the extension of liberty to the Black man but for the protection of the liberty of the white" and tried to alert free Blacks to the danger.[89]

Most Northern whites assumed that Blacks were not fitted for free labor. Abolitionists believed that after emancipation, combining free labor with rehabilitation would permit former slaves to climb the economic ladder. They rejected the idea of workers as producers (farmers or artisans) who owned the means of production and sold what they produced to willing buyers. To abolitionists and Republicans, free labor meant self-ownership of one's labor: workers were commodities who sold their labor to employers in a competitive labor market. According to Jonathan Glickstein, the Whig culture that nourished most abolitionists saw the freedom to sell one's labor as the "key to both the indefinite material and intellectual improvement of the individual and the attainment of the just society." As champions of industrialization and ardent believers in the "equality" of exchange in labor markets, abolitionists denied that exploitation could be a problem. William Lloyd Garrison argued that the ability to freely contract one's labor was the very definition of liberty. The necessity of selling one's labor also disciplined workers. Henry Ward Beecher preached that free labor "inspires . . . by hope of fruition, and intensified it by the fear of non-fruition. . . . The northern system intends to punish those who will not work. It is not a system calculated for slaves nor for lazy men."[90]

Abolitionists understood rehabilitation as a necessary adjunct to free labor. In part, this view reflected their understanding of the disciplinary qualities of free labor. Nobody captured it better than Lydia Maria Child. In the *Anti-slavery Catechism,* she asks whether it would be dangerous to just free the slaves. She answers:

> "[The abolitionists] merely wish to have the power of punishment transferred from individuals to magistrates; to have the sale of human beings cease; and to have the stimulus of wages applied instead of the stimulus of the whip. The relation of master and laborer might still continue; but under circumstances less irksome and degrading to both parties. Even that much abused animal, the jackass, can be made to travel more expeditiously by suspending a bunch of turnips on a pole and keeping them before his nose, than he can by the continual application of the whip."[91]

Grounded in a crude understanding of how work environments and incentives shaped behavior, Child's view represented that of most abolitionists. She remonstrated that if "negroes are treacherous, cunning, dishonest and profligate," their behavior was shaped by their experience as slaves.[92] Even so, many white Northerners took a dim view of the capacity of emancipated slaves to succeed in a free-labor economy. Many believed that Child was wrong: former slaves would not work hard without the threat of the whip. (In this sense, one can read Child's argument as a challenge to antiabolitionists.)

Equally common among Northerners was the view that the former slaves could not thrive in a free-labor economy because their capacities had been dulled by the mindlessness of slave labor. "The stupid, plodding, machine-like manner in which [slaves] labor," Frederick Law Olmsted declared, "is painful to witness." In an editorial, the *Springfield Republican* made explicit the racist assumptions of Olmsted's view, arguing that Blacks were not fit for industrial work: "It is perilous to the peculiar institution to set negroes about any business which requires so much intelligence, and is so mentally stimulating, as the process of manufacturing.... If anything is settled in regard to the peculiar institution, it is that negroes must be employed only in the roughest labors, where the least amount of intelligence and skill are required." Ignoring the skilled nature of slave labor on sugar and rice plantations, the paper mocked the idea that former slaves could staff Southern industries. Most former Whigs and Republicans thought that Blacks were simply inferior and must prove themselves before they could be equal citizens. In 1855, Horace Greeley's *New-York Tribune* claimed, "Blacks are indolent, improvident, servile, and licentious," and the *Philadelphia North American* wondered whether the problem of Black menial employment was not "something deeper[:] ... the constitution of the negro himself."[93]

Although abolitionists preached the language of equality of opportunity and mobility, they also believed that the redemptive qualities of manual labor constituted one of the virtues of their idea of free labor and assumed that Blacks were best served by embracing manual labor. These beliefs reflected a mid-nineteenth-century supposition that the characteristics of social groups determined their suitability for specific kinds of work—exactly what Douglass, Delany, Garnet, and other Black abolitionists were arguing against.[94] What free labor and free soil would mean for the freed people became apparent only during Reconstruction.

TWO

"What Shall We Do with the Negro?"

RACE AND LIBERALISM IN THE FREEDMEN'S BUREAU, 1865–1872

Do nothing with [the freedmen], but leave them just as you have left other men, to do with and for themselves.... We ask nothing at the hands of the American people but simple justice, and an equal chance to live.... What you have done with us thus far has only worked to our disadvantage. We now simply ask to be allowed to do for ourselves.

FREDERICK DOUGLASS,
"The Black Man's Future in the Southern States, 1862"

Your authority over the Freed Negro is just about this: you have the right to prevent any injustice being done him by anyone, even himself. Therefore, if you see him throwing away opportunity for helping himself, you should use measures to force him to the road to improvement. In effect, the Freedmen's Bureau already occupies the same relation to the Negro that the Indian Bureau does to the aborigines.

SAMUEL THOMAS,
Assistant Commissioner, Mississippi Freedmen's Bureau, 1865

We gwi wuk! We gwi wuk all right. De Union general dee done tell us tuh com back f'om follin' arter de army an' dig greenbacks under de sod. We gwi wuk fuh ourselves. We ain't gwi wuk fuh no white man! ... We ain't gwine nowhere. We gwi wuk right here on dis land where we wuz born and what belongs to us.

FREDMAN SPEAKING
to a planter who demanded the return of "his" land, Sea Islands, Georgia, 1865, quoted in myrta avery, *Dixie after the War*

RECONSTRUCTION OPENED THE QUESTION of racial equality in a way impossible before the Civil War. The war settled the question of whether African Americans were citizens, and the idea of colonization—the forced emigration of African Americans—was discarded. Republicans debated racial equality as questions of legal, political, and social equality. The first two were incorporated into the Thirteenth, Fourteenth, and Fifteenth Amendments to the Constitution, but social equality, white Southerners and Northerners agreed, was out of the question. Both the Thirteenth Amendment and the Civil Rights Act of 1866 presumed that the now-free African Americans had equal rights to own property, to contract their labor for a wage, and to enter marriage contracts—in short, to avail themselves of whatever economic opportunities they could find. But most Republicans and many Northern whites doubted that such equality could be achieved without remaking the Southern economy in the image of the free-labor North and uplifting the freed people. It fell to the Freedmen's Bureau to implement this vision. Reconstruction was the moment when race and equality of opportunity became matters of public policy and law.

Where did the freed people fit into Republicans' free-labor vision of Reconstruction? The role and operation of the Freedmen's Bureau and its relationship to the freed people turn on this question. Black abolitionists aspired to equal civil and political rights and equal economic opportunities. Many white abolitionists thought the abolitionist struggle was over once Union troops had secured victory, leaving Black abolitionists lamenting that Northern whites either did not fully grasp what was needed to achieve equal rights and opportunities for African Americans or did not really support full equality. Charles L. Remond feared that Blacks were caught between the "fires of rebellion in the South, and this hatred of the colored man in the North."[1]

What concerned many Black abolitionists in the battle over Reconstruction was white paternalism, which they thought was just another word for Black inferiority. Frederick Douglass's 1862 speech calling for the freed people to be left alone was less a suggestion that they be allowed to succeed or fail on their own than a defiant assertion of Black independence and capacity. Douglass believed it was necessary to forestall any notion of Black dependence, which would only reaffirm whites' belief that Blacks were fit only to be slaves. Douglass was not opposed to federal policies that would help the freedmen make the transition to freedom. He proposed a land redistribution scheme whereby the government would purchase land and resell it to the freedmen.[2]

Henry Highland Garnet made a similar argument in a speech he delivered to a joint session of Congress after passage of the Thirteenth Amendment, but he went much further in elaborating Blacks' principles and ambitions for Reconstruction in a speech he delivered to the Colored Citizens of Norfolk, Virginia, in June 1865. Ever the fiery Black nationalist, Garnet attacked white supremacy and asserted that the Thirteenth Amendment did very little to overturn the many Southern (and Northern) laws that restricted Black people's lives. Garnet recognized that freedmen faced not only white paternalism but also the obduracy of former slaveholders who had no intention of giving up their power and control. Like Douglass and other Black abolitionists, Garnet demanded suffrage and equality before the law, but he made two additional demands. One was for labor associations to bargain for fair wages and enforce legally binding contracts; the second was for land cooperatives that would raise money for the purchase of land for individual freedmen and their families. Without ownership of land, most Black abolitionists believed, emancipation would fail. For James McCune Smith, the problem of Reconstruction was a matter of social class, because slaveholders would still be in power and, if anything, stronger. This was a "condition of society in which capital owns labor," he wrote, and only by making the "freedman owner of his own labor, and also an owner of a fair share of the land," could the promise of Reconstruction be realized.[3]

The conflict between freedmen and planters is often understood as class conflict, just as Smith predicted. As in the Caribbean islands, emancipation opened a protracted struggle between planters and freedmen over the conditions and terms of their labor. The necessity of jump-starting the Southern economy, a priority for the Union Army during the war, put the Freedmen's Bureau at the center of this conflict after emancipation. Gerald Jaynes, among other historians, interprets the relationship between planters, freedmen, and the bureau as analogous to the transition experienced earlier by the English working class as peasants became industrial workers in a capitalist economy. Although Southern planters may have slowly recognized that slavery was gone, they continued, as James Roark writes, "to display a passionate fidelity to slavery and their proslavery beliefs."[4]

Southern whites rejected any conception of free labor. What mattered to planters was control over the freedmen. Every assertion of agency and independence on the part of freedmen inspired fierce opposition from planters. If this conflict has the marks of a class struggle between landowners and agricultural workers, it was just as much a fight to reinstate white superiority and subordinate Blacks. As one planter sharply observed, Freedmen's Bureau agents were unable to "comprehend the difference between the n——r freedman and the white northern laborer." Planters often displayed a deep visceral hatred of Blacks, wishing to reenslave them or let them die. One Florida planter, an agent reported, threatened to "poison every damned one" of his former slaves rather than free them, and he had his wife put strychnine in their food.[5]

Carl Schurz, a journalist who toured the South at the request of President Andrew Johnson in the fall of 1865, explained why it was impossible to see the problem of emancipation as only a labor conflict. He told Congress that even though "the former owner has lost his individual right of property in the former slave," he believed "the Blacks at large belong to the whites at large." Blacks existed for the well-being of whites, Schurz commented; a Black person was not property, but white Southerners did not admit that "he has a right to become his own master.... The negro exists for the special object of raising cotton, rice and sugar *for the whites,* and ... it is illegitimate for him to indulge, like other people, in the pursuit of his own happiness in his own way."[6] The Southern labor problem, as most Black abolitionists and activists realized, could be addressed only if southern Blacks had political rights and power. Both the freed people and the planters understood that economic opportunities and rights were inextricably tied to political rights. This was not true of the administrators and agents of the Freedmen's Bureau.

The Freedmen's Bureau was the leading arm of the Republican campaign to remake the Southern economy and society. Despite assumptions that it was either irredeemably racist or excessively deferential to planters and their allies, it was neither a tool of planters nor a weak agency charged with restarting cotton production and mediating labor conflict: it was the leading edge of a radical program to embed free labor in a society hostile to the very idea. Free-labor ideology and the concomitant idea of rehabilitating the freed people are important to understanding the aims of the Freedmen's Bureau and the actions of its agents. Freedmen's Bureau agents preached a free-labor gospel to hostile planters and suspicious freed people that an individual's labor was a commodity whose purchase could be secured only through inviolable labor contracts.

The abolitionists' template for emancipation combined free labor with rehabilitation. The Freedmen's Bureau, from Commissioner Oliver Otis Howard down to field agents, saw rehabilitation as the path to self-reliance and equality of opportunity. Hard work, frugality, and access to land and wage labor would open economic doors, banish the evils of slavery, and transform the Southern economy. Northern Republicans believed that the success of Reconstruction depended on freed people cultivating the habits necessary to function as upwardly mobile wage workers. Labor contracts were the agency's tool to rehabilitate the freedmen. Agents sought to use this instrument to strip away the damage of slavery, reconcile the conflicting interests of freed people and planters, and place hardworking freed people on the first rung of an agricultural ladder that would allow them to eventually become landowners. If the freed people wanted land, they would have to work for it.

The conception of equality of opportunity among freed people was very different. As a freedman explained to a planter trying to reclaim his plantation in the Sea Islands along the Georgia coast, the freed people would work for no one but themselves, and they laid claim to the land they had worked as slaves. Their vision of autonomy and collective self-determination, which eschewed simple notions of possessive individualism, was indebted to the producer ideology of Jacksonian Democrats. They demanded access to land, whether it was confiscated from former Confederate landowners or made available for sale. The freedmen regarded labor contracts as a betrayal after their exploitation as slaves and their loyalty to the Union. Their demands drew on the discourse of antiprivilege egalitarianism.

Free-labor ideology and rehabilitation conflicted with the aspirations of the freed people and elicited hostility from planters. To the Freedmen's Bureau, equality meant that freedmen and planters were treated as equals in the language and terms of labor contracts. But contracts did little to alter the imbalance in power between the two groups. Faced with Southern white intransigence to free labor, the bureau adopted policies and practices to regulate Southern labor markets and evolved into a powerful federal agency that belied the assumptions and goals of its creators.[7] Its ideological commitment to rehabilitation reinforced nineteenth-century conceptions of racial hierarchies while failing to institutionalize a free labor market.

ORIGINS OF THE FREEDMEN'S BUREAU: RACISM AND BLACK SUBJECTIVITY

Initially set up in 1865 as a temporary expedient to cope with the chaos at the end of the Civil War, the Freedmen's Bureau was charged with the "supervision and management of all abandoned lands, and the control of all subjects relating to freedmen from rebel states, ... under such rules and regulations as may be prescribed by the President."⁸ The agency was embattled from the outset—Congress reauthorized it in 1866 only after overriding two presidential vetoes—and never had a secure source of funding. It was a national agency staffed mainly by former military officers spread across the South, usually working alone. They were young (most were between twenty-six and thirty years of age), Protestant, and overwhelmingly from Pennsylvania, New York, or New England. At least one-fifth were Union officers who had served with one of the all-Black regiments during the war. There were fifteen African American agents, most of them stationed in South Carolina, Georgia, and Louisiana.⁹

The agency was the brainchild of the American Freedmen's Inquiry Commission (AFIC). Created by Secretary of War Edwin Stanton in March 1863 at the suggestion of Senator Charles Sumner of Massachusetts, the commission was charged with investigating "the condition of the [emancipated] colored population ... and what measures will best contribute to their protection and improvement." Led by Robert Owens, Samuel Gridley Howe, and James S. McKaye, the commission produced two reports that some historians characterize as a blueprint for Reconstruction.¹⁰ The reports set out an ambitious agenda that included a constitutional amendment outlawing slavery, political rights for the freed people, land reform, and an agency that would preside over the emancipation of Southern slaves at the end of the war.

Although the reports were remarkably radical for the time, they landed in the middle of a long-standing argument over slavery and its effects on slaves. The reports reflected the tension and contradictions of the emerging debate over Reconstruction and what policies the federal government should adopt to assist freed people in the transition from slavery to freedom. This debate turned on the competing views of freed people as lazy, docile dependents in need of guardianship and as sturdy, independent workers who would do just fine when free. The debate was predicated on white assumptions of Black subjectivity, drawn from perceptions of free Blacks in the North, Samuel Gridley Howe's report on former slaves in Canada, and interviews with former slaves or refugees in the South.¹¹

Most Northern whites embraced a dismal view of Black slaves, whom they regarded as brutalized and degraded by slavery into becoming mindless, plodding workers incapable of self-direction and discipline. Abolitionists believed emancipation would permit former slaves the opportunity for self-improvement and mobility. Black liberation, they insisted, required rehabilitation to overcome the brutal legacy of slavery. For abolitionists and many antislavery Republicans, citizenship and economic self-sufficiency were not self-executing propositions.

By the time the AFIC addressed the question of emancipation, Northern white attitudes toward Southern Blacks were changing. In her analysis of the reporting and commentary of Northern newspapers during and after Reconstruction, Heather Cox Richardson suggests that this shift resulted mainly from the performance of Blacks during the war: "As they redefined slaves as good workers, Northern Republicans began to describe the bondsmen as quintessential examples of ideal workers who would work hard, support themselves, and gradually rise."[12] Bolstering these conclusions were the reports of army officers dealing with contrabands (Blacks fleeing slavery) in the Mississippi Valley, which dismantled stereotypes of lazy, feckless Blacks who would not respond to market incentives or economic opportunity.[13]

Recognizing this shift, the commission's final report took issue with Alexis de Tocqueville's gloomy assessment of the future of race relations in America, arguing that once there was a constitutional amendment banning slavery, "there is little reason to doubt that [the Negro] will become a useful member of the great industrial family of nations." Intent on countering any suggestion that the freedmen would become a burden on the public, the commission wrote, "The enfranchised negro is as capable of taking care of himself and his family as any other portion of our people." The self-reliance of the freed people was not in question: "No fear is more groundless than that the result of emancipation will be to throw the negroes as a burden on the community." The freedmen should be given a fair shot at success. It was important that "we secure to them the means of making their own way. . . . If, like whites, they are to be self-supporting, then, like whites, they ought to have to rights, civil and political, without which they are but laboring as a man labors with hands bound."[14] Frederick Douglass could not have said it more clearly.

The commission set out an elaborate agenda for the Freedmen's Bureau that included supervision of labor contracts between freedmen and planters, the power to settle disputes, and responsibility for the education of the freed people.[15] The three commissioners were aware of the necessity of land redistribution to the success of Reconstruction. In a letter to Senator Charles Sumner, McKaye, the most radical member of the commission, argued that "any plan that separates the care and disposition of the freedmen, from the disposition of abandoned lands, at the South, will be a great mistake." McKaye had a very dim view of Southern planters: "Many of the [planters] at the end of the war," he reported, were "even more rampant to enslave the negro than ever before." He favored land confiscation, though the commission would not go that far.[16]

The commissioners also foresaw the power of racism to impede Reconstruction and the necessity of integrating the freed people into American society. Prejudiced actions were "not only a breach of humanity, an offense against civilization," they wrote in their preliminary report, but "also an act which gives aid and comfort to the enemy." Yet the final report put the burden of integration on African Americans, advising them to "refrain from settling in colonies or suburbs by themselves" if they wanted to "take off the edge of national prejudice."[17]

Although the commission seemingly endorsed a model of emancipation that was similar to Douglass's conception of independence—granting the freedmen equal civil and political rights and then allowing them to make their own way—its reports embodied a conception of Black subjectivity that led it to espouse a form of guardianship or rehabilitation. If the commission did not endorse a full-blown argument for rehabilitation, their report certainly flirted with it and justified it. The AFIC reports clearly reflect the fusion of free-labor ideology with rehabilitation. In its preliminary report, the commission embraced a historicist conception of Black subjectivity, one that Northern abolitionists and antislavery Republicans largely accepted. It attributed the "vices and immorality" reported among some former slaves, who had fled plantations to the Union Army lines, to the institution of slavery: "Men who are allowed no property do not learn to respect the rights of property." Theft was common, lying a necessity of survival. Where slavery was most brutal, these men displayed "a stolid, sullen despondency [that attested] the stupefying influence of slave-driving."[18]

Yet the AFIC mingled this historicist conception of race with an essentialist view, arguing that whereas whites were hard-headed and calculating, Blacks were "genial, lively, docile, emotional, the affections rule; the social instincts maintain the ascendant.... It is a knowing rather than a thinking race. Its perceptive faculties are stronger than its reflective powers.... It is not a race that will ever take a lead in the material improvement of the world; but it will make for itself, whenever it has fair play, respectable positions, comfortable homes." The AFIC believed the freedmen had to be guided to freedom, though such guidance should be temporary and humane. The freedmen had much to learn from sympathetic Northern whites, the commission wrote. "They will gain in force of character, in mental cultivation, in self-reliance, in enterprise, in breadth of views and in habits of generalization. Our influence over them, if we treat them well, will be powerful for good."[19]

It was common for white abolitionists and antislavery Republicans to infantilize the freed people. James Yeatman, the president of the Western Sanitary Commission and a staunch abolitionist, referred to them as "new born children of freedom" who had to be protected and guided in their "infancy." Yet doing too much for the freedmen was as unwise as doing too little. "We must not treat them as stepchildren, ... [but] let us beware the temptation to treat the colored people with less than even justice, because they have been, and still are, lowly and feeble."[20]

Public debate in Congress initially centered on General Nathaniel P. Banks's controversial plan for the contrabands in the lower Mississippi Valley. Intent on embedding free labor in the lower South during the war, Banks devised a plan to put contrabands to work on plantations under the supervision of their former owners and Union officers, in conditions that many considered similar to slavery. The former slaves contracted their labor at wages set by the Union Army and worked in gangs, just as they had when enslaved. They were confined to the plantation unless given authorization to leave and were required to work nine- and ten-hour days for the duration of the contract, usually one year. Banks required planters to provide food, clothing, and shelter for the former slaves, but he allowed planters to dock their pay for insubordination and violation of army regulations.

In subordinating emancipation to political and economic stability, Banks's plan effectively cultivated and promoted the interests of planters. Banks justified his labor regulations as a means of rehabilitating former slaves. He regarded labor as a "public duty" and saw disciplined work as the only path out of slavery. "It has required the legislation of four centuries to give white labor the freedom it enjoys in contracting for employment," Banks said, and it would likely take as long for Blacks.[21]

Douglass was furious when he learned of this plan. In a passionate 1865 speech, he denounced Banks's approach as a form of "absolute slavery" that mocked the Emancipation Proclamation by denying the freed people one of the basic rights of freedom: the right to choose where and when to work. Wendell Phillips wrote in the *National Anti-slavery Standard* that Banks's regulations reduced "the negro [to] a serf, punishable at will, hireable at the will of the government. No manhood."[22] But the fiercest denunciation of the regulations appeared in the pages of the *New Orleans Tribune*, arguably the major Black newspaper in the South during Reconstruction, founded by Louis C.

Roudanez. Its editorials reflected the views of the free, largely Creole population of New Orleans. The paper was distributed to members of Congress daily, and once the war ended it became the official paper of the Republican party in Louisiana. The *Tribune's* editors were pro-freedmen and assumed that emancipation required "the beginning of a great social, economic, and political revolution for the Negro." They demanded that Black workers have "self disposal of themselves. We want that they be as free as white men in contracting for their labor, going from place to place, and enjoying the earnings of their toils. " Like Garnet, but unlike Douglass, the paper's editors encouraged Black workers to form associations to bargain for wages, or worker-run cooperatives that would own and manage plantations. The editors called the Banks plan "tutorage." They pointed out that the army's rules for Black labor were more like rules for apprentices than free labor, and they referred to Louisiana as the "Apprentice State" instead of the "Free State." They complained that the "freedman must confine himself within the walls of the plantation like a prison"; a position in which a worker was unable to bargain for wages, the *Tribune* proclaimed, "is still servitude." The paper's editors argued that the rules were counterproductive to instilling the attitudes needed for freedom.[23]

The congressional debate over the Freedmen's Bureau in 1864–65 pitted plans for guardianship against laissez-faire emancipation, or a stripped-down version of Douglass's idea of combining independence with civil rights (most Republicans were not prepared to accept voting rights in 1865). Abolitionists and radicals rejected the Banks plan but favored guardianship. They proposed giving the Freedmen's Bureau the authority to mediate disputes and act as "advisory guardians" for the freedmen, protecting them from malicious white Southerners and ensuring they honored the terms of their contracts. Senator Charles Sumner set out the elements of guardianship in a June 1864 speech justifying his revisions to an earlier House bill authored by Thomas Eliot. According to Sumner, "the freedmen are not idlers. They desire work," but "in their helpless condition they have not the ability to obtain [work] without assistance. They are alone, friendless, and uninformed." Sumner's idea of guardianship was based on voluntary labor contracts and protecting the rights of the freedmen. But as he pointed out, his bill did not provide any support for the freedmen; it provided only the means "to [secure] them the opportunities of labor according to well-regarded contracts ... under the friendly advice of agents of the Government, who shall take care that they are protected against abuse of all kinds." White abolitionists widely advocated some form of guardianship in 1864–65.[24]

Republican senators opposed to Sumner's idea of guardianship thought it resembled the Banks plan, and they opposed the creation of a federal agency to supervise the freed people. Any number of senators believed the government lacked the constitutional authority to create a Freedmen's Bureau with the power to intervene in labor disputes in the South. Echoing Black abolitionists' concern for Black independence, they declared that freedmen should be left to fend for themselves. James Grimes of Iowa asked Sumner, "Are they free men, or are they not? [And] if they are free men, why not let them stand as free men?." Grimes had a point; both the Eliot bill and Sumner's revision appeared to envision the freedmen as working on government-operated or privately leased plantations under voluntary contracts and made no provision for the freedmen to acquire land of their own. Others worried that the Freedmen's Bureau would operate like the Bureau of Indian Affairs and degrade the freed people. Henry Wilson, the other Republican senator representing Massachusetts, complained that the land section of Sumner's bill "very much [looked] as though it were to take care of the plantation instead of the freedmen." Grimes and other senators forced Sumner to amend his bill to give the freedmen the power to reject the terms of leases, give the Senate the power to confirm bureau commissioners, and hold army officers accountable for their treatment of the freed people. The Senate approved Sumner's bill, but the House refused to act. There matters stood until the end of the war was in sight and the Thirteenth Amendment had passed the House.[25]

The Freedmen's Bill that Congress approved in March 1865 rejected the Banks idea for government-supervised plantations but added a provision for land that could be rented or leased to either refugees (dispossessed white Southerners) or freedmen with an opportunity to purchase it. There was never any intention to *give* land to the freedmen, despite General William Sherman's Field Order No. 15. In February 1865 Thomas Eliot and Charles Sumner put forth a revised guardianship plan in a House-Senate conference report that added language giving freedmen the opportunity to rent or lease land. Otherwise, the bill was much the same as Sumner's 1864 version. Republican moderates rejected the conference report because they feared, among other concerns, that the bill contradicted Black abolitionist ideas about freed people's independence.[26] The disagreement was resolved with a vaguely worded bill that appeared to reject any form of paternalistic supervision but gave the Freedmen's Bureau broad but ill-specified authority over the freedmen and the power to distribute land under federal control to the freedmen. All language referring to contracts and supervision was stripped out. The other significant addition to the 1865 law was the addition of refugees to the bill. Herman Belz believes that the law would not have passed Congress without an explicit commitment to aid needy white Southerners in addition to the freed people.[27]

The original law creating the Freedmen's Bureau expired after one year and provided no budget: the bureau was supposed to fund itself with donations from missionary and relief societies and fees levied on planters. Congress extended the life of the bureau in 1866 in response to white Southern opposition to Reconstruction—particularly the Black Codes that Southern legislatures passed in 1865–66, laws that all but reenslaved the freedmen—and President Andrew Johnson's decision to undermine the bureau. The 1866 bill, passed over Johnson's vetoes, expanded the agency's powers, giving it the authority to punish state officials opposing reconstruction and providing a $7 million appropriation to hire agents. It also assigned the bureau the responsibility for building and staffing schools and awarded it jurisdiction in cases where Blacks were denied basic civil rights.

The 1866 Freedmen's Bureau bill was a companion to the 1866 Civil Rights Act. Both bills established fundamental rights, such as the right to enter into contracts and the right to marry. Congress also attempted to put a bureau agent in every Southern county and make more land available to the freedmen. Neither of these provisions survived Johnson's vetoes, but one crucial change in the July 1866 bill bears on the question of rehabilitation. The civil rights and contract provisions of the bill point in the direction of equality, but section 2 of the July 1866 bill said: "Supervision and care of said bureau shall extend to all loyal refugees and freedmen, so far as the same shall be necessary to enable them as speedily as practicable to become self-supporting citizens of the United States, and to aid them in making the freedom conferred by proclamation of the Commander-in-Chief, by emancipation under the laws of States, and by constitutional amendment, available to them and beneficial to the Republic." This wording, which appears nowhere in the 1865 law or the February 1866 bill, appears to enjoin the Freedmen's Bureau to undertake rehabilitation, though the language implies some discretion: "as ... necessary."[28] Although the idea of guardianship was defeated in 1865, it reappeared as a statutory matter in 1866.

Launching the Bureau: Soldiers and Freedmen

For all the volatility of the Congressional debate, the vaguely worded 1865 statute gave Commissioner Howard and his agents enormous latitude over the implementation of the bureau's mission. Rehabilitation remained the template for its free-labor mission in the South, which bureau officials presumed would open economic opportunities for the freedmen. Abolitionist and Union Army views of free labor were pervasive, and not just because of the influence of abolitionists on bureau policy. During the crucial first year of its operation, Union Army officers who had absorbed the army and abolitionist interpretation of free labor staffed the bureau and set its policies. Assistant commissioners issued orders on taking office that described the bureau's mission in language that could have been drawn from the Thomas-Sumner conference report. Thomas Conway, the assistant commissioner for Louisiana, who was known to be pro-freedmen, produced labor regulations that mirrored Banks's wartime regulations. Union army commanders wrote the first labor regulations in some states and were influential in developing policies for the freed people, especially in Alabama and South Carolina.[29]

General Robert E. Lee's surrender at Appomattox did not end the war. The South remained occupied and governed under the war powers of the federal government for almost a decade.[30] The Civil War could not end until civil authority was reestablished on terms Congress could agree to. Republicans understood that emancipation and Reconstruction required the military occupation of the South, of which the Freedmen's Bureau was one instrument. At the end of the war, the Thirteenth Amendment had not been ratified. Many white Southerners believed slavery was still legal and were willing to use violence and intimidation to reinstate it. In the view of Republicans and army leaders, the freed people's liberty depended on the power of soldiers to enforce the peace. H. H. Alvord, the agent in charge of the Orangeburg district in South Carolina, reported that whites harbored a visceral hatred of Blacks and a desire to either reenslave them or let them die out. "Justice to the Blacks will not be rendered by any court or magistrate of this state.... It can only be done by the power of the U.S. Military force." Even as the Union army demobilized, Union generals marched their troops into the heart of the plantation South, into counties with large numbers of freed people. These were the counties in which slaves had made up 55 percent or more of the prewar population—the very counties where the bureau would later set up agencies. In Mississippi, Assistant Commissioner Samuel Thomas aligned the bureau's districts and subdistricts with military districts to ensure proximity to Union soldiers.[31]

At the end of the war, only 22 percent of the approximately 268,000 Union troops were stationed in the five states of the Deep South (see table 2).

Beginning in June 1865, Union soldiers swarmed into these states, many penetrating into areas of the rural South that had escaped the brunt of the war (southwestern Georgia and southern Alabama, for example). As total troop numbers declined, Union soldiers were concentrated in these states. As of June 1865, there were 121,699 troops in the Deep South, and by August their numbers exceeded those in the upper South. From June to December 1865, the number of troops dropped sharply, but 47 percent of all troops—52,562 soldiers—were stationed in Deep South states at the end of 1865. At same time, the army increased the number of army posts in the Deep South from 91 in May 1865 to 202 by September. Army posts in the Deep South states constituted 60 percent of all army posts by the end of the year (125 posts), compared to 27 percent in the upper South (56 posts).[32]

Figure 1 illustrates the movement of Union troops into the main plantation regions in the Deep South from June 1865 to May 1866. In Alabama, for example, Union soldiers marched into Montgomery County and then dispersed east and west into the plantation counties. By August, more than seven thousand troops were stationed in the eight Black Belt counties—43 percent of all troops in Alabama. In Georgia and South Carolina, the army moved fifty thousand troops into key plantation counties with large Black populations. In Georgia, Union troops in these counties accounted for an average of 42 percent of all troops. In South Carolina, Union troops were concentrated initially in the Sea Island counties and Charleston, where slaves had made up over 70 percent of the 1860 population.

There was less dispersion in Mississippi because most troops were stationed in the Mississippi Delta counties, mainly in Vicksburg, Natchez, and Jackson Counties, where cotton plantations were concentrated. There were very few troops in eastern Mississippi. In Louisiana, most of the Union troops were stationed in the plantation counties along the Red River, in the cotton plantations of the lower Mississippi Delta, and in New Orleans. The number of troops in these Louisiana counties averaged over fifteen thousand—73 percent of the total number in the state from June to December 1865.

Freed people and planters first encountered Union troops during the summer of 1865, when there were few Freedmen's Bureau agents in the field. The number of troops in plantation counties sharply declined by late spring 1866 as troops were moved to population centers. But by the time they left, Freedmen's Bureau agents had penetrated the interior of the Deep South, replacing soldiers as the main representatives of the North to freed people and planters. In August 1865 only 393 men had signed up as agents, almost all

TABLE 2 Numbers of Union Troops and US Army outposts, May–December 1865

	May	June	August	September	October	November	December
				UNION TROOPS			
All Confederate states	267,822	317,606	228,889	189,906	148,587	125,207	111,288
Deep South states	59,208	121,699	87,105	81,015	62,294	54,669	52,562
Alabama	8,169	50,843	18,632	18,051	10,963	11,299	9,678
Georgia	1,764	26,862	17,441	15,779	12,328	10,086	9,403
Louisiana	25,981	11,660	25,811	23,747	19,434	15,667	16,644
Mississippi	21,674	18,292	14,914	13,796	10,895	9,619	9,099
South Carolina	1,620	14,042	10,307	9,642	8,674	7,998	7,738
Upper South states[b]	200,424	195,907	84,174	56,764	46,892	38,854	32,854
Troops in Deep South as % of total	22.1	38.3	38.1	42.6	41.9	43.6	47.2
Troops in Upper South as % of total	74.8	61.7	36.8	29.9	31.5	31.0	29.5
				US ARMY OUTPOSTS			
Confederate states (excluding Texas & Florida)	165	217	312	324	287	246	208
Deep South states	67	91	196	202	173	156	125
Upper South states	91	115	102	98	77	65	56
Deep South outposts as % of total[a]	40.6	41.9	62.8	62.4	60.3	63.4	60.1
Upper South outposts as % of total[b]	55.2	53.0	32.7	30.3	26.8	26.4	26.9

SOURCE: Gregory P. Downs, Mapping Occupation Troop Locations Dataset, 2015 (www.mappingoccupation.org); Gregory P. Downs, *After Appomattox: Military Occupation and the Ends of War* (Cambridge, MA: Harvard University Press, 2015). appendix 1, 3. Calculations by author.

[a] Deep South states: Alabama, Georgia, Louisiana, Mississippi, South Carolina.
[b] Upper South states: Arkansas, North Carolina, Tennessee, Virginia.

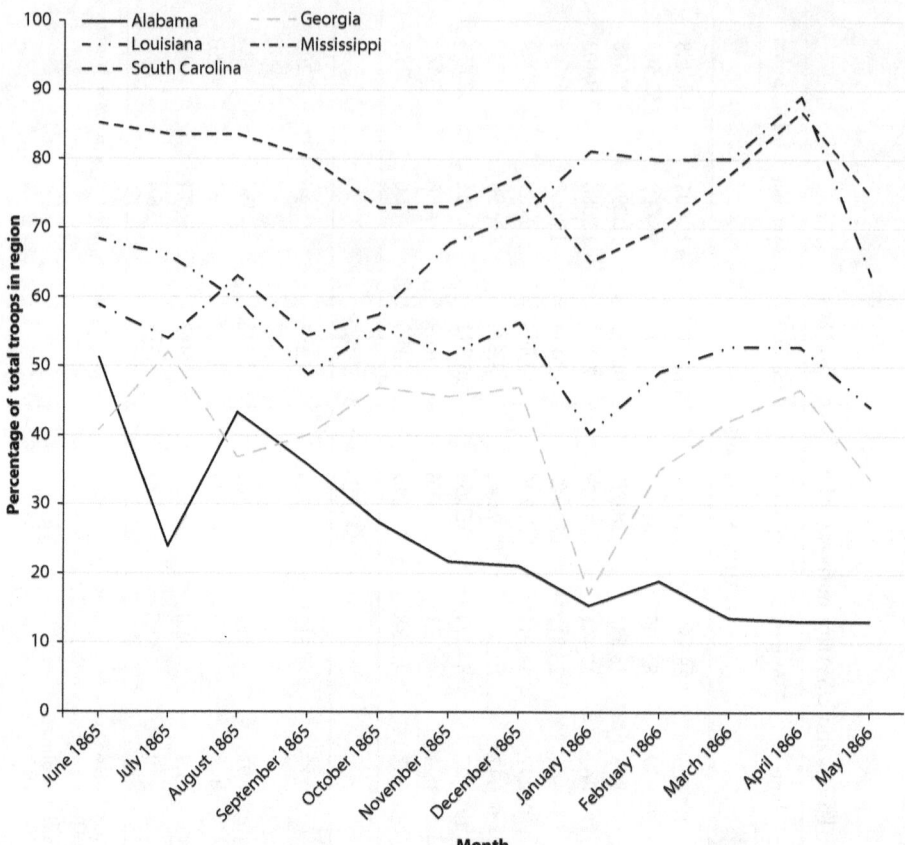

FIGURE 1. Deployment of Union troops in plantation regions, 1865–66.

of them Union Army officers or former officers. By the end of the year another 519 were added. Of the 912 agents serving in the bureau in 1865, 43 percent were in the five Deep South states and most of the rest in the upper South—mainly in Virginia, which had 24 percent of all agents.

The Freedmen's Bureau was a military operation from start to finish. It was under the jurisdiction of the Union Army, and it was staffed largely by army officers. Many agents who started out as Union officers later transferred to civilian status. Other officers became agents as they mustered out of the army. I estimate that 79 percent of agents in the former Confederate states were current or former military personnel; only 21 percent were true civilians who did not serve in either army (see table 3). Of the civilian agents, 76 percent were Southerners, and 10 percent of these agents were either former

TABLE 3 Military vs. civilian status of Freedmen's Bureau agents by state and region, 1865–72

	Total agents	Military (%)	True civilian		
			All civilian (%)	Southerners (%)	Northerners (%)
Deep South states	1003	70	30	26	4
Alabama	119	87	13	8	6
Georgia	361	28	72	67	5
Louisiana	202	98	2	1	1
Mississippi	177	92	8	3	5
South Carolina	144	92	8	3	5
Deep South States excluding Georgia	642	93	7	3	4
Upper South states[a]	787	89	11	9	3
Confederate states	2103	79	21	18	4

SOURCE: John A Carpenter Research Collection, Box 4, Schomburg Center for Research in Black Culture, New York. Calculations by author.

[a] Upper South states: Arkansas, North Carolina, Tennessee, Virginia.

Confederates or slaveholders. Freedmen's Bureau agents in Deep South states were drawn disproportionately from the regular army. Agents from the veterans' reserve accounted for only 28 percent of all agents, and most of these served in the upper South or Florida.[33]

The number of Southern civilian agents primarily in Georgia was clearly atypical among Deep South states. In Alabama, Louisiana, Mississippi, and South Carolina almost all agents (93 percent) were drawn from the regular army. In Georgia, however, Assistant Commissioner Davis Tillson recruited large numbers of Southern civilians, a decision driven by the paucity of Union troops stationed there by January 1866. Civilian agents accounted for two-thirds of the 242 agents in Georgia. They included local notables, ardent Confederates, and former slaveholders. Most Southerners joined the Georgia Bureau in the first six months of 1866, after a sharp decline in the number of Union troops in Georgia.[34] These agents were more inclined to represent the interests of planters than those of freedmen, and they believed, as one said, that Tillson had hired them "to keep [all freed people] straight." Freedmen complained vociferously that civilian agents wanted to reduce them to "crouching servility," and many were unscrupulous and given to corruption.[35]

Operating as a semi-independent arm of an occupying army, Freedmen's Bureau administrators issued regulations and directives that could be enforced at the point of a gun, and often were. Initially, the Union generals who issued these regulations merely copied the labor regulations the army had devised to deal with contrabands during the war. These regulations reflected an ideological commitment to contracts as the foundation of a free labor market and the army's concern to restore a semblance of social order after the war, thereby forestalling planter violence and Black rebellion. Labor contracts were understood as a means of stabilizing agricultural production. In the absence of any statutory language specifying the mission and authority of the bureau, the army's model of contracts formed the heart of the bureau's operations.

Wielding these contracts as a tool of regulation, Freedmen's Bureau agents espoused the combination of free labor and rehabilitation forged by the abolitionist movement. Wendell Phillips, like many abolitionists, railed against General Banks's draconian labor policies, but he accepted that liberty entailed the right to sell one's labor as one chose and the right to quit any employer. Such ideas were common among Union army officers who joined the bureau. Almost half of Northern agents were from strong abolitionist states or states where the Liberty Party flourished: the New England states, New York, Pennsylvania, and Ohio. Evangelical principles and antislavery influenced the outlook of Howard and the bureau's commissioner of education, John Alvord, as well as many of its assistant commissioners. Rufus Saxton, the assistant commissioner of Georgia and South Carolina, grew up in an abolitionist family in Massachusetts and was known for his antislavery and free-labor views. The bureau also cultivated a close relationship with the American Missionary Association, an organization that E. Allen Richardson characterizes as based on the fusion of the "tenets of... Christian abolitionism, free-labor thought, and the evangelical beliefs that evolved from... the Second Great Awakening."[36]

Yet the free-labor ideology espoused by the bureau remained chained to Northern assumptions about racial hierarchies and Black capacities. It was never a project geared to disciplining "preindustrial" workers to carry out the imperatives of industrial capitalism. Despite the language of equality of opportunity, Bureau policies and administrative regulations assumed, as the final AFIC report concluded, that, "once released from the disabilities of bondage, [the freedman] will somewhere find, and will maintain, his own appropriate social position."[37] What this meant for the freed people would depend on not just the bureau's regulations and actions but also, and more importantly, on African Americans' assertion of agency and demand for autonomy.

LABOR CONTRACTS: THE LANGUAGE OF REHABILITATION

The idea of the contract was the "metaphor of freedom" during Reconstruction, Amy Stanley observes. It was the antithesis of slavery, and in the hands of abolitionists it became "the language of insurgent popular politics."[38] In the hands of Freedmen's Bureau agents, contract was the language of rehabilitation and uplift. But it was not the only path to freedom. The alternative, as many historians have pointed out, was redistribution of land. Within the army and the Freedmen's Bureau, some military commanders and agents believed, along with radical Republicans like Thaddeus Stevens and George Julian, that it was not possible to implant free labor in the South solely by means of instituting contracts for wage labor: breaking up plantations and redistributing land were also necessary. In a report on conditions in northern Alabama at the end of the war, a Union army captain, Richard Hinton, wrote, "Small farms destroys [sic] the serfdom of capital, such as must exist in the south, if you only give personal freedom, secure no political or civil rights, and leave the freed class to struggle out of the slough the best way they can with the narrow plank of free labor." Hinton recommended allotments of twenty to forty acres and suggested that the army provide the necessary stock for these farmers, a form of capital investment. Samuel Thomas wrote Howard that he believed "the freedmen will never be thoroughly emancipated til they are allowed to own land and work for themselves at any branch of industry their inclinations may lead them to pursue." Thomas was influenced by his experience with the freed people at Davis Bend, Mississippi, a wartime experiment that set up 1,750 freed people on five thousand acres of land that had belonged to Jefferson Davis's brother Joseph and gave them control of farms of twenty to forty acres.[39]

The bureau understood the land question as a matter of equality of opportunity and assumed that the freedmen's acquisition of land was something that had to be earned through wage labor. The freed people conceived the land question very differently. For them, land was both a just restitution for their exploitation and the foundation for their civil and political rights.

The Land Question

President Andrew Johnson unilaterally overturned the land provisions of the 1865 Freedmen's Bureau law and ordered the bureau to restore abandoned lands to Southern planters. In doing so, he closed off land ownership as a path to freedom and scotched any chance of distributing most of the 858,000 acres of land the bureau controlled at the end of the war. Howard responded defiantly by issuing an order asserting the bureau's legal authority to distribute land under its control. He did this to protect freedmen already occupying lands on the Sherman Reserve in Georgia and South Carolina—those counties subject to General Sherman's Special Order No. 15 granting land to freedmen—and to speed up distribution of bureau-controlled lands. Johnson rescinded Howard's order and forced him to issue a circular commanding assistant commissioners to distribute land to "rightful" owners. Howard waged a rearguard battle to delay the process as long as possible, lobbying Congress to overturn Johnson's policies.[40]

Army commanders usually sided with Johnson, leaving assistant commissioners caught between the generals and the commissioner. In Mississippi, where the bureau controlled just 43,500 acres, General Henry Slocum pressured Samuel Thomas to return the land as quickly as possible. Uncertain of his authority, Thomas was reluctant to act on his own, though he did complain to Howard and requested authority to distribute three thousand acres of land owned by Confederates to freed people in Davis Bend. Thomas tried to keep control of the land he had in his possession, but he stopped taking possession of any more land. He told Howard that of the 251 plantations under his control, he had leased 170 to white farmers and 81 to Black farmers. In Alabama, where the bureau held only 3,400 acres, returning land to freedmen was not an issue. In Louisiana, the Treasury Department leased land to Black farmers during the war and set up Black cooperatives in St. Charles and Lafourche Parishes. By 1867, most of the 62,528 acres leased to freed people had been restored to pre–Civil War owners.[41]

Of all the land held by the bureau, half of it, 435,000 acres, was in Georgia and South Carolina. The sharpest conflicts over land took place in the Sherman Reserve in Georgia, where forty thousand former slaves and their families had acquired land by August 1865. In order to implement Johnson's order there, Howard and his agents set out to dispossess the freed people of land they occupied and believed they legitimately and deservedly possessed.

Johnson's decision to return land to planters who had received a pardon reinforced the bureau's preference for labor contracts; without contracts, they feared that massive numbers of freed people would be cast out with no means of employment or financial support and become dependent on government aid. This was one reason Howard did what he could to forestall seizure of land held by freedmen. He told Saxton to return land only on the "stipulation that the Planter shall absorb the labor now occupied in tilling the soil." But many planters had no intention of signing contracts before their land was returned. Nor were the freedmen willing to sign contracts; they rejected agents' appeals to do so and thereby give up any claim to land, and they threatened to leave the state rather than sign a contract. One said, "If a man got to go crost de riber, and he can't git a boat, he take a log. If I can't own de land, I'll hire or lease land, but I won't contract."[42]

Freedmen regarded the bureau's actions as a betrayal of the government's promises, which left them at the mercy of planters. A committee of freedmen on Edisto Island, South Carolina, wrote to Howard saying the government "now takes away from [the freedmen] all right to the soil they stand upon save such as they can get by again working for *your* late and their *all time ememies* [sic]." The army had suffered casualties during the war, but the freedmen were suffering oppression and exploitation: "The man who tied me to a tree & gave me 39 lashes... & who will not let me stay In His empty Hut except I will do His planting & be satisfied with His price... knowing I would not Have anything to do with Him if I Had land of my own—that man, I cannot well forgive." They asked Howard why the traitors and not the freedmen were being rewarded. Howard's reply evaded their question. He told the committee, "You are right *in wanting homesteads* and will *surely be defended in the possession of every* one which you shall purchase or have already purchased." Freedmen could not believe the government would betray them in such a way. But when Howard explained the bureau's land policy to a group of freedmen in North Carolina, one commented, "Dat no Yank; dat just some reb dey dressed up in blue clothes and brought up here to lie to us."[43]

But the freed people did have allies in the South Carolina bureau, two of whom were African American agents. Martin Delany became an agent after serving as a Union officer during the war. When he arrived in the Sea Islands in early June, he told the freedmen to "get up a community and get all the lands you can—if you cannot get any singly." He also told them there was no need to sign labor contracts, as their slave labor had enabled planters to "lead the idle and inglorious life." Even though he believed strongly in land redistribution, by the fall Delany was encouraging the freedmen to sign contracts.[44] Tunis Campbell, the other African American agent stationed in the Sea Islands, opposed contracts, and he preserved land for the freed people by setting up self-governing Black cooperatives in Beaufort County. He was joined by Aaron Bradley, a former slave who had escaped to Boston and become a lawyer. Both Campbell and Bradley were radicals: Bradley's fierce advocacy of land redistribution, through confiscation if necessary, set him apart from most Black leaders. He encouraged freedmen to resist dispossession, and his strident advocacy on behalf of the freed people brought him into conflict with Davis Tillson (who became assistant commissioner in Georgia after Johnson fired Rufus Saxton) and other bureau agents. One agent described Bradley's speeches as "insendiary, and bad teachings [sic]," and another charged he was a "dangerous man." Bradley was arrested and charged with using "insurrectionary and seditious language before public assemblages of colored people." The army convicted Bradley but allowed him to remain in Savannah on parole, subject to severe restrictions on his movements and speech.[45]

Although Howard and many agents worked to avoid dispossessing freedmen who had a valid claim to land, hoping Congress would rectify matters in the 1866 Freedmen's Bill, they remained committed to the idea that a free-labor economy in the South could be erected only on a foundation of wage-labor contracts. When failure of land redistribution left contracts as the main tool for building a free-labor economy, the bureau was already committed to contracts for both ideological and hard-boiled economic reasons. Tillson viewed the freedmen's resistance to contracts as irrational; he thought they would be better off working for wages, as the demand for labor was high. He told Howard that the policy requiring contracts "satisfactory to freed people prior to restoration" undermined any effort to convince them to sign contracts. Tillson believed that freedmen were not capable of farming successfully on their own.

This view was widespread in the bureau. General James Beecher, who oversaw the Combahee River plantations in South Carolina's Colleton district and adamantly opposed land redistribution, asserted that "the allotment of land *as now existing* is a curse, and no blessing to the freed people" because they had no incentives to accept reasonable wages. They had only insecure titles to the land, and they would be dependent on the government. Tillson believed the failure of the freed people to sign contracts and give up land would result in "large numbers of able-bodied people being fed in idleness by the government, while, throughout other parts of the State, labor is scarce at good wages." After explaining the virtues of contracts to a group of freedmen, an agent reported that they refused to sign contracts, as that would "bring them back into a state of slavery again," and they requested that the government sell them land on credit or induce planters to do so. The agent interpreted this position as a refusal to work and a desire to be taken care of by the government. Tillson did issue an order that gave some freedmen the right to stay on land and required planters to sign bureau-approved contracts. He, like most agents, failed to understand why the freed people resisted signing contracts.[46]

For the freed people, as many historians have pointed out, acquisition of land was fundamental to their conception of Reconstruction and freedom. African Americans passionately asserted their freedom and used every weapon at their disposal to attain it. At the center of their vision of freedom was autonomy: the ability to go where and when they wanted, and to work as they wanted. The desire for land ownership was based on an expectation, as a committee of former slaves stated, that "they would agree 'to work for no one but themselves.'" Although the freed people said over and over that they were willing to pay for land, they also believed land was owed to them. Their demands derived from an appreciation of their collective exploitation—the clearly correct idea that America was built on the backs of slave labor for the benefit of all white Americans, north and south. Bayley Wyat, a Virginia freedman, expressed the vision behind Black aspirations better than anyone in a speech to a gathering of freedmen. He charged the government with betrayal for refusing to accede to freedmen's claims for land, but he put their case not as a matter of charity or help but as one of obligation:

> I is not here to ask de Government to help me nor my family. I has never asked any help from de Government nor from friends, and I never has received any.... I owes no man any thing, but my people cannot do all this. Dey has been bought and sold like horses; dey has been kept in ignorance; dey has been sold for lands, for horses, for carriages, and for every thing their old masters had.... And den didn't we clear the land, and raise de crops of corn, ob cotton, ob tobacco, ob rice, ob sugar, ob every ting. And den didn't dem large cities in de North grow up on de cotton and de sugars and de rice dat we made? Yes!..... I say dey has grown rich, and my people is poor. We lives in slab cabins, on ground for floor, and many of us has not food, and we goes ragged and most naked.... Now, we must be united; we must take care of ourselves, and protect ourselves.... We must form societies to help each other who cannot help demselves, and we must show to the nations dat we can support ourselves.[47]

The freed people espoused a credible version of the producer ethic dear to Jacksonian Democrats. Just as Jacksonians argued that the product of their labor had been unjustly appropriated by nonproducers, so the freed people believed that nonproducing slaveholders had stolen the products of their labor. They associated freedom with economic independence. Ownership of land was the bulwark of freedom; it was a question of social power. Echoing James McCune Smith, Henry Highland Garnet, and the antimonopoly land reformers of the 1840s, the Committee of Freedmen on Edisto Island asserted that "land monopoly is injurious to the advancement of the course of freedom."[48]

In claiming land, the freed people expressed their own version of antiprivilege egalitarianism, a vision of equality of opportunity that combined land redistribution with uplift—Negro agrarianism. Wyat believed that the freed people would prosper only if they helped themselves. Tunis Campbell, drawing on the radical Black abolitionist discourse of the prewar period, aimed to provide the freed people with real and human capital—land and education—and believed that property rights could not trump citizenship or workers' rights. Negro agrarianism was a producer ideology, but unlike the Jacksonian conception of antiprivilege egalitarianism, it did not entail an individual entitlement to land. Instead, land was seen as a resource for all that could be used in common instead of a commodity. The bureau's conception of wage labor, Julie Saville points out, conflicted with the freed people's view of justice; the idea of individual payments for piecework made no sense to them. The preference for cooperative instead of individualistic work routines was underpinned by kinship ties. The chief manifestation of this view was the effort, led by Black women, to organize the sharing of ownership and work within families. These communal values led to the proliferation of schemes for the collective purchase of land and cooperatives or rotating credit associations.[49]

Union army officers and Freedmen's Bureau agents rejected this view of labor and ownership as deluded. Major General Hartsuff, commander of the Union Army in Petersburg, Virginia, accused the freedmen of believing that they "acquire individual rights in the property of their former masters, and that they are entitled to live with and be subsisted by them, without being obliged to labor or give any remuneration for their support." Such comments were ubiquitous among agents. J. E. Cornelius, an agent on Edisto Island, wrote, "Our great trouble is that they have been preached to about '*their rights*' until they are persuaded that nobody else has any rights, and until they learn better no dependence can be placed upon them as laborers." Assistant commissioners were relentless in trying to quash freed people's claim to land, instructing agents to disabuse the freed people of their "delusions."[50]

Underlying these clashing beliefs was a conflict between the freedmen's conception of justice and the bureau's understanding of equality of opportunity. Ownership of land had to be earned. A member of the Freedmen's Aid Commission, W. H. Allen, asked, "Why should a worthless vagrant, because he is a negro, receive the gift of a farm, that value of which a hard-working farmer's son in New England would think himself fortunate to acquire in ten years?"[51] Many agents believed freedmen would be better off working for wages and were incapable of planting and raising profitable crops on their own. Cornelius, Beecher, and other agents assumed that the freedmen were suited to be laborers, not owners, and would have to work their way up the economic ladder. Samuel Thomas, who believed land ownership was necessary for emancipation, nevertheless thought the way to deal with the freedman was "to place his labor on an equal footing with white labor.... Guard him against imposition, give him his just dues at the end of each month, and if there is one able to carry on business for himself so construct the rules as to assist him, and let him work his way up."[52] There was no strong desire to just give land to the freed people. Like many antislavery advocates and moderate and Radical Republicans, the administrators and agents of the Freedmen's Bureau did not see the freedmen as former slaves who had been exploited but as poor Blacks, an underclass in need of guidance and uplift.

The Freedmen's Bureau was not opposed to freedmen renting or buying land, provided they could come up with the cash. In Louisiana, for example, the assistant commissioner issued an order stipulating that abandoned or confiscated land could be given to freedmen only if they had sufficient money to pay for living expenses and sufficient capital such as "animals, tools, seeds, &c."[53] Absent land redistribution, freed people organized themselves into collectives or cooperatives to purchase land in the Sea Islands; Lenoir County, North Carolina; and Wilkes County, Georgia. In Louisiana, Black soldiers organized to purchase a large plantation. Howard encouraged agents to assist freedmen in acquiring land. Davis Tillson believed that Black landowners would "exercise a powerful influence over others, inducing habits of thrift and carefulness." Tillson proposed to Howard that the bureau set up a colony in southwest Georgia occupied by freedmen who wanted to purchase land.[54]

But there were limits to what the bureau could do to help freedmen buy or rent land. There was no national land-purchase program outside of the 1866 Homestead Act, even though Frederick Douglass and others had proposed such policies. And many agents objected on the grounds that freedmen would not be able to purchase plots of land large enough to be economically efficient and productive. More important, the bureau faced strident opposition from white planters. In Edgefield, South Carolina, for example, planters sought to deny freedmen access to land: if "all the 'land is owned by the white man and the negro is unable to get possession of it—he must work or perish.'" Some Southern whites proposed a tax on any man who sold, rented, or otherwise enabled Blacks to get a hold of land. Bands of white terrorists forcibly displaced Black farmers trying to cultivate their own land. Black dependence was predicated on ensuring that Blacks were landless and would be forced into contracts backed up by the Black Codes, thereby reestablishing a labor system tantamount to slavery.[55]

There was an additional reason why the bureau never provided the freedmen much help in acquiring land. The Civil War destroyed most of the capital in the South, which after all consisted largely of slaves, and after the war there was a credit shortage. In the absence of sufficient capital to launch viable farms, the likely outcome was the proliferation of subsistence farms that were inefficient and unlikely to produce an exportable crop like cotton. Some agents and assistant commissioners advocated that the Freedmen's Bureau provide food rations along with other resources to the freedmen working their own land so that they could get through the growing season, in effect capitalizing their work. But the predominant view was that the bureau should not lend capital to the freedmen, even though such a strategy would have been vital to establishing them as independent farmers. Howard adopted a policy banning any loans or investment, writing, "Extreme suffering cannot well exist among the able bodied when labor commands fair wages. An advance would no doubt in many instances result advantageously to the freed people, yet it would virtually amount to a loan of capital." If the freed people were to acquire farms, they would have to do it on their own.[56]

Even when the Union Army or the bureau tried to distribute land and set up the freedmen as independent farmers, they exercised close supervision. The best example of this policy is the wartime Davis Bend settlement. The results of this experiment and others like it were very favorable, and there is evidence that they worked better than labor contracts. Colonel John Eaton, seeking to promote the plan, wrote to a friend asking why the freedmen could not cultivate land outside the plantation system but "under the kindly but faithful care of some worthy friend of this race helping them to adjust any difficulties arising among themselves to obtain them [sic] provisions not easily within their reach quickening their enterprise and prompting their general input holding himself responsible to authorized Government supervision." Even Tillson was reluctant to let freedmen farm without supervision, telling Howard, "It would be a great wrong to induce these people to make the purchase and invest their money and then leave them without aid or direction to secure their success." In other words, any land redistribution had to be supervised by Freedmen's Bureau agents and guided by the need for rehabilitation.[57]

Work, Discipline, and Opportunity

The bureau's conception of labor contracts assumed a hierarchy whereby individuals could rise above manual work only through hard labor and frugality. Howard and the assistant commissioners believed it was the bureau's responsibility to inculcate these virtues in the freed people. Tillson believed his job was to educate freed people "to habits of thrift and industry." Rufus Saxton counseled freed people to "go to work at whatever honest labor your hands can find to do.... Try to show by your good conduct, that you are worthy of all." Orlando Brown, the assistant commissioner in Virginia, told the freed people in a letter, "Now you are to direct and receive the proceeds of your own labor and care for yourselves." Wager Swayne, the assistant commissioner in Alabama, believed that without contracts the freedmen would not have planted cotton: "Idleness," he told Howard, "was extremely prevalent and contracts... might restrain this disposition."

What bureau officers (and Southern planters) interpreted as laziness was the freedmen's refusal to work as they had been forced to work under slavery. When a Northern philanthropist said that Blacks would not work unless forced to, a freedman told him, "Don't know what for, sir, anybody think that. The colored folks, what been keeping up the country. When they had to work all day for the masters, they work all night and Sundays for themselves. Now when its all day to themselves don't know what for they lie down and starve."[58]

Contracts, the indispensable tool of rehabilitation, were wielded in the name of equality of opportunity. Samuel Thomas, who believed that freedmen and planters had coincident interests, made it clear that contracts were a way to reconcile conflicts between freedmen and planters. The contract was the bureau's tool to remake the freedmen and impose free labor on planters. "Contracts," wrote Stuart Eldridge, a lieutenant in the Mississippi Assistant

Commissioner's Office, "are not only useful to educate the freedmen, to secure to them justice, and to teach them how to deal with men; they also protect the planters by holding the people to steady work." Eldridge, like many agents and abolitionists, historicized slavery and justified rehabilitation as a way to help the freed people overcome the damage done to them. "Slavery has not taught them economy, but, on the contrary, has tended to make them extravagant and thoughtless. Having had no interest in the success of labor, the preservation of property, or even the care of their own persons, they have contracted habits in many which, if not corrected, will degrade, and ruin them. The dress, habits, language, and thoughts of slavery must be thrown off."[59] These attitudes were ubiquitous among agents and reinforced the idea of rehabilitation. A Georgia agent thought the "negroes are bad enough, ignorant enough—just as slavery had left them," but they needed to "be protected in their rights as well as punished from their misdeeds.... They need a guardian rather than a jailor or hangman."[60]

To throw off the legacy of slavery, according to bureau agents, the freed people must be made to understand self-ownership of labor. They were repeatedly told that the only thing they owned was themselves, and they were "not entitled to any share of [a] former master's land, or mules, or stock." Their only resource was their labor, and they ought not to expect any help from the government other than protecting their basic right to contract. But if they worked hard for a long time, army Captain W. Storer advised, they would be able to own land and hire men to work for them.[61]

Freedmen's Bureau agents also counseled that self-ownership entailed independence, by which they meant self-support. They advocated independence as an alternative to any form of relief, but they also understood slavery to have been a condition of dependence because of slaveholders' control over the lives and well-being of slaves. True freedom would entail throwing off the mantle of dependence. But freedmen could demonstrate independence only through the fundamental "conditions of a state of freedom, *a visible means of support and fidelity to contracts*," and education—not as farmers in possession of their own land. The principle of self-support applied not just to contracts or schools but also to health care. Union officers were reluctant to aid indigent Black mothers and their children, fearing they would become dependent on the government. Federal officials in Andrew Johnson's administration actively sought to undermine the bureau's medical division on the grounds that medical care only encouraged dependency. "The fear of dependency," Jim Downs writes, "ran like a cancer throughout the rhetoric of Union officials in the Civil War south."[62]

In antebellum America, independence gave rise to economic opportunity. "Independent citizens," Judith Shklar notes, "had a right to self-improvement, to education and unblocked opportunity for self-advancement." Citizenship depended on one's status as an independent earner and one's willingness to climb the ladder of economic opportunity. In the egalitarian discourse of the times, this was construed as less a matter of choice than one of obligation. Manual labor inculcated discipline and other ennobling characteristics, but the failure to rise above manual labor was a sign of individual defects. Horace Greeley accepted that "he is not the best workman in any department who is content to remain there evermore." The Freedmen's Bureau held out mobility as the reward for hard work and frugality but counseled patience. In an August 16, 1865, letter to the freedmen, Saxton wrote that in "freedom you must have an eye to the future and have a plan and object in life. Decide now what you are to do next year—where you are to plant in the spring, and how much." But as a recipe for equality of opportunity, Saxton's admonition was hardly applicable in the war-torn South. Reports from bureau agents are littered with statements that all the freedmen needed to do was husband their resources and plan for the future. "If you do not obtain all your rights this year," Saxton advised the freedmen, "be content with part; and if you act rightly, all will come in good time." At best, this was an utterly myopic view.[63]

Contracts were both the vehicle and an expression of equality. Howard told both planters and freedmen that "equality before the law is what we must aim at."[64] Equality meant only that contracts must be freely entered into. The bureau's approval of contracts was contingent on fair treatment of the freedmen and the absence of provisions favoring one side other the other. Agents were enjoined to protect the freedmen from false charges, unfair wages, unjust punishments for contract violations, and illegitimate control over the freedmen's behavior. Bureau officers insisted that contracts were color-blind and applied equally to Black or white workers and to planters. Contract violations undermined the idea of equality before the law. Planters were told that they could sue freedmen who violated a contract, but it was more important, as the Arkansas assistant commissioner said, that "no rules or regulations can be made for the government and control of freedmen that do not legally apply to whites."[65]

The bureau aimed for formal equality, and it usually assumed that the interests of freedmen and planters were harmonious—at least at the outset of Reconstruction. But as planters mounted ferocious efforts to reinstate something like a slave regime, and the freedmen complained about being cheated or subject to brutal treatment, bureau officers maintained that with time, both would come to see that cooperation was in their mutual interest. Even so, some assistant commissioners maintained that the freedmen would have to be taught where their true interests lay. Howard assured the freedmen that if they worked hard for planters, "all prejudices will be overcome, all differences reconciled, and the land will prosper and bloom like the rose."[66]

The struggle between planters and freedmen over authority in the workplace illustrates what contractual equality meant in practice. Most planters assumed that free-labor contracts allowed them to dictate freed people's movements and behavior just as they had under slavery. A Tennessee labor contract stipulated that "freedmen shall not leave the farm at any time without the permission of the employer. But he shall grant them indulgence when he thinks it not prejudicial to the interests of the farm, or the *quite [sic] of the county.*" Planters tried to regulate the lives of their workers down to dress, manners, and etiquette, in addition to behavior on the job. One planter went so far as to draw up a contract that required a Black woman to "conduct myself as when I was owned by him as a SLAVE."[67] Contracts that permitted whippings and beating were not uncommon.

As initially written, most of these contracts gave planters enormous leverage and allowed them to dismiss freedmen without paying any wages. A Mississippi subassistant commissioner reported that contracts were written to planters' advantage and "contain provisions which may be used to excuse almost any form of injustice or oppression." These contracts allowed termination for "disrespect" or any other manifestation of surliness. Many contracts were very detailed, specifying the rules for field work, how many and what kind of animals the freedmen could keep, behavior outside work, access to garden plots, and a list of fines and penalties for violation of the rules. Many contracts were also vaguely written or oral, leaving any interpretation open to dispute. The agent in Lauderdale, Mississippi, regarded contracts as "one-sided affairs" that had only one object: "To get the farm cultivated by the freedmen and pay nothing; making them do all manner of work for weeks and months not specified in the contracts."[68]

Although these contract disputes smack of the class conflict endemic to labor-capital relations the world over, the struggle was about race as much as social class. An observant Florida agent reported that planters "have known the freedmen—heretofore only as their slaves, from which they could expect nothing but implicit obedience, no matter what tortures they chose to inflict, they are instilled with a feeling of power and despotism over this race which they cannot erase." The monthly reports submitted by subassistant commissioners in these states contain voluminous accounts of the racial hostility, rapaciousness, and violent actions of planters. Garnet Nagel, a South Carolina agent, wrote that the "avarice of some [planters] has led far beyond the limits of ordinary cheating. These animals accuse the freedmen of theft, laziness, and ignorance." Samuel Gardner, the agent in charge of the Selma, Alabama, district, observed that the "natural expression of feeling [among whites] is a bitter . . . hatred beyond language to describe toward the whole black race. The general practice is to take advantage of their ignorance and need." Gardner reported that thirty-five to forty freedmen had been murdered since the military occupation began, and no one was convicted.[69]

Disputes over contract violations usually involved allegations of wage theft and other forms of monetary cheating. One agent reported that 20 percent of planters were breaching contracts, and 25 percent of freedmen were doing the same. But planters, he pointed out, violated contracts in order to "swindle" freedmen, while freedmen broke contracts in search of higher wages.[70] Wage theft was the most common complaint among freedmen and one of the many reasons they were reluctant to sign contracts.

Planters used three different tactics to deny freedmen their wages. The most common was illegal firing or dismissal. The subassistant commissioner for Montgomery County, Alabama, reported 411 illegal dismissals from July 1867 through September 1868. Dismissals peaked after planting, in March and April and again after the cotton was harvested. Planters also moved the cotton bales in order to deny freedmen any share. There were 453 complaints of this form of wage theft, with 280 reported in December 1867. Most of these contracts were for share wages, which agents almost uniformly detested, believing that monetary wages made it easier to curtail wage theft.[71] The third tactic involved cheating freedmen at the time of settlements.

Many contract disputes turned on the extent of planter control and authority and the freedmen's demand for autonomy and respect. When freedmen on a plantation refused to work for a white overseer, an agent reported, the freedmen told him, "They would not have a superintendent to direct them as they knew how to do work as well as any white man."[72] On issues of punishment, the length of the working day, and the extent of planter authority after hours or after the crop was planted and harvested, bureau agents and officers usually came down on the side of freedmen. They also sided with freedmen on more contentious issues, such as whether the freedmen were required to undertake additional work, such as repairing fences or clearing brush and forest. But on the question of planter authority during working hours and on the plantation, they defended planter prerogatives and power. Equality was served when, as one agent put it, the government has made "the freedman an *equal party* in the matter of contracts."[73]

The bureau's conception of formal equality was undermined in two ways. One was the ambiguity of most contracts: the line between planter authority and freedman obligation was usually vague, particularly in oral contracts. Some agents sympathized with freedmen, one commenting that "clearly, all of the freed people who were discharged from plantations had very little idea of what they contracted for. They were under the impression that when their usual tasks were finished, they were at liberty to do as they pleased." But other agents were prone to read freedmen's complaints as an excuse for idleness or improvidence. One agent in South Carolina went so far as to accuse the freedmen of acting in their own interest instead of the interest of planters.[74]

Second, the contract regime effectively tilted the playing field in the planters' favor, a point the *New Orleans Tribune* made over and over. Wager Swayne became so disillusioned with the contract system's bias against freedmen that he proposed abandoning it. Swayne believed that the freedmen would be best served by a unfettered labor market and aggressive legal protection of their civil rights.

Even so, the freedmen accepted the bureau as an ally, not an opponent of their freedom. In this respect, it is misleading to assume that the bureau always sided with the planters. Yet the freedmen could never be sure on whose side it would come down. One agent described the approval process for contracts "like a loaded ten-pounder, with its muzzle point blank at the freedman, who is perplexed, and overwhelmed, but not always satisfied that the barrier is safe on his side, or that the ten-pounder will point the other way, in case *his* rights are invaded."[75]

Freedmen saw the contract regime as tantamount to reenslavement, confining them to the system of gang labor that was reminiscent of slavery and a betrayal of their loyalty to the Union. They explicitly rejected the idea that their labor was merely a commodity that could be bought and sold. As one former slave told a Freedmen's Bureau agent, they were producers, not commodities. "If I am compelled to work for wages to support me," he asked, "wherefore is my condition bettered?" Admonitions to sign contracts only convinced the freedmen that agents were nothing more than "rebels in disguise." Yet most freedmen ended up signing contracts, as they saw no possibility of acquiring land. The freedmen often used the one tactic they had to increase their leverage over planters, which was to delay signing contracts for as long as possible. This behavior infuriated many agents, who all too often viewed it through the lens of racist stereotypes of a lazy, feckless people.[76]

The bureau's ability to convince freedmen to sign contracts depended on the approval process and agents' ability to enforce the terms of the contracts. Agents were likely to reject and rewrite contracts that were "defective and devoid of justice to the laborer." But given the shortage of money and manpower, the bureau lacked the capacity to approve or even monitor most contracts. One Georgia agent estimated there were one thousand labor contracts in his county, but he had seen only eighty-eight. An Alabama agent reported that he could monitor contracts only within a twenty-mile radius of his station. This was typically the case throughout the South. Planters avoided approval, if possible, which was easier in areas of the South with few agents or where the war had left most plantations untouched (for example, southern Alabama and southwest Georgia). The freedmen, on the other hand, understood that bureau approval of contracts increased their leverage.[77]

Contract approval protected the freedmen only to the extent that the contract could be enforced. This was clearly easier when an agent could call up Union troops, which was much more likely in the fall of 1865 and the spring of 1866 than thereafter. Agents reported that freedmen would move when soldiers were withdrawn from an area. Another complication was that many agents and assistant commissioners were initially uncertain of the extent of their authority to enforce contracts. Samuel Gardner asked Swayne, "How shall I make the lien [on the crop] effective, through the process of law only or by exhibition of arbitrary force, that is, a military detail?" There were formidable obstacles to enforcement of contracts, including the state laws enacting Black Codes and stay or debtor laws, and local officials' resistance. Civil authorities often refused to force planters to pay wages owed. One sheriff resigned, an Alabama agent reported, because he "would not attach white man's cotton at the suit of n——rs, and by such a trick the right of laborers to attach for their wages was rendered unavailing." Planters sometimes resorted to violence. In Demopolis, Alabama, planters staged a debtor's revolt, and when they could not stop civil cases for back wages, they burned down the courthouse.[78]

Some assistant commissioners used the language of rehabilitation to legitimize free labor and contracts and convince otherwise hostile white

Southerners of their benign intentions. In 1865, facing a deep shortage of agents, Tillson turned to recruiting Southerners to the bureau. Tillson told a crowd of three thousand whites in Milledgeville, Georgia, that the South would be better off once the freedmen were working under contracts and educated. Solicitous of Southern sensibilities, he told the audience that "large number of freedmen seem to imagine that freedom means relief from all labor or care, or the right to live a life of idleness and even of vice," and "this must be corrected [as the] Bureau has placed within their reach an opportunity for earning their own support." Tillson succeeded in putting many former Confederates on his payroll, but his plea did little to legitimize the bureau in the eyes of white Southerners or mitigate their hostility.[79]

THE ANTINOMY OF FREE LABOR MARKETS AND REHABILITATION

Rehabilitation was seen as the magic elixir that would transform freedmen into upwardly mobile workers and convince Southern planters of the benefits of a free labor market. In the event, however, it proved inadequate, leading the Freedmen's Bureau to attempt to reorder and regulate Southern labor markets. The bureau operated more like a powerful twentieth-century regulatory agency than a relief agency, even if it was not always successful in imposing its will on planters or protecting freedmen from white violence and rapacious, cheating planters. Howard and his assistant commissioners set up labor exchanges in the postwar South that shifted labor from counties with surplus labor to those with a deficit; they ordered agents to regulate the conditions of work; and they adopted policies that set wage rates and liens on the cotton crop that favored the freedmen. These actions were unprecedented in nineteenth-century America and ran counter to the bureau's commitment to free markets and federalism. But they were not unprecedented in the history of capitalism. Karl Polanyi pointed out long ago that free markets never emerge spontaneously: states always, everywhere, impose them. Laissez-faire is an end, not a means. Polanyi's great example was the 1832 English Poor Laws. By repealing the Elizabethan laws that provided the poor with a guaranteed income, the legislation transformed labor into a commodity. The Freedmen's Bureau attempted a similar feat, only to be undermined by its ideological enthrallment to the doctrine of rehabilitation and Northern aversion to deepening federal power in the South or investing the resources necessary to transform labor markets.[80]

By late fall 1865, many Freedmen's Bureau officers and agents had realized that their problem was not uplifting former slaves so much as dealing with angry, hostile planters who harassed and cheated the freedmen while complaining about laziness and insubordination. Agents interpreted such complaints as the residue of slavery—"it is hard," an agent reported, "for the planter to realize that the negro is free"—but more was involved than planter intransigence.[81] The bureau recognized that free labor markets required quit rights and living wages, neither of which planters were inclined to grant. Planters preferred contracts that lasted at least a year and thus limited freedmen's mobility, and they assumed freedmen should work as they had under slavery—six or seven days a week, from sunup to sundown. They also assumed they could violate contracts at will, a practice that dated from slavery and was upheld by Southern courts.[82] Planters quickly abandoned any pretense of supporting freed people who were too young or too old to work in the fields. Orlando Brown, assistant commissioner in Virginia, wrote to Howard that "large numbers of ex-slaveholders of this State are forcing from homes the destitute and helpless Freedmen living upon their estates." The subassistant commissioner for the Mobile, Alabama, district reported "indigent Negroes incapable of work are being thrust out and abandoned by their former masters." These planters claimed they could not support Blacks anymore, and Brown agreed. Other planters cast off so-called paternalistic obligations out of resentment. One complained that since the government had destroyed his property (that is, freed the slaves), he saw no reason why he should support freed people. If slavery had been destroyed for the good of the country, he said, "the Country ought to bear the expense."[83] A Florida agent believed that the collapse of paternalism had left the freedmen worse off than in slavery, mainly because the free labor market had unburdened planters of many of the obligations of slaveholders: "The planter has no interest in the freedmen's health."[84]

Freedmen resisted planters. They worked about three-quarters as many hours as they had under slavery and delayed signing contracts as long as possible. Waiting until late spring, close to planting time, to sign contracts gave them the opportunity to look for other work or work on their own plots in the interim, and it allowed them to bid up wages. Taking advantage of postwar labor shortages in the South, freedmen also formed proto–labor organizations and demanded higher wages and better working conditions. They argued that the abandonment of paternalism—slaveholders' obligations to provide for their families—constituted a loss of "earned rights" to the product of their labor. Using these strategies, freedmen increased their leverage.[85]

The radical version of free labor championed by the *New Orleans Tribune* and some assistant commissioners assumed that with viable quit rights and the ability of freedmen to organize, there was no need for contracts. "Free labor—in the full sense of the word—works better than any contract with half-free labor could do," argued the *Tribune* in a July 1865 editorial. "We, therefore, see no valid reason for making yearly agreements, while we see many not to draw any contract of any kind."[86]

In retaliation, planters resorted to food rationing, a practice dating from slavery. In 1865 and 1866 planter-dominated state legislatures used vagrancy and antienticement laws—the Black Codes—to coerce freedmen to sign contracts and work long hours. These laws permitted an arrest on almost any pretext. One freedman was charged with vagrancy because he would not work on Sunday. The Black Codes vitiated quit rights and undermined any possibility of a competitive free-labor market. A freedman complained to the bureau that "the [Mississippi] law says no man can hier himself out without first giving his old master the refusal.... if a Man is free and is not under or en Contract with Som one why Cant he hier himSelf to who he plese."[87]

As Howard, Thomas, Swayne, and others understood, quit rights are one of the foundations of a free labor market. Thomas believed the market, not laws, protected the freedmen. "This demand for labor protects the negro on the plantation from abuse," he wrote Howard, "when his employer is restrained from no other motive as the man who wants his work performed and knows that his neighbor wants to employ freedmen will not do anything that is likely to cause his laborers to leave." If Blacks could not quit when they wanted to, Howard thought, this would have a "tendency to check individuality, not sufficiently encouraging self-dependency." But this concern conflicted with his fear of the freed people's "dependency" on government relief and presumed unwillingness to work. In Virginia, General Alfred Terry issued an order that affirmed quit rights but stated that "vagrancy... will not be permitted—Neither whites nor blacks can be allowed to abandon their proper employment." Howard, adamant about work and determined to stave off dependency, instructed bureau officers and agents to enforce local vagrancy laws in the summer of 1865. He later justified this action by saying that he sought to avoid the impression that "the Bureau would 'feed n——rs in idleness'... [and] without doubt many freedmen and poor whites, from the seeming helplessness of their condition like pensioners, were ... expecting a permanent support."[88]

Most of the assistant commissioners followed Howard's orders, telling their agents, as Tillson did, that the freed people had the right to contract with anyone they wanted, but they did not have the right *not* to contract. Thomas thought he was countering the freedmen's belief of "a good time coming," when they would not have to work, by outlawing "idleness and vagrancy." Thomas Conway, the pro-Black assistant commissioner in Louisiana, told freedmen they had quit rights, but that if they were idle they would be subject to the enforcement of vagrancy laws. Only Rufus Saxton, who had some inkling of the idea of involuntary unemployment, took exception to the rigid enforcement of vagrancy laws. He issued a circular in the fall of 1865 that conformed to bureau policy regarding local vagrancy laws but hedged it by telling his agents: "The utmost care must be taken ... that no injustice is done to the freedmen who are idle from necessity and inability to obtain employment, and not from choice." The *New Orleans Tribune*'s assessment was more incisive. The bureau's policy on relief and quit rights, the editors asserted, was absurd; unemployment was not idleness, and if freedmen quit because of low wages or planter mistreatment, then planters caused vagrancy. The *Tribune*'s editors clearly understood that if idleness was not allowed, freedmen would be forced to work on terms dictated by planters.[89]

The bureau's policy on vagrancy and its weak response to the Black Codes undermined its own commitment to quit rights. Any vagrancy policy shifted the balance of power from freedmen to planters. Agents understood the problem such laws posed for quit rights and the ability of freedmen to negotiate better contracts: if the freedmen waited until late in the spring to sign contracts, they got a better contract but risked a vagrancy arrest. The passage of the Black Codes in late 1865 and early 1866 deepened their dilemma. In addition to draconian vagrancy laws, the Black Codes included laws that would bind freedmen to labor contracts and antienticement provisions designed to prevent competition among planters for workers. The bureau and Union Army officers rescinded the Black Codes in Mississippi and South Carolina because they were explicitly racist, applying to freedmen but not to whites. White-dominated Southern legislatures in these two states responded by passing laws that were superficially color-blind but accomplished the same purpose of subordinating Black labor to planters. Local agents continued to enforce vagrancy laws. The subassistant commissioner in Orangeburg, South Carolina, wrote, "In order to prevent vagrancy I have issued an order to my subordinates, that in case they find after the 1st of February colored men without occupation, they should report on the roads to work."[90]

In Louisiana, Absalom Baird, the assistant commissioner, tried to convince Howard to give him the authority to override the Black Codes, but Howard, fearing retaliation from President Johnson, was reluctant to do so. Baird did order his agents to prevent enforcement of vagrancy laws when they were used to coerce freedmen into unjust contracts. And he issued an explicit order recognizing quit rights. In an order he sent to planters in St. Martin Parish, Baird said that if freedmen decided to quit in the middle of the season, the bureau would not interfere but "may insist on the payment of wages for the work that has been performed."[91] In Alabama, Swayne tried to negate the more coercive punishments by ordering his agents to put freedmen to work on public works projects. He was able to convince legislators to repeal the vagrancy law. In Georgia, agents generally enforced the law. In fact, many of the local agents were quite willing to wield vagrancy laws as tools to enforce freedmen's adherence to contracts.[92] Committed to restoring Southern agriculture, many officers and agents disliked the freedmen's delaying tactics, even though they understood the rationale. Some agents tried to force freedmen to sign early contracts, but Howard put a stop to it.

If enforcement of vagrancy laws, which the bureau justified as a matter of rehabilitation, gave planters an advantage, the bureau's policies on labor mobility attempted to change the balance of supply and demand in many Southern labor markets and shift leverage back to the freedmen. Because Howard and others believed employment was the alternative to dependency, they were willing to try various schemes to increase the employment of freedmen. One of the most important was the establishment of labor exchanges that actively transported freedmen from areas with labor surpluses to areas with labor shortages. The idea was not new: the Union Army had forcibly moved freed people out of contraband camps to plantations at the end of the war. Samuel Thomas and Davis Tillson, the architects of this policy, believed that it offered a way to address the disequilibrium in Southern labor markets, bringing employers and laborers together. It was a way of sidestepping their dilemma over quit rights and vagrancy laws.[93]

Howard's General Order 139 of in September 1865 authorized transportation for destitute refugees and freedmen, and by early 1866 the bureau was operating labor exchanges and transporting freedmen and refugees to areas where there was work. A system of bonds was set up to guarantee that freedmen would not be exploited and that planters would honor the contracts. The bureau acted to seize plantations in some cases where transported freedmen were exploited. In Virginia, Howard and Orlando Brown hit on an alternative scheme to address the large surplus of unemployed freed people: using the 1866 Homestead Act to relocate freedmen from Virginia to Florida on land of their own. The plan failed because the bureau could not supply the capital that freedmen needed to get started on their own farms. Many of the Blacks who participated in this scheme had lost their land by 1870.

To transport Blacks to areas with jobs, the bureau had to actively intervene in labor markets to protect the rights of the freedmen. As William Cohen observes, it is remarkable that the bureau created "a system in which labor contracts made in Virginia really could be enforced in Louisiana a year later."[94] In order to resolve the dilemma between enforcement of vagrancy laws, to which the bureau was ideologically committed, and quit rights, the bureau actively intervened in labor markets.

To address the hardships arising from the collapse of paternalism, bureau agents demanded that planters support freed people's families just as they had under slavery. A Florida agent reported that planters "contract with the head of a family disregarding—his necessities in having to provide for a large family, which formerly was the care of the owner, and imagine that if the head of the family is fed that the rest require nothing." One military commander issued an order stipulating "the support of the laborer and his family is a just charge against the product of the land, and the owner cannot escape the payment, either as wages paid periodically, or by giving a fair proportion of the crop." The bureau's fear of "dependency" impelled harsh work and vagrancy policies, but it assumed that wages should support the freedmen's families, and it was not about to let planters off the hook.[95] The bureau's wage policies were motivated by the freed people's demand for a family wage as much as by any concern about planters' wage plans.

Planters tried to contract the labor of every member of a family, an expectation shared by many agents. The freed people refused. Massive numbers of Black women refused to work in the fields as they had been forced to do in slavery. Instead, they asserted themselves and the primacy of their families and demanded a family wage. Georgia's Black women withdrew from the labor market and, Susan O'Donovan argues, "refigured free labor by demanding that black men render the family the most basic unit of staple production." This determined the shape of labor contracts in southwest Georgia and elsewhere in 1866. One consequence of freedwomen's demand for family wage contracts is that Black men became solely accountable for the labor of the family and for holding planters to the agreed-on wage bargain. Settlement disputes often involved demands on behalf of "Self & wife" or "Self & Family."⁹⁶

The bureau believed that low wages and planters' failure to provide for families impaired free labor markets. Tillson thought that low wages were one source of disequilibrium in the labor market, saying, "It is useless to expect reliable and profitable labor for inadequate wages, or [to expect] a successful working of the free labor system." The bureau affirmed the responsibility of freedmen to support their families—in Mississippi, Thomas told his agents, "The available labor of the Freedmen must be made to support all who are legitimately dependent upon it"—but it also instituted wage policies that would enable freedmen to do so. Despite the bureau's strong inclination to let the market set wages, its agents ended up devising living wage policies.⁹⁷

Howard recognized that agents were often approving contracts stipulating inadequate wages. Abolitionists vigorously lobbied him for higher wages for freedmen. James Yeatman told Howard that neither Southern planters nor carpetbaggers could be trusted to take the freedmen's' welfare into account. He advocated a family wage and would have pegged wage rates to the wage rates of the antebellum South (presumably the rates that planters would have charged to rent out slaves). Howard was generally supportive of raising wages, but he was reluctant to set a minimum wage. He did adopt policies that required employers to furnish food or pay a wage that would allow families to purchase it. Many of his assistant commissioners went ahead on their own authority and established the equivalent of a minimum wage. Samuel Thomas issued an order to his agents stipulating that "no contract will be approved by the sub-commissioner that in any way recognizes slavery or fails to secure to the laborer wages that will provide food, shelter, clothing, and medical attention," though he later adjusted this policy to take account of differences in demand for labor. In Alabama, Swayne instructed his agents to require planters to provide supplies and food and pay a monetary wage, "proper compensation recoverable before any justice of the peace and for which he shall have a lien on the crop and damages in case he is compelled to leave by bad treatment."⁹⁸

Tillson went even further in trying to establish a minimum wage. He wrote Howard in January 1866 that he wished to establish a policy of rejecting all contracts that did not offer wages at the prevailing wage rates in Georgia, then $12 to $15 per month. "The free-labor system will inevitably fail," he wrote, "if fair, just wages are withheld." Tillson wanted to issue a circular to this effect, but Howard, reluctant to interfere with the workings of the free market, ordered him to confer privately with agents, saying he disagreed with "any course that would impair the nature of a contract." But Tillson went ahead and issued a circular ordering planters who refused to make written contracts to pay the highest prevailing wage in the event of a dispute. Howard made him remove that section. Tillson removed it but told Howard, "Start wrong, fail to secure for the freed people fair compensation for their labor, and the system of free labor, upon which almost everything depends, will be a *certain* failure."[99]

Howard ordered agents to protect freedmen "against avarice and extortion," and to stipulate that "wages had better be secured by a lien on the crops or land" that put the freedmen's claims first. Assistant commissioners followed suit, and most required labor liens in all contracts and instructed agents to give the freedmen's claims priority. The assistant commissioner of Texas (who was not known to be pro-freedmen) ordered that "in all cases *unpaid* wages will be regarded as an equitable lien on the crop or other products of the labor of the freedmen, and will be the *first claim paid*.... In such cases the *whole crop* will be regarded as liable for wages unpaid at the end of the Year."[100] Liens favoring the freedmen were adopted to prevent planters from cheating. As these established a floor for compensation, they were de facto minimum wages. Liens made more sense than a specific minimum wage, since contracts for a share of the crop had existed from the beginning of Reconstruction. By 1865–66, 72 percent of all labor contracts were based on share wages.

The bureau's policies on liens were among its most significant efforts to build free labor markets in the South. The policies established freedmen's rights to a share of the crop and thereby tried to shift the risks of crop failure or low prices to planters and creditors. But it is questionable how successful this policy was, since agents faced inordinate difficulties in enforcing it. In 1865 and 1866, under planter-dominated state governments, agents had no legal authority to force planters to pay up, and freedmen's attempts to recover stolen wages were blocked by stay laws. These laws prevented debt collection and were used to prevent freedmen from collecting monetary wages or their share of the crop. Many agents were able to impose settlements, and they advocated monetary instead of share wages on the assumption that it would be more difficult for planters to cheat freedmen of monthly wages. When freedmen asserted their property rights in the liens, including their right to take possession of their share of the crop before it was sold, the Freedmen's

Bureau backed them up. The bureau's wage policies were also undermined by its slavish opposition to collective action in favor of individual wage bargains.[101]

The bureau's policy of establishing schools for the freed people and increasing their literacy was aimed at giving freedmen leverage in bargaining over wages and crop shares. Literate Black farmers, as freed people understood, could sign contracts knowing what they were really agreeing to. The second Freedmen's Bureau Bill authorized financial resources for teachers' salaries, and the rental and repair of school buildings, and it created an educational division within the bureau. By 1869, the bureau, with the help of Northern aid societies, had set up about three thousand schools serving over fifteen thousand students. The Freedmen's Bureau schools had a demonstrable impact on the literacy of the freed people. The literacy rate among Blacks aged ten to fifteen increased from 11.8 percent to 25.5 percent between 1865 and 1870. According to one analysis, Freedmen's Bureau schools were responsible for up to one-third of this increase. But most schools were established in urban areas in the upper South states of Delaware, Kentucky, Maryland, North Carolina, and Virginia. There were very few in the Deep South, particularly in rural areas. Freedmen's Bureau schools likely had little effect on literacy in the rural, plantation South and thus were of little help to the freed people in challenging the exploitative contracts of rapacious planters.[102]

DU BOIS'S TRIBUTE TO THE FREEDMEN'S BUREAU

In his classic account of Reconstruction, W. E. B. Du Bois wrote, "The Freedmen's Bureau was the most extraordinary and far-reaching institution of social uplift that America has ever attempted.... It was a government guardianship for the relief and guidance of white and Black labor from a feudal agrarianism to modern farming and industry."[103] Du Bois's account of the origins and operation of the bureau may be thin, but his statement is a fair acknowledgment of the bureau's significance. The agency was neither a tool of planters nor an abject failure. Despite the pro-planter attitudes of some agents and assistant commissioners, the bureau gave freedmen some leverage in negotiating contracts and legal protection from predatory planters. Although Howard and his agents maintained that the agency was colorblind and evenhanded, after the first year the bureau adopted policies on wages, liens, and contracts that favored the freedmen. These changes were due to pressure exerted by the freedmen and their allies, the various relief organizations operating in the postwar South.

But Du Bois was wrong about the bureau's achievements. It failed to establish free labor markets in the South and was less the arm of an economic revolution than an underfunded regulatory agency with limited powers. It labored under constant opposition from President Johnson, who eviscerated land reform and sacked radical assistant commissioners and agents. It also faced Southern white opposition—Freedmen's Bureau agents lived under the constant threat of violence—and ultimately succumbed to the unwillingness of Northern Republicans to sustain deployment of Union troops in the South or to provide the capital investment necessary for developing the market economy they envisioned.

In the power struggle between freedmen and planters, the bureau's ideological commitment to rehabilitation proved irrelevant to the challenges of white opposition to the freedmen and their mission. Combined with a devout belief in the workings of free labor markets, rehabilitation assumed that no conflicts of interest or power stood in the way of equality of opportunity and that the interests of freed people and planters were fundamentally harmonious. But when confronted with planter power and freedmen's opposition, the bureau resorted to regulating labor markets in defiance of its commitment to free markets.

Reconstruction marks the forging of a political link between race and rehabilitation. White Northern cultural assumptions about Black inferiority and degradation were reproduced in an institution dedicated to freed people's emancipation and citizenship. It was not that Freedmen's Bureau administrators and agents accepted white Southern beliefs about Black inferiority and laziness. They did not. Instead, they projected their perceptions of the failings of Northern African Americans onto the former slaves. The irony of the Freedmen's Bureau is that an institution based on liberal assumptions about citizenship and inclusion and dedicated to Black liberation was infused with a racialized ideology.

The outcome of Reconstruction and the failures of the Freedmen's Bureau are well known. The struggle between freedmen and planters led to the emergence of labor-intensive agriculture based on sharecropping, which the Freedmen's Bureau could only bless with pro-freedmen liens on the crop. Sharecropping was not imposed on the freedmen and their families: it was their best alternative among the choices remaining once their dream of owning land had been effectively curtailed. Tenant farming provided freedmen and their families some autonomy, an alternative to gang labor under centralized control by planters. And although tenancy provided higher wages than could be obtained, at least initially, under wage contracts, it was a trap. The failure of Republicans to break up plantations and the vicious opposition of planters to Black landowning meant that land ownership remained highly concentrated after the war. Reconstruction governments did pass crop liens that favored tenants, but once the so-called Redeemer governments took power, these laws were repealed, giving planters control over Black sharecroppers and farmers. When combined with monopoly control of credit in the post-Reconstruction South, these measures inevitably led to debt peonage and exploitation.[104]

Not all southern Blacks were forced into tenancy. There was a second path out of Reconstruction. Negro agrarianism led to a rural Black struggle to acquire land, beginning in the late 1880s and extending until 1920. Out of this movement emerged Black enclaves, clusters of Black farm households dedicated to autonomy and security. Like tenancy, Black land ownership must be understood in light of the power of planters and merchant bankers in a rural society committed to white supremacy. For African Americans, autonomy and economic opportunity were always contingent.

I turn now to the New Dealers' efforts to overcome the legacies of the failure of Reconstruction, analyzing first how they tried to rescue sharecroppers during Franklin Roosevelt's agricultural revolution in the South. I then explore what the New Deal meant for those Blacks who became landowners in the first two decades of the twentieth century. Negro agrarianism remained a beacon for Black resiliency and independence for both tenants and landowners, a stark repudiation of the doctrine of rehabilitation.

THREE

Saving Sharecroppers?

BLACK TENANT FARMERS AND THE SOUTHERN
ENCLOSURE, 1934–1943

De landlord is landlord, de politicians is landlord, de judge is landlord, de shurf is landlord, ever'body is landlord, and we ain't got nothing.

WALTER ROWLAND,
Arkansas sharecropper, June 1939

The greatest efficiency of southern planters consists in securing government subsidy to uphold a system that might otherwise breakdown of its own weakness ... With one hand the cotton landlord takes agricultural subsidies and rental benefits from his government, with the other he pushes his tenants on relief.

RUPERT VANCE,
Letter to William Watts Ball, September 15, 1934

The [Resettlement Administration keeps] submarginal farmer(s) [tenants] ... on the land and ... prevented from swelling the steadily mounting ranks of the industrial unemployed, and likewise kept out of competitive production. In other words, the subsistence [farmer] will be lifted out of the mainstream of our economic life and laid upon an economic shelf to dry (rot).

RALPH J. BUNCHE,
"A Critique of New Deal Social Planning as It Affects Negroes," 1936

THE NEW DEAL WAS FOUNDED, President Franklin Delano Roosevelt often claimed, on the restoration of equality of opportunity for ordinary citizens. This was not the only way he and the New Dealers justified their massive expansion of government, but it was a recurrent theme of the president's speeches. Roosevelt characterized the New Deal as the fulcrum of a new economic and social order "in which class and privilege would be abolished." In his annual message to Congress on January 4, 1935, he invoked social justice as the aim of the New Deal: "We find our population suffering from old inequalities.... We have not weeded out the overprivileged and we have not effectively lifted up the underprivileged."[1] Roosevelt's rhetoric inspired workers and citizens, and there is no question that the Social Security Act and the Wagner Act, among other laws, put ordinary citizens on a new footing in a capitalist economy.

Seen from the perspective of the nineteenth-century conflict over slavery and its aftermath, the New Deal reinvigorated political commitments to equality of opportunity but failed to overturn the outcome of Reconstruction. Roosevelt recast the Jacksonian idea of antiprivilege egalitarianism as the political formula for equality in the New Deal. He attacked reactionaries and Wall Street financiers just as Jackson had attacked Eastern bankers to "protect the people against autocratic or oligarchic aggression." Roosevelt compared his pursuit of social justice to Jackson's: like Jackson he was fighting on behalf of the people against a "minority of business and finance that would 'gang up' against the people's liberties." Roosevelt proclaimed that the government sought to give the people "a square deal and a better deal—seeks to protect them, yes, to save them from being plowed under by the small minority of businessmen and financiers, against whom you and I will continue to wage war."[2]

In a speech in Little Rock, Arkansas, in June 1936, Roosevelt invoked Andrew Jackson as the patron saint of the New Deal: "We owe to Jacksonian democracy the American doctrine that entrusts the general welfare to no one group or class but dedicates itself to the end that the American people shall not be thwarted in their high purpose to remain custodians of their own destiny." At the same time, he clearly repudiated the antistate thrust of Jacksonian democracy: the times, he proclaimed, call "for measures of organized Government assistance which the more spontaneous and personal promptings of a pioneer generosity could never alone have obtained." In his speech, Roosevelt equated equality of opportunity with liberty: "Freedom is no half-and-half affair," he thundered. "If the average citizen is guaranteed equal opportunity in the polling place, he must have equal opportunity in the marketplace."[3]

As James Holt suggests, Roosevelt sought to regenerate the American value of equality of opportunity for a new era. He recognized that the expansive opportunities that (white) Americans had experienced in the nineteenth century were gone. It was no longer possible to move to another place to escape economic hardship: a "wise government seeks to provide the opportunity through which the best of individual achievement can be obtained, while at the same time it seeks to remove such obstruction, such unfairness as springs from selfish human motives." He pledged that the government would remove obstacles to success and seek "new means for the restoration of equality of opportunity."[4] One way to do so was by ensuring that American workers had security of employment and financial security in old age. Another was attacking entrenched privilege, a theme in many of Roosevelt's speeches. New Deal labor policy was based on the idea of antiprivilege egalitarianism. The Wagner Act put the authority of government behind the formation of unions and enabled workers to achieve a degree of equality with business so that fair bargaining could take place. Robert Wagner summarized the political formula: "This process of economic self-rule must fail unless every group is equally well represented. In order that the strong may not take advantage of the weak, every group must be equally strong." In the 1940s, Roosevelt's Justice Department brought a series of cases under the Thirteenth Amendment and the 1870 Civil Rights Act to ban debt peonage and other restrictions on the movement of labor. The Justice Department succeeded in doing what the Republicans could not do during Reconstruction: institutionalizing free labor in the South. By free labor, New Dealers meant not just quit rights, but the right for workers to organize into unions.[5]

The New Deal's commitment to equality of opportunity was also manifested in plans to restore opportunity through rehabilitation to those excluded from the main economic and social policies of the New Deal. The New Deal erased the partisan distinction between antiprivilege egalitarianism and rehabilitation that had defined the conflicting aims of Democrats and Whigs in the 1830s and 1840s. Rehabilitation inspired the shift from cash to work relief with the creation in 1935 of the Works Progress Administration (WPA) and the National Youth Administration, which ran student-aid and job-training programs for unemployed youth. It was also the rationale for creation of the Resettlement Administration (RA) and its successor, the Farm Security Administration (FSA).

For many African Americans, the New Deal was a cause for celebration. Arthur Mitchell, the lone Black member of Congress, declared, "I believe that under this administration the Negroes of the United States have the best opportunity that has come to them during my lifetime." But if Blacks were to benefit from New Deal reform, it would be as members of the working class, not as members of a racial group. Prominent New Dealers—Will Alexander, Harold Ickes, Frances Perkins, and Eleanor Roosevelt among them—all believed that the question of racism should be subsumed under the New Deal's economic reforms and its working-class agenda. New Dealers believed racial distinctions were irrational, "contrary to reason and derived from emotional and irrational attitudes which racists employed to separate blacks and whites and prevent them from recognizing a common economic and political destiny." Racial conflict would abate, they believed, as Blacks were incorporated into New Deal economic programs. Black economic gains would dissipate racial prejudice, and the "'Negro problem' would then be recognized to be individual and not racial." Will Alexander, who became head of the FSA in 1937 and disliked any expression of racial identity, told Black audiences in his speeches to be "more class conscious and less race conscious."[6]

Black leaders and activists recognized the significance of the economic changes afoot and the promise of the New Deal, but they also attacked the rampant discrimination inherent in many New Deal programs. John P. Davis, who helped form the Joint Committee on National Recovery, an umbrella group of civil rights organizations, exposed the discrimination in the National Recovery Administration's wage and hour codes and other programs. Ralph J. Bunche, arguably one of the most radical Black activists, excoriated the early New Deal programs as serving only "to crystallize those abuses and oppressions which the exploited Negro citizenry of America have long suffered under laissez-faire capitalism, and for the same reasons as in the past." The National Association for the Advancement of Colored People (NAACP) and the Urban League invoked the slogan "Not Alms but Opportunity—Jobs and Justice" to challenge New Deal policies that excluded Black workers and restricted assistance to Blacks to relief.[7]

Black politics in the 1930s traveled along two related tracks. One was elite-driven insider politics. The New Deal's Black Cabinet was the main avenue by which Black elites lobbied New Deal policy makers. Most federal agencies had Black advisers who kept track of and assessed the impact of New Deal policies on Blacks and tried to secure the appointment of Black administrators and officials to federal agencies. Mary McLeod Bethune was among the most successful of the Black Cabinet advisers. As one of the few who had meetings with FDR, she argued fiercely for a Black voice in the development of policy.[8] The second track of Black politics was the effort to align Black workers with the labor movement. Many Black leaders and elites believed that Black economic opportunity depended on an alliance with the white working class. Abram Harris, a militant young Black economist, challenged NAACP doctrine, arguing that "instead of continuing to oppose racial discrimination on the job and in pay ... the Association [should] attempt ... to get white workers and black to view their lot as embracing a common cause rather than antithetical interests." Bunche, who distrusted Black middle-class leadership and regarded race as an "American shibboleth," insisted that only an alliance with white workers, based on common economic deprivation, would alleviate African American suffering. A. Philip Randolph, who became the first president of the National Negro Congress, put his faith for the future of Black workers in the labor movement. In his keynote address as president, he contended that the New Deal was "no remedy" for Black workers because "it does not seek to change the profit system." Unlike Bunche, he insisted that Blacks were subordinated by both race and class oppression, a view shared by the Black tenants who formed the bedrock of the Southern Tenant Farmers Union (STFU). To one degree or another, Black elites and political organizations were pro-union and actively promoted alliances between Black and white workers. Even staid organizations like the Urban League formed Workers' Councils to convince Black workers to join unions, and the NAACP was a vocal ally of the STFU.[9] For many Blacks, antiprivilege egalitarianism was synonymous with building the power of the labor movement.

The notable dissenter to this shift in beliefs and political practice was W. E. B. Du Bois, who had concluded that racism was a "deeply entrenched" prejudice and that New Deal programs were unlikely to eradicate it. Du Bois advocated a "Black cooperative commonwealth," in which Black leaders and workers would rebuild Black communities. He believed that "if the leading Negro classes cannot assume and bear the uplift of their own proletariat, they are doomed for time and eternity.... It is not a case of ethics; it is a plain case of must."[10] Du Bois was not a late-blooming Black separatist. His turn away from integration in the 1930s was a brief for Black power and autonomy reminiscent of the demands of Black abolitionists and the Freed people. He had little faith that Blacks could transcend racism by assimilating white values, a process that was seen as integral to any program of rehabilitation. But Du Bois reserved his harshest criticisms for those Blacks championing an alliance with labor. He did not object to Blacks joining unions; he only insisted they should have no illusions. "White labor," he wrote, "has to hate scabs, but it hates black scabs not because they are scabs but because they are black."[11]

Nowhere was the New Dealers' faith that their economic policies could diminish the scourge of racism or the Black debate over race and class more consequential than in the South. Roosevelt fomented an agricultural revolution that transformed the Southern economy—at the price of dispossessing Black and white tenant farmers of land and entrenching the power of the dominant planter class. The Resettlement Administration (renamed the Farm Security Administration in 1937) provided needed loans and grants to some of the losers in this revolution: tenants, sharecroppers, and farm owners. As Aubrey Williams, one of the more radical New Dealers, explained, the agency's mission was "to take the landless, homeless, cashless farmer and set him up with the nucleus of a self-perpetuating subsistence. It can lend him land and make arrangements by which he can eventually buy it."[12] The agency was aligned with displaced tenants and landowners, whom it sought to rehabilitate, but it operated under rules of engagement dictated by Jim Crow. That meant the agency evaded the exploitation endemic to tenancy, sweet-talked Southern Democrats about the benefits of the Resettlement Administration for white Southerners, and avoided mentioning that the program would benefit Black tenants.

The STFU advanced a radical critique of tenancy that reflected the discourse of antiprivilege egalitarianism. Formed as a biracial union of Black and white tenants in the plantation counties of Arkansas, the STFU had a clear-eyed view of the pervasive exploitation of tenants. In a statement to the Arkansas Commission on Farm Tenancy, the Union asserted that Southern tenancy "combines the worst features of 18th century feudalism and 20th century finance capitalism. . . . [It] damns everyone and everything which it touches."[13] It was through the STFU that many Black and white tenants voiced their opposition to New Deal agricultural policies. The STFU believed the agency's rural rehabilitation policies only created a "subsidized peasantry" and advocated land redistribution that would create large cooperative farms. Along with the Louisiana Sharecroppers Union, the STFU lobbied the administration for written contracts for tenants and limits on planters' powers.

Instead of extending genuine economic opportunities, the FSA greased the wheels of Roosevelt's agricultural revolution. The New Deal marks the end of the Black quest for land. With the failure of the New Deal's land reform legislation, neither the Resettlement Administration nor the STFU could offer beleaguered tenants anything other than subsistence farming—they were put on the economic shelf to dry (rot), as Bunche put it—or migration to the industrial North. Black landowners succumbed to discrimination in the distribution of New Deal aid and ruthless dispossession of their land once Southern Democrats took control of the FSA in the 1940s.

EQUALITY OF OPPORTUNITY IN THE NEW DEAL'S SOUTHERN AGRICULTURAL REVOLUTION

The South was an object of New Deal policy long before Roosevelt issued his famous *Report on the Economic Conditions of the South*. By the early 1930s, the Southern economy was a stagnant, low-wage backwater in what was otherwise a high-wage, industrialized national economy. In 1929 the average per capita income in the eleven former Confederate states was half that of the rest of the country. In *The Souls of Black Folk*, Du Bois described Georgia's Black Belt as "an impoverished, debt-ridden land" where plantations were abandoned and "now only the black tenant remains." The South was dominated by a landed upper class who installed a repressive labor system after Reconstruction and promoted commercial agriculture but prevented industrialization. White racism and oppression of African Americans was the glue that held this system together.[14]

Southern planters and merchant bankers, often one and same, were allied with a weak middle class and depended on Northern investment in steel mills in northern Alabama and textile mills in North Carolina. There was no free labor in the South; that bourgeois dream went down in flames when Reconstruction failed. Southern poverty and economic degradation are often construed as a parable of class rule or the limits of a low-wage economy in a high-wage nation. Du Bois, however, understood that Southern backwardness was the result of Southern whites' need to maintain Black subordination and enforce racial hierarchies. The weight of Southern racism united white planters and white workers but dulled any incentive for the Southern ruling class to invest in factories, build schools, or nurture the land. In *Black Reconstruction in America*, Du Bois wrote, "It is impossible to disentangle the results of caste and the results of work and striving.... Why should we save? What good does it do to be upstanding? Who gains by thrift or rise by education?"[15]

Roosevelt launched his revolution from above, upending the Southern labor system but entrenching a ruthless planter class committed to white supremacy. His promise to eradicate privileged control of the economy gave way to the restoration of a landed elite in the name of "collective capitalism," the New Deal's euphemism for the system of crop controls and agricultural subsidies enacted in the Agricultural Adjustment Act of 1933. New Deal agricultural policy was America's enclosure act, and just like the enclosures of sixteenth-century England, its effect in the South was to ruthlessly displace Southern tenants and sharecroppers from the land and usher in capital-intensive agriculture—large farms in which cotton fields were plowed and planted with tractors and harvested with mechanical cotton pickers. The policies of the Agricultural Adjustment Administration (AAA) resulted in what David Harvey has called accumulation by dispossession, the acquisition of land and capital for planters at the expense of the tenant farmers, white as well as Black, who worked the land.[16] The AAA, in other words, was instrumental in preserving and injecting new capital into the planter-merchant coalition that had ruled the South since Reconstruction. Just as Rupert Vance had suspected, the New Deal rescued planters and absentee landowners from an antiquated agricultural economy and cast tenants aside. Roosevelt believed that a market economy could be saved only through a broader distribution of the fruits of economic growth. The "words 'freedom' and 'opportunity,'" he said, "do not mean a license to climb upwards by pushing other people down."[17] But that is exactly what the crown jewel of New Deal agricultural policy did.

The story of the FSA is the story of the New Deal's attempt to deal with the consequences of the agricultural revolution in the South. Created as a response to the protests of tenants and sharecroppers in Arkansas, Alabama, and Louisiana, led largely by Black tenants, the FSA was one of the many agencies that marched through the Jim Crow South in the 1930s, not as a conquering army but as a parade of aid givers and rural social workers.[18] Purportedly national in scope, in reality the agency was dedicated to alleviating the poverty of both Black and white tenants in the South. Roosevelt created the Resettlement Administration by executive order in April 1935. Harry Hopkins, who ran the Federal Emergency Relief Agency (FERA), defined the agency's mission when he decided to replace federal relief in the South with a policy of rural rehabilitation. Worried that tenants displaced by the agricultural revolution would migrate to cities already suffering from high unemployment, Roosevelt and Hopkins intended to use rural rehabilitation to forestall that possibility and ease the transition to capital-intensive agriculture.

In the FSA's view, rehabilitation would alleviate the suffering of downtrodden tenants and prepare them to climb the economic ladder to becoming landowners. Hopkins believed that Southern rural relief was a dead end, as it prolonged the destitution of displaced tenant farmers and the rural poor. He thought rural rehabilitation policies—combining loans to tenants with supervision—were the only solution to the traumatic poverty of the rural

South. What state relief officials should do, Hopkins told reporters, is "forget emergencies" and make the rural poor "self-supporting." His plan combined loans for various farming needs, education, and supervision with small grants to meet the subsistence needs of tenants. He regarded the policy as "preventative," unlike federal work-relief programs, which were "ameliorative," simply helping the unemployed maintain their livelihood. Hopkins believed that tenants' obligation to repay loans would preserve their moral character, just as work-relief wages saved the souls of the unemployed. "Our rural rehabilitation program is not predicated on charity," he said. Hopkins' concern for the moral character of displaced tenants had very little relevance to the reality of their lives. An FERA report on conditions in Dallas County, Alabama, caustically commented, "It appears that in many respects, government relief is less pauperizing [to tenants] than the cotton furnishing system of farming to which most of these people are accustomed."[19]

The 1930s idea of rural rehabilitation recapitulates that of the Whigs, the abolitionists, and the Freedmen's Bureau. Like the earlier versions, the New Deal's policy of rehabilitation was based on the idea of uplifting downtrodden tenants whose behavior was due to pathological cultural values that derived from their degradation and exploitation. Just as slavery had debased the freed people, tenancy had degraded its victims and sapped their capacity for independence, initiative, hard work, thriftiness, and economic success. Typical descriptions of the ills of the tenant system often concluded with vivid descriptions of the degradation of tenants' living conditions and habits—run-down shacks, poor diets, shabby clothing. All this, according to one study of tenancy, led to the "'gradual development of an inferior status [and] a loss of desire on the part of the disadvantaged persons to attain social well-being,' with the result that "the whole institutional, social, and cultural life of these communities is lowered.'"[20] Rural rehabilitation in the 1930s sought to change tenants' ingrained cultural habits, using loans and supervised reform of ill-suited farming and domestic practices to put them on the path to middle-class values and a semblance of prosperity. Without such assistance, tenants, especially Black tenants and sharecroppers, would not benefit from New Deal largesse, and any mitigation of racial antagonisms would be stillborn.

The cultural framework of the RA's rural rehabilitation policy originated with a group of Southern liberal academics and activists allied with the Commission on Interracial Cooperation, a group dedicated to managing race relations in the South. Led by Howard Odum and inspired by Rupert

Vance's work on regionalism, the group included three men instrumental to the formation and operation of the RA: Charles S. Johnson, Will Alexander, and Arthur Raper. Johnson and Alexander were among the authors of a searing description of the unraveling of Southern tenancy in the wake of enclosure, and Raper was deeply involved in studying tenancy.[21] The Southern regionalists were aware that tenants were exploited, but they believed the cultural pathologies they described derived from the legacy of slavery and the plantation system. Tenancy could not be changed, they believed, unless tenants assimilated to the values and culture of the Northern industrial economy and society.[22]

Both agricultural subsidies and rehabilitation loans were part of the New Deal's grand plans to remake the Southern economy and society and integrate it into the nation, collapsing the dual economy that had emerged after the Civil War. As Amanda Coleman astutely points out, New Deal reform "meant the economic and cultural integration of poor southerners into an emerging middle-class American mainstream."[23] Like the free-labor Republicans who sought to establish competitive labor markets in the South, New Dealers were intent on industrializing the South and implanting the cultural habits conducive to a consumer society.

The Farm Security Administration succeeded in improving the lives of those tenants who received loans and grants, but once legislation for land redistribution failed in 1935 and 1937, it was dedicated to preserving tenancy. Instead of creating economic ladders that tenants could ascend, the agency became the handmaiden to FDR's agricultural revolution. As for the tenants who received FSA loans or grants, put on an economic shelf, they survived on subsistence farms, paternalistically supervised.

TENANCY, THE SOUTHERN ENCLOSURE, AND THE FAILURE OF LAND REFORM

The crop-lien system of agriculture that emerged out of the struggle between the freedmen and white planters during Reconstruction had by the late nineteenth century evolved into an exploitative labor system that, despite its paternalistic veneer, led to debt peonage, degradation, and deep poverty. Because planters were able to hold the price of labor down, they had few incentives to buy machinery to replace tenants and sharecroppers, who plowed the land with mules and harvested by hand. Labor contracts distinguished between cash tenants, who paid a fixed rent; share tenants, who supplied mules, tools, seed, and most of the fertilizer needed; and sharecroppers, who contributed only their labor. Landlords furnished all the necessary work stock, tools, and seed for croppers but only part of the fertilizer for share tenants. Cash tenants received a fixed amount of cash or cotton, which they could sell; share tenants typically got two-thirds to three-quarters of the crop on the land they worked, and croppers only half. Cash and share tenants were better off than croppers. The wife of a Black Mississippi farmer who climbed the ladder from sharecropping to share renting recalled that once they had their own livestock and were renting, they felt like they were rich.[24]

Share tenants or share managers were tenants who had some measure of control over their labor, the land they rented. and the sale of the cotton crop. Croppers, who were legally akin to wage laborers, had no legal claim to a share of the crop before it was sold and no control over the labor process. Once white Southerners subverted Reconstruction and ended Black power, Redeemer legislatures rewrote African American–inspired lien laws to give landlords first claim to the crop and reduce croppers to the status of laborers who, a South Carolina Court ruled, do not "acquire any dominion or control over the premises upon which such labor is to be performed." By the 1880s, planters and their allies controlled the crop-lien system.[25]

Tenants made up almost 50 percent of all Southern farmers at the start of the twentieth century and 60 percent of farmers in the Deep South states. Most Black farmers were tenants. In 1910, when the Census Bureau first began counting tenant farmers, about 75 percent of Black farmers were tenants, compared to about two-fifth of white farmers. By 1930, 53 percent of white farmers in the Deep South states were tenants, up from 42 percent in 1910, and 85 percent of Black farmers were tenants. The descent of white farmers into tenancy as cotton prices collapsed in the 1920s did not go unnoticed by Southern politicians: it was one of the reasons they initially favored Roosevelt's rural rehabilitation and resettlement programs.

A color line is apparent in the status of tenants. In 1920, about 50 percent of Black tenants were typically sharecroppers rather than cash or share tenants, compared with 25 percent of white tenants. For Blacks these ratios sharply declined during the Depression; by 1940, 70 percent of Black tenants were croppers. Although the number of white croppers also rose in the 1920s, it declined in the 1930s. Figure 2 plots the ratio of tenants to croppers by race in six Deep South states from 1920 to 1940. In all these states, there were more white tenants and fewer Black tenants than croppers. The difference

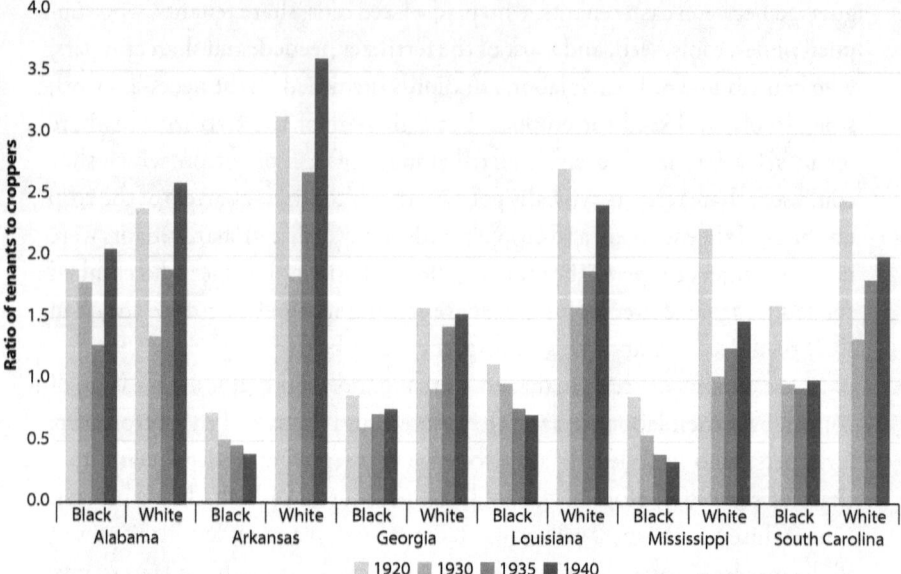

FIGURE 2. The tenancy color line in Deep South states, 1920–40.

was starkest in Arkansas, Georgia, Louisiana and Mississippi, where the color line between tenants and croppers is sharply drawn. Most Black farmers were croppers, not cash or share tenants, but the number of white tenants was two to three times that of white croppers. By 1940 Black tenants constituted 40 percent of croppers in Arkansas and 33 percent in Mississippi. Alabama is an exception, as the number of Black share tenants exceeded Black croppers and doubled by 1940.

The rise of Southern tenancy coincided with the emergence of "tenant plantations," mainly in the Mississippi Delta. The Census Bureau defined a tenant plantation as a "large tract of land worked by at least five tenants 'under the general supervision or control of a single individual or firm.'"[26] Many of these plantations, located in the Cotton Belt stretching from South Carolina to the Mississippi Delta, were in the same counties as antebellum slaveholding plantations and in which African Americans constituted 50 percent or more of the population. These plantations accounted for 82 percent of all plantation acreage in the South. Across the six Deep South states, where 43 percent of tenant plantations were located, over 65 percent of tenants in 1930 worked on such plantations. Black tenants were more likely than whites to work on plantations. Eighty-three percent of Black tenants worked on plantations, compared to only 54 percent of white tenants who often rented single-unit (nonplantation) farms. Many of these plantations were controlled by absentee owners, but regardless of ownership, their operations were based on the ruthless oppression of landless Black sharecroppers buttressed by violence and terror.[27]

Slavery's Legacy: Jim Crow Labor Discipline or Culture?

In 1933, Harold Hoffsommer, a sociologist, interviewed over one thousand tenants and seven hundred landlords in ten Alabama counties. All, he concluded, were enmeshed in a paternalistic relationship. "Landlords did not wish this relationship disturbed and tenants had developed psychological attitudes which made dependence a normal condition."[28] The relationship of master to slave in the antebellum South was supposedly a paternal one, but that description was never very convincing. In the 1930s, paternalism was widely understood as a legacy of the Civil War that defined the relationship between planters and tenants. Charles S. Johnson believed there was a straight line from slavery to tenancy. "The present Negro population of these old plantation areas," he wrote, "can best be understood by viewing it in the light of this plantation tradition, with its almost complete dependence upon the immediate landowner for guidance and control in virtually all those phases of life which are related to the moving world outside." Johnson thought Black tenants had never moved beyond slavery and were immobilized by a heavy-handed tradition of dependence and a nostalgia for paternalism. "The weight of generations of habit holds the Negro tenant to his rut." It was cultural attitudes, not exploitation, that mattered, Johnson argued. Conflict between landlord and tenant was mostly a matter of "misunderstanding."[29]

Arthur Raper described tenants as "childlike" peasants who were "dependent, servile, and landless" and "unaccustomed to responsibility." Tenants lacked any desire to save money: they oscillated between feast and famine, frivolously wasting whatever they accumulated, never saving for the future. Raper argued that tenants preferred to be in debt: in fact, they needed to be. Johnson and Raper were well aware of the exploitation endemic to tenancy, but they believed that changing tenants' attitudes, which had been molded by their servile position and the legacy of slavery, was the only realistic road out of tenancy. Otherwise, the only alternatives, Johnson wrote, were to "succumb or migrate."[30]

Paternalism is an inadequate description of the landlord-tenant relationship on the eve of the Depression. Consider Raper's cultural interpretation of tenants' debt. An intervention that appears paternalistic, say, a landowner carrying a tenant over for a year after a bad harvest, was simply a means to secure and sustain exploitation through indebtedness. Constance Daniels, sent by the FSA to Louisiana to investigate a resettlement project, concluded, "Many planters in the region will not keep a Negro as tenant who comes out ahead at the end of the year. The general practice seems to be to get the best tenants possible and keep them in debt." In some cases, white paternalism was a matter of taking care of a landowner's own progeny. Sharecroppers were clear that paternalism was nothing more than a planter fantasy. One former African American sharecropper succinctly characterized the legacy of slavery when he pointed out that planters "still have him in economic slavery, and they don't have to feed him, or cloth him or pay a doctor when he's sick." Whatever bonds existed between planters and their tenants were anchored by violence and terror. Paternalism, to the extent that it mattered to planters, was possible only because of the ever-present threat of a beating or worse.[31]

Like their nineteenth-century predecessors, twentieth-century planters believed that Blacks had to be forced to work: as one planter said, "We drive them hard and work them by the bell from 'can to can't' [dawn until dark]." Planters resorted to terror when necessary. Although Allison Davis and his colleagues thought that actual violence was less frequent than threats, the threats were reinforced by beatings, mainly of Black farmers. One planter described the use of another tactic widely used during slavery: "My father taught me how to handle the Negroes... He always told me to handle them through their stomachs.... When one starts getting smart on my place, I can just tell him to behave or get out. *If they won't act right, I can cut off the rations, and they quiet down.*"[32]

Tenants tell very different stories about their experiences, stories that belie their supposed lack of initiative and independence. Nate Shaw recounted that his efforts to fertilize his crops adequately were stymied by his landlord. His landlords would "furnish me what they wanted to; didn't leave it up to me. That's what hurt—they'd furnish me the amount of fertilize they wanted regardless to what I wanted."[33]

Credit was the main tool planters used to control their tenants. Black tenants in particular were often heavily dependent upon planters for credit. In his 1938 survey of tenant farmers, E. A. Schuler reported that 60 percent of Black tenants said owners controlled their credit, compared with 22 percent of white tenants.[34] CA, a Mississippi tenant, succinctly described the obstacles a Black farmer faced if he went to a bank and asked for money. The bankers assumed you were in debt, he said, and would likely pull up and aim a Winchester at you. Cash renters were better off than share tenants or croppers, but all Blacks were subject to the whims and caprice of whites. You were broke and you owed them, recalled HC of Yazoo City. An Alabama tenant said, "White folks take it when they git ready and you looking right at them." Black farmers were far more dissatisfied with their access to credit than white farmers. Schuler found that 50 percent of Black farmers complained about their credit sources, compared to 25 percent of white farmers.[35]

Not only were planters capricious in extending or withholding credit, but they were just as likely to cheat their tenants in the 1930s as they were during Reconstruction. They charged usurious interest rates of 20 to 35 percent and short-changed tenants whenever they could. Share contracts, which were typically oral contracts, were stacked against croppers. White planters, Allison Davis observed, "make half and steal half." Black tenants understood clearly what they were up against. One former cropper told an interviewer that his landlord either charged him for things he never got or doubled the price of something he did get. Tenants had no way of ascertaining what they owed a planter. Disputing a settlement often triggered a violent reaction. Aside from cash renters, many tenants lived in a cashless world where they could get much of what they needed from the company store but never knew what anything cost. To settle "debts," planters often just seized tenants' resources. AS, a Black tenant, recounted an incident when the planter came and took his cow and corn and told him his debt was settled. When he asked why, the planter said, because he could. If you asked for a record of what you owed, AS said, the planter would take you into the barn and whip you.[36]

Tenants were not completely defenseless. Planters were, after all, dependent on tenants for their labor, and there were limits to their power and control. Tenants pulled any levers of resistance they could, whether that meant "slow" walking, planting, and harvesting or deliberate forms of sabotage.[37] Moving was the simplest way to escape from a brutal, exploitative landowner, and tenants did move. Forty percent of Southern white tenants and 29 percent of Black tenants in 1930 had been farming the land they were on for less than a year. But 84 percent of those who moved stayed in the same county.[38] Although they claimed they took care of their tenants, once planters learned they could receive a federal payment to take land out of production, they threw tenants off their land fast as they could.

FDR's Agricultural Army Invades the South

AAA subsidy policies set in motion social and economic changes that destroyed the South's labor-intensive farming system. New Deal agricultural price supports and relief policies provided powerful incentives for Southern landowners to do away with sharecropping. Starting in 1933, the federal government paid farmers to take land out of production, usually 25 to 50 percent of a farmer's acreage, by "renting" their land. The US Department of Agriculture required planters to divide rental payments between landlord and tenant based on their agreed share in the crop. The USDA assumed the payments would be split proportionally, but landlords cheated tenants, simply refusing to share the rental payment with them. Walter Rowland, a Black Arkansas tenant, explained how this worked:

> You take de acre p'duction checks de gov'munt gives for not planting cotton: Fust dey wuz made out so's we couldn' git 'em thout de landlord—dey wuz even sent to him—an he mark 'em up en mark 'em down, en mark you up in de comm'sary en mark you down, en den we didn' git no checks, we jus' signed en git whut he say we had comin.' En de landlord think he ought to have all the acre p'duction checks, cause its his land, en we oughtn' to git nothin,' but de Tenant Farmers Union put up a kick, en now dey send us de checks—of we evah git anoth'un.

Southern cotton planters were the major beneficiaries of crop subsidies in 1933; they received $181 million, or 65 percent of total national rental and benefit payments that year.[39]

Sharecropper rebellions erupted in Alabama and eastern Arkansas in the wake of the rampant cheating and displacement of tenants from land taken out of production. The Alabama Sharecroppers Union (ASCU), launched in Tallapoosa County in 1931, saw its membership double, reaching six thousand members in several counties by March 1934, as planters evicted tenants and cheated them out of their share of rental payments. The union extracted some wage concessions but faced violence and repression from planters. In Arkansas, the STFU took aim at the rampant cheating of tenants and directly challenged AAA policies that favored planters. The union became the chief champion of land reform and critic of the FSA. It grew out of the efforts of H. L. Mitchell and Clay East, who started organizing tenants in Poinsett County, Arkansas. Driven by extreme poverty and planter violence and cheating, tenants flocked to the union.[40]

The STFU organized Black and white tenants and sharecroppers as an exploited class. It was unusual in the 1930s to bring the two racial groups into the same union. The STFU was a Black union with a white leadership. In Arkansas, Black tenants constituted two-thirds to four-fifths of its members: five Black-majority counties accounted for 63 percent of the union's membership in that state. Overall, Black tenants and sharecroppers made up the vast majority of rank-and-file members. Black tenants were better organizers than whites, and union membership grew faster among Blacks. The STFU locals were typically segregated, mainly because Black and white tenants lived in different counties. There were ninety-three Black locals and almost ten thousand Black members.[41]

African American union members were drawn to the class rhetoric of the union, but they had also absorbed the Black nationalism that was part of Marcus Garvey's legacy in the Deep South. The Black union locals recruited members from the Garveyite United Negro Improvement Association (UNIA) and NAACP chapters. There were twenty-six Garvey chapters spread across Arkansas and Mississippi in counties with union locals. E. B. McKinney, a Black minister and Garveyite, was part of the union's leadership. Members refused to see their oppression as exclusively a matter of social class. A 1937 Resettlement Administration survey of both Black and white tenants in Jefferson county, Arkansas, asked them, "What *class* of people do you think is worse off?" White tenants answered with references to social class, but Black tenants complained about "not getting equal rights," "inadequate pay," and "they don't get justice." These Black tenants understood the dimensions of white planters' class power, but they were clear that racial oppression mattered to them as much as, if not more than, the power of planters.[42]

Black and white sharecroppers in fact had very different aspirations and demands. In fact, the surge in Black membership in the STFU led white tenants to refuse to join the union. They told Mitchell that the way to boost white membership in the union was to form separate unions for each race. In the end, Southern racism undermined the union's biracial coalition. This weakness would later affect the STFU's attempts to undo the ravages of tenancy.[43]

The STFU took the AAA to court, challenging rental contracts and the exclusion of tenants from crop-subsidy payments. In 1934 the USDA wrote new contracts that gave tenants a share of the rental payments, but these paved the road to Southern enclosure. The department left it up to landlords to allocate shares among different classes of tenants: they were not required to share any of the payments on land they farmed with wage labor, or to retain tenants. WDS, a Black Mississippi sharecropper, explained that once the USDA changed the contracts, tenants could receive a check for their crops. But when that happened, he said, planters let the tenants go, hired wage hands, and drew all the government checks.[44]

In 1934, AAA subsidy payments represented 39 percent of net income for owners of plantations and 4 percent for tenants. Even when tenants received a crop subsidy, landlords and merchants typically grabbed the money, claiming it as payment for unpaid debts and furnishing. Harold Hoffsommer's 1935 survey of Alabama tenants and landowners found that in 60 percent of the tenant households receiving a government payment, all of the money went to pay debts. Black tenants were more likely to give up their payments: "86 percent … reported paying a part or all of their governmental money to the landlord and in nearly one half of the instances claiming that the payment was forced." Landlords coerced 58 percent of Black tenants, but only 23 percent of white tenants, to fork over their crop subsidies or cash relief.[45]

As cotton tenancy sank under the pressure of the Depression and the AAA's price-support policies, landowners realized they could shift the burden of supplying sharecroppers and wage laborers with the necessities of life during the off-season onto the federal government. As planters expanded and mechanized their farms, they had little need for tenants. Any semblance of paternalism went up in smoke at this point. L. C. Gray told Henry Wallace, Roosevelt's secretary of agriculture, "The relief system has greatly accelerated the disposition on the part of the dominant classes to divest themselves of individual responsibility for the tenant class." For planters it was a sweet deal: they got government money, replaced their tenants with day laborers, and foisted responsibility for their former tenants onto the government And as farm prices went up, they could buy more land and tractors.[46]

Henry Wallace and Chester Davis, head of the AAA, vigorously denied that crop subsidies displaced tenants. Yet it was clear, as leaders of the STFU pointed out, that the New Deal's enclosure act was throwing tenants off the land and intensifying poverty in the South. There is no question that the AAA displaced tenants. In cotton-producing counties, the number of sharecroppers declined by 10.5 percent during 1934–35. AAA policies overturned tenant farming during the next decade, reshaping the plantation system as planters added tractors and land while also replacing both share tenants and croppers with hired farm hands. By 1945, there were 301,541 fewer tenants in

TABLE 4 Displacement of tenants in the Deep South, 1930–45

	Total tenants		Black tenants		White tenants	
	Number	Mean change	Number	Mean change	Number	Mean change
1930–35						
Share managers	19,891	40.35	−36,954	−74.95	56,845	115.3
Sharecroppers	−26,426	−53.60	−5,565	−11.29	−20,861	−42.3
Net change	−6,535	−13.26	−42,519	−86.25	35,984	73
1935–45						
Share managers	−198,228	−402.10	−57,033	−115.7	−141,195	−286.4
Sharecroppers	−103,313	−209.56	−54,431	−110.4	−48,882	−99.2
Net change	−301,541	−611.65	−111,464	−226.1	−190,077	−385.6

SOURCE: Deep South New Deal Dataset (see appendix). Calculations by author based on 1930, 1935, and 1945 US Agricultural Censuses for all 493 Deep South counties.

the Deep South states, and wage workers supplied 40 percent of labor on plantations or multi-unit farms (large farms containing small acreages (subunits) worked by tenants or wage labor).

Black share mangers were the main victims of the initial phase of the enclosure. By 1935, their number had declined by almost 37,000, an average of 75 per county in the Deep South. The number of white share managers surged by 56,845. (See table 4.) There was significant displacement of white croppers but not Black croppers. In many plantation counties, a sizeable decline in Black share managers coincided with a slight increase in Black croppers. In Morengo County, Alabama, for example, Black share managers declined by 1,089, but croppers increased by 695.[47] By 1945, however, share managers accounted for two-thirds of all displaced tenants. The number of share managers declined by 42 percent, compared to 23 percent for croppers.

The plantation system survived and even prospered, particularly in the Mississippi Delta, where the size of plantations increased. In Alabama, Georgia, and South Carolina, there was a noticeable decline in the size of plantations. Nevertheless, by 1945 the remaining croppers, who were disproportionately Black, labored on plantations or multi-unit farms, where they accounted for 73 percent of tenants. Share managers were more likely to be working on nonplantation or single-unit tenant farms; 77 percent of

TABLE 5 Percentage of tenants on single-unit farms, by state, 1945

	Share managers		Sharecroppers	
	Black	White	Black	White
Alabama	29	51	6	15
Arkansas	23	57	6	14
Georgia	26	43	11	20
Louisiana	37	46	8	10
Mississippi	42	36	9	12
South Carolina	39	38	12	12
All Deep South states	32	45	9	14

SOURCE: Deep South New Deal Dataset (see appendix). Data from 348 Deep South counties.

all tenants on single-unit farms were share managers, and they were disproportionately white. White tenants accounted for 60 percent of tenants on single-unit farms and over half of all share managers on single-unit farms in Alabama and Arkansas (see table 5). There were very few Black sharecroppers on single-unit farms. These farms were relatively small, averaging 92 acres across the Deep South, compared to an average of 370 acres for plantations.[48]

A "New" Deal for Tenants and Sharecroppers?

Roosevelt's executive order creating the Resettlement Administration merged the FERA rural rehabilitation program with two smaller programs and funded it with money drawn from the massive relief appropriations bill Congress had approved. Senator Richard Russell (D-Georgia) introduced an amendment to the relief bill to fund the RA, indicating the importance Southern Democrats attached to the plight of white tenants.[49] Roosevelt intended to give the new agency control of the land-purchase program then pending in Congress. Both the 1935 Bankhead Bill (S. 2367), sponsored by Senator John Bankhead (D-Alabama), which passed the Senate but failed to get a hearing in the House, and the 1937 tenancy legislation that created the FSA were policies intended to redistribute land to eligible tenants. Both plans proposed that federal agencies would buy up land from insurance companies and banks that had foreclosed on the farms and then resell it on generous terms to tenants. The 1935 scheme was the work of Johnson, Alexander, and Frank Tannenbaum, a land economist. Tannenbaum deemphasized the creditworthiness of buyers in favor of the need for supervision of them, and thus the land-purchase scheme aligned with rural rehabilitation. L. C. Gray, a USDA land-use expert and adviser to Henry Wallace, incorporated these ideas into the USDA's framework for the 1935 Bankhead Bill.[50]

The 1935 bill was the USDA's response to the STFU, which was driving Wallace crazy. For Wallace and the Senate majority leader, Joseph Robinson (D-Arkansas), the aims of the legislation were to pacify Arkansas sharecroppers and undermine the STFU. In his Senate testimony on the bill, Wallace branded the tenant unions as radicals intent on undermining the New Deal: "The present condition in the South provides fertile soil for Communist and Socialist agitators," he told senators. "The cure is not forced violence or legislation to curb these activities but rather to give these dispossessed people a stake in the social system . . . to provide these refugees of the economic system with an opportunity to build and develop their own homes and to live on the land which they may call their own."[51] Bankhead, Robinson, and other Southerners also saw the program as a way to direct more federal dollars to the South. Rexford Tugwell, a member of Roosevelt's Brain Trust, believed that all the Southerners cared about was making land loans, "which are as bad as nothing without planning for economic independence and for supervision of farm management to secure some kind of success." Southern Democrats in Congress had no fear the program would undo Jim Crow, and so long as it did not interfere with price parity between agricultural and industrial products and continued to pump money into the South, they went along with it.[52]

Rural rehabilitation and resettlement were less about creating ladders of economic opportunity than about relieving the destitution of tenants displaced by Roosevelt's Southern enclosure. Gray assumed that only a small number of Southern tenants could become independent farmers, and that they would be subsistence farmers at best. He thought the government should try to establish a system of tenancy that "would be benevolent rather than exploitative in intent." He envisioned creating nonprofit corporations that would purchase land and then supervise the tenant farmers. Along these lines, he advocated a program of compulsory savings "to enable the tenant to escape from dependence on credit advances for subsistence from year to year while making a crop." Gray recognized that any land-purchase program would be costly: he proposed 1,500 resettlement projects over three years for 130,000 family holdings and federal expenditures of $450 million.[53]

Gray was not given to the expansive language of equality of opportunity that Hopkins and his deputy Aubrey Williams favored, but he thought his plan, like their rural rehabilitation scheme, would establish a path for some tenants to farm ownership—though not necessarily of a commercially viable farm. The administration's plan was limited less by the ability of tenant farmers to succeed than the USDA's intention of replacing tenancy with large farms and capital-intensive agriculture. The USDA crafted the legislation to ensure that the land-purchase policy did not conflict with the administration's price-parity policy. The legislation required the corporation to purchase land for tenants and to prevent the new owners from planting and harvesting controlled agricultural commodities. In effect, the administration proposed a plan that would create subsistence farms.

The 1935 Bankhead Bill was attacked from both the right and the left, often for the same reasons. A widespread and accurate criticism was that the program would create a subsidized peasantry, since tenants would be unable to produce commercial crops. Some of the harshest criticism came from African American allies of the STFU, notably John P. Davis of the National Negro Congress, and the NAACP. Both were concerned Black tenants would suffer. Their objections rested on the inherent contradiction in the New Deal's agricultural policies: the plan would subsidize the purchase of small farms, while federal policy was dedicated to reducing farm acreage in the South and consolidating the remaining land into large farms or turning it into forests. Davis wrote Walter White of the NAACP that the bill "as it now stands is seriously damaging to Negroes" and should be opposed. Without amendments, the bill would simply "bail out landlords and leave the tenant high and dry." White was worried that the plans would "fasten tenant[s] to inferior land, and chief effect will be to enable impoverished plantation owner to get rid of his unproductive land at government expense." At its 1935 annual convention, the NAACP passed a resolution stating that it was "unalterably opposed to the present form of the Bankhead farm tenant corporation bill" unless adequate safeguards were written into it. Gardner Jackson, of the National Committee on Rural Social Planning, a key ally of the STFU, argued that without amendments, the bill would restrict tenants to peripheral land adjacent to plantations, "thereby furnishing a permanent supply of cheap labor for plantation owners."[54] This view was not restricted to the STFU and left-wing critics of the bill. Agricultural economists in the administration believed that a land-purchase program would do nothing to resolve the conditions that produced abusive tenant relationships: "Low prices, inadequate incomes, poor credit facilities, high interest rates and the like."[55]

Both the STFU and the Nashville Agrarians, a Southern reform group, launched radical challenges to the New Deal's embrace of large, mechanized cotton plantations using wage labor and the paltry, self-defeating elements of the administration's schemes for tenants. Both campaigned to break up plantations and reduce economic concentration in the South.[56] But it was the STFU that launched the most sustained attack on tenancy and the administration's rural-poverty policies. It repeatedly said that both Black and white tenants had been "equally exploited." And the STFU flatly rejected the New Deal's commitment to a benign system of tenancy and the idea that tenants could be guided to become landowners through paternalistic supervision. It attacked the prevailing belief that tenants were "worthless, lazy and shiftless, incapable of simple management, and cannot be helped." They pointed out that tenants did not suffer from a cultural legacy of slavery that warped their character: rather, the incentives of tenancy crushed individual effort. The STFU believed the administration's policies would raise the income of some tenants while making it unlikely that they could become viable landowners. This was not only unjust: it was futile.[57]

To compete with the large, capital-intensive farms that were emerging in the Delta and elsewhere, the STFU argued, a new type of farm organization was required, one that would permit individual farmers to flourish. The STFU argued for cooperative ownership and farming operations based on mutual assistance between former tenant farmers. This would permit the use of tractors and other necessary machinery, the application of technical expertise such as crop rotation and diversification, division of labor among the owners, and a "high type of rural community." Group ownership would afford equal opportunity for all families; the cooperative's income would be divided among members based on the hours and quality of their work. Although individual ownership of land would not be permitted, the desire for individual ownership, the union insisted, could be met with a house and personal garden.[58]

This vision of cooperative farms conflicted with STFU members' strong desire for individual ownership of land. Most of the tenants who joined the union had done so hoping it would help them gain control of land and get them out from under the thumb of landlords. Even in the 1930s, the aversion to contracts for wage labor remained strong. Like the Negro agrarians of Reconstruction, tenants demanded that they, not planters, should receive the value of their labor. Nate Shaw's observations about his experience as tenant reflected the views of many. He recalled: "If you don't make enough to have some left you ain't done nothin, except givin the other fellow your labor. . . . That white man gettin all he lookin for. . . . But what am I gettin for my labor? I ain't gettin nothin." Lula Parchman, a member of the STFU, told Mitchell that landlords "don't regard my rights at all. . . . I want only a chance to make my own living and not the other get the profit of my labor and I suffer."[59]

Aware of these views, the STFU leadership conducted a survey of its members, asking what type of farm organization they preferred: sharecropping for a government landlord (this was the plan of the 1935 Bankhead Bill); renting land from the government; cooperative farming (STFU's plan); or individual landownership. Not surprisingly, 58 percent of the union members named individual ownership as their top preference. Nineteen percent preferred cash renting from the government. Both these options gave tenants considerable independence from oppressive landlords and ensured that they would reap the gains from their labor. Sharecropping for the government was chosen by just 6 percent and cooperative farming by 16 percent of respondents.[60]

The impulse for ownership among STFU members was driven mainly by Black tenants, who made up the vast majority of union members. They were eager to become "government farmers." They were not bound to a tradition of dependence or reluctant to make their demands known, as all too many RA/FSA officials assumed. In Louisiana, Black farmers eagerly worked with Black extension agents to implement home and farm management plans, apply new farming techniques, and diversify their crops. One Black tenant farmer said: "If I can just have the chance, I sure would like to buy this farm. . . . I can work 40 acres or more. If I can get a little piece with the government, I know I can defend myself."[61] E. A. Schuler's survey of tenant attitudes revealed that Black tenants had a stronger preference than whites to be owners, they were more optimistic of their abilities to handle larger farms, and they were more likely to be dissatisfied (not surprisingly) with their inability to get credit. He found that 80 percent of Black renters thought they would be better off as owners, and 90 percent said they were looking for a place to buy. The comparable figures for white renters were 62 percent and 75 percent, respectively. The divide among croppers was far greater: 75 percent of Black croppers thought they would be better off owning, compared to just 49 percent of whites. Black tenants were far more likely to say they wanted help in finding a farm and advice on how to run it. The power of Negro agrarianism persisted into the 1930s, spurring Black tenants' demand for landownership.[62]

The NAACP and John Davis may have made a strategic mistake in opposing the 1935 bill. The legislation contained the seeds of a significant land-distribution program, and in addition to a $50 million appropriation, it included the authority to issue $1 billion in bonds, raising enough to redistribute substantial acres of land to tenants.[63] It gave the federal government the authority to purchase land and then select farmers for loans instead of simply giving farmers loans and letting them decide where to purchase land. In this respect, it was far more radical than the tenant-purchase program Congress created in the 1937 Bankhead Bill, which gave loans only to "creditworthy" farmers and shifted control over land purchases from the federal government to Southern bankers and landowners. The failure of both the 1935 Bankhead Bill and the SFTU's plans for land reform in 1937 ended any alternative tenant policy based on antiprivilege egalitarianism. It left the RA's rural rehabilitation and resettlement programs as the only federal policies of any assistance to tenants.

TUGWELL'S VISION AND SOUTHERN REALITIES: TENANCY AND THE ANTINOMIES OF REHABILITATION

For Rexford Tugwell the heart of the RA was rural resettlement, not rehabilitation loans. Tugwell was not interested simply in solving the tenant problem: he thought agricultural land should be subject to national planning, like the industrial sector of the economy. This would require both shifting rural populations in order to take bad land out of production and moving farmers to better land or off the land altogether. Skeptical of schemes to encourage land ownership, Tugwell envisioned the agency as acquiring wasted or marginal land from federal land banks and insurance companies and resettling tenants on the land "with adequate farm equipment and technical supervision." This was Tugwell's vision for rural resettlement, a plan for rural renewal or, if you like, rural slum clearance.[64]

Rural rehabilitation, Tugwell believed, would be an "extensive and widespread monument to government folly." He saw no point in using federal resources to set up the benevolent form of tenancy that Gray and others believed was the only way to aid tenants. Simply giving downtrodden tenants loans would be a surrogate relief policy that would produce rural slums. Tugwell believed the government needed to help people who were displaced because of AAA policies, but he thought it could only be done by reorganizing Southern agriculture "so that there will be some recourse for the people who will be thrown out of employment by the reduction in cotton and by the new efficiencies in agriculture."[65]

Despite Tugwell's aversion to the loan business, as he called rural rehabilitation, it became the most important and largest of the three programs in the agency. From its beginning in June 1935 to June 1941, the RA/FSA spent over $600 million in rehabilitation loans and grants but just a fraction of total spending for resettlement projects. These loans and grants were redistributive. By 1943, the agency had developed 133 resettlement projects nationwide at a cost of $72 million, far less than the $450 million Gray had envisioned. Resettlement projects were enormously difficult to launch and highly controversial. Rural rehabilitation loans, on the other hand, were highly popular, especially in the South, where rural banks and merchants saw them as a promising source of income. In the dustup in Congress over the agency's 1936 budget allocation, Southern legislators came to its defense, largely because of what rural rehabilitation loans meant to the region's businesses and white voters.[66]

The standard rural rehabilitation loan had a five-year repayment period and a 5 percent interest rate (far below the usurious rates of 20 to 35 percent typically charged by landlords and merchant bankers). Loans were contingent on borrowers agreeing to a farm and home management plan. They were made only to farmers who could not obtain credit elsewhere, either from local banks or New Deal agencies such as the Farm Credit Administration. The agency made 959,351 rural rehabilitation loans in Southern states, representing 52 percent of all its loans in the US between 1935 and 1941. The six Deep South states received over one-third of all rural rehabilitation loans, worth $124 million, though the average loan was $186, far below the $346 average in non-Southern states (see tables 6 and 7). Yet the money the RA/FSA pumped into the South amounted to less than 4 percent of all federal expenditures in Southern states—a minuscule sum compared to the lavish amounts devoted to agricultural subsidies. The agency never had enough money to meet the demand for loans or grants to tenant farmers.[67]

Initially, the Resettlement Administration was staffed by 10,074 administrators and rural social workers drawn from the state relief corporations. Tugwell colonized these corporations, mostly in the South, and replaced them with a centralized agency that was unlike the FERA or the AAA, whose funds were allocated by county committees controlled by large landowners and county extension agents. Tugwell understood that his agency

TABLE 6 FSA loans and grants, FY1935–FY1941

	Amount (% of FSA total)	Number (% of FSA total)	Average amount
Loans			
Deep South states[a]	$123,717,407 (23.8%)	663,676 (35.8%)	$186
States of the Confederacy	$194,315,072 (37.4%)	959,351 (51.8%)	$203
Non-Southern states	$325,177,745	893,271	$364
Grants			
Deep South states	$13,193,896 (10.6%)	585,679 (9%)	$23
States of the Confederacy	$19,608,870 (15.7%)	880,892 (13.6%)	$22
Non-Southern states	$104,967,955	5,591,646	$19

SOURCES: *Monthly Report of Loan and Grant Activity by States, Territories, and Regions*, FSA Report No. 13 (RG 96, RP 520, Box 32, NA), tables 3, 7, 10. *Hearings, Select Committee of the House Committee on Agriculture to Investigate the Activities of the Farm Security Administration*, House of Representatives, 78th Cong., 1st sess., part 1 (Washington, DC: US Government Printing Office, 1943), 1014-15, 1021-22.

[a] Alabama, Arkansas, Georgia, Louisiana, Mississippi, South Carolina.

TABLE 7 FSA loans and grants in Deep South states by county, FY1935–FY1939 ($)

	Total Amount	County Mean	County Maximum	County Minimum
Alabama	15,420,120	230,151	560,465	53,806
Arkansas	13,869,759	184,930	322,994	79,916
Georgia	14,261,715	89,696	375,424	226
Louisiana	8,946,501	139,789	469,990	10,159
Mississippi	13,524,881	164,937	329,525	23,953
South Carolina	8,650,876	188,062	364,003	12,134
All Deep South states	74,673,852	151,468	560,465	226

SOURCE: County Reports of Federal Expenditures, 1935–39.

would run into conflict with the USDA's agricultural extension service, which was closely allied with the Farm Bureau and wealthy landowners. "So, in order to help our people and the poor farmers," Tugwell recounted years later, "we really had to set up a parallel organization to the county agents, because they wouldn't do anything for anybody but their own clients." Power resided with the RA's regional directors, who were directly responsible to

Tugwell.⁶⁸ For the first two years of the its operation, the agricultural extension service had very little influence over RA operations. This changed when Congress passed the 1937 Farm Security Act, which gave county committees statutory authority. But even then, the FSA displayed independence.

Rescuing Sharecroppers, Preserving Tenancy

The intent of rehabilitation loans, Tugwell and other administrators claimed, was to put tenant farmers on an "independent basis." When RA/FSA administrators talked about Southern tenancy, they assiduously avoided any mention of debt peonage or exploitation; instead they resorted to vague statements about how the "people have ruined the land, until finally the land has backfired and is ruining the people." Their dismal description of the incapacity of tenants to be independent farmers ignored the degradation of tenants that was a consequence of exploitation and instead trafficked in invidious cultural and racist stereotypes.⁶⁹ An RA farm specialist informed the assistant director of rural rehabilitation for Alabama that his clients needed help not because the farm depression and exploitation had crushed their ability to make any money "but because of [their] inability to manage money." He added, "Rather close supervision has been and will continue to be necessary if our clients are to be rehabilitated. Very few of the clients are literate and they will not be able to succeed unless they are closely supervised." Illiteracy and lack of education were clearly impediments for many tenants. Across the South, 20 percent of African Americans were illiterate in 1930, compared to 4 percent of whites. Over half of all borrowers in the Deep South states had no more than a sixth-grade education, compared with one-third of borrowers nationwide.⁷⁰

Administrators pushed a vision of equality of opportunity for tenant farmers that was predicated on undoing the "cultural pathologies" of sharecroppers, especially Black sharecroppers. The Southern regionalists' description of Black tenants as chained to a tradition of dependence and exhibiting a "dull, sometimes fatalistic, and unquestioning dependence upon the landowners and the soil [and] muffled with vast apathy" was widely accepted as a rationale for supervision and farm education.⁷¹ Although RA/FSA officials often said that paternalism held Southern tenants back, they imposed their own version of it on their clients. Instead of creating ladders of opportunity, administrators and farm specialists sustained tenancy, just as Gray had predicted. Still, they did constrain the power that landowners and merchant bankers could wield over tenants.

The RA/FSA administrators drew sharp distinctions between tenants they believed could climb a ladder of economic opportunity and those who could not. They guided the latter toward subsistence farming instead of cash crops. Tugwell believed that "one of our best claims for support is just these people we have kept from borrowing money." A Florida administrator reported that "the field men have been urged to promote subsistence on a conservative basis rather than production for profit. Cash crops have been sanctioned only where experience warranted approval." Since tenant farmers had no collateral to speak of, loans were granted on the basis of subjective assessments of the character of the borrower and backed up by supervision, which had a fiduciary meaning, as well as monitoring tenants' adherence to farm and home management plans.[72]

The RA divided borrowers into four groups, depending on their need for supervision. Those deemed most in need of supervision had larger families and fewer resources, were more likely to have received a rehabilitation grant in addition to a loan, had been in the program longer, were more likely to be tenants, and, not surprisingly, were more likely to be Black. RA staff regarded almost 75 percent of African American loan recipients as requiring extensive supervision; only 57 percent of white borrowers were so classified. Agency officials described Black tenants as "timid in making their needs known," a failure they ascribed to paternalistic landlord-tenant relations. Black recipients of rehabilitation loans had to deal with the racist assumptions white supervisors brought to the table. One supervisor said of her clients, "You can watch it every time: the ones [in the Negro group] who do the best work have white blood in them." In home reports, Black tenants were described as having "difficulty in carrying out instructions." Another tenant was described as "independent but not original," someone who "nurses a deep dislike for supervision." Arthur Raper, who supervised a rehabilitation project in Greene County, Georgia, believed that a little coercion was necessary to force tenants to overcome the unproductive cultural attitudes they had acquired.[73]

Rehabilitation loans were used, like the Freedmen's Bureau contracts, as instruments to change the behavior of tenants. Supervision was a form of loan collateral, and independence in this context had a very practical meaning: a borrower was classed as independent when the loan was paid off and he could survive without government assistance. Many FSA agents saw paying off debt as the tenants' primary obligation, even it meant they had to forgo making improvements to their land or buying basic necessities. According to Carl Taylor, rehabilitation "paid in 'remade personalities and lives' and not just in the government's balanced books." But the home and farm plans imposed by agents often left tenants and their families worse off than the terms of the "furnish" that planters and merchant bankers had imposed. Under the old system, tenants had some flexibility in choosing what to spend. Sam Bishop, a tenant in Greene County, Georgia, complained, "Before I got on FSA, I could make a debt and get some clothes for my family, but since I been on FSA I plant cotton, pick it and gin and don't never see no money. They won't let me have any for the things I need most.... I haven't got a dime for clothes this year."[74]

Despite the inherent paternalism of supervision, many agents disapproved of "spoon-feeding clients." Some supervisors deposited the checks given to clients (particularly Black clients) in banks and then required them to obtain a supervisor's countersignature in order to withdraw the funds. This practice provoked a policy letter that instructed field supervisors not to monitor clients' withdrawals of funds. Nor, despite complaints from disgruntled landlords or merchants, would the RA stand behind a tenant's debt to merchants who had extended credit in anticipation of cashing in on a rehabilitation loan. The RA put out a policy statement stipulating that it only provided "a loan to the client who, in turn, spends it independently of the Resettlement Administration, except that expenditures must be in line with the farm plans of that client." Merchants in Mississippi demanded "that rehabilitation clients be given separate orders for groceries fertilizer and hardware and every dealer be given equal opportunity to get their share of business," but Tugwell demurred, insisting that the agency's policy was to give checks for grants or loans directly to the client and "that he make his own purchases." In this regard, RA officials construed independence as a way to shift the balance of power between tenants and overseers, whether they were merchants or landlords. And that meant diminishing planter control over credit and debt.[75]

The Louisiana Share Croppers Union (LSCU) and the STFU demanded written, fair contracts and credit for tenants, and they lobbied the RA and Roosevelt to outlaw usurious interest rates and protect tenants from the exploitative lien system. In a 1936 letter to Roosevelt, the STFU demanded that "no contract between Federal agencies and landowners be approved" that would require tenants and croppers to "purchase ... supplies from a commissary store" and that the RA make production loans with tenants, not planters or merchant bankers. The union also wanted long-term written contracts and arbitration boards to settle contract disputes. Clyde Johnson of the LSCU made similar demands, though he wanted contracts that would establish "the tenant's rights on the land [and] elliminate [sic] a good part of the robbery of the tenant class so common today." The LSCU also advocated for written contracts and loans for mule teams and tools (both a form of capital investment), crop production loans, purchasing cooperatives, and tenants' right to organize.[76]

In voicing the demands of Black tenants and sharecroppers, both these unions belied the RA's notion that Black farmers were timid. Schuler's survey of tenants found that 60 percent of Black tenants were dissatisfied with their contracts and wanted changes; this was twice the number of dissatisfied Southern white tenants. They wanted written contracts, and both Black and white croppers wanted contracts that would increase their share of farm income.[77] The STFU and the LSCU never got the statutory changes they wanted, but the RA/FSA used rehabilitation loans to take control of credit, shifting tenants' debt obligations from planters and bankers to the federal government. Loans to tenants offered independence in some measure from landlords and thus ran right up against the source of planter power.

Yet all too many RA officials were more concerned about the stability of tenants' contracts than about exploitation. They believed vague, unfair contracts led tenants to move and thus undermined their chances of improving their farming practices (through supervision) and moving up the economic ladder. Although administrators avoided any mention of exploitation, much less the pervasive racism that structured Southern tenancy, they did recognize that rehabilitation would fail unless they raised tenant income and mitigated exploitation.

In practice, using loans to minimize planter power over credit meant that the agency gradually took over furnishing tenants receiving rehabilitation loans. Paul Maris, who was one of the top administrators in the Division of Rural Rehabilitation, deplored this practice because it would "accomplish very little in the way of bettering the condition of the client.... We have repeatedly stressed the evils of permitting our program to degenerate into a mere system of annual furnishing." But T. Roy Reid, the regional director for Arkansas, Mississippi, and Louisiana, saw rehabilitation loans as a substitute for furnishing, and he believed this was the only way to raise the income of tenants. In a report to Tugwell, Reid wrote, "An important step in correcting one of the hardest drains on the income of tenant farmers, who must obtain crop production credit on the basis of a crop lien, is to make possible a wide participation in loans of the type of Rural Rehab. loans." Reid distinguished between borrowers who were on a path to ownership and those who were not, believing that the RA must "have a cheaper crop credit to meet the needs of many worthy people who must remain tenants." Because interest rates on rehabilitation loans were much lower than typical furnishing rates, they would enable tenants to save money. Tugwell approved what amounted to a policy of furnishing, telling Reid that when farmers could not obtain credit from any other source and "their standard of living is such that they may be considered to require public aid," the agency would assist them with rehabilitation loans. Tugwell in effect converted rehabilitation loans into a cash transfer.[78]

There is indirect evidence that the agency engaged in recurrent financing of tenant farmers in Deep South states that was tantamount to furnishing and income redistribution. One measure of RA/FSA furnishing is the proportion of original loans relative to supplemental loans. A high rate of supplemental loans suggests furnishing, since it entailed continued support of owners and tenant farmers. As table 8 shows, this rate was higher in the Deep South than in the rest of the country. In Deep South states, 59 percent of all rehabilitation loan dollars (and 75 percent of all loans) were supplemental loans. In non-Southern states, supplemental loans accounted for 39 percent of loan dollars and 60 percent of all loans. Many farmers received more than one supplemental loan. In the three FSA region 6 states along the Mississippi river, 89 percent of all borrowers received more than one loan, and 74 percent received two or more. In region 2, comprising three states in the upper Midwest, only 42 percent of borrowers received any supplemental loans at all. Multiple loans to individual borrowers declined by the late 1930s, but even then, 29 percent of Delta borrowers received more than one loan, compared to 4.5 percent in the upper Midwest.[79]

Another indication of furnishing is that rehabilitation loans were more likely to be used for operating and family expenses than for investment in capital goods such as farm equipment or work stock and debt servicing. In the six Deep South states, borrowers used 48 percent of their first or original loan for operating and family expenses; outside the South, borrowers used only 30 percent of their loans for this purpose. Operating and family expenses consumed 69 percent of supplemental loans in the Deep South states, compared with 57 percent outside the South. Borrowers in the Deep South had fewer resources than borrowers elsewhere in the country, received smaller supplemental loans, and were more likely to have their debts refinanced. Yet Olaf Larson points out that despite their lack of resources, sharecroppers were just as likely as owners to receive loans for capital goods. Rehabilitation

TABLE 8 Purpose and distribution of FSA rural rehabilitation loans, 1936–44
(Percentages of number of loans and dollar amounts)

	South[a]	Deep South[b]	Non-South[c]
	Distribution of loans, 1936–44		
Original loan dollars	44	41	61
Supplemental loan dollars	56	59	40
Number of original loans	28	25	40
Number of supplemental loans	72	75	60
	Purpose of loans, 1936–39		
Original standard loans			
Capital goods and debt service	58	52	70
Operating and family expenses	42	48	30
Average standard loan amount	$269	$277	$773
Supplemental standard loans			
Capital goods and debt service	36	31	43
Operating and family expenses	64	69	57
Average supplemental loan amount	$142	$134	$357

SOURCE: Olaf F. Larson, *Ten Years of Rural Rehabilitation in the United States* (Washington, DC: Bureau of Agricultural Economics, USDA, 1947), Appendix Tables 34–37, 46.
[a] South: FSA regions 4–6, 8 (Upper and Deep South states plus Texas and Oklahoma).
[b] Deep South: FSA regions 5-6 (includes Florida).
[c] Non-South: FSA regions 1-3, 7, 9-12.

loans were also sharply redistributive. The ratio of the median loan amount to the median capital net worth of the farmer when the loan was approved was 1.34 for full owners but 1.98 for share tenants and 3.83 for croppers.[80]

The RA/FSA clearly tried to use its control over credit to curb planter power and augment tenants' income. Tugwell also succeeded in convincing Wallace that clients of the agency, whether they were farm owners, tenants, or sharecroppers, should be eligible for crop subsidies under the 1936 agricultural conservation program. In 1934, Southern tenants' annual net income was $263, of which 4 percent ($11) was derived from AAA subsidies. Department of Agriculture 1935 contract revisions made a small but significant difference to tenant's net income by 1937: it had risen to $300 annually, and agricultural payments accounted for 9 percent of net income ($27) (see table 9). In the upper Mississippi Delta, agricultural subsidies accounted for the entire increase in net tenant income; in the Louisiana interior and central Arkansas, subsidies were about 20 percent of net income. Subsidies

TABLE 9 AAA crop subsidy payments to tenants and planters by agricultural region

(percentages of tenant and planter annual income)

	Tenants, 1934 (%)	Tenants, 1937 (%)	Planters, 1937 (%)
All plantations	4	9	23
Atlantic Coast Plain	5	5	20
Black Belt A[a]	4	6	22
Black Belt B[b]	4	11	17
Upper Delta	4	6	18
Lower Delta	2	5	20
Interior Plain	4	20	34
Mississippi Basin	5	15	25
Red River	4	10	36
Arkansas River	4	18	35

SOURCE: William C. Holly, Ellen Winston, and T. J. Woofter Jr., *The Plantation South, 1934–1937*, Works Progress Administration, Research Monograph 22 (Washington, DC: US Government Printing Office, 1940) 94–95, tables 21, 23; 44, table 27.

[a] Black Belt A: Regions in which share tenants and sharecroppers constituted a majority of all tenants, as of 1930.

[b] Black Belt B: Regions in which cash renters were a majority of all tenants as of 1930.

for landowners were massively larger, but they accounted for only 23 percent of planter net income, down from 38 percent in 1934.

By 1937, partly in response to sharecropper union agitation, the FSA began requiring written contracts between planters and tenants. Compelled to respond to charges that clients were being forced to accept unreasonable terms for leases or being placed on submarginal land, Julian Brown, the director for Alabama, said, "Our supervisors will not accept any rental agreement where the lessor attempts to place unreasonable or unfair restrictions on our clients." Announcing two years later that any tenant receiving a loan would need a written contract, the FSA reported that 80 percent of rehabilitation loan borrowers had a written contract, and 20 percent of them had multiyear contracts. Written contracts were more common in the Deep South: in the Mississippi Delta, where most of the STFU chapters were located, 48 percent of tenant borrowers had written contracts. The agency's model contract prescribed that tenants should have gardens, acceptable housing, and credit for improvements, but many landowners ignored these requirements.[81]

FSA administrators had no doubt of the effectiveness of their policies in mitigating exploitation. An FSA internal report stated that "one of the most important achievements of the rehabilitation programs has been the liberation of negro and white tenants from bondage to the 'furnish' system under which tenants paid an average of 20% to 50% for production credit and were consequently kept in perpetual debt—or perpetually in flight from unpaid obligations."[82] Their policies, FSA officials claimed, led to higher tenant incomes and an average increase of 47 percent in the net worth of second- and third-year clients. Olaf Larson's assessment was less laudatory, suggesting that landlords often ignored or subverted contracts, but he acknowledged that written contracts had begun to change landlord-tenant relationships.

A USDA study of loan borrowers revealed that 83 percent of borrowers who started out as croppers moved up the ladder to become share tenants, a clear improvement in their economic status. But only 5 percent of borrowers who started out as share tenants became owners. White croppers were more likely to move up the economic ladder. Even so, African American tenants and sharecroppers recognized that rehabilitation loans could undercut the planter-dominated credit and furnishing system. A Black sharecropper recalled many years later that the FSA gave him a fair deal, and that once you covered your debts, you got to keep the rest of what you made. Now they were nice, he said.[83]

Whom Did the Resettlement Administration Rescue?

On what basis did the RA/FSA distribute the meager resources they had, and who benefited? Did the agency mainly help downwardly mobile white farmers, those who descended into tenancy in the Depression? Did Black farmers benefit, and if so, to what extent? Walter White of the NAACP made it clear in the lobbying over the 1935 Bankhead Bill that the "total amount expended in the purchase of land or in administration in any given state should not be less for Negroes than the percentage of Negro population." FSA administrators and officials acquiesced to Jim Crow, but the unacknowledged policy of the agency, Carl Taylor told the president of the Kentucky State Industrial College for Colored Persons, was "our desire to have the Negro population receive an equitable share of the benefits that come from the activities of the Resettlement Administration."[84]

Other than a vague national policy that farmers receiving loans or grants should either be on relief or marginally destitute and should be "worthy," there were no criteria for eligibility. Nor was the program restricted to tenants: about a quarter of borrowers were owners or part owners. In the Deep

South, the program served extremely poor farmers; their median yearly cash expenditures were $115 (equivalent to $2,578 in 2023 dollars). In non-Southern states the median was about $360. One-fifth of tenants receiving rehabilitation loans in the Deep South were croppers, compared to 2.5 percent in the rest of the country.[85]

Regional directors and county staff decided who received loans and grants, and they had broad discretion in allocating the money across counties. Deep South counties received an annual average of $151,480 in RA/FSA loans and grants during the five years from the onset of the enclosure (FY1935–FY1939). Mean dollars allocated were highest in Alabama counties, which is not surprising given Senator John H. Bankhead's influence over the agency, and lowest in Georgia (see table 7). Whether a borrower benefited from the program depended on where the money went. There is a big difference between an Alabama county that received over $530,000 (Dallas) and a county receiving $54,000 (Jackson). In distributing loans, RA administrators were responding to the wreckage of Roosevelt's enclosure, and they intended to use rehabilitation loans to keep tenant farmers on the land instead of moving to large towns or cities. This motive suggests that RA administrators invested money in those counties with large declines in the number of share managers and croppers. In selecting tenants for loans and grants, RA/FSA staff tended to prioritize tenants occupying small single-unit farms, since plantation owners were shedding tenants and had no interest in loans to tenants working on their land. Borrowers in Deep South states worked small farms: the median size of borrowers' farms was fifty-two acres, just over half the national median of ninety-nine acres, and 80 percent worked farms of less than one hundred acres. These borrowers were also more likely to be white tenants or croppers than Black.

What predicts the distribution of FSA loans and grants across the 493 Deep South counties is the mean decline in the number of Black share managers from 1930 to 1935 and the number of single-unit farms in a county. Southern rural counties contained a mixture of single unit (nonplantation) and multi-unit farms or plantations In order to test this hypothesis, I regressed total RA/FSA loans and grants for the years FY1935–FY1939 on the mean decline in Black share managers between 1930 and 1935, the number of single-unit farms in a county, and a measure of the distribution of plantation acreage across the six states. I also included a variable for state effects.[86]

The decline in the number of Black share mangers and the number of single-unit farms, combined with controls for plantation acreage, cotton acreage in 1935, and state effects explains 38.2 percent of the adjusted variance in the distribution of rehabilitation loans and grants. I estimate that a decline of one hundred Black share managers between 1930 and 1935 is associated with an increase of about $8,000 in RA/FSA loans and grants. This money largely went to single-unit farms. (See table A.1.) RA/FSA money went disproportionately to counties across the Black Belt of the Deep South, where there was substantial displacement of Black share managers from plantations, and to tenants renting and working single-unit farms. Dallas County, Alabama, is a striking example. The number of Black share managers declined by 1,688, and the county received $531,688 in loans and grants by FY1939. This pattern reflects that of the ten Alabama Black Belt counties, in which the number of Black share managers declined by an average of 631, and the counties received an average of $357,160 in loans and grants.

Although white tenants, who constituted a large majority of tenants working single-unit farms by 1945, accounted for over two-thirds of borrowers across the Deep South states, FSA administrators attempted to ensure that Black farmers got a share of loans. The agency adopted a policy that access to rehabilitation loans and resettlement projects for Black farmers should be roughly proportional to their number in a state or across the South. The agency was clearly aware of the political consequences of giving loans to Black tenants. It avoided labeling resettlement projects as Negro projects on the grounds that "there should be no restriction of participation in governmental projects on the basis of race and color." FSA staff went out of their way to "whitewash" the program by portraying needy tenants to the public as white. Under the direction of Roy Stryker, head of the historical section, FSA photographers were instructed to avoid publicizing pictures of Black tenants. The reluctance "to lead the agency in a crusade against racial disparity" came from the very top of the USDA. Will Alexander recalled that Henry Wallace was terrified of confronting racial discrimination. "You never could get him to stand up on that issue," Alexander said. "When I went to take leave of him when I left the department, the last thing he said to me—he looked up and said, 'Will, don't you think the New Deal is undertaking to do too much for Negroes?'"[87]

Despite the FSA's aversion to publicizing its proportionality policy, the agency claimed in 1937 that the distribution of rehabilitation loans in the four Southern regions was proportional: Black farmers, who made up 21.3 percent of farmers received 20.6 percent of the loans In the Deep South states, however, Blacks made up 37 percent of farmers but received just 31.5

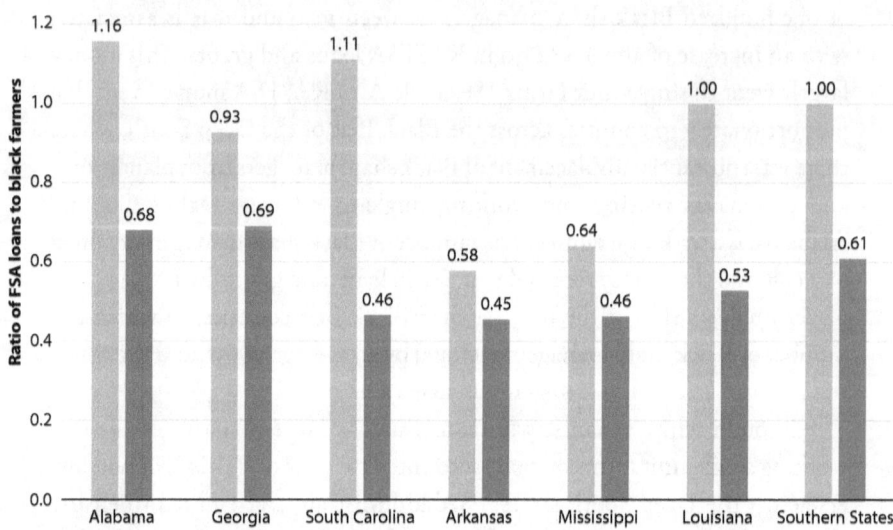

FIGURE 3. Distribution of FSA loans to Black farmers.

percent of loans. There were stark differences between the states. Loans to Black farmers exceeded the proportion of Black farmers in Alabama and South Carolina; they were proportional in Louisiana but not in Georgia, Mississippi, and Arkansas (see figure 3).[88] Arkansas had the lowest ratio. Reid reported that Black farmers there, including tenants and croppers, received only 8.6 percent of standard rehabilitation loans, even though they made up one-third of all Arkansas farmers and most tenants and croppers. In Arkansas and Mississippi, the two states where the STFU was strongest, Black farmers fared the worst. By contrast, in Louisiana, African American farmers constituted 40 percent of farmers and received 40 percent of loans, mainly because the LSCU mobilized Black tenants to apply for rehabilitation loans or resettlement projects. In Point Coupee Parish, which had many LSCU locals and received $462,856 in loans and grants from 1935 to 1939 (the highest amount of any county in Louisiana), 80 percent of African American farmers received an FSA loan.[89] In South Carolina, Black farmers, who accounted for 50 percent of farmers, received 50 percent of FSA loans, the highest proportion of any Southern state.

Yet there were significant racial disparities in the distribution of loans across the Deep South. African American loan recipients were more likely to be tenants or croppers, whereas white borrowers were more likely to be full or part owners. Seventy-two percent of Black farmers receiving loans were tenants, compared to 57 percent of white farmers. Black owners accounted for 23 percent of Black loans, white owners 30 percent. There was no difference in the proportion of Black and white croppers who received loans, but Black share tenants were more likely to receive a loan than white share tenants. Tenant purchase (TP) loans, created by the 1937 Farm Security Act, were not proportional; across the South, the ratio of the proportion of Black tenants receiving a loan to the proportion of all Black tenants was .61.[90]

ENCLOSURE'S HANDMAIDEN

The Farm Security Administration was an anachronism. The agency, Pete Daniel noted, "represented the old culture [of Southern agriculture], not the new." The agency's mantra, restoring economic opportunity by rehabilitating individual tenants, was the symbolic face of a program geared to enabling a transition to capital-intensive agriculture in the South. Propping up beleaguered tenants with rehabilitation loans and grants and farm-management plans on small plots of land was less a path to the future than a holding action. L. C. Gray, more than any other New Dealer, articulated the underlying rationale of the program: providing aid to the victims of the Southern enclosure while preventing them from moving to cities in the middle of the Depression. This policy entailed keeping tenants on the land and making them self-sufficient, or as Gray put it, enabling, "for those now largely self-sufficing, a more intelligent self-sufficiency, including a larger degree of cooperation, supplemented by appropriate institutional readjustments and forms of public assistance." This was a recipe for a cultural makeover of tenants using rehabilitation loans without promoting equality of opportunity. Jason Manthorne concludes that "each component of the rehabilitation program served a dual purpose: to improve people's lives on basically humanitarian grounds but also so they could work harder and better."[91]

Yet it would be a mistake to write off the RA/FSA as a failure. Although Jim Crow set the rules of engagement in the rural South, the agency, was able, at least for a time, to prevent landowners and their allies in the federal extension service from controlling its decisions, and it forestalled Southern opposition with cash. For tenants lucky enough to receive a loan or get a place on a resettlement project, the program raised their incomes and gave them some leverage against rapacious landowners and merchant bankers. Many Black tenants nevertheless expressed their dissatisfaction with onerous supervision and never gave up their desire for their own land.

There was no land redistribution. Given FDR's reliance on the votes of Southern Democrats, radical reform was never a serious possibility. One agrarian radical acidly commented that Southern members of Congress and New Dealers favored rural rehabilitation "because nearly all minds are used to thinking in terms of subsidies and humanitarian uplift; but other types of [reform such as land] distribution and agrarianism ... met shocked incomprehension, sheer refusal to discuss."[92] Had the 1935 Bankhead Bill passed, the outcome might have been different. By the late 1930s, the idea of cooperative farms was moribund, the agrarians had retreated, and the STFU favored individual homesteads for rehabilitated tenants, though they were far less successful in this initiative than the LSCU.

The STFU was hampered by planter violence and hostile politicians, but it was also weakened by the failure of H. L. Mitchell and others to confront racial antagonism among union members and between the leadership and Black members. Many Blacks believed the union's leadership disregarded their complaints of ill-treatment and segregation within the union. STFU's white leaders, notably Mitchell, had difficulty understanding that the struggle over tenancy was as much about race as about social class. E. B. McKinney, one of the Black leaders in the union and a militant Garveyite, led many Black members out of the STFU and into the Congress of Industrial Organizations (CIO). McKinney's rebellion anticipates the rising Black militancy of the 1940s and A. Philip Randolph's fight against discrimination in the war industries.[93]

The FSA faced relentless attacks from the Farm Bureau and its allies among agricultural extension agents and hostile Southern Democrats. Even though the FSA extolled the virtues of promoting equality of opportunity through loans and supervision, Southerners attacked the program as a giveaway to deadbeat tenants. Harold D. Cooley (D-North Carolina), chair of the select House committee convened in 1943 to investigate the FSA, thought the program led to the "individual becoming the ward of the government and dependent entirely upon the Government for his livelihood," unlike AAA subsidies, which he saw as "money earned ... as compensation for soil-building practices which inure to the benefit of the general welfare." The real source of the committee's ire was their belief, spread by Ed O'Neal, head of the Farm Bureau, that the FSA was paying poll taxes for poor farmers.[94]

Despite their limitations and flaws and their very different remedies for the tenancy, the STFU and RA/FSA responded to the hopes of Black farmers and tenants to become landowners. Negro agrarianism remained just as powerful in the 1930s as it had been during Reconstruction. From Black landowners who formed self-contained enclaves in the three decades before the Depression to the Southern Black tenants and sharecroppers who had long engaged in rural agitation and organizing, African American farmers and their families strove to carve out independent lives free from terror and violence. The African American quest for land never expired after Reconstruction, because land was never just a means of economic survival. Land ownership meant autonomy and leverage against rapacious whites. It was also a repudiation of the Freedmen's Bureau and FSA policies of rehabilitation. In order to understand why Negro agrarianism and Black tenants' demands for land remained so powerful in the 1930s, we need to examine the struggle of Black farmers to acquire and hold onto land after Reconstruction. The growth of Black landowning in the Deep South from 1880 to 1920 and the significance of the New Deal farm tenant and credit policies for the fate of Black landowners is the question to which I now turn.

FOUR

Black Enclaves and the African American Quest for Land, 1880–1950

> My purpose in writing this sketch is to show those whose capital, given to them in brain and muscle by the Great Ruler of the Universe, has been ignored and trampled underfoot by the moneyed aristocrats of this nation; for while it is eminently proper that each individual should be protected in all their lawful rights of property, yet they should never have any paramount claim on that ground over any other person.
>
> TUNIS CAMPBELL,
> *Sufferings of the Rev. T. G. Campbell and His Family, in Georgia*, 1877

> The reason I have always wanted to be a farmer is because I believed then and believe now that the farmer is the only free man we have in our race.
>
> BENJAMIN CARR,
> farm owner, 1914, Macon County, Alabama

REFLECTING ON THE FAILURES of Reconstruction in a 1880 speech in Elmira, New York, Frederick Douglass declared, "To the freedmen was given the machinery of liberty, but there was denied to them the steam to put it in motion.... The old master class was not deprived of the power of life and death, which was the soul of the relation of master and slave." Had Thaddeus Stevens or Charles Sumner prevailed in their attempts to confiscate land from the former slave owners, Douglas averred, the outcome would have been different: "The negro today would not be on his knees, as he is, abjectly supplicating the old master class to give him leave to toil."[1] As Douglass suggested, owning land was not only about restitution for the collective debt owed African Americans for their labor in building America. Nor was it grounded in a narrow vision of equality of opportunity. It was the foundation of their independence and self-determination.

For the freed people, freedom was not a "thing" or a "place," Thavolia Glymph points out, but the embodiment of the "understandings and intuitions of those who seek it or live it." Freedom was the specific claims Black people made to overturn the social relations of slavery. It was also a repudiation of rehabilitation—the idea that they, the former slaves, had been degraded by slavery and were thus in need of repair. Land hunger was driven by African Americans' "positive self-concept."[2] The failure of land distribution during Reconstruction was not the end of Black farmers' desire for land. Negro agrarianism, the freedmen's version of antiprivilege egalitarianism, flourished after the end of Reconstruction, spurring a quest for land to own and farm. As Jim Crow took hold across the South, Black landownership increased, belying white beliefs in Black inferiority.

Black landowners were usually the social and economic pillars of their communities. More significantly, their experiences and aspirations represent a counterpoint to the dogma of rehabilitation that characterized not just the Freedmen's Bureau and the Farm Security Administration but the plethora of reformers and Southern liberals who sought to undo the "damage" of slavery and tenancy. Negro agrarianism, an ideology grounded in the nineteenth-century doctrine of producerism, flourished in the first four decades of the twentieth century. "Black farmers," Jarod Roll writes, "sustained well into the 1930s an idealized agrarian vision, rooted in the rural black movements of the late nineteenth century, which held sacred the right of small producers to independent livelihoods on the land they worked."[3]

When Reconstruction ended, Blacks owned just 9.8 percent of cultivated acreage in the cotton South and 7.3 percent of farms.[4] By 1900, 23.4 percent of Black farmers in the eleven former Confederate states were landowners. From the end of Reconstruction to the early twentieth century almost two hundred thousand Blacks became landowners across the South. Ownership was higher in the Upper South, where almost 40 percent of Black farmers were landowners, but Blacks in the Deep South had also made impressive gains in ownership. In the five Deep South states, the number of Black landowners increased from approximately 12,451 in 1870 to 63,001 by 1900, 17 percent of all Black farmers. By 1920, over 105,000 Black farmers in Deep South states were either full or part owners, an increase of 23 percent from 1900, exceeding the 15 percent increase in the number of white landowners.[5]

Black-owned farms typically clustered in zones of autonomy that were vital for protection from predatory whites and held out the possibility of economic mobility. In his study of rural Blacks, Carter Woodson observed,

"Negroes' best opportunities for struggling upward [were] in settlements and towns largely restricted to the black population." These Black enclaves were hotbeds of Garveyism in the 1920s. But if they were socially autonomous, they were nevertheless subject to the strictures of white supremacy. Black farm owners were economically dependent on white-controlled banks and economic infrastructure, such as cotton gins and marketing facilities for their cotton. And they were exposed to the ever-present threat of white violence.[6]

The typical picture of Black landowners in the Jim Crow South is of struggling farmers eking out a living on marginal land they acquired only through the paternalism of a white benefactor. This picture is not so much wrong as it is misleading. Peggy Hargis pointed out its flaw some time ago, arguing that the evidence of Black farmers who prospered is obscured by treating them as "victims rather than agents" and focusing on the marginality of their land instead of their success. Because Blacks acquired land at a higher rate than whites in the early part of the twentieth century, their rate of wealth accumulation, measured as the growth in the value of their land and buildings, was higher than that for white farmers. In Georgia, Robert Higgs calculates that the comparative value of white property declined from thirty-six times that of Black property in 1880 to sixteen times by 1910. Even though this still represented a large gap in wealth, it was a significant gain for Black landowners.[7]

The location of the land purchased affected the relative gains in Black wealth. Buying land in plantation counties with extensive cotton acreage and low rates of illiteracy was conducive to Black wealth accumulation. In 1925, there were 48,505 Black landowners in plantation counties across the Deep South. They owned 3.6 million acres of land, of which the value (including buildings) was $89 million. By comparison there were 32,442 Black landowners in nonplantation counties, farming 2 million acres of land worth $38 million.[8]

Some Black landlords employed tenants, sharecroppers, cash renters, and day laborers on thirty-five-acre farms, and others farmed plantations of one thousand acres or more. In the Yazoo-Mississippi Delta, about fifty Black landlords operated profitable farms that offered Black laborers an alternative to working on white-owned plantations, creating the semblance of a competitive labor market. As one Black farmer told an interviewer, "Blacks who could not get work with a Black landlord was in good position to bargain with white planters for higher wages, 'cause those white boss men knowed that as soon as the Black landlord got more land, he was gon' encourage Black laborers to work for him."[9]

There is no point in embellishing the status of Black landowners in the Jim Crow South. All were at a disadvantage compared to whites. In the Georgia–South Carolina Piedmont and southern Mississippi, Black landowners struggled to farm mostly unproductive land. In plantation counties in 1925, Blacks owned just 17 percent of the available land, their farms were half the size of white-owned farms on average, and the value of their land and buildings was 43 percent of that of the white-owned land. They were exposed to threats of whitecapping and lynching, charged exorbitant interest rates, and exploited by merchants. The landowners of Promised Land, a Black enclave in Abbeville County, South Carolina, managed to avoid falling into tenancy by minimizing cotton production in favor of consumable crops. They evaded poverty but never produced enough cotton to turn a profit.[10]

Black land ownership, just like tenancy, must be examined in light of the power and ruthlessness of white planters and bankers and ever-present threat of violence. It should also be understood as a result of the powerful force of Negro agrarianism that emerged from Reconstruction, and the diffusion by 1900 of doctrines of self-help and racial solidarity as the path to economic well-being. In this context, landowning was, as Manning Marable points out, "an ideological imperative of black thought."[11] Most Blacks during and after Reconstruction understood land to be the foundation of the racist political economy in the South and realized that without land ownership their freedom would always be elusive. The enduring strength of this understanding explains why Black tenants sought to be farm owners and how Black landowners survived during Jim Crow and into the New Deal. Even after tenants and landowners lost their access to land and during the cauldron of the civil rights movement, these beliefs informed conceptions of Black power.

Marable suggests that a Black petty bourgeoisie emerged in the early twentieth century, supported by Black retail stores and Black banks that supplied much of the capital needed for Black landownership. Growth in Black landownership took a very different path in the South Carolina and Georgia Sea Islands than in the Georgia Piedmont, the Alabama Black Belt, or the Mississippi Delta. With the arrival of the boll weevil and the collapse of cotton prices after World War I, many Black and white landowners lost their land in the bitter 1920s. The number of both Black and white landowners rose between 1935 and 1945, when New Deal agricultural policies took hold. After twenty-five years of upheaval in the rural South, there were eight thousand fewer Black landowners in the Deep South states and almost thirty-five thousand more white landowners. By the end of World War II, Black landowners made up 17 percent of all landowners in the Deep South, about the same proportion as in 1900. But after 1945 large numbers of Black landowners were dispossessed of their land. The recovery and decline of Black landownership is a consequence of the way New Deal agricultural policies, including the Resettlement Administration, changed the Southern landscape.

Beginning with the 1914 Smith-Lever Act, Southern Democrats built a segregated agricultural welfare state based on federally subsidized agricultural extension services and financial aid to white farmers. Distribution of these resources was controlled by state legislatures or planter-controlled county committees.[12] With the exception of funds from the Resettlement Administration, Black landowners had scant access to the enormous sums of federal money the New Deal poured into Deep South rural counties. From 1933 to 1939, federal loans and AAA crop subsidies amounted to $890.5 million, almost one-quarter of all federal dollars flowing into Deep South states.[13] New Deal agricultural loan and subsidy policies were aimed at fostering or sustaining landownership, but Black farmers received scant help from the government and were left to fend for themselves after 1935.

The Black quest for land ended with the New Deal. Although the FSA succeeded in establishing Black resettlement projects for a very few Black farmers, their efforts to aid Black landowners faced white opposition. After World War II, white Southerners took control of the Farmers Home Administration, the agency that replaced the FSA in 1946, and any gains Black famers made in the 1930s were lost. To understand why, we first need to understand how and why Black Farmers gained a foothold in the Jim Crow South after Reconstruction.

BLACK LANDOWNING AFTER RECONSTRUCTION

The freed people, along with Northern abolitionists and some radical Republicans, understood the acquisition of land as a matter of power, the chief way to forestall economic coercion by planters. Delegates to the 1871 Southern States Convention in South Carolina resolved "that every possible legitimate means be taken by the laboring masses of the country to overthrow this cruel barrier to our progress—the monstrous land monopoly of the South." This statement reflected their concern that Southern planters refused to sell land or even farm implements to the freed people so as to keep them "in as dependent a condition as possible."[14] Antimonopoly rhetoric was pervasive among delegates to the Southern Black conventions and lay at the heart of the debate about the future of freed people. Many Blacks participating in the conventions believed that without the economic power of land ownership, civil rights "conferred not only as an act of justice, but as a rational safeguard, and for his self-protection, [invited] aggression, which he cannot repeal, and his political privileges become to him the source of personal peril."[15] This rhetoric drew extensively on the Jacksonian antimonopoly discourse Black abolitionists used in the 1840s and 1850s to challenge Northern racism and slavery. Combined with the demand for autonomy, it recapitulated the idea of antiprivilege egalitarianism.

The freedmen and their allies demanded land not only to secure their autonomy but also in the belief that land redistribution would invigorate the Southern economy. Martin Delany, the Freedmen's Bureau subassistant commissioner for Hilton Head Island, South Carolina, set out an economic program based on the equitable distribution of land that he believed would be the foundation for Black economic success and a path to prosperity for the South. In a news article, Delany wrote, "In the apportionment of small farms to the freedmen, an immense amount of means is placed at their command, and thereby a great market opened, a new source of consumption of every commodity in demand in free civilized communities." His scheme envisioned a triple alliance among Northern capital, Southern planters, and the labor of freed people in which the profits would be shared equally by the three parties. "It is a fact ... in political economy," Delany wrote, "that a given amount of means divided among a greater number of persons makes a wealthier community than the same amount held or possessed by a few." Both planters and freedmen would benefit, he told Senator Henry Wilson, a Massachusetts Republican, in a letter of March 7, 1871: "What the freedman wants is land of his own, with time to pay for it. What the landowner wants is cash for his surplus lands." But the freedmen lacked the capital, Delany added, to purchase the land, and neither wage labor or renting would provide it.[16]

Confiscation of Southern plantations was one way to supply the needed land for freedmen, but it was never a realistic possibility. Thaddeus Stevens, George Julian, and their allies never had the votes for confiscation. During the House debate over the 1866 Freedmen's Bureau bill, Stevens proposed an amendment that "forfeited estates of the enemy" be made available to freedmen. The amendment was defeated by a vote of 127–37; eighty-six Republicans opposed it, including many Radicals. Many Black leaders, other than radicals like Aaron Bradley, also opposed it. Even Frederick Douglass opposed confiscation (his 1880 speech marked his admission that he had been wrong). In his study of the Union League, Michael Fitzgerald concluded that neither Alabama freedmen nor the Union Leagues advocated confiscation.[17]

Republicans responded to the failure of their confiscation policy by creating a homestead policy tailored to the South. The Southern Homestead Act, which had the unanimous support of Republicans in Congress, allocated forty-six million acres in Southern public land states for homesteading. Most of the land was swampy and timber laden, with poor soil, and over half of it was in Florida. Neither Georgia nor South Carolina was a public land state, which meant there was very little land available to Blacks. Although Republicans intended the law to benefit freedmen, the final version of the law opened eligibility to anyone and added a nondiscrimination provision. The law failed to provide land to any but a very few freedmen. Three years after its enactment, only four thousand freedmen had made applications to acquire land—just one-fifth of all applicants—and three-quarters of these were in Florida. In the end, only one thousand freedmen obtained a title to homestead land in the South.[18]

Planter opposition to Black landowning was only one obstacle; another was a dearth of working capital and credit. Roger Ransom believes that subsidized land purchases—exchanging land for government bonds—could have provided planters and bankers with the liquidity needed to finance land purchases and make working capital available to Black farm owners. Southern Black leaders and freedmen insisted that there were planters who would sell land to freedmen, if only because they had to.[19]

Delegates to Black conventions insisted that land-purchase schemes were essential to Black freedom and economic success. Richard Cain, a Black abolitionist and ordained minister who moved south after the Civil War, introduced a resolution at the 1868 South Carolina constitutional convention demanding that Congress appropriate $1 million to purchase land in the state. Cain told delegates the plan would bring "capital to the State ... [and] such a measure will give to the landholders relief from their embarrassments financially and enable them to get fair compensation for their lands." He argued that landowning would relieve the suffering and poverty of the freed people and would promote equality of opportunity. Freed people were thrown on their own resources, Cain said, "I know the philosopher of the New York Tribune says, 'root hog or die'; but in the meantime we ought to have some place to root. My proposition is simply to give the hog some place to root." Cain, who clearly foresaw the possibility of debt peonage unless the freedmen acquired land, made an argument that would have been familiar to late-twentieth-century welfare reformers. Land purchases, he told the convention, would obviate the need for relief or welfare, as well as the Freedmen's Bureau. The resolution passed the convention by a vote of 101–5, but Henry Wilson told the delegates to forget it, as Congress would not appropriate the money.[20]

He was correct. Republicans were unwilling to invest federal money in the South, and abolitionists and radical Republicans believed that granting freedmen the franchise was sufficient to ensure their freedom and prosperity. Wall Street bankers, the core of the Republican coalition after the war, detested radical reconstruction and were adamantly opposed to land redistribution, which they believed could not be limited to the South. Radical reconstruction would entail an expansion of federal authority and preclude the fiscal retrenchment they thought necessary for tax cuts.[21]

Voting rights were the only alternative to land redistribution to secure Black freedom. James M. Ashley, a radical, pronounced on the House floor, "If I were a black man, with the chains just stricken from my limbs . . . and you should offer me the ballot, or a cabin and forty acres of cotton land, I would take the ballot." This widely accepted view was the linchpin of Douglass's understanding of what Black freedom required. Without the vote, freedmen would lack power, and the Black individual, Douglass argued, would be "the slave of society, and hold his liberty as a privilege, not as a right. He is at the mercy of the mob and has no means of protecting himself." Delany, like Tunis Campbell and Aaron Bradley, both Black radicals, could not have disagreed more. Without land, Delany believed, Blacks would never gain their freedom.[22]

The Advent of Black Land Ownership in the Deep South

Despite these failures, Black landowning took off after 1880, driven by Negro agrarianism and the availability of land in the Mississippi Delta, the Alabama Black Belt, and the Piedmont of Georgia and South Carolina. Blacks established collective or cooperative schemes to finance land purchases or rental agreements. Land was the basis of community building, enabled in many cases through Black kinship networks. In some cases, renting land was a path to ownership. During radical Reconstruction, some states adopted crop liens that gave Black farmers property rights to a share of the crops. As a result, Orville Burton shows, an agricultural ladder emerged in the South Carolina counties he studied, and there was substantial movement among Blacks from laborer to farmer: 59 percent of African Americans who were laborers in 1870 had become farmers by 1880. A similar economic ladder emerged in the Mississippi Delta in the 1890s and in the Alabama Black Belt, though for different reasons.[23]

There was one statewide land experiment during Reconstruction: the South Carolina Land Commission. Republicans in the state crafted a program that would enable Blacks to purchase land, mainly as a way of protecting up-country Blacks who lived among sizeable white majorities. Recognizing the threat that landless Blacks, who would be subject to white economic retaliation if they tried to vote, posed for their electoral majorities, one Republican politician announced that unless Blacks could purchase land, "it would be a great stumbling block in the next election." The Commission purchased 168 plantations in 1871 and divided them into 1,992 small farms. Almost ten thousand Black farmers and their families settled on the farms. Although the program was marred by fraud, the Land Commission had distributed over one hundred thousand acres by the time it closed.[24]

Collective purchases of land by Blacks were sometimes assisted by the Freedmen's Bureau. Such purchases usually occurred in or near lands Black farmers already occupied. In the Sea Islands and in Louisiana, for example, Black soldiers saved their money when they left the Union army and used it for collective land purchases. One regiment saved enough money to buy four of the five largest plantations on the Mississippi River. The *New Orleans Tribune* steadfastly campaigned for schemes to raise money for land purchases. Blacks also created rotating credit associations and cooperatives to purchase land. The collective land purchases that took place toward the end of Reconstruction anticipate the emergence of rural Black enclaves anchored by a small Black landowning class.[25]

The growth and success of Black land ownership varied with the development of the post–Civil War plantation economy in the first two decades of the twentieth century. In the older plantation regions, mainly the Georgia and South Carolina Piedmont, most plantations had absentee owners, and many were mismanaged or broken up and decaying. Over two-thirds of the thirty-nine thousand plantations that went out of business by 1940 were in

Georgia, South Carolina, and eastern Alabama. Most of these had absentee owners. By contrast, the Mississippi Delta, a region Rupert Vance described as "Cotton obsessed, Negro obsessed ... the deepest South," was the site of modern, centralized plantations. A third region, the Sea Islands, was populated with large rice plantations and small farms based on subsistence agriculture.[26]

The autonomy of Black owners, and with it any possibility of economic stability, let alone success, depended on their location and relation to white owners and to tenants (Black or white). W E. B. Du Bois pointed out that "the real question [about Black owners] is, what are the surrounding influences on the Black farmer?" Generalizations based on nothing but the proportion of Black landowners in a county obscure the varied patterns of ownership and the context in which they were marginally prosperous or eked out at best a meager living. A county with a high proportion of Black owners usually had a small Black population and very few Black tenants. In the sixteen Mississippi counties in which Black owners made up 50 percent or more of all Black farmers, there were just 571 Black tenants.[27]

It mattered whether a Black landowner was farming land in the rich soil of the Mississippi Delta, where there were large numbers of Black tenants, or the sandy soil of southeast Mississippi, where there were few tenants. Plantations were typically located on the most fertile and thus the most productive land, which translated into higher valuations of land and buildings. Landlord farms had more than twice the improved acreage of tenant farms, and the value of land and buildings was substantially higher. In 1910, plantation farms cultivated thirteen million acres, which constituted 39 percent of improved land. Mississippi and Arkansas had the most plantations, Georgia and South Carolina the fewest. In these same plantation counties, there were smaller nonplantation farms cultivating twenty million acres of improved land. Black owners often acquired these nonplantation farms. There were almost one million small farms outside the plantation system, about half of them located in nonplantation counties. Many of these farms were on rocky, unfertile land.[28]

No matter where Blacks tried to buy land, they had to deal with white planters, merchants, and bankers. Southern whites were reluctant to sell land to Blacks, believing that it would "demoralize" labor—a euphemism for undermining their control of tenants. Black landowners, usually considered "uppity," faced the threat of whitecappers, who surged in the two decades from 1890 to 1910 and attempted to dispossess them of their land. According to Isaiah Montgomery, the founder of the Black enclave Mound Bayou, whitecappers singled out independent Black renters and landowners because they were "sober, industrious, and reliable ... [and] because they prospered, and their example was likely to be helpful to others." In other words, they threatened the system of tenancy.[29]

But in the early twentieth century whites did sell land to Blacks. In his study of Greene and Macon Counties, Georgia, Arthur Raper concluded that "landownership by a Negro in the Black Belt is the culmination of a business transaction based on a personal equation." Acquisition of land depended on a white sponsor: white landowners could choose their Black landowning neighbors. Whites typically initiated a purchase, according to Raper, and preferred a docile farmer who would stay in his place.[30]

Raper's view of land transactions across the color line is a common one, but it hardly explains the forty-year surge in Black land accumulation that started in the 1880s. Some whites had compelling reasons to sell land to Black farmers, who then availed themselves of Black-owned banks. Distributed across the Deep South, there were eleven such banks in Mississippi, seven in Alabama, and two in Georgia that together made loans of $20 million in 1910. In some parts of the Deep South, Black tenants were eventually able to purchase land. Black agricultural colleges were established; the Tuskegee Institute was the best-known. Besides offering technical training, some of these colleges facilitated land ownership by acquiring capital from Northern philanthropists and setting up land-improvement companies that would buy up plantations, subdivide them, and sell the land to Black farmers.[31] The surge in Black landowning cannot be understood independent of Black self-determination and autonomy, the ideology of Negro agrarianism that persisted well after Reconstruction. To this, Booker T. Washington added an ideology of self-help, uplift, and accommodation.

Washington has been variously described as a Black capitalist, an advocate of Black power, and the progenitor of the idea of race relations.[32] He should also be understood as following in the path of Black abolitionists in the 1830s who believed that uplift would compel recognition of Black aspirations and eventually equality. Washington's advocacy of self-help and uplift is a throwback to the 1830s conception of rehabilitation, but devoid of any link to civil and voting rights—in other words, he rejected any conception of antiprivilege egalitarianism. Washington was certain that even though Blacks were starting at the bottom of the heap, they would eventually rise. He famously said, "When Race gets Bank Book, its Troubles will Cease." Yet he preached uplift without challenging white supremacy. Long ago, Robert Allen pointed out that Washington's dream of creating a class of Southern Black small business owners, teachers, and landowners was premised on separatism. The famous line from his Atlanta Exposition speech, "Cast down your buckets where you are," becomes, Allen says, "We must build an independent economy in the Black community." But Washington's ideology was double-edged. It was not only a public declaration that reaffirmed white planters' and merchants' belief in white supremacy and their derogatory view of Blacks but also a stalking horse for independent land ownership.[33] As such, it appealed to many Black farmers in the rural South.

Washington built the Tuskegee Institute around the dream of creating a generation of rural Black yeomen by setting up land-purchase schemes and using the institute's cooperative demonstration service to help landowners become successful farmers. The initiative resonated with many Blacks across the Deep South, connecting the Negro agrarianism of Reconstruction with the dire realities of Jim Crow. The very notion of self-help and uplift was understood by many Blacks to be subversive, a challenge to the Southern white beliefs in Black inferiority and a claim to independence. Whether this belief was subversive is questionable, but the idea did resonate with many Black farmers.

Alternative Paths to Black Landowning

Distinctive patterns of Black land acquisition corresponded to the changing contours of the plantation South and the land available for purchase. To analyze Black land gains, I have constructed a typology of counties based on three ratios: (1) the ratio of Black farm owners to white farm owners; (2) the ratio of Black tenants to Black farm owners; and (3) the ratio of white tenants to Black tenants. Combining these ratios yields four geographical configurations of landowning and tenancy for Black and white farmers (see table 10). These point up the different paths that Black farmers took to landowning and their relative success. My baseline is 1920, a high point for Black land ownership.

Black Enclaves Seven counties that had a high number of Black owners relative to white owners and a very small number of tenants are located along the Georgia and South Carolina sea coast. This is the region of the Sherman Reserve, where Blacks acquired some land during Reconstruction. Black

TABLE 10 Southern farm owners by race and farm region typology, 1920

	Black enclave	Plantation Black enclave	White plantation	White tenant
Deep South farmers				
Total	16,382	229,135	588,643	565,532
Percentage of white farmers	24	17	44	83
Percentage of Black farmers	77	83	56	17
Deep South farm owners				
Total	12,303	43,754	188,701	293,389
White owners	2,858 (23%)	20,304 (46%)	140,747 (75%)	268,697 (92%)
Black owners	9,445 (77%)	23,450 (54%)	47,594 (25%)	24,692 (8%)
White owners as percentage of all farmers	17	9	24	48
Black owners as percentage of all farmers	58	10	8	4
White owners as percentage of all white farmers	74	53	55	57
Black owners- as percentage of all black farmers	75	12	14	26
Change in number of owners from 1900 to 1920				
White owners	446 (19%)	−1,297 (−6%)	7,207 (5%)	48,978 (22%)
Black owners	391 (4%)	6,099 (35%)	10,052 (27%)	2,840 (13%)
Cotton acreage in farm regions				
Mean cotton acreage	7,415	64,609	41,961	22,719
Percentage of land in cotton	4	29	20	11
Number of counties (excluding urban counties)	7	51	187	232
Number of plantation counties	0	44	138	54
Percentage of plantation counties	0	86	74	23

SOURCES: Deep South Farm Owner Dataset (see appendix); 1920 Agricultural Census; Michael Haines, Price Fishback, and Paul Rhode, United States Agriculture Data, 1840–2012, Inter-university Consortium for Political and Social Research ICPSR35206, v. 4, August 20, 2018, https://doi.org/10.3886/ICPSR35206.v4.

farm ownership was very high in this area: 72 percent in Beaufort County, South Carolina, for example, and 81 percent in Bryan County, Georgia. It was in nearby McIntosh County that Tunis Campbell organized the Belle Ville Farmers Association on 1,250 acres of purchased land. There were 9,445 Black owners out of 12,303 owners in these seven counties by 1920, a ratio of Black owners to White owners of 3.3, and just 3,033 Black tenants. But white-owned farms were almost ten times larger on average than Black-owned farms, 268 acres compared to 28 acres. The area was characterized by small Black farms amid the remnants of rice and cotton plantations.

Before the Civil War these Sea Island counties had been the site of large rice plantations based on an intricate division of labor, manned by skilled slave labor, and planters cultivating Sea Island cotton. Blacks acquired some of this land during Reconstruction either by staking a claim to land abandoned by planters during the war or through the South Carolina Land Commission, which allocated 32,367 acres to three Black enclave counties: Beaufort, Charleston, and Georgetown. By 1879, Black landowners cultivated most of the cotton produced in this region. But much of the land was acquired later, as a result of labor conflict between rice planters and freedmen. Black workers on rice plantations resisted planters' attempts to impose stringent discipline and wage cuts. There were numerous labor strikes in the 1870s; one of the largest occurred on rice plantations along the Combahee River in 1876. Faced with labor strife, Black solidarity and militancy, Black political power in South Carolina, and competition from Louisiana rice plantations, Sea Island rice planters gave up and began to rent or sell land to Black farmers. Land was usually purchased out of savings from wages and cash crops.[34]

The rice plantations that remained depended on wage labor, which for most Blacks supplemented their own small-scale, largely subsistence, cultivation. These farms were not particularly prosperous; the average value of land and buildings per farm for Black-owned farms in 1925 was $650, compared to $5,786 for white-owned farms (a difference that stems from the high value of the remaining rice plantations). Yet these farms provided a significant measure of independence for former slaves, who, as William Harris noted, "owned small plots of land and operated in a peasant like economy in which autonomy meant more than success."[35]

Plantation Black Enclaves The fifty-one counties I identify as plantation Black enclaves were located mainly in the Mississippi Delta; thirty-three of these counties were adjacent to the Mississippi River, mainly in Mississippi and Arkansas. Ten of these counties were in the Black Belt of Alabama. The story of Black landowning in these counties is very different from that in the Sea Islands, though both types of Black enclaves had high numbers of Black owners. The difference is that in the Mississippi Delta and Alabama Black Belt enclaves, significant numbers of Black owners farmed in the shadow of large plantations worked mainly by Black tenants. In 1920 there were 23,450 Black owners in these counties, constituting 53.6 percent of all farm owners, and 166,772 Black tenants, about 91 percent of all tenants.

Black landowning in this area began with migration to acquire land in the mostly undeveloped, heavily forested parts of the Delta after Reconstruction. Delta plantations occupied a narrow strip of land along the Mississippi River, and much of the land to the east was uninhabited. Delta planters faced the same challenge as other planters across the South—obtaining a dependable supply of labor. Initially, they resorted to using prison labor or recruiting tenants. Many Black tenants owned livestock and farm implements and largely escaped furnishing. The backcountry became a magnet for ambitious Black farmers, who cleared the land in exchange for the right to cultivate it for up to three years free of any charge. The landowners, many of them planters, agreed to this deal in order to avoid foreclosure as taxes went up after the war. By agreeing to give a Black farmer three years' free use of the land if it was cleared and brought into cultivation, planters avoided losing ownership of the undeveloped land. Such agreements created an opportunity for Black farmers to eventually purchase the land they cleared. They wasted no time taking advantage of it. John C. Willis writes: "By their labors these men and women, most of whom had once been someone's chattel property, accumulated cash and credit to buy their own land, investing the purchase with their hopes of attaining some economic independence with which to make their legal freedom ring true."[36]

Willis shows that an agricultural ladder developed in the Delta that enabled renters to accumulate enough capital to buy land and prosper. He analyzed the average age of croppers, tenants, and owners over time, assuming that if it remained constant, it was an indication of no upward mobility. By 1900, he found, Black croppers were younger and owners older, indicating that Blacks had been able to move up from sharecropping to renting to owning. Many of these owners did not survive, however, after cotton prices collapsed in the 1890s and white landowners asserted their dominion. Willis argues that the structure of Delta farming changed, and it was more difficult to move up from renting to owning. Black land purchases in Washington County, Mississippi, declined from an annual average of 5.22 in the 1880s to 1.33 by the start of the twentieth century.[37]

Delta planters destroyed as much of the agricultural ladder as they could by replacing renters with sharecroppers. One hard-nosed planter, Alfred Holt Stone, believed that renting to Black farmers "allows the Negroes privileges which he too often abuses." A Black renter did not, he wrote, "take kindly to suggestion or direction as to what he shall plant[, and] he thinks he should be left free to work his crop when and as he pleases."[38] Even so, planters were unable to put down every enterprising Black farmer. The number of Black landowners in the sixteen Mississippi plantation Black enclave counties grew from 4,324 to 5,474 between 1900 and 1920, a 27 percent increase. In the same period the number of Black landowners in the Arkansas Delta rose from 3,758 to 6,217. Black landowners in the Delta made up about half of the landowners in all the plantation Black enclaves.

In the Alabama Black Belt, the number of white landowners in the ten plantation Black enclaves decreased by 15 percent during this period, while the number of Black landowners rose by over 40 percent, from 3,271 to 4,613. It appears that Black farmers took advantage of opportunities to buy land as white farmers decamped. In Macon County the number of Black landowners rose from 211 to 455. About one-third of the gain in Black landownership is attributable to the various land purchase schemes launched by Booker T. Washington. Using the grants he secured from Northern philanthropists, he subsidized the purchase of forty-acre farms on large tracts of land. The land companies he established were tied to farm extension programs run by the Tuskegee Institute. Not all these schemes succeeded, as they ran up against white Southern control of credit and planters' exploitation of Black labor, but these farmers formed the nucleus of Black enclaves across central Alabama.[39]

White Plantations The counties I designate as white plantation counties were dominated by white-owned plantations worked mainly by Black tenants. Almost half these counties were in the Georgia and South Carolina Piedmont. Black owners, while more numerous overall than those in Black enclaves or plantation Black enclaves, made up only a small proportion of farm owners. In 1920 there were 47,594 Black owners in the 188 white plantation counties, one-quarter of all farm owners, working amid 283,774 Black tenants. These counties fit the stereotype of plantation counties in the Deep South Tenant Purchase—large plantations worked by scores of tenants with few Black landowners—but they were already in decline when the boll weevil wiped out cotton production.

Black landowning in these counties was a consequence of the decline of plantations. In Greene and Macon Counties, Georgia, Arthur Raper found that Black owners after 1900 emerged mainly where plantation agriculture was disintegrating. Most Black farmers were able to acquire land only in areas occupied by renters, not by croppers or wage laborers—in other words, land that the plantation owners did not want because plots were too small, unproductive, or difficult to oversee. In white plantation counties there were 5,318 fewer farms of five hundred acres or more by 1920. This was a decline of 58 percent of all such farms in the Deep South. As large farms broke up because of indebtedness or mismanagement, both Black and white cash renters, many of whom had accrued savings as the price of cotton soared during World War I, were able to purchase land. In Greene County, two-fifths of new owners paid cash, much of which was accumulated by renting.

Of the cash renters in the Deep South in 1910, 179,000 were in white plantation counties. Raper thought the advent of cash renting reflected the demise of the plantation system; it also meant that a significant number of renters were able to acquire land.[40] By 1920 there were about 54,000 fewer cash renters in these counties, and although some likely migrated north to flee Jim Crow, it is plausible that many acquired land of their own. Black farmers made large gains in land owning in white plantation counties, but they paid above the market value of the land they purchased. These Black landowners were clearly better off than tenants or wage labor, but Raper thought the breakup of plantations led only to an increase in small Black farms that were not economically viable. "Thus does peasantry emerge when the Black Belt plantation collapses," he concluded.[41]

White Tenants About half the counties in the Deep South (232 of 493) were dominated by white owners of small farms. In these counties there were almost as many owners as tenants—268,697 owners and 270,196 tenants. The Black population was small, about one-fifth of residents in 1930, and there were 24,692 Black farm owners, who made up 8.4 percent of all owners. Only about 25 percent of tenants were Black. The average number of Black tenants in these counties was 299, compared to 1,463 in white plantation counties and 3,270 in Black plantation enclave counties. The number of Black owners increased by only 13 percent from 1900 to 1920, and those gains were spread across all the counties. There were four times as many Black owners in the plantation Black enclave counties as in the white tenant counties, even though almost all of the counties in which Black owners were more than 50 percent of Black farmers were white tenant counties. In most of these counties, Black farm owners worked on poor land in an ocean of white owners.

The counties I refer to as Black enclave counties were disproportionately the home of Black landowners, who accounted for 77 percent of owners and 58 percent of all farmers. In plantation Black enclave counties, by comparison, Black owners made up 54 percent of all owners but just 10 percent of farmers. At the other extreme, Black landowners constituted 8 percent of all owners in white tenant counties and only 4.4 percent of farmers. Between 1900 and 1920, as table 10 shows, the largest gains in Black ownership occurred in the two types of plantation counties. These counties added over 16,000 Black landowners, compared to 3,231 in the other two types of counties, a gain of 30 percent compared to just 4 percent. Black farmers seeking land gravitated to plantation counties either because land was readily available, as absentee owners gave up farming, or because new land opened in the Mississippi Delta and Alabama Black Belt. Marable argued over forty years ago that as cotton prices rose, Blacks migrated to counties with a history of violence and lynching—the plantation South—but these counties were also disproportionately populated by Blacks and dedicated to planting and harvesting cotton.[42]

Under the Shadow of Jim Crow: The Ideology and Politics of Black Landowners

Black landowners' ideology of self-reliance, mutual aid, and separatism was a bulwark against white violence and oppression during the Jim Crow era. They lived in geographically concentrated clusters, often connected through kinship ties (and often on poor land), amid plantations. These enclaves permitted Blacks to pursue lives outside white control. One Black enclave, Promised Land, occupied four square miles of land in Abbeville County, South Carolina, purchased through the South Carolina Land Commission. Starting with 48 families in 1872, it grew to 250 households by 1890. Promised Land was not a town or even a village, but, like many Black enclaves, it developed a vibrant community life centering on churches, benevolent societies, and schools. As in many other Black enclaves, its landowners paid taxes but suffered from poorly maintained roads and the lack of any other public services or support. John Lewis, whose father was a landowner, described life in

Dunes Chapel in the Alabama Black Belt, where he grew up: "We had unpaved roads," he recalled in a 1983 interview, "and for many years the county refused to pave the major road. They paved it up to where the black section of the county started." Homes also lacked electricity and indoor plumbing.[43]

These communities were usually isolated from merchants, cotton gins, banks, and the other institutions of the cotton economy. Although many of the landowners were farmers who had established secure titles to their land, they had little possibility for upward mobility. But they were able to become economically self-sufficient, avoid slipping into debt, and thus evade the tentacles of tenancy. And they were better off than tenants. Black landowners in Promised Land planted about as much cotton as tenants and croppers—15.9 acres, compared to 14.4 for tenants—and produced slightly more cotton (3 bales compared to 2.5)—but reaped twice as much money, $216.41 compared to $108.39, each year. What made the difference for landowners was avoidance of the lien system and using their land to produce their food instead of growing cotton on every acre.[44]

Some all-Black towns flourished for a time. At the start of the twentieth century Mound Bayou, in Bolivar County, Mississippi, deep in the Delta, was a beacon of Black economic success. Isaiah Montgomery launched the enclave in the 1880s by telling would-be landowners that "they might as well buy land and own it and do for themselves what they had been doing for other folks for two hundred and fifty years."[45] These Black migrants were able to purchase land from the railroad and started with seven hundred acres. By 1907, Mound Bayou was a thriving community of four thousand people who owned thirty thousand acres of land and cultivated between five thousand and six thousand acres. They were producing about three thousand bales of cotton each year, aided by the Bank of Mound Bayou. The leaders of this all-Black town did their best to keep whites out. Janet Hermann reports they created the Mound Bayou Loan and Investment Company to keep whites from buying land in the area.[46]

Black landowners struggled, some sinking into peasantry, others eking out a very modest living, and a few prospering. The average Black landowner in the Deep South farmed 75 acres of land that was often poor, hilly, and rocky; the average white landowner farmed 157 acres. The value of land and buildings for white-owned farms was almost three times that for Black-owned farms: $4,505 per white owner compared to $1,666 per Black owner. Table 11 presents data for the value of land and buildings for Black and white farm owners in

TABLE 11 Farm land value and size by farm region typology and race of owner, 1925

Percentile	Value of land and buildings ($)			Farm size (acres)	
	White owners	Black owners	Ratio white-owned/ Black-owned	White owners	Black owners
	BLACK ENCLAVE COUNTIES				
25	2,938	522	5.6	242	24
Median	3,939	687	5.7	263	33
75	4,689	812	5.8	441	43
95	18,497	827	22.4	469	44
Ratio of 95th to 25th percentile	6.3	1.6		1.9	1.8
	PLANTATION BLACK ENCLAVE COUNTIES				
25	4,770	1,366	3.5	152	55
Median	6,410	1,904	3.4	224	63
75	13,661	2,671	5.1	324	88
95	27,457	4,137	6.6	464	108
Ratio of 95th to 25th percentile	5.8	3.0		3.1	2.0
	WHITE PLANTATION COUNTIES				
25	2,858	1,282	2.2	120	69
Median	4,013	1,731	2.3	149	83
75	5,247	2,089	2.5	189	100
95	8,063	3,069	2.6	334	153
Ratio of 95th to 25th percentile	2.8	2.4		2.8	2.2
	WHITE TENANT COUNTIES				
25	2,009	1,021	2.0	91	49
Median	2,598	1,323	2.0	107	64
75	3,687	1,811	2.0	136	78
95	6,383	2,665	2.4	235	107
Ratio of 95th to 25th percentile	3.2	2.6		2.6	2.2

SOURCES: Deep South Farm Owner Dataset (see appendix); 1925 Agricultural Census.; Michael Haines, Price Fishback, and Paul Rhode, United States Agriculture Data, 1840–2012, Inter-university Consortium for Political and Social Research ICPSR35206, v. 4, August 20, 2018, https://doi.org/10.3886/ICPSR35206.v4.

1925 in the four types of counties at different percentiles. These values are a measure of the *gross* wealth of landowners and as such are a limited, even crude measure. Unfortunately, data on mortgage debt or income by race of the owner are unavailable. The census data, however, are fairly accurate and convey the differences in the status of Black and white landowners at different levels of wealth.[47] In plantation Black enclave counties, the median white-owned farm was 3.4 times more valuable than the median Black-owned farm. The difference was even greater in the seven Black enclave counties in coastal Georgia and South Carolina, where median white-owned farms were almost six times more valuable. The difference was lowest in white tenant counties, where it appears that both Black and white landowners farmed poor land. The median value of white-owned farms was about $2,600 and that of Black-owned about $1,300. Regardless of location or percentile, white-owned land was more valuable than Black-owned land. White supremacy circumscribed the fortunes of Black landholders at every turn.

Black landowners' status and chances of succeeding as farmers varied greatly across the rural South, depending on where they obtained land. Despite the risks of violence and harassment from white planters, the farms of Black landowners in plantation Black enclave counties were more valuable than those in other counties: the median value of Black-owned farms in these counties was $1,904, compared to $1,731 in white plantation counties and $1,323 in white tenant counties. Black landowners in the seven Black enclave counties had the lowest-value and smallest farms, a legacy of the conflict over land and labor in the Sea Islands during and after Reconstruction. The median value of their land and buildings was just $687 and the median farm size thirty-three acres.

Whether Black landowners were reduced to subsistence farming or able to make a modest living depended on whether their farms were in the Mississippi Delta or an older plantation region such as the Georgia Piedmont. Even after the boll weevil invasion and the collapse of cotton prices after World War I, land in the Mississippi River Delta was far more valuable than land in other regions. In Coahoma County, Mississippi, for example, the value of white-owned land and buildings was the highest in the ten counties of the Mississippi Delta ($31,378). Black-owned farms there were small, at an average of thirty-five acres, but they were among the most valuable Black-owned properties in the Delta, worth an average of $3,548. In Greene County, Alabama, deep in the Black Belt, the average Black-owned farm was ninety-two acres and valued at just $1,358, just over one-third the value of Coahoma

County farms. From the 25th to the 95th percentile, Black landowners in the two types of plantation counties occupied more valuable farms than those in Black enclave or white tenant counties, both of which had very high proportions of Black landowners and low numbers of Black tenants.

The value of white farms vastly outstripped that of Black farms. But there was a sharper class divide between white landowners than between Black landowners. One way to measure this difference is to compare the ratio of the value of land and buildings at the 95th percentile and the 25th percentile for each group of landowners. In the two Black enclave counties, farm value for the white landowners in the 95th percentile is about six times that of white owners in the 25th percentile. For Black landowners, the gap between the 95th and 25th percentiles is narrower. These data show that the large planters occupied the best land and from there ruled the Deep South.

Louis Harlan argues that Booker T. Washington conceived the Tuskegee Institute as "a mighty engine of black self-help" based on creating a class of land-owning Black yeomen. As a path toward Black self-determination, Washington's land-owning schemes failed, Harlan asserts, because the "whole system of racial subordination and labor exploitation on which the cotton growing economy rested went counter to such efforts." Mound Bayou, which was in decline by 1920 after the failure of its bank and Isaiah Montgomery's attempt to set up a cottonseed-oil plant, is often cited as a failed attempt to a create self-sufficient economic community.[48] Landowning was never an alternative to the tenant system, and Tuskegee had nothing to offer tenants. The cooperative demonstration program that Washington created was an early version of extension work that began with the Smith-Lever Act, and it anticipated the rehabilitation programs of the Resettlement Administration. In the 1920s, the very idea of self-sufficient Black farmers was subversive, a challenge to white beliefs in Black inferiority. Planters opposed extension work for tenants, who understood why. As one said, the tenant system was intended to make sure Black farmers "don't have no way to help ourselves."[49] But for those Blacks able to acquire land, neither self-determination nor self-sufficiency was an empty ideological slogan, despite their lackluster economic prospects: it was the point.

What mattered for Black farmers and their families in Black enclaves were independence and freedom from coercion. Economic accumulation was secondary to autonomy. Nothing makes this so clear as the reception of Garveyism in the 1920s, after Washington died and chapters of the United Negro Improvement Association (UNIA) proliferated across the rural South. Marcus

Garvey's message was one of economic independence, social separation, and Black autonomy. The *Negro World,* the newspaper of the UNIA, editorialized, "We believe in the farmer and in ownership in the soil as the most independent life," and advised Black farmers "to own land wherever they can and to raise their own home supplies, and thus become independent of the country storekeeper and the credit system." Mary Rolinson suggests that Garvey's message and its appeal to rural Blacks facing the exploitation and violence of Jim Crow can be traced to the nineteenth-century Black nationalism espoused by Martin Delany and Henry McNeal Turner. But its appeal also derives from the power of the Negro agrarianism that grew out of Reconstruction and the idea that land ownership was the only means for Blacks to attain the independence necessary to resist white oppression. Owning land, Tunis Campbell recognized, was a source of power. During Reconstruction, he aimed to equip the freed people with real and human capital—land and education. He was dedicated to uplift and self-reliance but had absorbed the lessons of antiprivilege egalitarianism, and his speeches often sounded like those of a Jacksonian Democrat decrying the corruption of monopoly charters. Campbell set up the Belle Ville Farmers Association, a venture in cooperative farming, and created an early Black enclave in McIntosh County, Georgia, which remained an island of Black power in a sea of white supremacy for nearly forty years after the so-called Redeemers railroaded him into convict labor.[50]

In Black enclaves, farmers were already practicing what Garvey preached. Roy Roberts, a Black farmer in Hancock County, Georgia, a Black enclave populated by 182 owners, understood the leverage that owning land gave him. He told an interviewer, "Most black people hired themselves out to whites. If they said, 'get up at six o'clock and go to work,' they had to get up. If they said, 'fifty cents a day,' that's all they got. But we didn't have to get up for nobody because we were home. We had our own land—our own everything—and it made a difference." As Elizabeth Bethel points out, subsistence agriculture gave the farmers of Promised Land and their families "a degree of independence and self-reliance unknown to most other Negro families in the area."[51]

Isaiah Montgomery, like Garvey and others, was convinced that Black progress could occur only in segregated communities. He was the sole Black delegate to the 1890 Mississippi constitutional convention and voted in favor of disenfranchising Blacks. He ignored the withering national criticism he received, responding that he was not sacrificing Black voting or civil rights, since Blacks faced danger and even death if they tried to vote. Mound Bayou, Janet Hermann concludes, was "an oasis of freedom and autonomy for oppressed Negroes ... for at least twenty-five years, when black esteem was being severely buffeted by the fiercest forms of white bigotry[, and] a thriving, well-publicized example of a successful Negro colony."[52]

These self-contained Black enclaves were vital to protection of Blacks from violence, whitecappers trying to dispossess them, and rampaging white lynch mobs. Abbeville County, South Carolina, was notorious for its violence during and after Reconstruction, but Promiseland was an island of protection. Recalling how the people of Promised Land repelled an attempted KKK attack, one resident said, "Any white man come in to Promise land to beat the n——rs up, some body going to die. They'll fight 'til hell freezes over. You Phoenix rats go back to Phoenix."[53] And they did. Both Hancock County and Promised Land experienced very little violence. Macon County, Alabama, the home of the Tuskegee Institute, was an "oasis of racial peace" after 1890. Bolivar County, where Mound Bayou was located, became deadly in the 1920s, when the price of cotton declined and many white yeoman farmers descended into tenancy. Montgomery believed Mound Bayou was safeguarded against marauding whites, though he recognized that he needed to keep influential whites on his side to prevent terrorist attacks.[54]

Grounded in self-defense and racial pride, Garveyism flourished in precisely those counties with high levels of violence, especially toward Black women, and exploitation. The slogan "God, Garvey, and a gun" captures the appeal of Garveyism in the rural South. It is no accident that UNIA chapters were concentrated in the Mississippi Delta and southwest Georgia, mostly in all-Black communities in cotton-growing counties. Almost half of rural UNIA chapters were in Arkansas and Mississippi, states with very high rates of lynchings in the early twentieth century. Jarod Roll suggests that UNIA chapters were dominated by "small landowners, successful renters, aspiring sharecroppers, teachers, and preachers." Many share tenants and croppers were also attracted to Garveyism. Although men often dominated the chapters, Black women were key organizers.[55]

A NEW DEAL FOR BLACK LANDOWNERS? RESETTLEMENT AND DEBT RELIEF IN THE DEEP SOUTH

Garveyism was a response to the upheaval in the rural South as cotton prices and exports declined during and after World War I. Along with more than forty-seven thousand white farmers, almost twenty-one thousand Black landowners in the Deep South lost their land between 1920 and 1925. When Garveyism collapsed in the late 1920s, Black landowners gravitated to the National Federation of Colored Farmers (NFCF). Under the leadership of Leon Harris, the NFCF sought to forge an alliance between landowners and tenants. Black farmers, Harris asserted in a 1933 speech, needed to work together: "You will remain the Lazarus of American Farmers and continue getting only the crumbs from the table until you become organized." Although the NFCF started out as a cooperative organization of successful farmers, it organized its first local chapter in Holmes County, Mississippi, in 1929, among share tenants and croppers. This was the only county in Mississippi where a Black resettlement project was established. Harris sought to alert the "whole nation" to the "evil" of tenancy and the "misery and unhappiness" of men who watched their wives and children toil as "cotton-patch slaves." The NFCF lobbied the Roosevelt administration to aid Black tenants and to make "every effort ... to widen land ownership by Race farmers." Similarly, Black extension agents were demanding that the administration help Black farmers by buying up large plantations, subdividing them into smaller farms, and selling them to tenants.[56]

The number of Black and white farm owners increased by 113,010 between 1930 and 1945. Most of the growth in ownership came between 1935 and 1945, as New Deal farm programs took hold. The number of part owners decreased by 21 percent between 1935 and 1945. In the six Deep South states, there were almost fifteen thousand more Black full owners by 1945, a gain of 21 percent, and over one hundred thousand more white full owners, a gain of 35 percent.

What did New Deal land and agricultural policies mean for the livelihood and status of down-and-out farmers and tenants in the Deep South? Did New Deal policies contribute to Black land ownership, or did white farmers scoop up all the benefits?

The failure of New Deal land redistribution plans in 1935 and 1937 left the administration with three policies to create opportunities for tenants and downwardly mobile farm owners to acquire land. The centerpiece of these policies was its resettlement program. By 1937, the agency owned 772, 217 acres of land, most of it in the South. The Resettlement Administration (RA) purchased much of this land from banks, insurance companies, and individual landowners who were deep in debt. Resettlement entailed taking submarginal land out of production and relocating displaced farm households on single-owner farms. This was one arm of the US Department of Agriculture's plan to reorganize Southern agriculture as a capital-intensive enterprise. If rural rehabilitation aimed to keep starving tenants off relief and mitigate exploitation, rural resettlement aimed to demonstrate the power of Roosevelt's Southern agricultural revolution. The RA was not just rehabilitating tenants; it was rehabilitating the South.[57]

The other two programs were credit policies. FDR tried but failed to get Congress to approve a land-purchase policy modeled on the 1935 resettlement bill. What he got was the tenant purchase (TP) program, a weak credit policy that benefited very few farmers. Proponents of a credible land-purchase program that would redistribute land to tenants never had a chance. Dominated by Southern Democrats, the House Committee on Agriculture created a credit policy instead of a land-purchase program and slashed the $50 million appropriation the administration requested to just $10 million for farm-purchase loans. To double the insult, the committee gave county committees the authority to approve loans, thus ensuring that funding was under the control of white planters, agricultural extension agents, and local bankers. The committee also imposed severe limitations on the eligibility of borrowers: preference was given to those farmers who owned some equipment or livestock and could make a small down payment. Marvin Jones (D-Texas), the committee chair, quipped that the committee's action "takes the government out of the picture as a land purchaser." With the federal government's role reduced to monitoring the TP program after 1937, white men dedicated to upholding Jim Crow governed the allocation of loans.[58]

Blacks were aware of the perils of local committee control of the loan program. Charles Houston wrote Will Alexander, "I have the gravest misgivings that Negroes will not receive impartial consideration." Walter White of the NAACP lobbied the administration for the appointment of Blacks to the FSA, telling USDA administrators that "experience has shown unmistakenly that in a great many counties of the South Negroes will be the victim of gross discrimination if such decisions are left wholly to local boards." The 1937 Bankhead-Jones Act put Black tenants at a significant disadvantage for access to TP loans.[59]

Driven by money lust, Southern states were ahead of the pack in setting up local committees and processing loan applications. By the end of 1937, nine Southern states had set up county committees, including all the Deep South states but Louisiana. Applications exceeded the number of available loans. As of January 30, 1938, there were 19,500 applications (80 percent of the national total) for just 1,932 loans available in the four Southern FSA regions. But the South captured two-thirds of all loans. Southern senators and members of Congress were always quick to take credit for the program.[60]

The third New Deal landowning policy was the establishment of the Farm Credit Administration (FCA). The agency comprised the twelve existing federal land banks (FLBs), which were private but government sponsored, and the land bank commissioner (LBC). These two government banks originated loans and refinanced existing loans for land and crops in response to the wave of farm foreclosures in the 1930s. Their main instrument of debt relief was interest-rate subsidies. FCA interest rates averaged 3.5 percent, about 1.5 percentage points lower than commercial rates during the 1930s. The FCA made $135 million worth of loans between 1935 and 1939 in the Deep South states, almost 11 percent of all its loans. Criteria for lending included the valuation of the farm property. In the context of the New Deal preference for large-scale, capital-intensive agriculture, loans for small farms were rejected.[61] Black landowners were not usually the intended beneficiaries of FCA loans.

Resettlement projects and TP loans provided vital assistance to some farmers, but the programs helped very few farmers in the Deep South, whether tenants or landowners. The FCA was another matter: along with the federal crop subsidies, it greased the wheels for the emergence of capital-intensive agriculture.

Turning Tenants into Landowners: Who Benefited and Why?

The RA's resettlement projects across the South were lavish ventures that combined rural social work with the construction of model farms intended to rehabilitate the land and the people. Members of Congress from Mississippi, Louisiana, and Arkansas lobbied the administration for resettlement projects for their districts. The projects were a source of jobs and of income for bankers, merchants, and white Southerners. At the opening of the Plum Bayou project in Arkansas, Senator Joseph Robinson (D-Arkansas) endorsed resettlement, saying, "Nothing... is better calculated to sustain the fundamental institutions upon which society and government... rest than the effective encouragement of home ownership." Alabama and Mississippi's senators were all strong advocates of the Resettlement Administration, seeing the program as a boon to white farmers.[62] But it was less the benefits of home ownership than the lust for federal dollars that lay behind Southern enthusiasm for resettlement projects. Money could override even white objections to black resettlement projects.

The resettlement projects are salient examples of what might be called concentrated redistribution. For each project, the RA invested significant financial resources in the construction of homes, farm buildings, schools, and community centers. The agency built a small number of full-blown farm communities that took down-and-out tenants and farm owners and set them up to become successful farmers. Some resettlement projects established individual farms scattered across several counties in a state; there were a total of fifteen "infiltration" projects in the Deep South. Another twenty-eight were community projects located in one or two counties in a state. In some cases, the agency acquired existing plantations; in others it developed farms from the ground up, clearing land and erecting farmhouses, barns, community buildings, and schools. There were thirty-nine counties with community projects and ninety-seven counties with scattered projects.

These were not cheap undertakings. Between 1935 and 1943, the RA invested $26.7 million to purchase land and develop over four thousand farms, averaging sixty-six acres in size, in the six Deep South states, at an average cost of $622,023. The projects resulted in 258,000 acres of farmed land. Resettlement projects received a disproportionate share of the FSA's resources (see table 12). Farmers relocated to these projects received $6.6 million in rehabilitation loans, with loans averaging almost $1,700, far more than the standard rehabilitation loans. Counties with resettlement projects received one-third of FSA's expenditures for loans and grants ($24.5 million), though not all of this money went to tenants. In Alabama, Arkansas, and South Carolina, resettlement counties received over 43 percent of FSA loans and grants in the three states. Resettlement counties received an average of $180,563 for loans and grants, compared to about $140,384 for counties with no projects. The RA also leveraged funds from the Farm Credit Administration and the Works Progress Administration (WPA). Counties with resettlement projects received an average of almost $353,000 in FCA land and emergency loans, one and half times the amount distributed to counties without resettlement projects. The average land loan was $2,100. Administrators anticipated that projects would be "self-liquidating" as loans were paid off, and that resettlement farmers would become self-sufficient through a combination of subsistence agriculture and the sale of cash crops.[63] These projects amounted to a significant infusion of resources into a small number of Deep South counties.

TABLE 12 Resettlement Administration loan amounts, farm areas, and costs for Deep South projects, 1935–43

	Total loan amounts ($)	Average loan ($)	Farmed acres	Average farm size (acres)	Average project cost ($)
Black RA projects	1,413,266	1,570	49,089	54.5	530,060
White RA projects	2,774,614	1,789	90,139	58.1	694,810
Infiltration projects	2,399,078	1,651	118,599	81.6	595,987
Deep South Total	6,586,958	1,687	257,827	66.0	622,023

SOURCES: United States Congress, *Hearings before the Select House Committee of the House Committee on Agriculture to Investigate the Activities of the Farm Security Administration*, House of Representatives, 78th Congress, 1st Sess. (Washington, DC: US Government Printing Office, 1943), 1033–99; Richard Sterner, *The Negro's Share: A Study of Income, Consumption, Housing, and Public Assistance* (New York: Harper and Brothers, 1943), 423–25.

Resettlement projects replaced tenant plantations with group farms that were privately owned but collectively managed. As the RA described them, these projects were "group farming paternalistically controlled." The RA retained control of resettlement property and had the authority to sell or lease land. A loan required a 15 percent down payment and a forty-year term at 3 percent interest, but since almost none of the tenants could meet these requirements, the RA just gave them a five-year trial lease that could be converted into a sale or another lease. These leases were, in effect, interest-free loans. Homesteader payments were limited to 25 percent of their income, and the RA subsidized the costs of maintenance, farm operations, and local taxes. Roosevelt approved all these policies.[64] Tugwell restricted the kind of farming clients could undertake to a "maximum 'live at home' type of farming, and minimum cash crop type of farming." This was nothing more than a recipe for subsistence farming, and it undercut any notion of creating self-sustaining farmers. Resettlement projects were not vehicles for land ownership but models for a future that many tenants would never experience, one that was being undermined by the New Deal's aid to large, capital-intensive landowners. A resettlement project was indeed a step up for farmers, but whether it was an economic opportunity is questionable.[65]

In selecting tenants or former owners for farms in a resettlement project or TP loans, administrators claimed they were looking for farmers who could be independent—that is, able to produce enough to feed their family and pay off the loan. Administrators preferred young farmers who met desired social or cultural criteria. Selection based on "nationality, race, or creed" was prohibited, but the agency did consider "the desirability of homogeneity with the particular group": in other words, projects would be segregated. Agency policies appear to have excluded sharecroppers, preferring families who "possess sufficient stock and equipment to efficiently operate the units." Yet many of the tenants selected were destitute. They were drawn from the relief rolls or from among farm families displaced from land purchased and cleared by the RA.[66]

Tugwell and Alexander made a concerted effort to set up all-Black resettlement projects. Out of the forty-three Deep South resettlement projects, ten, comprising forty-nine thousand acres of farmed land, were designated solely for Black farmers. The RA invested $5.3 million in these projects, one-fifth of all resettlement funds in the six states, and resettled 814 African American families in community projects. Another 229 Black families were given farms in scattered tenant-security or infiltration projects spread across multiple counties (see table 13). In setting up these projects, RA officials catered to Southern white racism and the power of local white elites and politicians. Robert Hudgens explained to Alexander: "If it is realized that we are constructing homes and outbuildings for low income negroes deep in the black-belt of Alabama that are far superior to the improvements that the most of the better class of white people enjoy . . . extreme caution must be exercised and . . . constant missionary work must be done with the leading white element in that section, in order that our plans will be tolerated and carried out to a satisfactory conclusion." Despite the RA's efforts, there was substantial white opposition whenever it tried to acquire land for Black farmers. Agents often did not place Black tenants on farms because, as one South Carolina agent reported, to do so "it would have been necessary to option land of very poor quality."[67]

One strategy the agency used to evade white opposition was to look for land that was isolated and unoccupied by white farmers. Gee's Bend, Alabama, located on an isolated part of the Alabama River, appealed to the RA because it was isolated enough to be developed without white interference. "The project, therefore, is ideal for a negro development insofar as the racial question is involved," according to a report. The land in question had had a single owner and been farmed by the same African American families since Reconstruction. The agency also developed Black projects that were loosely affiliated with African American agricultural colleges in order to give the projects some legitimacy and allow farmers access to Black extension agents. The Prairie Farms settlement in Macon County, Alabama, was

TABLE 13 Summary data for Deep South Resettlement Administration (RA) projects

	Number of Black clients in RA projects	Total number of farm units	% Black farmers in RA projects	Number of farms occupied	Number of farms sold to occupant	% of farms sold to occupant	Average selling price	Number of RA projects
Black RA projects	814	951	85.6	900	470	52.2	$2,957	10
White RA projects	43	1659	2.6	1551	598	38.6	$5,965	18
Infiltration projects	229	1496	15.3	1453	639	44.0	$2,998	15
Deep South total	1086	4106	26.4	3904	1707	43.7	$3,805	43

SOURCES: United States Congress, *Hearings before the Select House Committee of the House Committee on Agriculture to Investigate the Activities of the Farm Security Administration*, House of Representatives, 78th Congress, 1st Sess. (Washington, DC: US Government Printing Office, 1943), 1033–99. Richard Sterner, *The Negro's Share, A Study of Income, Consumption, Housing, and Public Assistance* (New York: Harper and Brothers, 1943), 423–25.

affiliated with the Tuskegee Institute and described by participants as "a Government answer to the plea of the late Booker T. Washington, Tuskegee's founder, for a live-at-home, crop-rotated salvation for the American farmer."[68] Flint River Farms, the only Black resettlement project in Georgia, started with a request from the Fort Valley Normal and Industrial School, and the project in Orangeburg, South Carolina, was tied to the Vorhees Normal and Industrial School. Both were Black colleges created after Reconstruction.

White Southerners were never of one mind about Black resettlement farms, but money lust frequently trumped white supremacy. Resettlement projects, whether for white or Black farmers, were a source of cash for landowners and merchants, and building barns and schools provided jobs for working-class whites. Politicians usually let the RA know what they thought about a project. Senator James Byrnes (D-South Carolina) told officials he was in favor of the Orangeburg project, and the local congressman, Hampton P. Fulmer, wrote Carl Taylor to say that he was "deeply interested in securing prompt and favorable consideration of this very meritorious project." Fulmer appeared to be less interested in whether Blacks would occupy the farms than in who would benefit from the sale of the land.[69]

It was not uncommon for a local chamber of commerce to write the RA in support of a resettlement project. In the case of Flint River Farms, the local ruling class—white bankers, merchants, and landowners—with the aid of Senator Richard Russell (D-Georgia), staved off white opposition to the project, although the RA was forced to move it from Peach County to Macon County. Opponents objected that the project would demoralize farm labor on adjacent farms. What they meant was that wages might go up and undermine the exploitative wage contracts they imposed on tenants. The Flint River opponents were not opposed to RA projects, but what they wanted was the tenant purchase program, through which local landowners could sell land to tenants who had been given loans issued by local white bankers and merchants. In other words, they wanted control of the program.[70]

White opponents acting in the interests of local planters often challenged projects on behalf of white tenants. The eviction of Black tenants from Transylvania Farms in East Carroll Parish, Louisiana, and the demise of the Mississippi Delta project show the lengths to which white Southerners would go to evict Black farmers and replace them with white tenants to keep Black tenants under the thumb of planters. Southern senators and members of Congress were the chief instigators of opposition to both these projects. The RA purchased the Transylvania plantation from an absentee owner in Memphis and planned to subdivide the six-thousand acres into family-owned or rented farms, to be made available to some of the 252 Black tenants who were already working the land. The agency added a blacksmith and mechanic for tenants and planned to distribute any profits from the community store to the tenants. FSA subsidies, Packard told Will Alexander, would "increase the patronage dividends to the clients from these operations."[71]

This was a sweet deal for the Black tenants— so sweet that white landowners and tenants promptly complained. T. G. Biggs, the mayor of Lake Providence, Louisiana, demanded that the "proposed colored units of East Carroll Parish be changed to a white project." A local plantation owner complained to Senator Allen Ellender that the project was creating "a rather bad feeling on account of the fact of the great difference that farming operations are being handled by the United States and the surrounding neighbors." Planters objected to the diminution of their control over Black tenants whom they could easily exploit. They were quite willing to see white tenants moved onto a resettlement project.[72]

Facing white opposition to resettling Black farmers on the Transylvania plantation, the agency reluctantly decided to move the Black tenants to another plantation, called Mounds. This move provoked opposition from the LSCU and NAACP. The *Pittsburgh Courier,* a nationally known African American newspaper, ran a story on Transylvania with the headline "Two Hundred Fifty Families Tricked into Signing Away Homes They Occupied for 100 Years." Alexander and others viewed the plan as merely switching black and white tenants to comparable plantations, but Charles Houston and

Thurgood Marshall thought Black tenants, many of whom had farmed the land since the late nineteenth century, were being dispossessed of property they had improved and a church and school they had erected. They had little reason to trust the FSA. They believed, correctly, that displaced tenants would end up under the thumb of a notorious landowner and that funds for Black schools would be diverted to white schools. The FSA's plan entailed moving white tenants from Mounds as well, but this provision led Newt Mills, the local congressman, to fiercely oppose selling any farms to Black tenants.[73]

The FSA ended up trying to move white and Black tenants to different but segregated plantations and investing the same amount in each—about $870,000. It is unclear how many of the original Black tenants occupying Transylvania moved to Mounds, mainly because the local agent in charge of selecting families rejected many of these tenants, leaving them no alternative but working for local planters. The FSA told Houston and Marshall they were doing everything they could on behalf of the Black tenants and asserted that the land at Mounds was just as fertile as that on Transylvania. In fact, T. Roy Reid, the regional director, reported that twice as many white tenants as Black tenants got farms.[74]

Mississippi Delta Farms, in Sunflower County, started out as a Black project, but Alexander, under pressure from Theodore Bilbo and the fiercely racist white residents of the small town of Drew, decided to set up a white project that required evicting Black tenants working the plantation. The grand master of a local Black Masonic lodge, John L. Webb, complained to Alexander that the local FSA agent tried to "frighten these Negroes and cause them to throw up their contracts and move away and thus make a white project" by telling them that if they did not move, they would not receive loans. Alexander tried to move Black tenants to a project at Mound Bayou in Bolivar County, but Will Whittington, the congressman representing Delta counties, sabotaged the effort because "thoughtful citizens now regard it as a hot bed of radicalism and as a breeding place for the agitation of discord between landlords and tenants." Mound Bayou was never completed, and the land and some of the tenants became part of an infiltration project in northwestern Mississippi. The FSA was able to set up Mileston Farms, a successful Black project in Holmes County, with 110 tenants.[75]

Although resettlement projects demonstrably increased farm ownership among both Black and white tenants, whites benefited far more. Black farmers were much more likely to purchase their farms than white farmers—52

TABLE 14 Resettlement Administration farm loans, increase in farm ownership, and land values by counties with RA projects, 1935–43 (mean values)

	Federal loans by type ($)			Increase in number of owners		Change in land values ($)	
	FCA[a]	FSA[a]	TP[a]	White[a]	Black[b]	White[b]	Black
Counties with RA projects	352,828	180,563	30,011	198	39	2,904	929
Counties with no RA projects	239,958	140,384	20,064	113	20	1,641	832

SOURCE: Deep South New Deal Dataset (see appendix).
[a] Difference in mean values significant at 0.0000.
[b] Difference in mean values significant at ≤ 0.009.

percent of Black farmers had purchased resettlement farms in community projects by 1943, compared to 39 percent of white farmers (see table 13). But in counties with RA community or infiltration projects, the average number of new owners was significantly higher. The mean increase in the number of full farm owners between 1935 and 1945 in resettlement counties was 198 for white farmers and just 39 for Black owners. White owners in resettlement counties ended up with property that was almost twice as valuable as that of white farmers in counties with no project—an average value of $2,904 compared to $1,641 (see table 14). Being in a resettlement county made little difference in the value of land obtained by Black farmers: all these farms were small and potentially uneconomical.

FCA loans for land augmented resettlement money. In counties with resettlement projects, the dollar amount of FCA loans was 70 percent higher than in counties without them. Tenant purchase loans were another matter. There were very few TP loans in Deep South counties. Congress limited the number of loans that could be issued in any single county, with the result that 473 counties, mostly in the South, could approve no more than five loans. But TP loans averaged $4,400, far higher than the average of $186 for rehabilitation loans. Local committees allocating TP loans favored white tenant farmers and landowners who benefited from a reverse means test in which access to loans depended on an applicant's eligibility for credit. This usually required that tenant farmers own farm equipment such as plows and mules, which was more likely for white than for Black tenants. The upshot was that TP loans, unlike rehabilitation loans, did not conform to the FSA policy of proportionality between Black and white farmers. The ratio of TP loans to Black farmers in all Deep South states was 0.54, compared to a ratio of 0.85 for rehabilitation loans. Rehabilitation loans were proportional to the number of Black farmers in Alabama, Louisiana, and South Carolina. TP loans were not proportional in any of the Deep South states.[76]

Rehabilitation loans and resettlement projects were redistributive; FCA loans for land or crops were not. FCA loans went to high-income counties and large farms.[77] Black landowners were far less likely to receive an FCA loan than white owners. White planters and bankers, who exerted tight control over the FCA loan program in the South, had little interest in bailing out Black landowners. Blacks were excluded from white credit unions, and because their property was usually underappraised, their loan applications were denied or they received only paltry loans. In Greene and Macon Counties, Georgia, Arthur Raper found that 291 white landowners received a total of over $700,000 in FCA loans, compared with 34 Black landowners who received loans totaling $37,000. The average loan amount to white landowners was more than twice that to Black farmers.[78]

That Southern Blacks received anything at all from the FCA is partly due to the efforts of Henry A. Hunt, who was the Black Cabinet representative to the FCA. Hunt was an important figure in Southern Black agriculture, running demonstration and outreach programs at Fort Valley State College in Georgia. In his capacity as the Black adviser to the FCA, Hunt tried to inform Black landowners of the FCA's loan programs and help them form credit unions, which were necessary to access loans.[79]

Both Black and white farmers made gains in ownership between 1935 and 1945. To gauge the effect of New Deal loans on farm ownership, I estimated the change in the number of full white and Black owners between 1935 and 1945 as a function of the two FCA loan programs and FSA's rural rehabilitation and tenant purchase loans. I also included variables for cotton acreage, the number of white or Black farmers in a county, the number of farm-owner failures in 1934, and whether there was a resettlement project in a county. The results show that FCA loans had a significant effect on gains in white ownership but a negligible effect on gains in Black ownership. A 10 percent increase in the value of FCA loans is associated with an increase of eight white farm owners. Rural rehabilitation loans were associated with the increase in Black ownership, but the effect was not large. A 10 percent increase in the value of rehabilitation loans was associated with an increase of 1.5 Black owners. (See table A.2). Whether an owner was in a resettlement county had a slight effect on gains for white owners but no effect for Black owners. An increase in white ownership was more likely in counties with a large number of cotton producers and white owners. Cotton acreage across the Deep South declined after 1930, but cotton prices shot through the roof during World War II, spurring gains in ownership.[80]

There is one striking difference between Black and white landowners. White landowners made their gains in counties with few Black farmers; white owners' gains are negatively associated with the percentage of Black farmers. For Black landowners the case was just the opposite. Although a small number of Black farmers acquired land from rehabilitation loans, white farmers were the major beneficiaries. Roosevelt's tenant policies set up some Black farmers on subsistence farms with rehabilitation loans, but New Deal land purchase policies did little to help them. If Black farmers acquired land in the late 1930s and early 1940s, as many did, they did so on their own.

AN EPITAPH FOR THE FARM SECURITY ADMINISTRATION

The end of World War II in 1945 marked the peak of Black land ownership after the Depression. Black-owned farm acres declined from 12 million in 1950 to 5.5 million by the late 1960s.[81] While some of this loss can be explained by economic factors, a major cause of the decline in Black landownership in the South was racist exclusion of Black landowners from government programs, notably from the agricultural subsidies distributed by the Soil Conservation Service (SCS) and the FHA, the successor to the FSA. It is a profound irony that the very agency that enabled Black farmers to acquire or keep their land in the 1930s became the instrument of their decline after 1945.

When Congress axed the FSA in 1946 and replaced it with the FHA, the agency was enfolded into the burgeoning Jim Crow welfare state that Southern politicians were building. The FHA acquired control of the original TP program (renamed the Farm Ownership Program) and the authority to make production loans, a form of capital investment. Along with the farm-subsidy programs of the SCS, the FHA was one of the main sources of credit for Southern farmers. By the 1960s, it had abandoned any pretense of aiding poor farmers and embraced the USDA's mission of promoting large, scientifically managed farms. FHA administrators ran a Jim Crow farm program that was of little help to Black farmers. In a 1965 report on farm programs in the South, the US Civil Rights Commission concluded: "During the quarter century since the farm credit program of the New Deal undertook to help tenants achieve ownership and to help small farmers enlarge their operations, the position of the Negro farmer relative to white Southern farmers has steadily worsened."[82]

The pattern of discrimination started in the late 1930s, when Black farmers were shut out of subsidy programs, usually by the SCS and other federal agencies' failing to inform them of benefits they were legally entitled to or actively discriminating against them. County committees controlled the allocation of FHA credit and assistance, and before 1965 there were no African Americans among the 3,600 state and county committee members. The FHA employed few Blacks in the South, and those who did work for the agency worked out of segregated offices. The FHA was one of three agricultural programs dedicated to subsidizing white landowners at the expense of Black farmers. Black landowners faced discrimination from extension agents. SCS committees controlled access to crop subsidies and systematically denied Black landowners information about them. A Black farmer applying for a subsidy would not receive one unless a white landowner vouched for them.[83]

Even when they received government loans, Black farmers got shafted. In a study of thirteen Southern counties with large numbers of Black farmers, the Civil Rights Commission reported that white farmers constituted one-third of all borrowers receiving loans but received two-thirds of the money. Black farmers accounted for two-thirds of borrowers in thirteen counties but received just one-third of the money. The FHA gave larger loans to white farmers than Black farmers, and the poorest white farmers received loans four times as large as the poorest Black farmers. Capital loans, which allowed farmers to acquire land and improve their farms, went disproportionately to white farmers: Blacks were more likely to receive loans for operating and living expenses. Black farmers were also less likely to receive needed technical assistance or supervision (this was a reversal from the 1930s).[84]

FHA officials rationalized their discrimination by citing the small size of Black farms or alleging ignorance and incompetence among Black farmers. In a civil rights hearing, an Alabama FHA agent admitted that he withheld information about available loans from Black farmers and on average gave loans of $7,000 to white farmers and $700 to Black farmers. He explained this discrepancy by saying that he has "about 5 white operating boys over there, and they are big cotton farmers." The Alabama FHA director, Robert Bamberg, was more explicit. Black farmers needed less money, he explained at the hearing, because "in many cases our n——r population has small acreage," a misleading statement that ignored historic white opposition to Black landowning. Walter Lewis, who ran the Civil Rights Commission's federal program division, exposed the racism underlying FHA loan practices. "There is a widespread belief," he wrote of the FHA, "that Negroes cannot profit from the programs being offered—be it education, job training or technical assistance in farming—and this self-defeating conviction acts as a bar to the success of the program with Negroes."[85] The history of Black landowning in the twentieth century clearly belies Bamberg's assertion.

The historian Pete Daniel argues the FHA served mainly wealthy farmers and used its power to drive Black farmers off the land. This is where racism merged with the mandate for large, capital-intensive farms. Daniel writes that in the minds of FHA staff, "purging Black farmers became an agenda item in maintaining white supremacy, and they eagerly pushed Blacks off their land, unconcerned about their hopes and aspirations." They did this by allowing Black farmers to run up debt and then foreclosing on their farms. A Black minister commented that federal loans had "become an evil tool against Negroes because the system of farming and white domination has always kept the Negro in debt."[86]

Though their numbers were diminished, the Black landowners who survived into the 1960s, many of them beneficiaries of the resettlement program, became civil rights activists and pillars of rural Black communities.[87] Postwar dispossession of Black landowners marks the disappearance of Negro agrarianism as the ideological core of antiprivilege egalitarianism. But the idea of land ownership endured as the symbol of the Black struggle for equality and freedom. In perhaps one his most important speeches, "Message to the Grass Roots," Malcolm X put land and the autonomy it signified at the center of his conception of a Black revolution.[88] Land was also important to the Southern civil rights activists struggling for a measure of control over federal financial resources in President Lyndon B. Johnson's War on Poverty.

FIVE

The Revolution Stalled

THE SOUTHERN WAR ON POVERTY AND
THE CIVIL RIGHTS MOVEMENT, 1964–1972

> The Federal Government places money into the hands of the lowest level governmental agency capable of doing the job, thus placing government into the hands of the people closest to the problem. This is more radical even than states rights. It is city rights, so to speak. It is the New England town meeting all over again. Would you believe it's John C. Calhoun democracy!—without segregation.
>
> SARGENT SHRIVER,
> *Letter to Eugene Patterson,* April 24, 1967

> If OEO were sincere, it would not demand that poor Negroes sit down with their oppressors, including members of the Ku Klux Klan and Citizen's Councils. OEO is not responding to the needs of the poor Negro because the poor Negro does not and cannot trust the white power structure.
>
> REVEREND JAMES MCREE,
> president, Child Development Group of Mississippi, June 16, 1966

> Civil rights is taking on a broader definition. Reconstruction taught us the lesson that there can be no civil rights—no social or political equality—without economic security. Increasingly, therefore, the civil rights struggle will find itself concerned with economic criticism, social welfare, and public planning.
>
> A. PHILIP RANDOLPH, December 18, 1963

ASKED WHAT HE MEANT by equality for African Americans prior to the 1963 March for Jobs and Freedom, Martin Luther King Jr. replied, "The untrammeled opportunity for every person to fulfill his total individual capacity without any regard to race, creed, color or previous ancestry." For King and other civil rights leaders, this demand went beyond civil rights: it meant access to decent jobs at a living wage, education, and housing "to escape the penalty imposed" on African Americans because of their "high visibility"—their skin color. King's demand was widely shared by other African American leaders at the time. Whitney Young Jr., head of the National Urban League, went further and demanded reparations for 250 years of oppression. Echoing Frederick Douglass's capacious understanding of equality of opportunity, Young said, "The scales of equal opportunity are now heavily weighted against the Negro and cannot be corrected . . . simply by applying equal weights." Young called for a domestic Marshall Plan, a massive government effort to overcome and compensate for racial injustices. Though he represented a conservative Black social services organization, Young's demand was radical. One hundred years after Abraham Lincoln issued the Emancipation Proclamation, King, Young, A. Philip Randolph, Bayard Rustin, John Lewis, and many others declared that formal civil rights without some compensation and genuine equality of opportunity were meaningless.[1]

This assertive Black public discourse was an expression of the rising militancy of the civil rights movement, Black impatience with condescending white advice to go slow, and the northward spread of civil rights demonstrations and protest in the spring of 1963. A revolution erupted that spring and summer, King wrote, with a "power . . . and fervor [that] displayed a force of a frightening intensity."[2] The year 1963 marked a turning point in the civil rights movement. Black leaders abandoned any vestige of the New Deal's racial liberalism and replaced it with an agenda that combined economic justice with equal citizenship and civil rights, which they announced during the March for Jobs and Freedom. No one expressed this new assertiveness more clearly than A. Philip Randolph, who had long refused to accept any separation between a racial and an economic agenda for the civil rights movement. Randolph believed that Black freedom and equality required fundamental structural changes to America's economy and society. That summer he told a congressional committee, "We cannot have fair employment until we have full employment. Nor will we have full employment until we have fair employment."[3]

Civil rights leaders in the major civil rights organizations and Black activists in the Congress of Racial Equality (CORE) and the Student Non-violent Coordinating Committee (SNCC) wanted a national civil rights law that outlawed labor market discrimination and established voting rights. But they believed civil rights laws would achieve little without a massive federal commitment to create jobs and provide needed investment in Black communities. King bluntly stated that the proposed civil rights act was incapable of addressing "the magnitude" of Black unemployment and "sub-standard housing conditions." The *Pittsburgh Courier* editorialized that "equal opportunity is essential, but not enough, not enough." One of the demands of the March for Jobs and Freedom was a federally funded jobs program. Randolph insisted that "Negro labor needs and is entitled to special preferential treatment in the form of preparation in training and education," an assertion compatible with Whitney Young's call for a Marshall Plan, which Randolph endorsed. Young made clear what was at stake when he warned Congress that civil rights must be "buttressed by the resources with which people can take advantage of equal opportunity; to provide equal opportunity without providing a deprived, a historically deprived group of citizens with the resources by which they may take advantage of the opportunity, is to me to invite upon them disillusionment, frustration, and despair."[4]

President John F. Kennedy and members of his administration were certainly aware of the inadequacy of civil rights for Blacks without equality of opportunity. Senator Hubert Humphrey commented that civil rights laws would fail if Blacks lacked the education and training necessary to get and hold jobs. Kennedy's secretary of labor, Willard Wirtz, echoed Randolph's demands when he told a Senate committee, "It will be a hollow victory if we get the 'whites only' signs down, only to find 'no vacancy' signs behind them." In a special message to Congress, President Kennedy responded to the yawning gap between civil rights law and Black economic need with a slew of modest policy changes to alleviate unemployment and lack of opportunity for African Americans. He asked Congress to augment federal funding for job training, vocational education, and youth opportunities and to focus these programs on unemployed Black men in Northern cities. His response to racial strife in the summer of 1963, though tepid, put the federal government on the side of civil rights activists and publicly committed the federal government to attacking Black poverty, unemployment, and discrimination.[5]

Kennedy's modest redirection of federal social policies formed the template for President Lyndon B. Johnson's War on Poverty. But instead of responding to civil rights leaders' demands with robust jobs programs and economic change, Kennedy's initiative committed the federal government to policies intended to rehabilitate the victims of Jim Crow. Many of the War on Poverty's signature programs derived from Kennedy administration legislative proposals. Both the Job Corps and Neighborhood Youth Corps, two of the Office of Economic Opportunity's signature programs, were imported from Hubert Humphrey's Youth Opportunities Bill, which was then languishing in Congress. OEO's work-training program was lifted from the Department of Health, Education and Welfare. To these policies the Johnson administration added programs for destitute farmers tailored for the South, and grants or loans for small businesses. Little consideration was given to the question of Southern rural poverty outside Appalachia. Although administration officials claimed retrospectively that African Americans did not figure in their planning of the War on Poverty, these policies were the liberal response to the March for Jobs and Freedom.[6]

Kennedy-Johnson liberals described their aims for the poverty program with the same language of rehabilitation that Harry Hopkins and Aubrey Williams had invoked when they justified the rural rehabilitation program. Johnson's economic advisers proclaimed, "A federally led effort is needed, with special emphasis on prevention and rehabilitation." What they meant by rehabilitation would have been familiar to any 1830s Whig politician or 1860s Freedmen's Bureau agent. They stripped their technocratic language of the religious connotations of reform liberalism, but the demand for self-improvement and discipline remained. Rehabilitation, the Kennedy-Johnson economists believed, was the remedy for "inadequate motivation to utilize fully one's earning potential and employment opportunities" and for "low earning potential."[7]

The moral reformers of the 1830s, white abolitionists, Freedmen's Bureau agents, the architects of the New Deal's rural rehabilitation program, and the War on Poverty planners all shared the assumptions that freed people, sharecroppers, and poor African Americans were deficient in ways that mattered for economic opportunity and citizenship, and that this deficiency could be remedied only through training and supervision. Kennedy-Johnson officials assumed that a tangle of negative self-reinforcing cultural traits and attitudes—dependency, lack of motivation, failure to defer gratification, lack of impulse control—prevented poor people from adapting to modern society and taking advantage of economic opportunities. Sargent Shriver, whom President Johnson appointed to lead the Office of Economic Opportunity, was advised by the influential psychiatrist Leonard J. Duhl that "the critical problem is that [poor] people do not have . . . the basic skills of living in our society; attitudes to jobs, money, and education. . . . The lack of skills comes both from their own attitudes and culture and from the very methods used by the institutions responsible for services they could use, e.g., welfare increases dependency."[8]

Like the New Deal interpretation of tenants' cultural deficiencies, which were attributed to the toxic legacy of slavery, the War on Poverty version assumed that the cultural pathologies of the poor were self-reinforcing and passed from generation to generation. Poor people, and the Black poor in particular, were depicted as cultural outsiders. Michael Harrington, who more than anyone else made poverty a national issue, wrote of the poor that they were like an "underdeveloped nation.... They are a different kind of people. They think and feel differently; they look upon a different America than the middle class looks upon." The answer lay in rehabilitation.[9]

Shriver took a similar view. He believed the intense experience of the Job Corps was necessary to change "the emotional outlook, the intellectual capacity, the character of kids who spent the first 16 years of their lives in a slum environment." Adam Yarmolinsky, a key adviser to Shriver who had as much to do with creating the War on Poverty as anyone, believed their program was "aimed at people in trouble.... [I]t would cut not one but all the chains that hold them down" and permit them to "achieve independence."[10] Rehabilitation, inextricably linked to equality of opportunity, would supposedly give Blacks the capacity to climb the economic ladder and develop their capacities as democratic citizens so that they could assume their rightful place in society.

Civil rights leaders initially assumed that poverty programs could provide the resources and jobs they demanded. Adam Clayton Powell Jr. regarded the "anti-poverty bill [as] more important than the Civil Rights Act."[11] In a speech at a conference on integration, Shriver declared that the War on Poverty "will make an important step toward the complete emancipation of the Negro." Yet Johnson's poverty program was far more limited than King and others initially realized. Johnson rejected the main demand of the civil rights movement—a massive public investment in jobs—and put his faith in the massive federal tax cut that he and his aides believed would create the needed jobs. He had no intention of launching a massive spending program. By early 1965 King had recognized that the War on Poverty was inadequate to remedy the "violence" of poverty and undo "the institutionalized consequences of color" that limited Black opportunities.[12]

What distinguished the 1960s antipoverty program from both the Freedmen's Bureau and the Farm Security Administration was the community action program. This was also the most controversial element. Regarding local governments as unresponsive to the poor, Johnson's planners intended to create independent nonprofit agencies that could coordinate the delivery of federal dollars. Unlike any other federal program, the War on Poverty operated out of the Executive Office of the President, with a direct financial pipeline to cities and communities across the country. Johnson's aides envisioned the agency as a funnel that collected funding from other federal agencies and then coordinated its distribution to local constituencies. The bill Johnson sent to Congress proposed an authorization of $500 million for community action and other OEO programs, and another $400 million drawn from other agencies. He and his aides intended to shift money from ongoing federal programs—job training and vocational education, for example—to the War on Poverty, a policy strategy that amounted to redistributing money from middle-class to poor communities.[13] It was an audacious concept. Republicans and Southern Democrats had no illusions about the scheme: they attacked the director as a "Poverty Czar."

The community action agencies (CAAs) could be either public or private nonprofit entities, and the law required the "maximum feasible participation" in these agencies by the people who were served by the program. Added during the drafting stage for the legislation, the participation requirement was considered part of the process of coordinating the allocation of federal funds. Since none of the planners understood it as a radical innovation, they were surprised by the conflict it generated. The reason is not hard to find: the antipoverty law permitted OEO to fund private nonprofit agencies that were not under the thumb of local politicians. This language was purposely inserted into the law to address the "Southern problem." Johnson's planners were keenly aware that without this provision, white racists running local governments would either block establishment of CAAs or set up segregated agencies.[14]

The idea of an agency based on technocratic coordination of public money and programs, with the active participation of poor people, always posed political problems, and in the context of the Southern civil rights movement and rising Black anger in Northern cities it was a recipe for conflict. Black activists, from radicals in CORE and the SNCC to moderates in the NAACP and the Urban League, saw the antipoverty program as an avenue to acquiring influence and control over federal resources. Without their involvement, they assumed, the program would degenerate into a feckless array of paternalistic policies. African American residents of cash-starved Southern counties saw in the War on Poverty an extension of the civil rights movement, a source of needed resources, and a hope for a measure of autonomy.

Southern Democrats, aware that the War on Poverty might enable African Americans to escape white economic coercion, decried the establishment of a national program that bypassed states and could lead to Black control of the delivery of federal resources. White Southerners in Congress regarded antipoverty grants and CAAs as empowering civil rights activists. In the Senate debate, Strom Thurmond (D-South Carolina) commented acidly that "this bill is pregnant with racial overtones," and fulminated that "the poverty czar would not only have the power to finance the activities of such organizations as the National Council of Churches, the NAACP, SNCC, and CORE, but also a SNOOP and a SNORE, which are sure to be organized to get their part of the green gravy." Thurmond and other Southern Democrats, many of whom were on the receiving end of agricultural subsidies, never hesitated to red-bait the program. But not all Southern Democrats were opposed to the bill: they were less likely to support it than Northern Democrats but more likely than Republicans. In the Senate, Southern Democrats were evenly split, eleven voting against the bill and eleven voting for it. In the House, forty Southern Democrats voted against the final bill, a vote that was positively correlated with the Black share of the population in their districts.[15]

Inevitably, the fate of the War on Poverty in the South, arriving as it did in the interregnum between the Civil Rights Act and the Voting Rights Act, was tied to the battle to tear down Jim Crow and the vestiges of white supremacy. While Shriver was setting up the poverty program in early 1965, Martin Luther King Jr. settled in Selma, Alabama, and launched protests intended to bring about the passage of a voting rights law. Klan violence and white opposition to integration and voting rights continued unabated. The Civil Rights and Voting Rights Acts settled the legal question of Southern apartheid but left open the question of what a new racial order would look like. Whites' entrenched commitment to white supremacy and the deep roots of Jim Crow set the stage for the next phase of the civil rights struggle. "Black people in [the Deep South] in 1967 were not writing on a clean slate," Frank Parker acutely observed in his study of African American voting rights.[16]

Black civil rights activists in the Deep South understood that any policy promoting economic opportunity would fail unless it established a foundation for Black autonomy. Like the freedmen's challenge to the Freedmen's Bureau's contract regime for wage labor, the struggle over community action and federal antipoverty dollars was a conflict between a technocratic version of rehabilitation and Black demands for significant economic change. Shriver believed OEO could bring Southern whites and Blacks together and preached integration of community action agencies. He assumed that arch-segregationists and civil rights activists could work together to allocate resources in local communities and manage the efficient implementation of educational and job training programs. Reverend James McRee, among others, pointed out Shriver's naivete. Shriver's demands, McRee said, would only reinforce white Southerners' intentions to maintain control and suppress Black aspirations for autonomy. What Black Southerners wanted and demanded was not just access to federal dollars but control over the allocation of the money. The War on Poverty presented that opportunity.[17]

Blacks' demand for control of CAAs, like the freedmen's claim that their political rights could be secured only by access to land, was grounded in ambitions for autonomy and self-determination. And both were expressed in the language of antiprivilege egalitarianism: in the 1960s this became the insurgent language of Black power and community control in urban ghettos and in Black communities across the rural South. The belief that civil rights laws would usher in integration collapsed midway in the decade amid growing Black militancy and white opposition to change. Many white Americans, alarmed by Black working-class revolts in Northern cities and facile press reports, assumed Black power represented hatred of whites and portended racial violence.[18] Southern Democrats stoked the fear of Black power to derail the War on Poverty. For most Blacks, Black power signified their growing independence and anger at what they regarded as a white betrayal of the promise of the civil rights revolution. It also divided civil rights leaders.

Both Rustin and Randolph excoriated Black power advocates for abandoning the idea of a biracial coalition that could bring significant change to American society. Stokely Carmichael and other activists strongly disagreed with Rustin's faith that coalition politics and integration would bring about significant change. In a letter to Rustin indicating SNCC's support for Randolph's Freedom Budget, Carmichael challenged Rustin's belief in a coalition with the labor movement, writing, "In regards to your statement that the only movement that is doing anything for Negroes is the labor movement, we would suggest that one of the major roadblocks to the freedom of black people is the labor movement as it is presently constructed."[19]

In the South, the lexicon of Black power and its political strategies evolved out of the organizing efforts of SNCC workers and local activists in the Mississippi Delta and, significantly, Lowndes County, Alabama, where

Carmichael worked with Black residents to organize the Lowndes County Freedom Organization. In devising practical strategies for Black empowerment, SNCC organizers were deeply influenced by rural Blacks' understanding of the "true meaning of black nationalism, [which] made clear to them the importance of black self-reliance." Black power represented a newfound consciousness of grassroots Black solidarity and identity. Black abolitionists in the 1840s, including Samuel Cornish, Martin Delany, Henry Highland Garnet, David Ruggles, and Samuel Ringgold Ward, would have understood what SNCC and local activists meant by Black power; in fact, they said many of the same things.[20]

For the activists fighting for control of the War on Poverty across the Deep South, Black power was not a slogan. Nor was it a demand for separatism. It was a fundamental part of their struggle to rewrite the rules of the Southern racial order. The Black women who started Mississippi's Head Start program, the Child Development Group of Mississippi (CDGM), devised preschool classes to give Black children a belief in their self-worth and independence and to cultivate a new generation of Black leaders through the involvement of working-class Blacks in the program. These women understood that control of Head Start and other antipoverty programs was a path to Black power and just as important as voting rights to overthrowing white supremacy.[21]

Despite his aversion to the slogan "Black Power" and his skepticism toward the idea of a Black political party, Martin Luther King Jr. recognized that power was necessary in order for the civil rights movement to accomplish its aims. "One of the great problems that the Negro confronts," he wrote, "is his lack of power. From the old plantations of the South to the newer ghettos of the North, the Negro has been confined to a life of voicelessness and powerlessness." King strongly believed that Black power was a "call to black people to amass the political and economic strength to achieve their legitimate goals" and that they could "never be content without participation in power."[22] Entwined with implementation of the Voting Rights Act and the Civil Rights Act, the outcome of the conflict between southern Blacks, federal poverty warriors, and white defenders of their racial privileges structured the post–Jim Crow racial order.

The contours of this struggle were shaped by the New Deal's Southern legacy: a welfare state dedicated to upholding segregation and white supremacy. Southern Democrats manipulated Federal grant-in-aid programs to Southern states in the early 1960s to privilege whites. This pervasive discrimination was one of the chief obstacles to any attempt by OEO to use the poverty program to influence the distribution of federal dollars in local communities. The outcome for African Americans depended on the depth of civil rights mobilization in a state and the strength of local movement organizations, many of which emerged independently of the major civil rights organizations.

THE NEW DEAL'S SOUTHERN LEGACY: A JIM CROW WELFARE STATE

Tersh Boasberg, an OEO staff member, informed Shriver that "any meaningful solution to the problem [in Mississippi] calls for massive Federal intervention, wholesale change in Mississippi politics, and huge programs planned and administered with Negro participation."[23] The level of poverty and degradation in Mississippi was severe but not unique. In the five Deep South states, 50 percent of families had 1960 incomes of less than $3,000 per year, compared to 21.4 percent across the United States. Twenty-eight percent of Deep South families had incomes of less than $2,000 per year. If anything, poverty was much worse in the ninety-nine Black-majority counties in the Deep South, where 63 percent of families had incomes below the poverty line. Annual per capita income in these counties averaged $722, compared to $1,036 in the Deep South states and $2,223 in the United States. Of the one hundred poorest counties in the United States at the time, thirty-five were in Mississippi and Alabama. Yet as the Mississippi Council on Human Relations (MCHR) concluded in a scathing report, "It is ... misleading to conclude that the problem of poverty in Mississippi is the result of farm mechanization and the [recent] minimum wage law. Most of the people who are poor now and are being dismissed from the plantations, were almost as poor when they were working. Even when they were employed, it was the food assistance programs that meant the difference in their being poorly fed or starving."[24]

By the 1960s, abject poverty and immiseration existed in the South alongside growing prosperity, fueled by federal dollars—the legacy of New Deal grant-in-aid policies. Southern Democrats were ardent New Dealers early on, but by the late 1930s they were more likely to oppose New Deal legislation. As Devin Caughey points out, this shift had to do with a conservative turn among white Southern voters after the 1938 elections, driven by their opposition to the emerging labor movement. Yet Southerners in Congress occupied a distinctive ideological ground, apart from both Northern Democrats and Republicans. On labor bills, Southern legislators voted with Republicans to limit union power, but many Southern Democrats then sided with Northern Democrats and voted against tax cuts and in favor of social-welfare legislation. Roosevelt and Northern Democrats adopted an explicit strategy of wooing Southerners with policies that allowed them to funnel federal money to the eleven former Confederate states and erect a Jim Crow welfare state. Northern Democrats agreed to tilt federal aid formulas southward in order to enact new social welfare legislation, but they paid a high price: they acquiesced to Southern demands to vote down the nondiscrimination amendments Republicans regularly attached to social-welfare legislation and permit local control of federal programs. Republican nondiscrimination amendments forced Northern Democrats to choose between striking a blow against Jim Crow and allowing the Southerners to build a racially segregated welfare state. Invariably, they chose the latter.[25]

The 1946 Hill-Burton Hospital Construction Act, championed by Senator Lister Hill of Alabama—a pro–New Deal, pro-labor, pro-segregation Democrat—was a prototype for the Jim Crow welfare state. The law provided money for badly needed hospitals but came with a nonintervention clause that prohibited federal control of the grant. Southern Democrats commonly attached nonintervention clauses to social-welfare legislation, and they used the authority to establish segregated federal grant-in-aid programs that mocked the assertion of "separate but equal." Equally salient, the funding formula for Hill-Burton distributed the largest federal grants to states with the lowest per capita incomes and gave rural counties priority. Southern rural counties were disproportionate beneficiaries of Hill-Burton funds, which were used to build ninety segregated hospitals by 1960—seventy-one for whites and nineteen for African Americans.[26]

In a meeting of the President's Economic Opportunity Council, Nicholas Katzenbach, Johnson's attorney general in the mid-1960s, identified the problem the Jim Crow welfare state posed for efforts to undo discrimination or, in the case of OEO, to direct the use and distribution of federal money. It "isn't a question, as it often isn't in a state like Mississippi," he said, "of sort of overt channeling of funds here rather than here, yet the net impact of this has a very pronounced discrimination because ... of other past discrimination built in."[27] OEO faced not only angry white Southerners defending their racial privileges but also the use of federal money to implant segregation deep into the structure of state agencies. Federal money given to the Department of Labor for manpower training or OEO's Neighborhood Youth Corps came under the jurisdiction of the notoriously racist state employment service. Head Start and other education programs required OEO to challenge segregated schools.

Understandably, African Americans were skeptical of federal policies predicated on the use of Jim Crow welfare departments to supply aid to poor Blacks in the South. Southern states were voracious consumers of federal public assistance grants, combining very low payments to individuals and families with high caseloads. An OEO report notes "ample evidence that the welfare program is discriminatory, punitive, dishonest and endowed with a feudalistic authority over human life and dignity." Southern welfare officials discriminated against Black families and put welfare and US Department of Agriculture surplus-commodity programs to work on behalf of planters, who wielded benefits as a tool of economic coercion against Blacks fighting for jobs and voting rights. Food distribution under the surplus-commodity program in Alabama reached just 50 percent of those in need, and there were no food distribution programs in Alabama's Black Belt counties.[28] Aaron Henry and Charles Evers, then field director for the NAACP in Mississippi, protested to Shriver and Secretary of Agriculture Orville Freeman that their attempt to use the Mississippi Department of Welfare to coordinate the distribution of surplus food perpetuated oppression. They demanded that funds be withheld, writing that the food program began "with the ingredients that have fostered segregation and discrimination against the Negro community in the past still in tact [sic]."[29]

Nowhere did the problem of racist state agencies loom larger than for the agricultural loan program, enacted as Title III of the Economic Opportunity Act. Johnson's poverty planners designed Title III to help "boxed-in" farmers who were elderly, poorly educated, or unable to move into other lines of work, along with "farmers without land." These policies were explicitly modeled on the New Deal rural rehabilitation grants and resettlement program.[30] Authority to implement the loan program was delegated to the Department of Agriculture, which meant that the agency in charge of disbursing the loans to poor Black farmers was the Farmers Home Administration (the successor to the Farm Security Administration). Johnson might as well have given control of the program to white Citizens' Councils. Local FHA officials used access to loans as a tool to punish Black civil rights activists and prop up white landowners. In hearings before the Alabama State Advisory Committee on Civil Rights on FHA activity in Greene County, Alabama, in 1965, Reverend Percy McShan said Black farmers were "told that they couldn't get a loan if the landlord didn't want them to have a loan."[31] FHA discrimination, combined with Black landowners' lack of access to agricultural subsidies, stacked the deck against Black farmers, whether they were landowners or tenants, and augmented the power of white planters.

African American farmers in the early 1960s faced not just discrimination but government-sponsored exploitation. In a May 1967 speech to officials of the federal Soil Conservation Service, Shriver said that Agricultural Stabilization and Conservation Service (ASCS) county committee decisions to decrease cotton and tobacco allotments had the effect of "turning marginal but viable farmers into impoverished farmers." These farmers were denied operating loans because they could not convince the FHA that they could repay the loans. ASCS officials had no need to overtly discriminate against Black farm owners: discrimination was built into the system, with the result that Black farmers could never gain from federal subsidies, and they always lost when subsidies were reduced. It would be hard to find a better example of structural racism.[32]

Title VI of the 1964 Civil Rights Act outlawed discrimination in the distribution of federal grants and income transfers on the basis of race or skin color. Title VI applied to any nonfederal agency or program receiving federal dollars, and federal agencies were empowered to enforce it by terminating the funding if necessary. Despite its national scope, the law was a dagger pointed at the heart of the Jim Crow welfare state The Department of Health, Education and Welfare used the law successfully to desegregate hospitals and schools by threatening to withhold funds for Medicare and the 1965 Elementary and Secondary Education Act. USDA officials, however, insisted that the law did not apply to either agricultural subsidies or FHA loans. They regarded the law as a joke and evaded enforcement by filing false compliance reports. Not only did OEO face formidable obstacles to coordinating federal funding, but control of one of its key programs of benefit to Southern African Americans was ceded to white racists.[33]

The success of Title VI enforcement in desegregating schools and hospitals obscures the extent to which federal aid dedicated to helping poor Blacks remained under the control of racist state agencies. What was at stake in the South was whether community action agencies would be folded into the Jim Crow welfare state or whether they would enable Blacks to acquire control over the federal resources flowing into cash-starved counties and gain some independence from white coercion.

THE RACIAL STRUGGLE FOR REPRESENTATION AND CONTROL OF COMMUNITY ACTION AGENCIES

OEO began setting up community action agencies across the South just as the ground of the civil rights movement shifted. With the success of the march on Selma and the impending passage of the Voting Rights Act in Congress, Martin Luther King Jr. began planning protests against segregation and poverty in Northern cities. Meanwhile, members of the SNCC realized that the pending voting rights legislation and the arrival of the War on Poverty in the South required that the economic needs of Black Southerners be addressed. Both Stokely Carmichael and Julian Bond, who was then campaigning for a seat in the Georgia state legislature, understood that after registering to vote, Black Southerners wanted jobs, decent wages, and a foundation for economic opportunity.[34] Yet it was clear that nothing would change unless African Americans gained power over their own lives and acquired the necessary leverage to force whites to recognize and treat them as equals.

Members of SNCC's Vine City project in Atlanta produced the clearest statement of what Southern activists meant by Black power, though initially it was not accepted by many SNCC organizers. Although the statement advocated separatism, its importance rested less on that prescription—which some SNCC members and certainly most rural Blacks did not accept—than on its analysis of white racism and the implications for the civil rights movement's campaign to overturn white oppression. The authors acknowledged the importance of white participation in the early stages, but with the advent of national civil rights and voting rights laws, they asserted, whites no longer had a place in the movement. Blacks now had the legal right to organize, and this could be done only by African Americans themselves: an "all-Black project is needed in order for the people to free themselves." Black solidarity was the first premise of the doctrine. The only way to confront the "reality of 180 million racists" was through cohesive, collective action based on awareness of a common racial identity.[35] Then and only then would Blacks be in a position to negotiate fair restitution for slavery and Jim Crow.

The second premise was that without Black solidarity and organization, integration would reinforce white paternalism and Black inferiority. Whether they knew it or not, the Vine City writers reproduced Frederick Douglass's vehement denunciation of white paternalism and his belief in the strength and resourcefulness of African Americans at the outset of

Reconstruction. They argued that involvement of whites in organizing Blacks would reinforce stereotypes of Blacks' inadequacy and their lack of the skills needed for citizenship, as well as whites' beliefs in their own superiority. Black abolitionists in the 1840s had had the same concern. Civil rights activists who espoused Black power understood the ravages white supremacy had wreaked on Southern Blacks, but they believed Black self-organization and learning offered the only path out of the racist wreckage. Thus Blacks, not whites, must define what equality meant for them. These were not solely the views of a small group of civil rights activists: they percolated down to the rural grassroots and influenced Black organizing and demands across the South. For Southern rural African Americans, Black power was not a call for separatism; it was a claim that undergirded their insistence on independence and control of their destiny.[36]

SNCC was skeptical of the War on Poverty. Some activists saw it as a tool to co-opt civil rights workers. H. Rap Brown told SNCC workers that the federal government was going to pour money into local communities, and SNCC should control the programs, but "if it is not possible to control them, then we should disrupt them."[37] Other civil rights organizations—NAACP, CORE, and the Southern Christian Leadership Conference (SCLC)—embraced the program and sought to shape it. More telling, rural and urban Blacks across the South gravitated to the program. In his history of organizing in Mississippi, Charles Payne observed that the program attracted local people because it could "provide work for people who had rendered themselves unemployable by their activism." The War on Poverty also drew in people who were not a significant part of the early SNCC organizing campaigns: ministers, teachers, farmers, women, and indigenous civil rights activists.[38]

In many Southern rural counties, indigenous Black civil rights organizations, such as the Lowndes County Christian Movement for Human Rights (LCCMHR) in Alabama and the Southern Consumers Education Foundation (SCEF) in southwestern Louisiana, took the initiative to contact OEO and submit proposals to form community action agencies and launch antipoverty programs. Dedicated to organizing poor people, SCEF mobilized a biracial coalition that, an OEO report commented, "caught hold and threatens to become a new force.... It has stirred an awareness among the impoverished." Black women in the Mississippi Delta were drawn to the CDGM's Head Start program. It offered not just a secure income but the opportunity to work "for principle," Anna Mae King of Sunflower County recalled. "We were working for freedom and to be able to govern our own affairs and our own businesses and to teach our own children."[39]

An OEO staffer described these early participants in the Southern War on Poverty as filling the "middle ground in the Negro communities" and noted that they "might be termed 'progressive liberals'—in comparison to SNCC at least."[40] This was *not* how activists saw themselves. For many of them, what mattered was the opportunity the War on Poverty presented for Black autonomy and control in the face of white oppression. In a way, entry into the War on Poverty was an extension of their civil rights activism and the pervasive influence of the tenets of Black power circulating throughout the South. The CDGM mobilized hundreds of poor Blacks in Mississippi, and, as the Reverend James McRee told Shriver, "We have been building competence and self-respect." Another activist, Mrs. Thelma Barnes, added that CDGM was the "first nonpaternalistic relationship we have had with our Government. Our people are feeling their self-worth."[41] These beliefs reflected the long history of Black organizing. Equality of opportunity, activists understood, was an empty vessel without a measure of autonomy and control—the evisceration of white supremacy.

For rural Blacks the issue of autonomy was closely tied to the money and jobs the War on Poverty offered them. Their demands could not be reduced, as some critics charged, to getting their hands on the OEO "pork barrel." The War on Poverty, LCCMHR activists stated in their application for a community action agency, was not part of the Jim Crow welfare state, where "billions of dollars have been appropriated [for schools and hospitals] and wonderful plans created, yet Negroes in our county remain victimized and shut out of these programs." Echoing the freed people one hundred years earlier, a Black farmer in western Alabama pointed out the stakes for Black people in the Deep South. Antipoverty programs, he said, created a "kind of economic basis by which people will be able to think for themselves. . . . [If] a man is able to feed himself he votes the way he wants to . . . [and] he does anything else he wants to." The alternative, he pointed out, was the persistence of the "master-servant relationship, [and] as long as it exists, you can control the very destiny of people."[42]

Despite OEO's urban bias, the agency invested heavily in Southern rural counties, especially in Mississippi. Shriver was required by law to allocate 78.4 percent of OEO dollars to states according to a formula based on the percentage of people unemployed, public assistance spending, and the number of children in very poor families. He could allocate the remaining

21.6 percent as he saw fit. OEO could invest in either single-purpose agencies such as CDGM or in community action agencies. Of the 1,050 CAA agencies, 700 were in rural counties, and 451 were in the South. But OEO shortchanged rural counties. In a meeting of his Economic Opportunity Council, Johnson demanded to know "why poor counties received fewer Federal resources for their poor than do the wealthier counties." From 1965 through 1968, Southern states averaged $11 million less in OEO funding than Northeastern states, though Mississippi, which received funding in excess of the formula, was a clear exception to this pattern. Even so, a significant amount of OEO money went to poor Southern rural counties with low or nonexistent public welfare budgets. Grants were made in eighty-three counties that as of the mid-1960s had no welfare spending.[43]

White Southerners were deeply opposed to the War on Poverty, but if they couldn't stop it, they intended to control it. They did not accept the logic of the poverty program and had no intention of integrating Blacks into the Southern economy if they could avoid it. Instead of addressing Black demands for voting rights and economic opportunity, white Southerners tried driving Blacks out of the South. In Hale County, Alabama, the thirteenth poorest county in the United States at the time, most whites believed the War on Poverty would deter Blacks from leaving the South. Frank Prial, an OEO staff member, told his superiors that the "important whites [in Hale County] are adamantly opposed to any antipoverty program on the quaint grounds that they hope to starve the Negroes out."[44] Semmes Luckett, the first chair of the CAA board in Coahoma County, Mississippi, and an arch-segregationist, believed the poverty program would upset Mississippi's racial hierarchy. "He thinks," wrote an observer, "that the real purpose of the OEO in Coahoma County is to interfere with the normal laws of supply and demand and to negate the out migration of Negroes from the Delta." Luckett feared that OEO's education programs would induce Blacks to stay in the Delta and render them unwilling to work on menial jobs.[45]

Defenders of segregation used various methods to control antipoverty programs. R. Leigh Peagues, the mayor of Marion (the county seat of Perry County, Alabama), told Frank Prial that he was willing to put Blacks on the CAA board, but they must all be handpicked. "If we let them pick their own representatives," he said, "they will pick the same ones who led those riots. . . . The whites in this county don't want the poverty program[, and] we sold it to them by assuring them we'd be in charge. Where would we be if we sold out now to that SCLC crowd?"[46] Alabama's governor, George Wallace, who saw the poverty program as a source of patronage, sought aggressively to take over community action agencies across the state. He threatened to veto projects and withhold state funding unless segregationist whites controlled the CAAs. Governors John McKeithen of Louisiana and Paul Johnson of Mississippi were equally hostile toward OEO. They intended to control the allocation of OEO dollars and ensure that no members of any civil rights organization or militant local Black leaders—of whom there were many by 1965—were able to influence agency policies. Southern county officials viewed the poverty program as just another federal program they could plunder. In Mississippi, where county authorities had wide powers, they set up CAA boards so that, according to OEO staff, "the county can get some of that money and the men in charge can feather their pockets."[47]

Across the South, white segregationists sought to control CAA governing boards by appointing malleable Blacks, who were typically outnumbered by whites, and installing a white director. Usually this meant picking African Americans who could be easily manipulated either because they were economically vulnerable or because they were regarded as "good" African Americans—men who had long ago knuckled under to Jim Crow and were unlikely to demand significant changes to the racial order. Members of the main civil rights organizations—SNCC, SCLC, CORE or NAACP—were automatically excluded, as were longtime Black residents if they challenged the racial order. Prial describes the white reaction to Louis Black, a well-known high school teacher and effective organizer in Hale County. Black was instrumental in forming a local civil rights group and had taken the initiative in submitting a proposal for a CAA agency. Though he was not affiliated with a major civil rights organization, he was not afraid of vigorously challenging whites. A local bank president, who described himself as a Johnson Democrat and a moderate, told Prial he was willing to form a community action agency with a biracial board, but he could not "foresee a day when he will have to deal with men like Black or Black's two close allies."[48]

White elites insisted that only whites should be appointed as directors of antipoverty agencies. Most were described as "politically affluent" or closely connected to state and local politicians. Robert Saunders, who monitored civil rights violations in the South for OEO, commented that "some of these directors have the personal blessings from persons in high political offices" and direct pipelines to these politicians. He reported that throughout the South, it was assumed that the "top man must be white in order to relate to the white community." This "rule" underpinned segregation within CAA agencies and permitted discrimination in hiring.[49] As of June 1967, there were only three Black CAA directors in the Deep South states.

Another strategy used by white elites to contain the War on Poverty was substituting relief programs, such as food distribution, for educational projects, job training programs, or economic development. Theodore Berry, OEO's director for community action, who was in charge of setting up agencies and approving grants, told Shriver that the "white political structure in Mississippi, Alabama, and even Georgia are [sic] following a clearly defined pattern, [doing] everything to block the educational programs," mainly Head Start and Adult Education, and asking for a "food distribution program in order to prove that they are not anti-Negro." This was the outcome in Lowndes County, Alabama, after a long, divisive struggle by LCCMHR to launch a program focused on employment and housing. White opposition to a viable poverty program resulted in grants totaling $1.8 million for emergency food and health care—badly needed resources that helped individuals survive hunger and sickness, but did little to create an economically viable and autonomous Black community. Whites were trading Black economic opportunities for welfare. Berry advocated that OEO invest more money in single-purpose agencies that could be funded directly from Washington and forestall governors' vetoes and local manipulation of programs.[50]

Shriver's Quandary

Caught between Black aspirations and militancy and white opposition, what did Shriver do? Shriver, it must be said, was ambivalent about community action and participation of the poor. Despite his public support for community action, often expressed to Johnson, he expressed serious misgivings to several people who had helped him develop the program. Even so, Shriver praised community action in a letter to Eugene Patterson, an Atlanta newspaper publisher, comparing it to a New England town meeting and observing that it that put money in the hands of local officials and gave control to "the people closest to the problem." He construed it as a form of John C. Calhoun democracy—a disturbing analogy. Dedicated to distributing federal dollars to local communities and to Blacks, Shriver was unprepared for the power struggle between white segregationists and rural Blacks.

For Shriver, community action was part of the struggle to integrate the South, an extension of the original goals of the civil rights movement. He was given to effusive praise for "integrated" community action agencies, telling

Johnson that a biracial CAP was operating in Senator James Eastland's home county—Sunflower County, Mississippi. "Twelve months ago," he observed, "no one would have given 10 cents for our chances of accomplishing this." Shriver demanded that OEO integrate its programs. He insisted on biracial CAP boards and integrated Head Start programs, which were among the first OEO programs launched in the rural South. During the controversy over his decision to defund the CDGM, Shriver issued a public statement chastising the Citizens' Crusade against Poverty, one of his most vitriolic critics: "We do intend to move as fast as possible away from the de facto racially segregated programs, such as CDGM, to racially integrated programs."[51]

OEO staff desperately wanted to avoid all-Black programs in the South because they believed they allowed white opponents to brand the War on Poverty as a Black program. Robert Saunders pointed out that white Southerners sought to undermine the program by creating "a state of irrefrangible gullibility in the minds of their constituents. These constituents, often among the very poor themselves, are led to believe that Poverty Programs are for Negroes only." He thought that the widespread belief, particularly among low-income whites, that the poverty program was under the control of Black radicals undermined its legitimacy.[52]

OEO's commitment to integration was not just moral and ideological; it was mandated by law. Like any other federal agency, OEO was subject to Title VI of the 1964 Civil Rights Act and was thus legally prohibited from discrimination in the funding and administration of CAAs. Title VI was a double-edged sword: it gave Shriver a tool to oppose white discrimination against Blacks, but when OEO demanded integrated boards and programs, it undermined Black control of agencies. Beyond a commitment to Black representation and a demand for integration, OEO's policy on representation was vague and ambiguous. CAP Memo 57, the existing policy regulation, committed the agency to representation of "minority group members" who made up a disproportionate number of residents of target areas, usually a county or several contiguous counties. The policy appeared to endorse some form of proportional representation, though OEO did not usually impose numerical quotas on the racial composition of CAA boards. But the vagueness of the policy allowed white Southerners and OEO staff to interpret the policy as meaning they could put anyone on the board, including handpicked, malleable "Uncle Toms," and exclude representatives of Black civil rights organizations. The white people setting up CAAs assumed that so long as there were people of color on governing boards, they were in conformity with the policy.⁵³

OEO's policies on integration put it on a collision course with the civil rights movement just as Black power became the reigning discourse of civil rights activists. Shriver and the Atlanta regional staff often sided with Black "moderates," typically Blacks who had few discernible connections to SNCC, CORE, or even the SCLC. Both Shriver and Maurice Dawkins, his chief emissary to Black civil rights organizations, were hostile to Black militants. Dawkins told Shriver that CORE had dropped any pretense of supporting integration, and he thought the movement was trying to "sell 'the establishment' on the idea that a Black community charting its own destiny independent of the white community will permit peaceful co-existence that would not be possible if the thrust toward integration is continued." He disparaged the Black Panthers and the SNCC, especially H. Rap Brown. Keen to demonstrate that OEO could bring Southern whites and Blacks together and overcome racial barriers, Shriver trumpeted integration whenever he could. He told Bill Moyers, an influential Johnson aide, that the OEO program in Clarksdale, Mississippi (Coahoma County), was an example of "what can be achieved when barriers fall—not just racial barriers, but barriers of petty personality conflicts and of political obstructionism as well." The Clarksdale board, a symbol of what Shriver thought the War on Poverty could do, included "14 members of the White Citizen's Councils, three white moderates, and 11 Negroes." Shriver seems to have regarded integration as a way to manage race relations. ⁵⁴

Civil rights activists and African Americans working to set up poverty programs in the rural South regarded Shriver and his staff as naive. Harvey Burg, who was helping local Black organizations in western Alabama, wrote OEO to try to dispel the notion that whites would work with Blacks on a "basis of equality." Burg thought that the only way to convince whites to cooperate on antipoverty programs was to fund Black programs separately. Only then, he believed, would poor whites be willing to seek benefits for themselves. Tom Levin, who was the inspiration behind the CDGM, averred that Shriver's penchant for integration of antipoverty programs was doomed to failure. In a statement he circulated to OEO staff, Levin said, "The black poor of Mississippi do not yearn to be 'integrated' by submission to the white power structure. They have their own communities, their own needs, and their own leaders." Levin believed that establishing CAP agencies only in one county or several adjacent counties in a state was arbitrary and served only to prop up the existing racial order. Blacks in rural towns were quite capable of forming alliances and building viable programs, but OEO's insistence on integrating powerful whites "into this new political womb would bring immediate abortion." Levin preferred statewide programs like CDGM, which operated in twenty-nine Mississippi counties and was a catalyst for the mobilization of poor African Americans, an achievement that even OEO staff recognized.[55]

OEO staff working in rural Mississippi recognized that white control of antipoverty agencies would lead inevitably to paternalism, or worse. Tom Heller, who worked in Mississippi, thought OEO should require a fixed percentage of whites on governing boards and then appoint Southern white liberals—a strategy most Blacks would have opposed. OEO should avoid working with county officials, who had no interest in viable programs. In fact, most OEO staff on the ground understood that the real difficulties OEO faced were not challenging an all-Black governing board or confronting advocates of Black power but rather preventing or undoing white manipulation of the racial composition of the board, appointing more African Americans, and blocking white maneuvers to stack antipoverty boards with compliant Blacks. White officials either went after OEO money without consulting African Americans or they challenged Black proposals and opposed the appointment of any African American they believed could not be manipulated.[56]

Some OEO staff were skeptical of or even hostile to Black control of agencies. Mary Grice, a member of the Atlanta regional staff working in Alabama's Black Belt counties, believed that Blacks were unable to do anything for themselves and that the antipoverty program should be run like other federal programs, with whites in charge and token Black participation. Tersh Boasberg told Shriver that it was "absurdly naive ... to assume that poor, uneducated and inexperienced rural Negroes and whites [would] suddenly meet together to plan and organize an effective CAP."[57] In other words, Black control should be forestalled until Blacks could demonstrate their capacity for self-governance. Yet many OEO staffers were well aware of the game Southern whites were playing, and their reports are larded with caustic comments about the appointment of compliant Blacks and the need to appoint Black militants.[58] Ironically, OEO policies and practices very often undermined Black representation and influence over antipoverty agencies.

Despite the rhetoric of Black power, most African Americans were not averse to working with whites and were responsive to OEO pressure for integrated governing boards. What they demanded was equal representation and the right to elect their own representatives to an antipoverty board. But Shriver faced unrelenting pressure, not just from hostile Southern governors but from also segregationist US Senators and members of Congress, to exclude any Blacks from CAP agencies who had even remote connections to the civil rights movement. Mississippi Senators James Eastland and John Stennis, rabid opponents of the War on Poverty, continually pressured Shriver over the composition of antipoverty boards and were instrumental in the campaign to defund CDGM in Mississippi. Nor were Southern whites averse to using Title VI to attack agencies. Representative Glenn Andrews (D-Alabama) demanded of Shriver "why the Lowndes County, Alabama grant was made without white representation on the board while in many cases to my knowledge OEO grants have been refused because the Board had no Negroes represented." Shriver testily replied, "The white community has shown a singular lack of interest in the series of overtures made by this group on behalf of its program."

Yet Shriver and his minions often folded in the face of white intransigence, angering African Americans. Wilcox County, Alabama, had a ratio of 3.5 Black residents to 1 white, but OEO proposed a CAA board made up of 10 Blacks and 13 whites. The Wilcox county SCLC antipoverty committee promptly denounced OEO's decision as "railroaded democracy." They added, "We still cannot believe that the whites are willing to work with the Negroes on an equal basis and with respect in Wilcox County."[59]

OEO policies for multicounty agencies in the rural South were an equally significant obstacle to Black representation and influence. OEO required any county with a population of less than twenty-five thousand to combine with adjacent counties in order to create agencies large enough to mount significant programs and make effective use of OEO money. Blacks were opposed to multicounty agencies because the inclusion of Black-majority counties within them effectively diluted the Black population and weakened Black representation. They demanded the creation of single-county agencies. Mrs. Lee, a member of the Wilcox County SCLC, told a member of OEO's staff, "Ala caps so drawn that N[egro] counties match with W[hite] so N counties lose majority." LCCMHR likewise accused Shriver of creating gerrymandered agencies.[60]

Originally, OEO provided 100 percent of agency funding only in counties with a per capita income below $750 annually. Because of this regulation, very few agencies had been set up by December 1965. To bolster and speed up the creation of agencies, OEO changed its regulations to allow 100 percent funding of agencies in counties with a per capita income of up to $1,000, or in which more than half the population was below the official poverty line (then set at an annual income of less than $3,000). The new regulation increased the number of counties eligible for 100 percent funding from 86 to 324 in the five Deep South states. As a result, almost four-fifths of Deep South counties received 100 percent funding from the federal government.

This policy change dramatically altered the racial balance of the population in eligible counties. Under the old regulation, Blacks made up 68 percent of the population in eligible counties; under the new, expanded standard, they made up only 45 percent. Theodore Berry had intended to include more white rural poor in the program, but in combination with OEO's policy on multicounty agencies, doing so effectively diluted the Black population in CAP agencies. Combined with white intransigence and opposition, this policy had significant consequences for Black representation on CAA boards and access to antipoverty funds across the South.[61]

By the end of the Johnson administration, OEO had set up 117 CAP agencies in 289 counties in the five Deep South states (69 percent of all counties). Table 15 shows the characteristics and distribution of OEO-funded agencies. South Carolina, a small state, set up agencies in 76 percent of its counties. Louisiana created the largest number of agencies, twenty-eight, but these covered only 58 percent of parishes (counties), the lowest percentage of the five states. Alabama and Mississippi covered 66 percent of counties and Georgia almost 75 percent. There were eighty-four rural agencies, of which fifty were multicounty CAAs. Louisiana favored single-county agencies, but in the other four Deep South states, 53 percent of the agencies were rural multicounty. There were thirty-three urban agencies, most of which were a single county.

I estimate that there were twenty-two gerrymandered agencies—CAAs in which predominantly Black counties (those with a Black population of 40 percent or more) were combined with counties with a large majority of whites.[62] For example, the Dale County, Alabama, CAA combined three counties. Two had large Black populations, and one had a large white and a very small Black population. Although Blacks considered Alabama the prime instigator of gerrymandering, there were only two gerrymandered agencies in the state. By comparison, there were six in Mississippi. Five of these agencies were clearly products of racial gerrymandering; the sixth, the Montgomery County CAA, included six counties, and the population was equally divided between Blacks and whites. Gerrymandering was most egregious in Georgia, which had nine gerrymandered agencies. Louisiana had

TABLE 15 Community action agencies (CAAs) and Black representation in Deep South states

	Alabama	Georgia	Louisiana	Mississippi	South Carolina	All Deep South States
Number of counties with CAAs	44	117	37	56	35	289
Percentage of counties	66	74	58	69	76	69
Number of CAAs	25	22	28	24	18	117
Number of urban county agencies	8	6	12	4	3	33
Number of rural single-county agencies	6	2	13	8	5	34
Number of rural multicounty agencies	11	14	3	12	10	50
Number of gerrymandered CAAs	2	9	1	6	4	22
Number of predominant Black counties[a] with no CAA	9	20	12	11	8	60
Number of predominant Black counties as percentage of total counties	43	37	52	26	35	37
Mean Black population, 1960 (%)						
Rural single-county CAA	60	39	35	57	46	47
Rural multicounty CAA	27	30	35	43	39	35
Urban county CAA	29	26	33	33	29	30
Mean number of families with income less than $3,000, 1960 (%)						
Rural single-county CAA	59	60	53	66	48	57
Rural multicounty CAA	51	50	54	61	48	53
Urban county CAA	33	28	35	36	33	33
Mean number of agricultural jobs, 1964 (%)						
Rural single-county CAA	25	18	20	36	24	25
Rural multicounty CAA	15	14	18	27	17	18

SOURCES: Deep South CAA County Dataset; Deep South FY68 Dataset (see appendix).
[a] Counties with 40 percent or more Black population.

only one gerrymandered district, mainly because there were only three rural multicounty agencies in the state.

Service areas with rural single-county agencies in Alabama and Mississippi, which African Americans preferred, had very large Black populations, averaging 60 and 57 percent, respectively, and were very poor. In Louisiana and Georgia, service areas with rural single-county agencies had populations that were slightly less than 66 percent white (Georgia had only two rural single-county districts), though the poverty level was about the same as in the service areas of Black-majority agencies in Alabama and Mississippi. The Black population was much lower, on average, in all service areas covered by rural multicounty agencies; in Alabama and Georgia it was less than 30 percent. There were no rural multicounty agencies in either Alabama or Georgia covering service areas in which Blacks were a majority of the population. Seven of the twelve rural multicounty agencies in Mississippi and four of the eleven in South Carolina covered service areas with majority Black populations. Alabama and Georgia set up multicounty rural agencies in service areas with significant white majorities.

Gerrymandering was one way for white opponents of the poverty program to diminish Black influence; another was to establish no CAAs at all in Black majority counties. In the five Deep South states, 60 of 164 predominantly Black counties had no poverty program. Louisiana excluded 52 percent of predominantly Black counties in the state; Alabama excluded 43 percent (see table 15). Georgia and South Carolina excluded 35 and 37 percent of all predominantly Black counties, respectively. This amounted to twenty counties in Georgia. Mississippi was the exception to this pattern: though it excluded eleven predominantly Black counties, these represented just slightly more than 20 percent of such counties in the state. In Mississippi, most predominantly Black counties were incorporated into an agency jurisdiction. These patterns reveal the differences in the outcome of representation struggles in the states of the Deep South: the similarity of Alabama and Georgia compared to Mississippi exceptionalism.

PATTERNS OF STATE OPPOSITION: ALABAMA VENALITY AND MISSISSIPPI EXCEPTIONALISM

Alabama's governor, George Wallace, was the chief instigator of opposition to Black control, aggressively challenging Black initiatives to set up agencies and wielding his veto. OEO staff, who recognized that Wallace was trying to take over the CAAs, concluded that the question facing OEO was "whether the governor can scare wavering communities into line with veiled threats of the veto, or cutting off other state funds to them, and gain absolute control of appointing boards." Wallace used Alabama's OEO-funded state technical assistance agency to wrest control of local agencies. The state OEO director, Claude Kirk, reached out to Wallace cronies in Coosa County, among others, and asked them to form a CAA, and he regularly asked Wallace who should be hired as directors or appointed to governing boards in different counties. Because of Wallace's early, aggressive interference, Alabama was one of the slowest states to set up CAAs: it had only twelve funded agencies by early 1966. Wallace shifted the leverage in conflicts over representation to white segregationists who gained control of agencies. All too often, the Atlanta regional office sided with Wallace and his cronies instead of Black activists.[63]

Many of the counties without CAAs in Alabama were those in which Black activists had tried to establish agencies but failed. White opposition to any agency at all, or to sharing power with Blacks, prevented Black organizations in Hale, Perry, and Wilcox Counties from establishing single-county agencies. In all three cases, Black opposition stopped an attempted gerrymander, but the county ended up with no agency. OEO regional staff, mainly Mary Grice and the staff of the Alabama state OEO office, tried to set up a five-county agency covering Hale and Perry Counties, which were 70 percent Black, and three white-majority counties. The Perry County Poverty Committee opposed this idea because of the lack of Black representation, telling OEO the agency should "*not* be funded in its present form." Black residents stated their willingness to join with whites on an equal basis, but after a public meeting, they reported, "Our white brothers would not vote to join with us man to man on a 50-50 basis to form a new, biracial community action program coordinating committee." Whites in Hale and Perry Counties saw the poverty program as a deterrent to their campaign to force Blacks to leave and were unwilling to accept a poverty agency unless they could control it. White officials in the three white majority counties wanted nothing to do with Hale and Perry Counties, and OEO eventually agreed to exclude them. When OEO tried to combine Dallas County with Wilcox and Morengo Counties, only Dallas County eventually got a program.[64]

The outcome of representation conflict in Georgia and Louisiana was similar to that in Alabama. In Georgia, the task of establishing antipoverty agencies was given over to county planning and development commissions controlled by white businessmen and the remnants of the courthouse gangs (local elites who ran Georgia counties under the county unit voting system). There was no Black representation—not that white Georgians wanted to hear from Blacks anyway. When the development commissioners of Worth County in southwest Georgia set up a CAA board made up of whites along with Black members who either did not know they had been appointed or could hardly participate because of physical and mental infirmities, an OEO investigator commented that the evidence "would tend to substantiate the charge that a bunch of Georgia crackers are trying to pull the wool over the eyes of the money-wielding yankees."[65]

White control of the process also stemmed from the weakness of the civil rights movement in rural Georgia—though not because activists did not try. Albany, in Dougherty County, was the site of extreme civil rights conflict and violence. Led by Charles Sherrod, the SNCC launched a voting rights campaign in twenty-three southwestern counties but abandoned it after encountering sustained white violence. Sherrod later said, "Southwest Georgia was far worse than Mississippi." White elites had little interest in poverty programs, leading one OEO official to conclude that a "broadly based OEO is not possible at this time." A state consultant to OEO simply said, "A lot of the white leadership is bad," and they would forgo OEO money if they had to integrate. But when local Blacks tried to secure funding for an antipoverty agency, white segregationists jumped at the chance to take over the program, which they viewed as a money tree they could harvest. A local Black activist, C. B. King, wryly observed they were acting to "maintain their position in this as in other things." OEO eventually set up a gerrymandered ten-county agency that excluded two of the poorest Black-majority counties in southwest Georgia. The heavily Black populated counties in central Georgia had no agencies.[66]

Louisiana failed to set up agencies in many predominantly Black counties, but unlike Georgia or Alabama, it funded very few rural multicounty agencies. It had two of the most aggressively pro-Black urban agencies in the South, in New Orleans and Shreveport. Twenty-two of the twenty-eight Louisiana antipoverty agencies were in single counties, many of them sparsely populated. The governor, John McKeithen, every bit as intransigent as George Wallace in Alabama or Paul Johnson in Mississippi, appointed an arch-segregationist, Shelby Jackson, as deputy director of the state technical assistance office, intending to gain control of local agencies just as Wallace had done. McKeithen wanted to use the funding for antipoverty programs to build roads, but Shriver refused to give him any money, and eventually he backed down. McKeithen then appointed a CORE activist and schoolteacher, Kacellious Bridges, to the state agency, but he left control in the hands of his ally Champ Baker, who stridently challenged OEO's demand for integrated programs. He wrote in the newsletter of the Louisiana Office of Economic Opportunity, "When the Head Start classes are not funded due to a lack of integration, the Negro children are penalized.... Let us not subordinate the interests of the poor to that of integration." Because of Baker's opposition, only seven Head Start summer programs had been funded by June 1967.

Indigenous Black mobilization across the state led to the formation of single-county agencies, several of them under Black control. Besides SCEF, both CORE and NAACP were active across the state, and the Louisiana civil rights movement was dominated by local activists, many of whom headed up NAACP chapters. By comparison, there was only one NAACP chapter in Alabama by 1964, and the national organization had written off Mississippi as too difficult. Louisiana gained twenty-two chapters between 1957 and 1964, while the other four Deep South states lost NAACP chapters. The state's congressional delegation was split. Otto Passman, a rabid segregationist and fiscal conservative representing Mississippi Delta counties, was a hostile opponent of the antipoverty program. But OEO had congressional allies in Louisiana—Hale Boggs in New Orleans and Gillis Long, a confidant of Lyndon Johnson—and both its senators typically backed Shriver.[67]

In Mississippi, representation struggles followed a different path because Shriver decided to set up a statewide Head Start program in 1965, run by the Child Development Group of Mississippi. His decision prevented the formation of CAAs for two years. Aside from a few locations such as Coahoma County, where there was no CDGM presence, OEO did not begin to fund CAAs in Mississippi until late 1966, after Shriver ended most of CDGM's funding.

OEO initially funded eighty-five Head Start centers with a $1.5 million grant for five thousand children and added a second grant of $6.4 million in 1966. There were CDGM centers in twenty-nine Mississippi counties, mainly in the Delta and Southern Mississippi. CDGM's director, Tom Levin, administered the program through Mary Holmes Junior College. He recruited activists, many of them women, who had worked in the state since the early 1960s.They included members of the Council of Federated Organizations (COFO), a coalition of civil rights organizations, and the Mississippi Freedom Democratic Party (MFDP). Of the top fifteen administrators in the program, thirteen had civil rights credentials. In Holmes County, where a vibrant local movement had emerged, almost all the CDGM staff members had been active in the MFDP. Charles Payne believes that CDGM generated "a level of emotional involvement comparable to the pre-1964 years," and OEO staff, who thought the program would become a model for other Head Start programs in the rural South, described it as "balanced, and imaginative" and "certainly the most grass-rootsy." From the outset, poor African Americans were deeply involved in the planning and direction of the program. By the summer of 1966, CDGM employed 2,382 people, most of them working-class Black women, of whom three-quarters lived in the towns and neighborhoods where Head Start centers were located.[68]

In mobilizing poor Blacks in rural Mississippi and in its deep commitment to Black autonomy and control, CDGM was unique among antipoverty programs in the rural South. Its centralized structure drew in activists across the state. To white Mississippians, CDGM represented a dire threat, and segregationists began attacking the program soon after the OEO grant was announced. Whites harassed CDGM staff relentlessly. Four Head Start centers were burned down in the first year under suspicious circumstances (bombing Head Start centers was a favorite pastime of KKK thugs). CDGM staff were threatened with violence—shots were fired into their homes—economic boycotts, and cross burnings. Many of them were arrested and jailed for driving while Black or on other flimsy pretexts. Hundreds of incidents were reported to OEO staff that summer.[69]

Mississippi's segregationist politicians weighed in. Senator John Stennis charged that the CDGM was funding civil rights activists and threatened OEO's budget. Governor Paul Johnson told Shriver that CDGM was "an effort on the part of extremists and agitators to subvert lawful authority in Mississippi and create division and dissension between the races." The Mississippi State Sovereignty Commission, a public agency that investigated opponents of white supremacy, placed two informants in a CDGM office, but OEO staff reported that although CDGM staff asked about individuals' civil rights activity, an investigation revealed that CDGM staff were not asking applicants about their prior civil rights activity.[70]

Conflict erupted in Mississippi when Shriver tried to break up the CDGM. After an acrimonious investigation, undertaken partly in response to pressure from Stennis and other opponents, Shriver decided to withhold funding from CDGM and dismantle the statewide single-purpose program.

Shriver acted on the basis of an OEO legal opinion that he could not continue to fund the program unless he could certify that CDGM was capable and qualified to administer the program. CDGM was accused of management deficiencies, running a daycare program instead of an educational program, and, importantly, of opposing the "development of bi-racial community action agencies which could mount the broader-based programs contemplated under Title II." Some allegations of financial irregularities were less a matter of corruption than of OEO's suspicion that Head Start dollars were being used to fund civil rights activity; the evidence for this was sketchy at best. OEO also objected, ironically, to CDGM's strategy of hiring local Blacks as a way to "spread the money among the poor," instead of hiring professionals. But Shriver's opposition to CDGM centered on its failure to establish integrated governing boards and integrated Head Start classes. He had repeatedly emphasized this concern to his many critics. CDGM was not the answer to addressing Mississippi poverty, he wrote to Archibald Cox of Harvard Law School, because it was not "truly a community action organization.... [W]e are more disposed to any organization which would provide true community action and true compliance with the laws of the nation."[71]

Shriver created a new entity, Mississippi Action for Progress (MAP), to take over the remnants of CDGM and set up community action agencies across the state. OEO awarded MAP a $3 million grant for a full-year Head Start program for 1,500 children and created an eighteen-member biracial board stacked with Delta luminaries, planters, and industrialists. Aaron Henry, president of the statewide NAACP conference and an influential member of COFO, was the was the only Black activist of any importance on the board. Control of MAP rested with practical segregationists. Shriver's staff set up task forces throughout the state to preside over the establishment of CAAs and the incorporation of CDGM Head Start centers into the new agencies. Although several counties had submitted proposals by September 1966, the boards of these proposed agencies were "almost always handpicked and packed in favor of [Governor Paul Johnson]. Negro representation is always 'Tom' and target area representation is never present."[72] Like Wallace, Paul Johnson was a practical segregationist who sought to maintain white control over local agencies, and he was ready and willing to veto proposed CAAs.

Local county commissions remained under control of members of white Citizens' Councils. These local elites sought to create white-dominated boards stacked with compliant Blacks, but they were opposed by local

CDGM staff and veterans of the Mississippi civil rights movement. Shriver's decision to defund CDGM drew OEO into a conflict between Black "moderates" and "radicals." CDGM's central staff in Jackson threw a spanner into the transition by encouraging local CDGM staff and local supporters to refuse to cooperate with local CAPs and OEO staff. Robert Moore reported on "CDGM representatives in each area with orders from Jackson to be disruptive and work for CDGM or nothing." Faced with the prospect of losing their Head Start programs, and the jobs that went with them, unless they worked with OEO, many local CDGM groups agreed to work with CAPs, mainly as delegate agencies, once new by-laws were enacted that required agencies to include Black representatives through elections, not by appointment. Even so, conflict with white segregationists trying to control CAAs was overlaid with conflict between different African American groups.[73]

Shriver's decision to dismantle CDGM and establish community action agencies was one of the most controversial decisions he made. He faced criticism not just from civil rights activists in Mississippi and national antipoverty organizations but also from his staff. Ted Berry told Shriver that OEO should refuse to fund MAP in the twenty-eight counties where CDGM was previously located; if OEO did fund MAP in any of those counties, it should be required to work with existing community organizations there. Berry, unlike Shriver, favored single-purpose agencies. He was also worried that MAP would not employ CDGM workers.[74]

John Dittmer argues that Shriver caved to Stennis and other segregationists. There is no doubt that Shriver faced pressure from Stennis, who was an influential member of the Senate Appropriations Committee. Shriver and his staff were concerned that Stennis could mobilize a coalition of Republicans and Southern Democrats who could defund OEO and disperse its programs to other agencies. Shriver was not reluctant to withhold money or override a governor's veto of a grant when he thought it was necessary, but he did go out of his way to pacify Stennis. Also, concerned that CDGM staff were agitating for civil rights, mobilizing Black voters, and recruiting members for the Mississippi Freedom Democratic Party, Shriver warned CDGM about potential violations of the Hatch Act, which prohibits federal employees from engaging in political action. This warning was prudent, since Congress added explicit language from the Hatch Act to the 1966 supplemental OEO appropriations bill. There is no convincing evidence that Shriver, at the behest of President Johnson, was taking sides in the acrimonious conflict between the MFDP and its rival, the Loyal Democrats. What drove him to defund CDGM was his ideological commitment to integrated programs and his hostility to Black power.[75]

Shriver made clear his ire at the lack of integration in a conference with CDGM staff in the fall of 1966. Along with many of his Atlanta regional staff, Shriver viewed CDGM as a cauldron of Black nationalists who subscribed to the tenets of the Vine City project, a supposition that was not entirely wrong. Tom Heller, of OEO's Mississippi staff, recommended that OEO take steps to challenge the Black power ideology of CDGM staff, dismantle centralized control, and facilitate infiltration of local Head Start centers "with local liberally inclined whites." When Shriver restored some of CDGM's money in 1967, he required that it appoint a "fixed percentage" of influential whites to its advisory council, prompting his chief civil rights administrator, Samuel Yette, to complain that Shriver was imposing a requirement on CDGM that applied to no other CAAs.

CDGM staff regarded Shriver's demands as a betrayal. John Mudd, who replaced Levin as the organization's director, acidly told the conference, "A facade of biracialism in substance still preserves the dominant-subordinate relationship, and it is regressive. It retards change." Reverend James McRee added that it was only through single-purpose agencies that Blacks could acquire the leverage needed to address poverty in Mississippi: "We can't compete with CAP Boards because we have no political power.... We want OEO to stop telling us to go thru CAP boards for what we want." Steve Lowenstein, who spent two days interviewing Black community leaders in Mississippi, told Yette of their "growing bitterness" over OEO's treatment of CDGM, which they believed was a "betrayal of the hopes raised by CDGM."[76]

In forcing the establishment of integrated CAP boards across Mississippi and dismantling a largely Black-controlled agency, Shriver fomented conflict between rival factions of Mississippi's African Americans. Both Payne and Dittmer argue that Shriver's decision gave an advantage to moderate African American organizations, such as the NAACP, throwing control to opponents of the MFDP, and quashed local leadership in favor of elite-driven programs. By this interpretation, the outcome of Mississippi's representational struggles was no different from the outcome in states like Alabama or Georgia. But it is precisely because of CDGM's presence that Mississippi CAAs were more likely to end up under Black control than agencies in any of the other four states. In Mississippi, where most of the counties included in CAAs had a history of vigorous civil rights mobilization and Black activists were running Head Start programs in many counties, many of the new CAAs were staffed by CDGM veterans or their allies.[77]

FIGHTING THE WAR ON POVERTY IN THE DEEP SOUTH

The Southern War on Poverty could be described as a program for Blacks run by whites. Despite Shriver's demand for integration, the programs served mainly Blacks because whites refused to participate or were threatened with violence if they tried to enroll in an educational program or send their children to Head Start. But control over agencies and the allocation of resources depended on the outcome of representational struggles across the Deep South. Substantial sums of federal money were at stake, and it is worth exploring where the money went and who decided on its allocation. It made a significant difference for rural Blacks whether OEO funded a single-county rural agency or a multicounty agency.

During the Johnson administration and the first three years of Richard M. Nixon's presidency, OEO distributed $471 million to the five Deep South states, of which $412 million (87 percent) was given to cities and counties through local CAPs (see table 16). The remaining $58 million was distributed through state economic opportunity offices (EOOs) and in one case a large grant to the Tuskegee Institute. About 30 percent of this money went to cover administrative costs and technical assistance, but it was also used to fund state-sponsored job training and educational projects, and in Mississippi, Head Start (CDGM). About 60 percent of all OEO funding originated from the Johnson administration.[78]

Mississippi received significantly more funding than other Deep South states: $124 million, or $72 per capita compared to an average of $38 in the other four states. Urban county agencies garnered about half of OEO funds in all five states, and rural multicounty CAAs received one-third. Yet, as table 16 shows, per capita funding was much higher in rural counties with a single agency, $78 per person compared to $33 in urban and $32 in rural multicounty agencies. It is the differences between the states that are most notable, however. At one extreme, in Georgia there was no difference in per capita funding across the different types of agencies, whereas in Mississippi OEO invested heavily in rural single-county agencies: the per capita rate was $139, compared to an average rate of $58 in the other four states. Mississippi also

TABLE 16 Total OEO expenditures in Deep South states, FY1965–FY1971

	Alabama	Georgia	Louisiana	Mississippi[a]	South Carolina	Total
			OEO expenditures ($)			
OEO CAA, total expenditures	76,605,324	99,238,574	83,954,134	88,258,506	64,142,918	412,199,456
State EOO, total expenditures	10,721,318	6,904,183	1,180,910	35,883,304	3,762,228	58,451,943
Total OEO expenditures	87,326,642	106,142,757	85,135,044	124,141,810	67,905,146	470,651,399
Johnson administration budgets, FY1965–FY1968 (% of total)	58	56	57	70	51	61
			Per capita expenditures by CAA type ($)			
Statewide	45	27	39	72	40	45
Urban county	27	27	37	37	40	33
Rural single-county	94	30	44	139	65	78
Rural multicounty	33	27	27	40	29	32
			Project allocation (% of total CAA expenditures)			
Administration	19.3	14.9	16.2	16.6	12.9	16.1
Community services	26.4	39.0	34.9	4.9	23.5	24.7
Head Start	22.2	15.6	26.3	51.8	21.2	29.1
Job training/adult education	15.9	12.5	7.9	15.2	15.5	13.4
Housing	1.5	0.7	0.1	0.2	0.7	0.6
Health	10.4	13.0	8.9	6.7	19.5	11.1
Emergency food	4.3	4.3	5.7	4.6	6.5	4.9

SOURCE: Deep South CAA county dataset (see appendix).
[a] Mississippi state OEO expenditures include CDGM funding.

had the highest per capita rate for funding rural multicounty agencies, and Georgia and Louisiana the lowest.[79]

Shriver, who naively believed that Head Start would bring Black and white Southerners together, got his way. Deep South agencies allocated 29 percent of OEO dollars to Head Start. The legacy of CDGM was apparent in Mississippi, where Head Start funding greatly exceeded that in all other states. Agencies allocated another 25 percent to community services, a total of $114 million. Although this money ostensibly funded neighborhood service centers, financial counseling, legal services, and programs for migrant farm workers, agencies had substantial leeway in how they used it. In practice the money was used for everything from needed services to make-work projects to a slush fund through which whites rewarded their friends and neighbors. Mississippi CAAs spent a paltry 5 percent on community services, compared with 39 percent in Georgia and 35 percent in Louisiana.

Blacks in the Deep South favored single-county agencies, which they were more likely to be able to control. To determine whether the type of rural agency—single- or multicounty—made a difference in the distribution of OEO dollars, I estimated per capita OEO funding across the five Deep South states, based on a dummy variable for type of agency. Control variables included Black share of the population, percentage of families with income below the $3,000 poverty level in 1960, the percentage of Black farm owners in a county, the ratio of agricultural to manufacturing jobs in 1962, and a variable for state effects. (See table A.3.) This model explains 45 percent of the variation in the distribution of per capita OEO dollars. Based on this model, I estimate that per capita OEO funding was on average $37 higher for single-county rural agencies than for multicounty agencies. This is 48 percent of the mean value of per capita funding in rural single-county agencies.[80] My analysis demonstrates just how consequential rural single-county CAAs were for Blacks and points up the distinctive pattern in Mississippi. The relationship between per capita OEO funding and type of agency is negative for every state but Mississippi.

Rural single-county CAAs were money magnets. They were more successful in attracting federal dollars from other federal agencies than multicounty agencies or counties with no agency. For example, child welfare grants from the Department of Health, Education and Welfare averaged $35,596 for service areas with single-county CAAs, compared to $19,756 for those with multicounty CAAs. Table 17 compares the mean dollar distribution of nine different federal grants-in-aid for service areas with rural single- and multicounty CAAs and rural counties with no agency. Federal funding is higher for service areas with rural single-county agencies than for those with multicounty agencies or counties with no CAA, and the mean difference is statistically significant in all but one case (grants for vocational rehabilitation). The differences in funding are substantial. Food distribution grants averaged almost $471,350 in fiscal year 1968 in service areas with rural single-county agencies, compared to $205,176 in service areas with multicounty agencies and $242,074 in counties with no agency. Both mean FHA farm loans and OEO farm grants under Title III were significantly larger in counties with rural single-county agencies. On the other hand, there was little difference in federal funding between service areas with multicounty agencies and counties with no agency, except in two cases: Department of Labor manpower grants and Aid to Families with Dependent Children (AFDC) grants.[81]

Charles Payne concluded that all local people got under MAP was "an educational program dominated at best by a traditional social-welfare mentality," a statement that could apply to all agencies in these states.[82] But who these agencies served and what they did with the money they received depended on the outcome of representational struggles. Conflict over representation and control resulted in four different types of agencies. In *white-controlled* agencies, local white elites usually initiated the request for funding and ended up with near-total control over programs and resources. White-controlled agencies were the result of a takeover of the process; often there was minimal conflict. *White-co-opted* agencies emerged out of conflicts between whites and their African American adversaries in which white elites gained control and secured funding from OEO by co-opting the opposition, appointing some African Americans to the board, and hiring some Black staff. Co-opted agencies did make some concessions to their Black opponents. *Black-controlled* agencies were just that: CAAs in which Blacks gained control of the board and were able to influence the allocation of resources. Finally, there were agencies in which a struggle for control ended in a *stalemate* or unclear control.

Neither white nor Black control was necessarily enduring or stable; changes in control and influence were not unusual. Some agencies shifted from complete white domination to a measure of Black influence because of pressure from Black activists and the OEO. In Amite County, Mississippi, an agency that started out under the control of African American activists reverted to a white-controlled agency following a concerted campaign of terror, violence,

TABLE 17 Comparison of federal grants in rural counties by CAA type, FY1968
(Mean dollar values)

	FHA farm loans	OEO farm grants	DOL manpower grants	OEO employment training grants	Vocational rehabilitation grants	Child welfare grants	Health services grants	Food distribution grants	AFDC grants
Single-county CAA	$624,988	97,189	52,738	198,303	75,669	35,596	225,895	471,350	211,790
No CAA in county	457,611	15,907	16,224	72,708	58,963	23,508	98,154	242,074	130,816
Significance (t-test)	0.023	0.000	0.054	0.001		0.003	0.004	0.000	0.000
Multicounty CAA	439,329	17,597	40,071	75,984	56,488	19,756	88,556	205,176	93,202
No CAA in county	457,611	15,907	16,224	72,708	58,963	23,508	98,154	242,074	130,816
Significance (t-Test)			0.056						0.005
Single-county CAA	624,988	97,189	52,738	198,303	75,669	35,596	225,895	471,350	211,790
Multicounty CAA	439,329	17,597	40,071	75,984	56,488	19,756	88,556	205,176	93,202
Significance (t-Test)	0.008	0.000		0.001	0.052	0.000	0.001	0.000	0.000

SOURCE: Deep South Federal Expenditures FY1968 Dataset (see appendix).

and economic pressure by KKK thugs and white elites. What determined the outcome was the ability of white segregationists, from governors on down, to control representation struggles; the power and influence of Black civil rights activists; and the position of OEO on the struggle, either acting to ensure Black influence and control or ceding control to white racists. When OEO was dithering about whom to back in Adams County, Mississippi, Tom Heller warned that failing to side with civil rights activists would be fatal. "Militant leadership was lost, and the situation went straight downhill," he wrote about an agency in Louisiana. "We now have an out-and-out white supremacist CAA... which takes OEO programs to keep Negroes in line."[83]

Using data drawn from OEO files and reports of community action agencies, I classify forty-seven of the one hundred agencies in Alabama, Mississippi, Louisiana, and Georgia. Table 18 describes the racial composition and financial allocations of these agencies.[84] The most interesting comparison is between Alabama and Mississippi. Of the sixteen Alabama agencies for which I have sufficient data, eleven were white-controlled or co-opted; only one CAA in the state was under Black control—in Macon County, home to the Tuskegee Institute. One of the two largest agencies in the state, Jefferson County (Birmingham), was stalemated. Mississippi could not have been more different. There were six agencies under Black control, four were co-opted, and three were stalemated. In two of the cases of white co-optation—agencies in Bolivar and Montgomery Counties—Blacks were able to secure control of delegate agencies in which the CAA ceded control of programs to a subordinate agency. Louisiana was an intermediate case, with nine white-controlled or co-opted agencies, four Black-controlled agencies, and three stalemated.

Blacks held about two-thirds of board seats in the agencies they controlled, but only one-third in white-controlled and about two-fifths in co-opted agencies. Agencies in gerrymandered counties were more likely to be white-controlled or co-opted, and those counties had smaller Black populations than counties in which agencies were controlled by Blacks. The difference between white-controlled and white-co-opted agencies depended on the scale of local Black mobilization. In Mississippi, agencies under Black control were entirely rural, but those in Louisiana were urban agencies, including two of the largest, those in New Orleans and Shreveport (Caddo and Bossier Parishes).

TABLE 18 Representation, control, and resource allocation of CAAs in Deep South states

	White-controlled	White-co-opted	Black-controlled	Stalemated	Total	% of total CAAS
All Deep South States	12	14	11	10	47	46
Alabama	8	3	1	4	16	60
Mississippi	(1)[a]	4	6	3	13	56
Louisiana	4	5	4	3	16	54
Georgia		2			2	9
Race of board members (% of total)						
White	60	57	35	53		
Black	34	40	65	47		
Number of gerrymandered CAAs	2	3	1	0		
CAA spending, FY1965–FY1971						
Rural agencies						
Total OEO funds (millions of dollars)	14.9	50.8	26.7	14.3		
Per capita spending (dollars)	39.3	71.2	89.5	78		
Urban agencies						
Total OEO funds (millions of dollars)	17.4	61.8	34.3	26.9		
Per capita spending (dollars)	32.8	46.2	44.5	46		
Percentage of Blacks in CAA service Area	33.5	41.8	48.1	38.5		
Percentage of families below poverty line in CAA service area	48.5	48.7	49.9	48.9		
Resource allocation (%)						
Rural CAAs						
Administration	12.7	12.9	15.2	8.1		
Community services	42.7	13.4	6.4	19.9		
Head Start	23.3	44.2	54.1	30.3		
Job training/adult education	8.5	9.8	20.1	10.7		
Health	2.7	12.8	1.0	22.5		
Urban CAAs						
Administration	8.6	11.9	17.4	12.0		
Community services	20.8	37.0	34.3	27.0		
Head Start	31.1	13.6	25.8	41.4		
Job training/adult education	12.7	11.9	10.0	12.0		
Health	21.6	23.7	10.6	5.4		

SOURCE: Deep South CAA County Dataset (see appendix); OEO CAA state data files, RG 381, NA.
[a] Amite County shifted from Black control to white control.

White-Controlled Agencies

White controlled agencies were disproportionately rural. Local officials usually initiated the proposal for an agency either on their own initiative or at the behest of a governor or state official, a practice that in some cases was clandestine. In Louisiana, segregationists launched agencies in Evangeline and Grant Parishes without participation of African Americans, though three handpicked token Black representatives were appointed to the Evangeline board. In Alabama, white-controlled agencies were more often the result of gerrymandering or the banding together of white-majority counties that resisted merging with Black counties. All these agencies served relatively small Black populations: Blacks made up an average of one-third of the residents in these counties. White-controlled agencies received $32.3 million from 1965 to 1971, substantially less than the other three types of agencies.

White Southerners running these agencies viewed Blacks with either "tolerant paternalism" or outright hostility. Agency staff were segregated, there were few Blacks in professional or administrative positions, and white staff were often hostile to the aims of the War on Poverty. OEO staff described the assistant director of the Chilton County agency as "completely insensitive and actually opposed to poor blacks, to whom he refers as 'agitators.'" Black political participation and organization were nonexistent in the three rural counties served by the Chilton CAA. There were no programs for job training, education, or housing, but the agency ran a large food distribution program and a home management program that may have been a vehicle to train Black maids for white families. In the Pike County CAA, Black home health aides were "relegated to traditional maid type service for white families, thus reinforcing the customary social status [of blacks]."[85] White-controlled agencies allocated more money to community services (43 percent) and less to job training or adult education (8.5 percent) than the other three types of agencies.

White-controlled agencies combined segregated programs with "absolute POLITICAL PATRONAGE," as one OEO report described the pattern, and diverted resources to influential whites, or in some cases poor whites. A Wallace ally in charge of the CAP agency serving Dale, Henry, and Barbour Counties in the southeastern corner of Alabama "built [his] strength among rural [white] politicians through patronage and favors." He allocated antipoverty funds to small-town mayors, dispersing authority and power across the three counties. The Dale County CAA used three-quarters of its funding for administration and community service, programs that facilitated racial discrimination and favoritism toward white allies. Dale was not unusual; the Conecuh and Chilton agencies did the same thing.[86]

KKK bombing of Head Start centers reinforced white control, driving away participants. Rural whites saw Head Start as a "despised symbol of federal power" and a tool of integration that had to be stopped. In East Carroll and Grant Parishes, Louisiana, in the Mississippi Delta, the KKK burned crosses at Head Start centers and terrorized participants. An OEO report estimated that in 1966, KKK terrorism in Delta parishes exposed 375 children and forty-five teachers (many of whom were white) to threats of violence. White opponents of OEO were not averse to taking antipoverty money; however, they sought segregated programs that would benefit only white children and adults. In some instances, Black complaints weakened white control by forcing OEO to appoint more Blacks to the board. In East Carroll, Louisiana, for example, Black pressure on OEO led to the CAA allocating more money to programs of direct benefit to poor African Americans (and relatively little on community services)—far more than the Evangeline or Grant CAAs, where Black opposition was suppressed.[87]

White-Coopted Agencies

Most white-co-opted agencies emerged out of protracted conflict between segregationists and civil rights activists. White elites usually took the initiative in angling for an agency, only to be challenged by local civil rights organizations. The outcome usually depended on where OEO came down in the conflict. Pressure to fund an antipoverty agency often outweighed concerns about whether or how intransigent white segregationists would run the agency.

Dallas County, Alabama (Selma), was an archetypical co-opted agency. The Selma mayor, Joe T. Smitherman, a diehard Wallace ally and opponent of voting rights, tried to set up an agency without Black participation, only to be rejected by OEO. Smitherman's gambit provoked Shirley Mesher, an SCLC organizer, to form an alternative organization, SHAPE (Self-Help against Poverty with Everyone). Mesher and the chair of SHAPE, the Reverend Ernest Bradford, set about building support among rural Blacks in Dallas County for an agency controlled by poor African Americans. An OEO inspection report commented that the effort led to the "most effective elections [of board members] by the poor that have been held in the South, and perhaps in the nation."[88]

Smitherman responded to SHAPE's campaign with a new proposal that included Black agency representatives and was clearly intended to divide Black opposition and co-opt Black community leaders unaffiliated with SHAPE. These leaders, many of them drawn from the Black middle class in Selma, proceeded to select their own representatives to the board and align themselves with Smitherman. Bradford and Mesher refused to go along, believing that the program had been taken over by the "white power structure" and those Blacks aligned with them. OEO threw its weight behind the new proposal, even though Smitherman retained control by appointing an acolyte as executive director. OEO staff were either unsympathetic to SHAPE's concerns or believed that SHAPE wanted to be the sole representative for poor people on the board. Eager to get a program up and running, OEO bypassed the concerns of the most vibrant civil rights organization in the county. The upshot was predictable: Dallas County lavished almost half its funding ($2 million) on administration and directed very little toward programs of direct benefit to poor African Americans or whites.[89]

A similar chain of events ensued in many of the other co-opted rural agencies. Three cases of co-optation occurred in gerrymandered agencies, two in Mississippi and a singularly egregious instance involving the Southwest Georgia CAP in Colquitt County, Georgia. A group of Blacks in Albany, led by C. B. King, prepared a proposal for a multicounty agency. Rather than let Blacks control an antipoverty agency, county commissions in the area prepared their own proposals. A Colquitt County official told OEO staff the counties were mostly uninterested in antipoverty programs, "but when word got around that the Negroes could get programs of their own, more interest picked up." In the end, white elites gained control of the program and appointed to the board Blacks who could be manipulated, in a "systematic effort," according to C. B. King, "to exclude Negroes who had anything to do with the movement."[90] In Louisiana, meretricious whites in St. James and St. Mary Parishes hijacked the process, handpicked the Black board members, and stacked the board with "political cronies of the Mayor." An OEO staff report lamented that St. Mary was "the same story of the region trying to make a good situation out of something which can hardly be made so."[91]

Black-Controlled Agencies

Black control of agencies emerged when strong local civil rights organizations and activists were able to direct how agencies were established and who administered them. In this respect, Mississippi was unique. In the aftermath of Shriver's decision to dismantle CDGM, activists migrated to delegate agencies or acquired full control of them. In Louisiana and Mississippi counties that were not affiliated with CDGM, Black-controlled agencies were established in counties with long-standing Black political organizations or aggressive local movements.

The struggle over Acadiana-Neuf in southern Louisiana illustrates how an indigenous Black movement succeeded in establishing its own agency in the face of powerful white opposition. Acadiana-Neuf started out as a six-county agency in south-central Louisiana, a largely Cajun or French-speaking region that remained sharply segregated in 1966. Originally the CAP board was composed of fourteen white men, one from each of the police juries and school boards in the six counties, and two administrators from the University of Southwest Louisiana. After OEO complained about the absence of Blacks on the board, two token members, widely regarded as "Uncle Toms," were appointed. The agency was opposed by Black members of the Southern Consumers Education Foundation (SCEF), a part of the Southern Consumers Cooperative. This was an organization with a membership of one thousand families that operated a loan company and had signed a contract with OEO to set up cooperatives and credit unions throughout southern Louisiana. SCEF filled a gap in a part of Louisiana where there were no civil rights organizations. It was aided by Marion Overton White, a militant former president of the state NAACP.[92]

OEO insisted on a reconstituted board as a condition of funding the agency, mainly because White demanded to know "why [OEO] had finally released funds to Acadiana-Neuf in spite of the fact they had run an admittedly segregated program." White elites reconstituted the CAA board but did so in a way that left whites in control. A year later the agency became enmeshed in conflict when the agency's director obstructed the operation of delegate programs operated by SCEF, including Head Start and an agricultural education and marketing program for Black farmers called the Sweet Potato Alert. The board's vice chair believed that SCEF should never run a program. White opponents red-baited SCEF and charged it with fraud and nepotism, allegations that were never proved. At the same time, SCEF was organizing advisory committees in Lafayette Parish that mobilized large numbers of poor people, mostly Black. When the white majority defeated OEO's proposed reorganization plans, OEO split the agency into a white-controlled operation in Acadia and Vermilion Parishes and a Black-run agency in Lafayette, Iberia, and St. Martin Parishes.[93]

Two cases in Mississippi—in Bolivar and Holmes Counties—pitted Black opponents, anchored by CDGM activists, against white segregationists attempting to set up agencies they could control. In both instances white elites remained in charge, but activists carved out some autonomy with delegate agencies. Both counties had deeply rooted civil rights movements, bolstered by the economic independence of Black farm owners. In Bolivar County, the board of supervisors, aligned with the local chamber of commerce, tried to set up an agency stacked with Blacks they could control, only to confront a group of parents from across the county who demanded 70 percent of the seats on the CAA board and urged CDGM to become a delegate agency. Given the choice of siding with white elites or acceding to the demands of Black parents, OEO split the difference, funding a CDGM Head Start program for six months alongside a program run by the Bolivar County agency.[94]

In the second case, the gerrymandered Central Mississippi agency, which served six counties and a population evenly divided between Blacks and whites, the conflict turned on a division between Blacks affiliated with CDGM and another group of Blacks aligned with so-called moderate whites—racists who may have been members of white Citizens' Councils but did not oppose a poverty program. Holmes County was the only county among the six with a long tradition of civil rights activism, bolstered by many Black farmers who had acquired land through the Farm Security Administration's resettlement project. (Blacks constituted 57 percent of all farm owners in the county.)[95]

OEO sided with the Black activists. It set up a six-county agency and funded it when CDGM was already operating Head Start centers in Holmes and Attala Counties. An OEO report pointed out that there was at least "one strong Negro voice representing the Negroes of each county" on the board but noted "a strong tendency for the whites and some Negroes to form a coalition which effectively blocked the more militant and representative Negroes." OEO negotiated an agreement between the Central Mississippi CAA and CDGM in Holmes and Attala Counties that resulted in a delegate agency with considerable autonomy. An OEO evaluation report noted that it was "understood by both parties that the CAP would not interfere in any way with the operation of the delegate agency." White conservatives on the CAA board were opposed to delegating Head Start to CDGM activists, but the board delegated control of eleven Head Start centers to the CDGM activists in the two counties.[96]

The transfer of CDGM Head Start programs to new CAP agencies invariably led to conflict, but Blacks prevailed in counties where local activists and former CDGM staff gained representation on the board and control of programs. Pearl River Valley Opportunities, in Marion, Walthall, and Lamar Counties, and Southeast Mississippi Opportunities, in Forrest County, are notable examples. In Walthall County, a local activist, E. R. McGee, the secretary of the local NAACP chapter and a "long-time leader of the hardcore disadvantaged" who was allied with CDGM, arranged the merger of CDGM and CAP staff. The resulting board was composed of nine white and eight Black members, augmented by nine former CDGM members elected from "private agencies with a prior concern for poverty"—that is, CDGM Head Start centers. A similar set of negotiations occurred in Forrest County (Hattiesburg), where civil rights activists linked to the MFDP, the Delta Ministry, and influential white allies overcame white opposition to antipoverty programs. The Forrest County activists successfully elected five board members, formed an association of Head Start mothers composed of individuals from both sides of a divided Black community, and evaded Governor Paul Johnson's efforts to control the agency. In both these cases, Blacks acquired influence and control of large programs in delegate agencies: the budget of the CDGM-controlled Head Start program in Forrest County was five times the size of the CAA budget.[97]

Blacks also succeeded in claiming outright control of some of the largest agencies in Mississippi and Louisiana, though that control was never entirely stable. Coahoma Opportunities in the Mississippi Delta is an example of an agency under stable Black control. The agency was the largest CAA in the state. Shriver told his staff that it represented "the biggest breakthrough against poverty (and for civil rights) in Mississippi history." Whether or not this was true, Coahoma Opportunities was well funded—it received over $13 million, far more than any other Mississippi agency. Coahoma County had a history of activism going back to the Black and Tan political organizations during Reconstruction and a mobilized civil rights movement. Aaron Henry saw its antipoverty program as a vehicle to get money to the Black community and led the campaign to get control of the agency.[98]

Initially, the CAA board was loaded with white segregationists, but Henry had an ally in Oscar Carr, a wealthy planter, former president of the Delta Council, and one of the so-called moderate whites. Carr thought the county should seek poverty money and acted as an intermediary between Henry and the county supervisors. Unlike most planters in the area, Carr advocated retraining displaced sharecroppers for the manufacturing jobs he assumed would be forthcoming. Initially, the CAA board was split between arch-segregationists and militant Blacks. Although Shriver thought of the board's composition as a breakthrough, it was unworkable, and Henry and his allies forced the segregationists off the board and took over.

Henry believed the antipoverty program would establish the basis for Black economic and political autonomy. An OEO-funded credit bureau, he said, would give people a "stature of independence and now they do not have to come with hat in hand, scratching when they don't itch and that sort of thing when they need to borrow money." Andrew Carter, a white planter who became chair of the board after the segregationists resigned, touted the program to Stennis as an alternative to civil rights radicals. Henry was no radical, despite his involvement in COFO, yet the Coahoma program stands out among Mississippi agencies for its efforts to create viable economic programs for sharecroppers and Black laborers, the victims of Southern agricultural modernization. Coahoma Opportunities allocated $6 million—47 percent of its funding—to job training and adult education.[99]

The New Orleans CAA was the one big-city agency in the South that came under Black control. Atlanta's was a case of white co-optation, and the Birmingham agency was mired in relentless conflict, a stalemate. But in New Orleans, Kent Germany argues, Black political activists used the CAP, and its opportunities for mobilization and political influence, to break down white resistance to Black power and achieve a modest redistribution of resources.[100]

The Caddo-Bossier Parish was another Louisiana agency where Black militants succeeded in taking over. Its largest city, Shreveport, was a notorious center of Confederate resistance after the Union Army consolidated control of Louisiana in 1862. It was known for white violence during Reconstruction, and in the 1960s it was a bastion of strident right-wing (Goldwater) Republicans. Initially, no county or city agencies were represented on the board, and in this respect the Caddo-Bossier CAA was like some Northern agencies in which insurgents took control before city officials struck back. Neither the NAACP nor CORE was active in Shreveport. The takeover was the act of a coalition of "liberal whites . . . and a group of progressive middle-class Negroes who are tired of the present white power structure."[101] They were opposed by a loosely aligned group of older, more conservative Blacks, the local labor organization, and white segregationists and arch-conservatives.

The Caddo-Bossier agency was the third largest agency in Louisiana, with a budget of over $8 million. It set up twelve neighborhood centers and embarked on an aggressive civil rights and antipoverty strategy. It imposed an antiracist litmus test for prospective employees and tried to take over an in-school Neighborhood Youth Corps program run by the segregated local school district. Believing that voter registration was a legitimate function of neighborhood service centers, it required service center employees to ask clients if they were registered to vote, and if not, to help them register. The agency registered seven thousand new voters, inspiring strident opposition from segregationists and the president of the Louisiana AFL-CIO.[102]

Bob Emond of OEO told Shriver that "the establishment is concerned about the growth of Negro political power as a result of the program." And that establishment struck back. Governor McKeithen's veto of a $600,000 Head Start grant led to a reorganization of the CAA board. Up to that point the agency had sole control over membership; after the reorganization, city and county agencies gained representation, diluting the power of the salt-and-pepper coalition running the agency. Even so, Emond reported, "the position of the poor and minority representation has been strengthened."[103]

One of the most egregious reversals in control occurred in Southwest Mississippi Opportunity, an agency covering Amite, Pike, and Wilkinson Counties. According to an OEO profile, the combination of the "fountainhead of COFO activity and the violent reaction of the local rednecks produce the sobriquet, Bomb Capitol of the USA." Amite and Pike Counties had CDGM centers, which the OEO folded into the new CAA. When white elites tried to take control, they were stymied by Black opposition, led by C. B. Bryant and veterans of the civil rights movement. Governor Johnson vetoed the initial proposal for the new agency because of the involvement of CDGM committee members, but Shriver overrode the veto and set up an agency with a thirty-six-member board that had twenty-two Blacks. The agency was initially a success. An OEO report credited the agency for "its efforts to coordinate poverty-related activities of existing public agencies," notably local schools. It exerted pressure on local authorities operating the local food-distribution program and was looking to start offering adult education and employment training.[104]

At the time, Pike County was the center of vigorous civil rights pressure. Activists defeated the white mayor in November 1966 and were able to desegregate the McComb County schools. In October 1967 OEO negotiated an agreement for a CDGM delegate agency to run Head Start with an initial grant of $822,500, but the relationship between Southwest Mississippi Opportunities, which was now dominated by white segregationists, and the delegate agency deteriorated over time. The Klan harassed Head Start centers for three years beginning in 1967, bombing centers and terrorizing participants. In the spring of 1970, the county attorney threw a rock through the window of the Head Start office. He was followed by "Night Riders" who "sped through Liberty, the Capital Seat of [Amite] county, and shot into the office." OEO staff reported that the white-dominated CAA used the agency "to contain and control blacks." Whites were unsympathetic to the goals of OEO and brought in police during board meetings to intimidate Blacks. White board members said they "would rather destroy the agency than have it comply with the law." The Head Start program, operated by the CDGM-staffed delegate agency, was the one bright spot. But by the summer of 1970, economic threats to their livelihoods had diminished the influence of the three remaining Black members of the Board. An OEO inspection report recommended defunding the agency.[105]

BLACK POWER AND THE SOUTHERN WAR ON POVERTY

The War on Poverty is often depicted as irrelevant to Southern Black economic gains, or as a vehicle for the political co-optation of radical civil rights organizations and a triumph for "pragmatic segregationists" seeking to limit the gains of the civil rights movement. Both arguments contain elements of truth, but both mislead. In the rural South, particularly during the interregnum between enactment of the major civil rights laws and their successful implementation, CAAs plowed needed resources into many beleaguered rural communities, providing jobs and a measure of autonomy from predatory whites. The program served as a conduit for federal grants-in-aid from other agencies to CAAs, especially to rural single-county agencies. Far from being an irrelevant sideshow, OEO supported independence for many Blacks facing the dehumanizing oppression of the Southern version of white supremacy. OEO's funding of CDGM "facilitated meaningful changes in Mississippi's racial and political status quo," Crystal R. Sanders concludes, "by circumventing ... politicians who benefited from African Americans' second-class citizenship."[106] But if the program delivered resources to some counties, it did so only because Black activists were able to gain control of

CAA boards and determine the allocation of resources. Such achievements were more likely in Mississippi, where CDGM activists gained control of agencies after CDGM was defunded, than in Alabama, where Governor Wallace, abetted by OEO regional staff, was able to set up multicounty agencies dominated by white racists.

Shriver and many of his national and regional OEO staff never acknowledged or really understood that they could neither alleviate poverty nor advance equality of opportunity in the rural South without empowering Black people. Instead, they assumed that OEO's success depended on integrating CAA governing boards and Head Start classes. They had legal and political reasons for preferring integrated programs, but all too often Shriver falsely equated demands for Black power and autonomy with white insistence on segregation. Amplified by OEO policies favoring the creation of multicounty rural agencies, Shriver's insistence on integrated boards—which appeared to establish equality between Blacks and Southern whites—played into the hands of practical segregationists and diluted the ability of Blacks to control governing boards and the distribution of resources. This was why Black organizers and activists demanded single-county districts.

For many whites, not just Shriver, the language of integration in the 1960s had little to do with questions of power and privilege. They understood integration as the path to racial harmony, and Black power as a recipe for conflict and failure. Bayard Rustin's belief in a coalition of poor Blacks and poor whites had little purchase in the Deep South —or the North, for that matter. The reason Head Start programs were not integrated was that whites would not participate in them—either because they hated the idea of integration or because they feared retaliation from KKK thugs and white opponents of the program.

Martin Luther King Jr. could not have disagreed more sharply with this understanding of integration as force for racial harmony. By 1967, he accepted neither Black nationalism nor a facile belief in the power of an alliance with white labor. Rather, King believed the civil rights movement could redefine the relationship between race and class by paving the way for a more inclusive form of social justice, which in turn would form the basis for integration. "In our kind of society," he wrote, "liberation cannot come without integration and integration cannot come without liberation.... When a people are mired in oppression, they realize deliverance when they have accumulated the power to enforce change."[107]

Antiprivilege egalitarianism is about power. Southern Black activists understood that successful opposition to white attempts at co-optation and control was contingent on the existence of viable local civil rights movements. Activists in the SNCC, SCLC, and CORE were involved in the struggle to take control of agencies, but much of the impetus came from indigenous civil rights organizations and Black activists, many of them women. Although the NAACP was often criticized as a force moderating civil rights activism, some of the fiercest local activists were NAACP members. These local movements succeeded when they were able to persuade OEO to intervene on their behalf. Mississippi stands out as an ironic case. Civil rights activists and some historians see Shriver's decision to defund CDGM as a betrayal of the civil rights movement, arguing that replacing a network of statewide Head Start centers with community action agencies co-opted the civil rights movement and substituted pork-barrel politics for real social and economic change. Shriver did betray the Mississippi activists, but they did not disappear; they ended up running community action or delegate agencies with large budgets. What subverted poverty programs in Mississippi and other Southern states was the tenacious white opposition to any assertion of Black autonomy, to which Shriver often acquiesced.

SIX

What Does Racial Justice Require?

> There cannot be ... a more dangerous, absurd, and immoral contradiction than political equality without social and economic equality. To enjoy equality in law but to be deprived of it in life is an odious injustice.
>
> ARMAND DE LA MEUSE,
> French National Convention, April 17, 1793

INDIVIDUAL AFRICAN AMERICANS MADE SUBSTANTIAL economic and political gains from the civil rights era to the twenty-first century. Yet deeply embedded racial inequality remains a formidable problem. Significant racial disparities in employment, poverty, wealth, access to health care, policing, and incarceration persist almost sixty years after the triumphs of the civil rights revolution. Americans are constantly reminded of the unfinished business of the civil rights era, and they are deeply divided over the legacies of slavery, Jim Crow, and civil rights laws and policies.[1] Movements to undo durable racial inequality and deep-seated white resentment confront each other within a society riven by widening inequalities of income and wealth and a collapse in the American vision of economic opportunity. Just 50 percent of children born in the 1980s could expect to have a higher income than their parents, compared to 90 percent of children born in the 1940s. African American children experience less upward mobility than white children and more downward mobility, a pattern that is independent of individual or family characteristics.[2]

Nowhere are these racial disparities more apparent than in the Deep South, where, amid an economic boom across northern Alabama into Georgia and South Carolina, Black poverty and degradation, especially in rural counties, remain interminably high. Even though civil rights laws and federal policies in the South overturned segregation and opened job and educational opportunities for African Americans, the legacy of slavery in the Deep South persists today in racially hostile attitudes of white Southerners toward Blacks and regressive state policies.[3]

The Second Reconstruction established political and legal equality for African Americans but failed to undo fully the harms of slavery and legal racial apartheid. Economic gains for individual Blacks mask deeply embedded group inequality, sustained by both overt racial prejudice and structural racism. Edwin Dorn calls this the paradox of procedural equality, a result of policies based on "weak biased opportunity." Groups that start out unequal will remain unequal, even though individuals may move up or down the economic ladder, and this disparity between individuals "threatens to trap blacks as a group into a position of permanent substantive inequality vis-à-vis whites." De facto segregation is one of the linchpins of sustained racial inequality today.[4] Black lives in twenty-first century America, regardless of an individual's income, are precarious, relentlessly insecure. All Blacks face greater risks of unemployment, personal threats from police officers or a frightened white person with a gun, and exclusion from many of the ordinary social and economic benefits that most white people take for granted, such as walking into a store without being seen as a possible thief.[5] As Martin Luther King Jr. recognized, abolishing legally segregated institutions may have been the easy part.

The white backlash that began in the late 1960s blocked the road to racial justice and led to a conservative resurgence that began with the election of Richard Nixon and has now resulted in the rise of a revanchist white nationalist movement that has taken over the Republican Party. Republican politicians came to power and forged a new national electoral majority on the back of white resentment at Black political mobilization, and they used their power to undermine civil rights and social policies of the 1960s. The Nixon administration diverted needed resources from the rural South and Northern cities; the Ronald Reagan administration and Supreme Court decisions rendered Title VII and affirmative action policies ineffective; and all too many politicians, Republicans and Democrats, replaced policies for equality with incarceration. This political movement recently resulted in the Supreme Court's decision to end affirmative action policies for college admissions.

An ideology of individual choice and personal responsibility and discipline, voiced by both Republicans and Democrats, superseded demands for racial justice and equality. Racial equality, it was said, required only a regime of political rights, formal equality before the law, and Blacks' acceptance of responsibility for their own fates. President Bill Clinton made this view explicit in his 1995 State of the Union Address. "All Americans," he proclaimed, "have not just a right but a solemn responsibility to rise as far as their God-given talents and determination can take them. Opportunity and responsibility: They go hand in hand. We can't have one without the other." There was nothing new in this statement: Clinton merely recycled the Whig orthodoxy of equality of opportunity. And like Whig programs in the 1830s, Clinton's welfare reform policy replaced responsibility with discipline.[6]

None of these developments are surprising considering my account of the history of national efforts to overcome racial inequality in the aftermath of slavery and Jim Crow. The inadequacy of formal equality without a measure of economic independence and autonomy is apparent, as is its injustice. So too are the deficiencies of any conception of equality of opportunity based on the policies and practices deriving from reform liberalism that I have labeled rehabilitation. Is the cultural and political tradition of antiprivilege egalitarianism a viable alternative? Or is equality of opportunity simply a dead end, an inadequate response to structural racism?

And, importantly, is racial justice possible without a large measure of social and economic equality across American society? Most Black leaders from the New Deal forward have assumed the necessity of both civil rights and economic justice for all American citizens. In a 1946 speech, Mary McLeod Bethune, one of the most prominent members of FDR's Black Cabinet, said, "Let us realize that full and fair employment are . . . desirable and that we cannot rest until *all* have the equal opportunity to work at the fullest capacity of their skills. . . . Educational, economic, and health conditions must be equalized for *all* peoples."[7] This was the premise of the 1966 Freedom Budget, an economic manifesto developed by A. Philip Randolph that was endorsed by all the major civil rights organizations, including the SNCC and CORE. The Freedom Budget revived the concept of a universal, egalitarian welfare state that had been moribund since the 1940s. It proposed a guaranteed annual income for all the poor; public investments in housing, health care, and education; and a full-employment economy. Civil rights leaders regarded the Freedom Budget as the foundation for civil rights, stating that it would "achieve the freedom from economic want and oppression which is the necessary complement to freedom from political and civil oppression." Randolph insisted that racial equality was impossible without broad economic equality for Black and white workers. The budget failed to gain traction with the Johnson administration, Congress, or the broader public, but it represented a clear commitment to the idea that civil rights and economic justice cannot be separated.[8]

THE FANTASY OF REHABILITATION AND ITS CONSEQUENCES

The Freedmen's Bureau, the Resettlement Administration/Farm Security Administration, and the War on Poverty were dedicated to integrating the freed people, tenant farmers, and the victims of Jim Crow and Northern racism into a market economy by extending equality of opportunity to them. As a set of cultural practices, rehabilitation embodied normative assumptions about what was necessary to integrate individuals into the economic opportunities presumably awaiting them. Its policies and practices were predicated on assisting individuals to become self-supporting citizens who were motivated to pull themselves up the economic ladder. All three agencies were predicated on opposition to relief or social welfare and preached the mantra of self-support and uplift. Rehabilitation underpinned the contract regime of the Freedmen's Bureau, OEO's job training and community action policies, and the loan and grant programs of the FSA. In each case, the goal was to create independent democratic citizens who, as Judith Shklar observed in writing about the political culture of the 1830s, would "not only be respected for working, they also [would have] a right to self-improvement, to education and unblocked opportunity for self-advancement."[9] Yet even though all three agencies justified their mission and legitimacy in the unmistakable terms of America's liberal political culture—uplift, individual success—their policies generated opposition from both Blacks and Southern whites.

White Southerners' visceral dislike of the Freedmen's Bureau stemmed from their belief that the agency, an arm of a hated and oppressive federal government, was an obstacle to their power and control over freedmen. In the 1960s, OEO impeded the goal of many white Southerners to drive Blacks out of the South; it represented a threat to white rule that had to be either contained or co-opted. During the New Deal, white planters and merchant bankers tolerated the FSA so long as it poured federal dollars into the South, but ultimately they turned against the agency. Southern Democrats replaced it with the Farmers Home Administration, an agency that became a tool of Southern whites for discriminating against Black farmers and driving them off the land.

Blacks saw these agencies as supporting their aspirations for independence and freedom, but invariably they opposed agency policies that they believed were thwarting their struggle for freedom. Their vision of their future derived from the fusion of demands for autonomy and freedom with the necessary ingredients for success—education and economic independence—forged in the antebellum struggle for abolition of slavery. In welding antiracism to Black economic independence, Black abolitionists appropriated the elements of antiprivilege egalitarianism, the Jacksonian antimonopoly credo, and turned it into a cry for Black freedom. Inspired by this vision, freedmen objected to the Freedmen's Bureau's contract regime and demanded land they could own and farm free of white control. It launched their struggle after Reconstruction to acquire land and build enclaves that gave them a measure of independence. It underpinned Blacks' demand for land reform in the 1930s. And it was behind Southern civil rights activists' opposition to OEO policies for representation on community action agency boards. Local civil rights activists believed, correctly, that white control or token representation on a CAA board obstructed their access to and influence over the distribution of federal resources.

As a policy strategy intended to open paths to economic independence, rehabilitation failed. This policy failure was endogenous. None of the agencies could deliver the promised independence and upward mobility to Blacks. Administrators assumed there was no conflict between cultivating economically independent citizens and reordering the Southern economy, though skeptics of these assumptions abounded: Freedmen's Bureau agents, who understood that land redistribution was the foundation of independence; the Southern Tenant Farmers Union and Black critics of the Farm Security administration, who challenged the failure of the New Deal to confront the reality of tenancy's exploitation and to redistribute land; and the critics of the War on Poverty in the South, who understood that Sargent Shriver's vision of integration was paternalistic and self-defeating.

The agencies did not fail because of administrative incompetence: all were run by capable and even creative administrators who were able to learn and adapt to the hostile environment of the Deep South, albeit not always successfully. O. O. Howard worked to rescind or at least delay President Andrew Johnson's orders to return land to former Confederate owners and to defend the bureau. He presided over policy changes calculated to shift leverage from planters to freedmen. Rexford Tugwell centralized power within the Resettlement Administration and evaded, insofar as he could, planter interference over the loan and grant program. Agency administrators used loans and grants with written contracts to minimize planter control over credit, and thus over tenants. where they could. Sargent Shriver proved willing and able to defy Southern governors trying to undermine the War on Poverty.

Rehabilitation failed in part because it was subordinated to economic and political agendas that had little chance to succeed absent massive federal investment in the Deep South and a commitment to establishing Black autonomy and power beyond formal political rights: that is, giving Blacks the steam to put in motion the "machinery of liberty" that Frederick Douglass said was missing from Reconstruction. The Freedmen's Bureau and most radical Republicans understood free labor as the need for fair wage-labor contracts instead of subsidized land purchases that would have established Black autonomy. The agency preferred a contract regime to land distribution, and Republicans, including most radicals, had no intention of investing federal money to secure the freed people's independence.

OEO's commitment to participation of the poor in administering antipoverty programs is usually assumed to have been based on the need to cultivate an agency constituency. But in the Deep South, Shriver's understanding of what integration required undermined a significant measure of Black control over CAA programs and federal resources. OEO's inability to set up viable policies of representation for CAA boards set Blacks in opposition to agency policies and facilitated co-optation of the civil rights movement in the Deep South.

The RA/FSA was different mainly because it operated under Jim Crow rules and was limited by Southern political power within the New Deal coalition. The doctrine of rehabilitation peddled by agency administrators masked its underlying purpose—keeping tenants displaced by New Deal agricultural policies from moving to cities. It was the handmaiden for the emergence of capital-intensive agriculture in the South. Independence was reduced to the idea that tenants were independent when they could pay off their loans. And many did, especially Black farmers. But neither Black tenants nor Black farm owners received a proportional share of either FSA loans or grants. Nor did the Farm Credit Administration loans do anything to help Black farmers purchase land or refinance their mortgages.

The most significant failure of all these policies lies in the underlying cultural assumptions of rehabilitation. Foremost is the assumption of Black deficiency, an assumption that derives from the belief, accepted by abolitionists, Freedmen's Bureau agents, and twentieth-century reformers, that slavery and Jim Crow had damaged Blacks, rendering them incapable of freedom, deficient in the capacity for independence and moral judgment. Freedmen's Bureau agents saw freed people as a damaged underclass, in need of guidance and supervision, who were incapable of becoming independent farmers. If

Blacks refused to sign contracts, Freedmen's Bureau agents assumed they were not rational economic actors and preferred "dependence" to labor. In refusing to supply freedmen with capital for their farms, Howard saw his policy as an antidote to dependence.

RA and FSA administrators and agents believed that tenancy had reduced most tenants to a state of docile dependency that left them capable of only subsistence farming. Instead of confronting how Southern tenancy ruthlessly exploited tenants, RA officials dwelled on tenants' cultural deficiencies and assumed that stringent supervision of their farming and household practices would put them on the road to success. Black tenants were more likely to be on the receiving end of close supervision. But the RA undermined the very premise of its policies by relegating tenants to subsistence farming, a practice grounded in the administration's decision to subordinate RA/FSA loans and grants to their price-parity agricultural policies.

OEO's community action program was premised on participation of clients, but this did not mean autonomous control of agencies. Shriver's integration policies tied Black activists to shared control with white segregationists or so-called moderates, paternalists who were intent on taming the civil rights movement. Some OEO staff assumed that rural Blacks lacked the capacity to set up and administer programs. No one characterized the trap of rehabilitation as well as Mrs. Thelma Barnes of the Child Development Group of Mississippi. Shriver, she believed, had betrayed Black people and his own commitment to improving their lives. Defending what CDGM had accomplished, she told OEO administrators during a meeting, "We have tried to run a program of which OEO can be proud. We agree that there has been a slippage of control. This is the first non-paternalistic relationship we have had with our Government. Our people are feeling their self-worth."[10] But Shriver ignored her and pulled the plug on CDGM.

A second failure of the doctrine of rehabilitation was its evasion of issues of power and conflicts of interest. Administrators and agents in the Freedmen's Bureau and the War on Poverty often assumed the interests of Blacks and Southern whites were harmonious, even in the face of white intransigence. Inclined to extol the virtues of cooperation between white planters and freedmen, or white segregationists and Black civil rights activists, to justify their agencies, Howard and Shriver often sounded plainly naive. Black people minced no words in telling both Howard and Shriver that they misunderstood the power struggle the agencies faced.

Freedmen's Bureau agents scrupulously administered formally equal-wage or share contracts, assuming these would result in a fair exchange, but freedmen and many agents recognized that such contracts gave the advantage in any bargain to planters, who clearly exploited it. Shriver did much the same thing in setting up CAAs in the South. He believed that the overriding goal of agency representation and control was integration, and therefore considered that Black control was as much a form of segregation as white control. Civil rights activists repeatedly told Shriver he misunderstood the nature of Black-white relationships in the South and that he was undermining any chance of success for the Southern War on Poverty. His assumption that integration required a measure of formal equality between white segregationists and Black civil rights activists often enabled Southern whites to either assume control or co-opt some Blacks into supporting the agency. Black representation was further undermined by OEO's policy favoring multicounty over single-county agencies.

Confronted by white Southern opposition and efforts to undermine federal policies, along with Black demands for changes in agency practices, all three agencies abandoned any semblance of formal equality. Faced with rampant cheating by planters, the Freedmen's Bureau turned toward regulating Southern labor markets. They tried to enforce quit rights for the freedmen, transported Black farmers to high-wage parts of the South, and adopted a policy of a living wage for freedmen and their families by giving freedmen legal claims to a share of the crop. The bureau's educational policies increased Black literacy but never reached into the rural counties of the Deep South. The FSA threw its weight on the side of tenants and tried to give them leverage against rapacious planters and merchant bankers with their loan policies and written contracts. OEO never abandoned its insistence on integrated CAA boards, but its staff did try to place militants on boards and forestall control by segregationists, even to the extent of dismantling some agencies. Shriver also proved willing to fund dedicated program grants for Black farmers and employment training projects that avoided Southern white control. Rural single-county CAAs in the Deep South were able to attract significant federal resources and invest them in Black communities at a time when it mattered.

None of these shifts in policy compensated for the inherent weakness of rehabilitation as a viable policy strategy to undo the devastating legacies of slavery and Jim Crow. Structural power undermines the very logic of reform liberalism. For many Blacks the insufficiency of rehabilitation was a betrayal of the promises of the two Reconstructions and thus an unjust restitution for their victimization. The meaning of justice, Judith Shklar insists, can be deciphered only by asking what constitutes injustice. And that requires taking account of the beliefs of victims. In a democracy, she writes, "the sense of injustice is taken to be an intrinsic part of our moral structure and an appropriate reaction to unwarranted social deprivation," and this means "crediting the voice of the victims." Injustice is a matter of betrayal, of broken promises that amount to "acts of public wrongdoing." The failure to distribute land to the freed people was a broken promise. So was OEO's failure to establish Black control of community action agencies to the extent possible. Shklar adds that paternalism leads directly to a sense of injustice, since it "begins with a view of the poor as so defective as to have no understanding of their own welfare."[11] In this regard, the idea of rehabilitation, despite the intentions of reformers but from the point of view of recipients, is itself unjust.

With rehabilitation, the sense of injustice was compounded by a related failure of any policy of equal opportunity. It is common for whites to ascribe continued racial inequality to the failure of Blacks to take advantage of the opportunities opened to them in the 1960s. Continued high rates of Black poverty and unemployment are the result, they say, not of racism but of a dysfunctional Black culture. John Schaar predicted this outcome. The canonical idea of equality of opportunity and the assumption that it gives people opportunities to develop their talents fully cause those who fail to suffer harsh judgment. "It leaves the losers," he wrote, "with no external justification for their failures, and no amount of trying can erase the large element of cruelty from any doctrine which does that."[12] The irony of rehabilitation is that it is incapable of providing individuals with economic independence and success, since it evades the structural impediments to opportunity but exposes those who lose to opprobrium. After the civil rights era, the doctrine provided a way for many white people to absolve themselves of any responsibility for durable racial inequality.

OVERCOMING DURABLE RACIAL INEQUALITY

The idea of equality of opportunity remains popular among Americans of all political persuasions but a matter of contentious disagreement among academics and intellectuals. Over three-quarters of Americans agree that society should do whatever is necessary to promote equal opportunities for individuals to succeed, and they reject, at least in public opinion surveys, policies that would lead to equal outcomes.[13] Over the last fifty years, equality of opportunity has generated a multitude of policy approaches from both conservatives and liberals, along with curt dismissals of the idea as a cover for a dog-eat-dog market economy.

I do not believe that any measure of racial justice is attainable unless it is based on equality of opportunity. The issue is what we mean by that idea and what kind of policies it should entail. No policies or programs will succeed in reducing inequality between whites and Blacks without efforts to overcome the structural impediments to opportunity— the privileges and institutional rules that sustain racial inequality—and enlarge the capacity of all Black people to choose how they will live. This is the point that Black leaders and activists have made over and over, from abolitionists to the Negro agrarians to the Black members of the two Southern tenants' unions to the civil rights movement to Black Lives Matter.

Almost all contemporary theories of equality of opportunity are indebted to the Whig conception of reform liberalism. Whigs based their conception of equality of opportunity on an early version of meritocracy and assumed that hard-working, talented individuals could climb up the economic ladder. They did not believe their rise would lead to deeply rooted economic inequality, because upward and downward mobility would even out. This might have been a plausible assumption in the 1830s, when Daniel Webster was preaching the virtues of reform liberalism, or even in the 1850s, but it was scotched by the rise of corporations by 1900.[14] The modern version of the Whig model of upward mobility accepts that it is a formula for inequality but tries to even out the chances for success, either by tinkering with the starting line or by redistributing opportunity to those who find themselves at the bottom of the ladder through no fault of their own. Luck egalitarianism, which has been endorsed by both mainstream liberals and putative socialists, divides the population between those whose social and economic advantages allow them the opportunity for upward mobility and those who are trapped at the bottom by external circumstance. The task of the omniscient equal opportunity planner is to turn the dials of opportunity in favor of the latter to compensate for the advantages of the former.[15] But these contemporary notions of equality of opportunity end up, paradoxically, demolishing any distinction between opportunity and results, as the approach requires enormous financial resources and an unlimited range of justified policies to succeed. In the end, it offers individuals only an equal chance to become unequal.

The Whig conception of equality of opportunity and its modern successors suffer from two fatal flaws. First, they generate resentment on the part of losers and arrogance on the part of winners. Those who make it to the top are inclined to see their success as due to their personal qualities—their superiority to others and their work ethic—but this self-righteous belief breeds resentment. Michael Sandel argues that the rise of angry populist resentment in America can be traced to the elites who created the "conditions that have eroded the dignity of work and left many feeling disrespected and disempowered."[16] Such arrogance among the winners is unwarranted, of course, since it is next to impossible to distinguish advantages of social class and family from ostensible indicators of merit such as standardized test scores. Moreover, with respect to the advantages of family and social class, any efforts to equalize the starting line, as Joseph Fishkin points out, only amplifies "past inequalities of opportunity." He characterizes the contemporary model as similar to a "big test society" in which future opportunities are defined by tests given to sixteen-year-old students. In a big test society, life is just a race, with zero-sum outcomes between competing individuals and in which being white or wealthy gives some individuals the edge.[17]

These flaws are compounded for African Americans. There is no reason to suppose that adjusting starting lines, using the algorithms of luck egalitarianism, or devising new policies to uplift individuals can compensate for African Americans' long history of exploitation or eliminate durable racial inequality. But is there a viable alternative? When combined with a more generous and universal welfare state and investment in Black communities, antiprivilege egalitarianism may offer a path forward. In effect, I advocate combining my conception of antiprivilege egalitarianism, which embodies Amartya Sen's capability approach, with redistribution of income, whether that takes the form of reparations to Blacks or public investment in Black communities and robust social welfare policies.

Antiprivilege egalitarianism attacks the structure of opportunities and seeks undo the structural impediments to individual development and opportunity. That was the Jacksonians' insight, one that Black abolitionists appropriated. The refusal of Republicans and the Freedmen's Bureau to aggressively redistribute land, whether through confiscation or subsidized land purchases, drastically limited the opportunities open to freed people. Great Society liberals made public investment in Black communities a priority and tied this to policies of formal equality that outlawed discrimination but did little to alter the structure of opportunities other than expanding public employment, which many Blacks took advantage of. Like Joseph Fishkin, I think we need to shift our focus "away from the decisions and perspectives of an individual actor and toward the shape of the overall opportunity structure."[18] But such efforts will succeed only if the vast disparities in income, wealth, and status in American society are substantially reduced, since white racial resentment feeds off class inequality.

Instead of trying to equalize starting lines, if that were even possible, we should shift our efforts to removing what Fishkin calls "bottlenecks" to economic opportunity. College entrance exams, for example, are a bottleneck that results in zero-sum competition, and given the ability of wealthy families to game the system, they change nothing. This bottleneck just narrowed with the end of affirmative action for college admissions. Bottlenecks are similar to unjust privileges; both are structural roadblocks to opportunity, and both diminish the life chances of individuals who face limited or nonexistent opportunities because of poverty, poor health, and racial discrimination and segregation, among other obstacles.[19]

The Jacksonians understood privileges as unjust legal and political advantages, but in the twenty-first century, privileges are not just legal but amount to exclusive "ways of taking advantage of the system," according to Pierre Rosanvallon. He defines privilege today as a "form of asymmetry in the relation of individuals to rules and institutions."[20] Some of these asymmetries are rooted in law—noncompete clauses in labor contracts, for example—but not all. The residential segregation of Blacks is the legacy of putatively neutral but effectively racist housing policies enacted during the New Deal that have resulted in large racial differences in home ownership and wealth accumulation long after the policies were repudiated. Another example of a contemporary unjust privilege or bottleneck is Charles Tilly's concept of opportunity hoarding, a phenomenon characteristic of modern labor markets: the ability of groups to monopolize resources or access to jobs or even occupations and exclude others. Opportunity hoarding is a compelling explanation for the persistence of labor-market discrimination. White advantages in labor or housing markets can become self-reinforcing leading to cumulative inequalities.[21]

The theory of racial accumulation and disaccumulation offers a broad-gauged way of thinking about the problem of unjust privileges and of how durable color lines are formed and reproduced over time. Whites can accumulate advantages in labor and housing markets that lead to higher incomes and wealth. To the extent that these advantages come at the expense of Blacks through labor-market discrimination or housing segregation, there is a corresponding process of disaccumulation or disinvestment in Black communities. The upshot is that Blacks are denied their full share of the gains of economic growth and are prevented from pursuing flourishing lives.[22] There is no more graphic example of this process than the history of Black landowning in the South. Land was at the center of Blacks' visions of autonomy and self-determination, and it remains so today. Yet despite their heroic and successful efforts to acquire land in the first decades of the twentieth century, Black farmers faced whitecapping, dispossession through theft, and the predatory and discriminatory actions of the Farmer's Home Administration. One recent estimate places the value of Black land lost to dispossession and discrimination between 1920 (the peak of Black landownership) and 1997 at $326 billion.[23] Much of this loss occurred after 1945 at the hands of the Farmers Home Administration. The federal government has yet to compensate those farmers who lost their land. Recent efforts at redress have been struck down by courts on grounds that they amount to reverse discrimination.

This brings me to a key flaw in most theories of equality of opportunity, including Fishkin's otherwise compelling theory of opportunity pluralism: they leave out issues of power and agency. Achieving genuine equality of opportunity is not a bloodless, benign process: it is always about power and control. Some bottlenecks or privileges may be removed without severe conflict, but the main obstacles to Black opportunity pose questions of redistribution, the diminution of white advantages in labor or housing markets, and questions about fairness. The tortured history of housing discrimination under the auspices of government officials, from local mayors to presidents of the United States, illuminates the difficulties of attempting to go beyond formal equality of opportunity to a vigorous campaign based on antiprivilege egalitarianism. Even after Congress outlawed overt housing discrimination, many cities used zoning laws to perpetuate white neighborhoods.[24] Today, the political and judicial obstacles to a full-throated campaign to attack structural racism are formidable.

A second issue pertains to money. Fishkin argues that opportunity cannot be reduced to money: human development requires dismantling the bottlenecks that prevent individuals from acquiring the skills and personal attributes that would allow them to flourish. That may be true, but doing so requires public investments in education, health care, and housing, along with social policies that can support all citizens in leading successful, prosperous lives. No program of antiprivilege egalitarianism can succeed absent policies of redistribution. John Rawls's theory of justice combined the idea of equal opportunity with the "difference principle," the idea any inequalities in a society should be to the benefit of the least advantaged members of the society. The difference principle may be unworkable as a policy principle, but there are certainly examples of capacious universal welfare states that endeavor to create and sustain the conditions in which their citizens can flourish. Genuine equality of opportunity for Blacks, indeed for all citizens, is impossible without greater social and economic equality across American society.

Racial justice demands public restitution to Black communities. This could be achieved through reparations to individuals for their long history of exploitation, public investment in Black communities, or some combination of both. Such investment is needed to compensate for and reverse the longstanding disinvestment in Black communities in big cities and the rural South. The initial versions of President Joe Biden's American Jobs Plan and the Build Back Better bill included investments directed to Black communities and other communities of color. Proposals for reparations are now before the California state legislature and the San Francisco Board of Supervisors, among other jurisdictions. Such restitution is not only a matter of justice. It is necessary to create a society where African Americans and their fellow citizens have the autonomy and resources to fully develop their human abilities—to cultivate "their physical, intellectual, aesthetic, and moral faculties," just as Black and white abolitionists demanded.

Equality of opportunity in America today is not just about enabling people to climb the ladder of success, grab the brass ring, or take the main chance. It is about building a multicultural democracy that allows *all* its citizens to flourish and receive the respect they are due. Martin Luther King Jr.'s vision of what equality could be still resonates and should inform any discussion. He envisioned not an emaciated version of a color-blind society but one where citizens could prosper regardless of their race or social class. I am under no illusions about the difficulty of building a society where, as Dr. King demanded, whites abandon, their "ontological affirmation . . . that the very being of a people is inferior" and a just restitution for the sins of America's racist past is made. But the arc of history will not bend toward justice unless we bend it.

Appendix

LINEAR REGRESSION TABLES

TABLE A.1 Allocation of Farm Security Administration loans and grants, FY1935–FY1939

	Coefficient	Std Error	t-Value	P>[t]
Change in number of Black share managers, 1930–35	−79.51449	23.94185	−3.32	0.001
Number of single-unit farms, 1940	38.47781	4.67968	8.22	0.000
Cotton acreage, 1935 (number of acres)	−0.6743524	0.271543	−2.48	0.013
Plantation acres, 1940 (percent)	−2088.322	3337.21	−0.63	0.532
Arkansas	−464.3201	16632.32	−0.03	0.978
Georgia	−68337.4	14274.48	−4.79	0.000
Louisiana	−58525.85	15559.88	−3.76	0.000
Mississippi	−40411.8	13471.18	−3	0.003
South Carolina	−28723.12	15318.04	−1.88	0.062
Constant (Alabama)	126509	16628.32	7.61	0.000

SOURCE: Deep South New Deal Dataset.
$N = 383$.
R-squared = 0.3966. Adjusted R-squared = 0.3821.

TABLE A.2 Change in number of full farm owners by race and type of loan, 1935–45

	White full farm owners			
	Coefficient	Standard error	t-value	P>[t]
FCA loans for land (log)*	80.81535	19.85265	4.07	0.000
FCA emergency loans (log)	−21.61212	14.55593	−1.48	0.139
Rural rehabilitation loans (log)	22.09894	22.48759	0.98	0.327
Tenant purchase loans (log)	26.13927	19.94487	1.31	0.191
% cotton acreage, 1935*	405.2196	195.6181	2.07	0.039
% Black farmers, 1935*	−384.9447	47.68584	−8.07	0.000
Farm failures per number of owners, 1934	−0.000215	0.0133096	−0.02	0.987
Resettlement projects**	38.22479	22.36222	1.71	0.088
Arkansas	−35.58086	44.34024	−0.8	0.423
Georgia	−18.8573	37.23803	−0.51	0.613
Louisiana*	−98.59357	43.23736	−2.28	0.023
Mississippi	−12.81465	33.73585	−0.38	0.704
South Carolina	−0.1640892	47.94645	0	0.997
Constant (Alabama)*	−983.9112	307.0616	−3.2	0.002
	Black full farm owners			
FCA loans for land (log)	5.468788	6.793603	0.8	0.421
FCA emergency crop loans (log)	5.629961	4.980921	1.13	0.259
Rural rehabilitation loans (log)*	15.35447	7.695283	2	0.047
Tenant purchase loans (log)	−9.654785	6.805163	1.41	0.158
% Cotton acreage, 1935*	−170.7638	66.94079	−2.55	0.011
% Black farmers, 1935*	81.14915	16.31816	4.97	0.000
Farm failures per number of owners, 1934*	−0.009174	0.0045546	−2.01	0.045
Resettlement projects	6.156187	7.652384	0.8	0.422
Arkansas**	5.203521	15.17329	0.34	0.0732
Georgia	−6.262732	12.7429	−0.49	0.623
Louisiana	−10.43862	14.79588	−0.71	0.481
Mississippi**	20.39017	11.54445	1.77	0.078
South Carolina	−14.51832	16.40734	−0.88	0.377
Constant (Alabama)**	−184.4147	105.0769	−1.76	0.08

SOURCE: Deep South New Deal Dataset.
$N = 312$.
White Farm Owners: R-Squared = 0.3160; Adjusted R-Squared = 0.2862
Black Farm Owners: R-Squared = 0.1746; Adjusted R-Squared = 0.1386
*$p < 0.05$.
**$p < 0.10$.

TABLE A.3 Per capita OEO dollars by type of CAA

	Coefficient	Std. error	t-value	P>|t|
Type of agency: single- vs. multicounty*	37.67348	11.49358	3.28	0.002
Percent Black population, 1960	73.12068	45.13405	1.62	0.109
Family income < $3,000, 1960	−0.6963562	0.7765498	−0.9	0.373
Percent Black farm owners	18.57101	62.44122	0.3	0.767
Ratio of agricultural to manufacturing jobs*	8.407521	3.61109	2.33	0.023
Alabama	−10.90473	14.63566	−0.75	0.459
Georgia	−20.20579	15.7176	−1.29	0.203
Louisiana*	−48.57956	16.40415	−2.96	0.004
South Carolina	−30.81313	17.04013	−1.81	0.075
Constant (Mississippi)	49.05221	39.39583	1.25	0.217

SOURCE: Deep South CAA County Dataset.
N = 84 CAAs
*p < 0.03.
R-squared = 0.4516. Adjusted R-squared = 0.3849.

STATISTICAL MODELS (LINEAR REGRESSION)

Distribution of FSA Loans and Grants

In estimating the allocation of FSA loans and grants for the period FY1935–FY1939, I hypothesized that the FSA allocated funds to counties where enclosure resulted in a significant decrease in the number of Black share managers, and to single-unit farms. The equation for this model is

$$Y = a + B_1{}^*X_1 + B_2{}^*X_2 + B_3{}^*X_3 + B_4{}^*X_4 + B_5{}^*X_5 + e$$

where Y is the value of total FSA loans and grants allocated to a county. X_1 is the decline in the number of Black share managers in a county from 1930 to 1935; X_2 is the number of single-unit farms in a county in 1940; X_3 is the 1935 cotton acreage in a county; X_4 is the 1940 percentage of plantation acreage in a county; X_5 is a categorical variable for state effects; and e is an error term. Because data for the number of single-unit farms and plantation acreage are not available for 1935, I have used the data from a survey of plantations included in the 1940 US Census. Since there was a very small decline in cotton acreage between 1935 and 1940, and the price of cotton plummeted after 1935, the 1940 data are a reasonable approximation of the 1935 values. This statistical analysis includes the state of Arkansas, as it is part of the analysis of the FSA in chapter 3.

Change in the Number of Black and White Landowners, 1935–45

In this analysis, I explain the increase in the number of Black and white landowners in the ten years after 1935 as a function of four New Deal credit programs created to assist farmers. I converted the four financial variables to log variables and estimated separate linear-log models for each type of farm owner. The equation for this model is

$$Y = a + B_1*\ln(X_1) + B_2*\ln(X_2) + B_3*\ln(X_3) + B_4*\ln(X_4) + B_5*X_5 + B_6*X_6 + B_7*X_7 + B_8*X_8 + B_9*X_9 + e$$

where Y is the increase in the number of Black or White landowners in a county from 1935 to 1945; X_1 is the value of FCA land loans; X_2 is the value of FCA emergency loans; X_3 is the value of FSA rural rehabilitation loans; and X_4 is the value of FSA tenant purchase loans. X_5 through X_9 are control variables. X_5 is the percent of 1935 cotton acreage; X_6 is the percent of Black or white farm operators, 1935; X_7 is the percent of farm failures of farm owners in 1934; X_8 is a dummy variable, where 1 equals the presence of a resettlement project in a county and 0 its absence; X_9 is a categorical variable for state effects; and e is an error term.

Distribution of CAA Dollars, FY1965–FY1971

In this model, I estimate the distribution of total CAA dollars as a function of the type of funding agency. I hypothesize that per capita OEO funding will be significantly higher in areas with single-county agencies than those with multicounty agencies. The unit of analysis is CAA agency service areas, single or multicounty, rather than counties. The equation for this model is

$$Y = a + B_1*X_1 + B_2*X_2 + B_3*X_3 + B_4*X_4 + B_5*X_5 + B_6*X_6 + e$$

where Y is total OEO dollars per capita in an agency service area, from 1965 to 1971; X_1 is a dummy variable, where 1 equals single-county agencies and 0 equals multicounty agencies. X_2 through X_6 are control variables. X_2 is the percent population who were Black in in an agency service area 1960; X_3 is the percent of families with an annual income of $3,000 or less in 1960; X_4 is the percent of Black landowners; X_5 is the ratio of agricultural jobs to manufacturing jobs in 1964; X_6 is a categorical variable for state effects; and e is an error term.

DATASET SOURCES

Reconstruction: Union Troops Dataset

The data on Union troops are drawn from Gregory P. Downs, *After Appomattox: Military Occupation and the Ends of War* (Cambridge, MA: Harvard University

Press, 2015). Downs's data on Union troop movements and locations are coded according to the location of army outposts. These data are estimates drawn from army records of troop deployments, and they should be treated with caution. Downs's methodology can be found in Gregory P. Downs and Scott Nesbit, *Mapping Occupation: Force, Freedom, and the Army in Reconstruction* (2015), (http://mappingoccupation.org).

I reaggregated these data by county for the five Deep South states that are the focus of this study. For each month beginning in May 1865, Downs reports the total number of troops in each state and the number in different outposts. I have built my county-level database from raw troop counts in outposts and regions. My totals are the total count of troops in Deep South counties. My state totals differ from those of Downs, especially for May and June 1865. As Downs explains, the exact location and department of many troops were uncertain at the end of the war. That said, the numbers and locations stabilized as Reconstruction took hold, and there is less discrepancy. (Downs, personal communication, December 11, 2015).

Reconstruction: Freedmen's Bureau Dataset

Data on Freedmen's Bureau agents are drawn from John A. Carpenter's unpublished study of the Freedmen's Bureau. The data are available at the Schomburg Center for Research in Black Culture, New York City Public Library, ScMG Box 4. The dataset is based on all 2,442 Freedmen's Bureau agents. Carpenter derived his data from Freedmen's Bureau records of agents' letters sent to assistant commissioners, reports of their superiors and bureau inspectors, and biographical data drawn from pension records. His data on the number of agents in each state differs from figures given in most historical accounts, which are based on assistant commissioners' manifests. Carpenter recorded agents' dates of enlistment instead of the number of agents on duty. That approach, combined with the rapid turnover of agents during the first six months, may account for the differences. In any case, appropriate caution must be taken in interpreting these data.

Deep South New Deal Dataset

This dataset combines federal expenditure data with demographic and political data for all Deep South counties. The unit of analysis is the county. These data were used for the quantitative analysis of the Farm Security Administration and the Southern enclosure. The data are drawn from the following sources:

1. *Report No. 10, Vol. 1: County Reports of Federal Expenditures;* March 1933–June 1939. United States Office of Government Reports, Statistical Section, 1940.

2. *Final Statistical Report of the Federal Emergency Relief Administration,* Works Progress Administration. Washington, DC: US Government Printing Office, 1942, table 14.
3. Charles S. Johnson, *Statistical Atlas of Southern Counties: Listing and Analysis of Socio-economic Indices of 1104 Southern Counties.* Chapel Hill: University of North Carolina Press, 1941.
4. Mary G. Rolinson, *Grassroots Garveyism* (Chapel Hill: University of North Carolina Press, 2007), 197–99.
5. Michael R. Haines, Historical, Demographic, Economic, and Social Data: The United States, 1790–2002. Inter-university Consortium for Political and Social Research [distributor], 2010-05-21. ICPSR 02896. V. 3; US Censuses for 1930 and 1940.
6. Michael Haines, Price Fishback, and Paul Rhode, United States Agriculture Data, 1840–2012, Inter-university Consortium for Political and Social Research ICPSR35206, v. 4, August 20, 2018, https://doi.org/10.3886/ICPSR35206.v4; US Agricultural Censuses for 1930, 1935, 1940, and 1945.

Deep South CAA County and FY1968 Dataset

The unit of analysis in this data set is community action agency (CAA) service areas rather than counties. Data on county-level demographic, occupational, non-OEO expenditures (e.g., child welfare grants) have been aggregated to CAA service areas. Any agency with two or more counties includes the total of non-OEO data of each variable for all counties served by that agency. Single-county agencies include only data for the specific county. Data from the FY1968 expenditures database have been integrated into the data set. Data are drawn from the following sources:

1. Community Action Program, Funded Program Account and Grantee Organization Master Files, 1964–1971, RG 381, NARA.
2. Federal Outlays, FY1967–1980, NN3-381-73-157, RG 381, NARA.
3. Michael R. Haines and Inter-university Consortium for Political and Social Research, Historical, Demographic, Economic, and Social Data: The United States, 1790–2002. Inter-university Consortium for Political and Social Research, May 21, 2010. ICPSR 02896. v. 3; US Censuses for 1960 and 1970; County Data Book, 1962, 1967.
4. Michael Haines, Price Fishback, and Paul Rhode, United States Agriculture Data, 1840–2012, Inter-university Consortium for Political and Social Research ICPSR35206, v. 4, August 20, 2018, https://doi.org/10.3886/ICPSR35206.v4; US Agricultural Census, 1964.

Black and White Landowners Dataset

Michael Haines, Price Fishback, and Paul Rhode, United States Agriculture Data, 1840–2012, Inter-university Consortium for Political and Social Research ICPSR35206, v. 4, August 20, 2018, https://doi.org/10.3886/ICPSR35206.v4; US Agricultural Censuses for 1900, 1910, 1920, 1925.

NOTES

INTRODUCTION

1. King, *Where Do We Go from Here?*, 8; "The Other America," speech by Martin Luther King Jr., April 14, 1967, Aurora Forum, Stanford University, 4–5. The history of white backlash is powerfully rendered by Carol Anderson, *White Rage: The Unspoken Truth of Our Racial Divide* (New York: Bloomsbury USA, 2016).

2. Zackary Okun Dunivin, Harry Yaojun Yan, Jelani Ince, and Fabio Rojas, "Black Lives Matter Protests Shift Public Discourse," *PNAS* 119, no. 10 (2022): 1–11. The number of whites who consider racism a matter of public concern has declined somewhat since the summer of 2020, but the change in beliefs has persisted. See Carrie Blazina and Kiana Cook, "Black and White Americans Are Far Apart in Their Views of Reparations for Slavery," PEW Research Center, November 28, 2022, 3, www.pewresearch.org/short-reads/2022/11/28.

3. Quoted in Michael D. Shear, Alan Rappeport, and Stacy Cowley, "Biden's Push for Equity in Government Hits Legal and Political Roadblocks," *New York Times*, June 26, 2021.

4. Judith N. Shklar, *American Citizenship: The Quest for Inclusion* (Cambridge, MA: Harvard University Press, 1991), 8, 13.

5. Exemplary studies include W. E. B. Du Bois, *Black Reconstruction in America, 1860–1880* (New York: Atheneum, 1992); Rogers M. Smith, *Civic Ideals: Conflicting Visions of Citizenship in U.S. History* (New Haven, CT: Yale University Press, 1998); Gretchen Ritter, *The Constitution as Social Design: Gender and Civic Membership in the American Constitutional Order* (Stanford, CA: Stanford University Press, 2006).

6. Jennifer L. Hochschild, *Facing Up to the American Dream: Race, Class, and the Soul of the Nation* (Princeton, NJ: Princeton University Press, 1995), 60; King, *Where Do We Go from Here?*, 8. Hochschild does not analyze the content of Black beliefs about equality, and she begs the question of what different terms mean to each group. She says that both Black and whites endorse "self-sufficiency" but assumes they mean the same thing by the term (55). Melissa Harris-Lacewell points out that

Black self-reliance has a distinctive shared meaning and is clearly distinguished from bootstrapping, or individual self-reliance. Melissa Victoria Harris-Lacewell, *Barbershops, Bibles, and BET: Everyday Talk and Black Political Thought* (Princeton, NJ: Princeton University Press, 2004), 141. Desmond S. King and Rogers M. Smith, *Still a House Divided: Race and Politics in Obama's America* (Princeton, NJ: Princeton University Press, 2011) provides a historical account of "racial policy alliances."

7. *New-York Tribune*, May 25, 1865, quoted in George M. Fredrickson, *The Black Image in the White Mind: The Debate on Afro-American Character and Destiny, 1817–1914* (New York: Harper & Row, 1971), 182. Charles Sumner, "A Bridge from Slavery to Freedom," speech to the Senate of the United States, June 13 and 15, 1864 (Washington, DC: H. Polkinhorn & Son, Printers, 1864), 2. Wyat is quoted in Gerald David Jaynes, *Branches without Roots: Genesis of the Black Working Class in the American South, 1862–1882* (New York: Oxford University Press, 1986), 283.

8. Chimamanda Ngozi Adiche, *Americana* (New York: Anchor, 2014), 341, quoted in Eddie S. Glaude Jr., *Democracy in Black: How Race Still Enslaves the American Soul* (New York: Crown, 2016), 23.

9. Robert L. Carter, "A Reassessment of Brown v. Board," in *Shades of Brown: New Perspectives on School Desegregation*, ed. Derrick Bell (New York: Teachers College, Columbia University, 1980), 23–24, emphasis in original; Michael C. Dawson, *Black Visions: The Roots of Contemporary African American Political Ideologies* (Chicago: University of Chicago Press, 2001), 243, 255.

10. Michael K. Brown, Martin Carnoy, Elliott Currie, Troy Duster, David B. Oppenheimer, Marjorie M. Schultz, and David Wellman, *Whitewashing Race: The Myth of a Color-Blind Society*, 2nd ed. (Oakland: University of California Press, 2023).

11. See William Darity Jr. and A. Kirsten Mullen, *From Here to Equality: Reparations for Black Americans in the Twenty-First Century*, 2nd ed. (Chapel Hill: University of North Carolina Press, 2022); Tommie Shelby, *Dark Ghettos: Injustice, Dissent, and Reform* (Cambridge, MA: Harvard University Press, 2016); Charles W. Mills, *Black Rights/White Wrongs: The Critique of Racial Liberalism* (New York: Oxford University Press, 2017); Melvin Oliver and Thomas Shapiro, *Black Wealth/White Wealth* (New York: Routledge, 1997); Peniel Joseph, *The Third Reconstruction: America's Struggle for Racial Justice in the Twenty-First Century* (New York: Basic Books, 2022).

12. King and Smith, *Still a House Divided*, 17.

13. Lincoln set out his justification for the war in his message to Congress of July 4, 1861. Abraham Lincoln, *Lincoln: Speeches and Writings, 1859–1865* (New York: Library of America, 1989), 259, quote on 624.

14. Abraham Lincoln, "Speech at New Haven, Connecticut, March 6, 1960," in *Lincoln: Speeches and Writings, 1859–1865*, 144; "First Lincoln-Douglas Debate, Ottawa, Illinois," in Abraham Lincoln, *Lincoln: Speeches and Writings, 1832–1858* (New York: Library of America, 1989), 301–2, 512. In his reply to Douglas, Lincoln said that Blacks were entitled to the rights enumerated in the Declaration of Independence as much as any white man. See also Harold Holzer and Norton Garfinkle,

A Just and Generous Nation: Abraham Lincoln and the Fight for American Opportunity (New York: Basic Books, 2015), chapter 3.

15. Remarks to members of the President's Committee on Equal Employment Opportunity, July 7, 1964; remarks at a reception for participants in a planning session for the White House Conference; "To Fulfill These Rights," Commencement address at Howard University, June 4, 1965, all available at American Presidency Project, www.presidency.ucsb.edu/documents.

16. Paul K. Conklin, *FDR and the Origins of the Welfare State* (New York: Thomas Y. Crowell, 1967), 55.

17. Remarks at the White House Conference on Equal Employment Opportunities, August 20, 1965. The War on Poverty encompassed more than just the OEO; it included many of the programs enacted or redirected as part of the Great Society.

18. Imani Perry, *South to America: A Journey below the Mason-Dixon to Understand the Soul of a Nation* (New York: HarperCollins, 2022), 371; George Breitman, ed., *Malcolm Speaks: Selected Speeches and Statements* (New York: Grove Press, 1965), 9. Black acquisition of land was a prominent part of the early calls for reparations for slavery and Jim Crow in the 1960s. See Robin D. G. Kelly, *Freedom Dreams: The Black Radical Imagination* (Boston: Beacon Press, 2002), 120–21, 124–26.

19. Judith N. Shklar, *The Faces of Injustice* (New Haven, CT: Yale University Press, 1990), 83, 108. The sense of injustice, Shklar writes, is "the betrayal that we experience when others disappoint expectations that they have created in us."

20. Du Bois, *Black Reconstruction in America*, 183; W. E. B. Du Bois, *The Souls of Black Folk* (New York: Norton, 1999), 95.

21. Martin Luther King Jr., *Why We Can't Wait* (New York: Signet Classics, 1964), 13; King, *Where Do We Go from Here?*, 8. In his final sermon before his assassination, Dr. King returned to this theme. See "Remaining Awake through a Great Revolution," in James M. Washington, ed., *A Testament of Hope: The Essential Writings of Martin Luther King Jr.* (New York: Harper and Row, 1986), 271.

22. *Proceedings of the National Colored Labor Convention*, Washington, DC, 1869 (Washington, DC: New Era, 1970), 30. Dona C. Hamilton and Charles V. Hamilton, *The Dual Agenda: Race and Social Welfare Policies of Civil Rights Organizations* (New York: Columbia University Press, 1997), 141–52. The Freedom Budget contained policies of benefit to both Blacks and whites, such as a guaranteed income.

23. For a critique of the War on Poverty in the South, see Gavin Wright, *Sharing the Prize: The Economics of the Civil Rights Revolution in the American South* (Cambridge, MA: Harvard University Press, 2013).

24. Leslie McCall, *The Undeserving Rich: American Beliefs about Inequality, Opportunity, and Redistribution* (New York: Cambridge University Press, 2013), 43, 216–17, 224.

25. Frederick Nietzsche, *Basic Writings of Nietzsche*, trans. and ed. Walter Kaufmann (New York: Random House, 1992), 516.

26. Pierre Rosanvallon, *The Society of Equals* (Cambridge, MA: Harvard University Press, 2013); Nick Bromell, "Where the Distinction between Action and

Knowledge Vanishes: Pierre Rosanvallon's 'Philosophical History of the Political,'" *Political Theory* 44, no. 4 (August 2016): 578–85.

27. Richard Ashcraft, "Liberal Political Theory and Working-Class Radicalism in Nineteenth Century England," *Political Theory* 21, no. 2 (1993): 249–72.

28. Carol A. Horton, *Race and the Making of American Liberalism* (New York: Oxford University Press, 2005), 4–10, 37–60.

29. Sanford F. Schram, "Contextualizing Racial Disparities in American Welfare Reform: Toward a New Poverty Research," *Perspectives on Politics* 3, no. 2 (June 2005): 253–68. I am drawing on insights from Nikhil Pal Singh, *Black Is a Country: Race and the Unfinished Struggle for Democracy* (Cambridge, MA: Harvard University Press, 2004), 42–45, and Thomas C. Holt, *The Problem of Race in the Twenty-First Century* (Cambridge, MA: Harvard University Press, 2002), 76.

30. J. David Greenstone, *The Lincoln Persuasion: Remaking American Liberalism* (Princeton, NJ: Princeton University Press, 1993), 53–55, 59–62; Isaiah Berlin, *Four Essays on Liberty* (New York: Oxford University Press, 1969), 122.

31. Greenstone, *The Lincoln Persuasion*, 44; Lisa Wedeen, "Conceptualizing Culture: Possibilities for Political Science," *American Political Science Review* 96, no. 4 (December 2002): 713–28.

32. Greenstone, *The Lincoln Persuasion*, 59. I am defining rehabilitation as an element of reform liberalism. My conception is broader than simply restoring someone to a previous state, as in the rehabilitation of an individual suffering an injury.

33. Quoted in Greenstone, *The Lincoln Persuasion*, 245.

34. J. David Greenstone, "Against Simplicity: The Cultural Dimensions of the Constitution," *University of Chicago Law Review* 55, no. 2 (Spring 1988): 445, 447–48. We do not know how Greenstone would have addressed the question of the relationship between reform liberalism and race had he been able to do so. He passed away before he finished *The Lincoln Persuasion*. He had planned chapters on Frederick Douglass and Lydia Maria Child that would have permitted him to examine this issue.

35. Shklar, *Faces of Injustice*, 119. This was Isaiah Berlin's concern with positive liberty. The danger, he argued, lies with the capacity of policies based on positive liberty to coerce individuals and with its (apparent) paternalism. Berlin, *Four Essays on Liberty*, 141–54.

36. Philip Green, *Equality and Democracy* (New York: New Press, 1998), 59–61. Green puts the matter succinctly: "Truly equal chances for everyone, but even more importantly, privileges for no one, is the essence of egalitarianism."

37. George is quoted in Herbert McClosky and John Zaller, *The American Ethos: Public Attitudes toward Capitalism and Democracy* (Cambridge, MA: Harvard University Press, 1984), 87.

38. Herbert Croly, *The Promise of American Life* (Boston: Northeastern University Press, 1989), 181, 183.

39. Henry Wallace, quoted in James Holt, "The New Deal and the American Anti-statist Tradition," in *The New Deal: The National Level*, ed. John Braeman,

Robert H. Bremner, and David Brody (Columbus: Ohio State University Press, 1975), 40.

40. Brown et al., *Whitewashing Race*, 186–87, 190–91; McCall, *Undeserving Rich*, 209–213, 217.

41. Amartya Sen, *The Idea of Justice* (Cambridge, MA: Harvard University Press, 2009), 233.

42. Sen, *The Idea of Justice*, 22, 254–55. John E. Roemer, *Equality of Opportunity* (Cambridge, MA: Harvard University Press, 1998), advocates a technocratic solution to the question of equality of opportunity.

43. Franklin Delano Roosevelt, acceptance speech for the renomination for the presidency, Philadelphia, PA, June 27, 1936, www.presidency.ucsb.edu/documents/acceptance-speech-for-the-renomination-for-the-presidency-philadelphia-pa.

44. Sen, *The Idea of Justice*, 146.

45. Charles Postel, *Equality: An American Dilemma, 1866–1896* (New York: Farrar, Straus, and Giroux, 2017).

46. "All forms of political organization have a bias in favor of the exploitation of some kinds of conflict and the suppression of others because *organization is the mobilization of bias.*" E. E. Schattschneider, *The Semisovereign People: A Realist's View of Democracy in America* (New York: Harcourt, Brace, Jovanovich, 1975), 69, emphasis in original. Schattschneider used this idea to analyze the structure of interest-group politics, but it applies to administrative agencies as well. For an application of the idea to an administrative agency, see Martha Derthick, *Policymaking for Social Security* (Washington, DC: Brookings Institution, 1979).

47. Jefferson Cowie, *Freedom's Dominion: A Saga of White Resistance to Federal Power* (New York: Basic Books, 2022), 5, 166. Cowie argues that freedom for Southern whites meant freedom to dominate, and they believed that "any increase in Black freedom meant a decrease in white freedom" (119–20).

48. James D. Schmidt, *Free to Work: Labor Law, Emancipation, and Reconstruction, 1815–1880* (Athens: University of Georgia Press, 1998), 67.

49. Reva Siegel, "Why Equal Protection No Longer Protects: The Evolving Forms of Status-Enforcing State Action," *Stanford Law Review* 49 (1997): 1111–48. The supposition that Blacks were entitled to equality before the law was never a reality before the civil rights revolution.

50. Reva Siegel, "The Racial Rhetorics of Colorblind Constitutionalism: The Case of Hopwood v. Texas," in *Race and Representation: Affirmative Action*, ed. Robert Post and Michael Rogin (New York: Zone Books, 1998), 31–32.

51. Reva Siegel, "Discrimination in the Eyes of the Law: How 'Color Blindness' Discourse Disrupts and Rationalizes Social Stratification," in *Prejudicial Appearances*, edited by Robert Post, K. Anthony Appiah, Judith Butler, Thomas C. Grey, and Reva B. Siegel (Chapel Hill, NC: Duke University Press, 2001), 119–20. Under this concept of equality of opportunity, Siegel notes, "It is the essence of 'individualism' to categorize persons and to discriminate among them on the basis of . . . 'socially relevant characteristics.'" Shklar, *The Faces of Injustice*, 78–82, shows the absurdity of this view.

52. Siegel, "Discrimination in the Eyes of the Law," 132. Racism, in this sense, is "a scavenger ideology, which gains its power from its ability to pick out and utilize ideas and values from other sets of ideas and beliefs in specific socio-historical contexts." John Solomos and Les Black, *Racism and Society* (Basingstoke, UK: Houndsmills Palgrave MacMillan, 1996) 18–19, quoted in George M. Fredrickson, *Racism: A Short History* (Princeton, NJ: Princeton University Press, 2002), 8.

CHAPTER 1. THE POLITICAL INVENTION OF EQUALITY OF OPPORTUNITY

1. Sean Wilentz, *The Rise of American Democracy: Jefferson to Lincoln* (New York: Norton, 2005), 511.
2. Lee J. Benson, *The Concept of Jacksonian Democracy: New York as a Test Case* (Princeton, NJ: Princeton University Press, 1961), 103.
3. Wilentz, *The Rise of American Democracy,* 513; Daniel Walker Howe, *What God Hath Wrought: The Transformation of America, 1815–1848* (New York: Oxford University Press, 2009), 582–83.
4. Gordon S. Wood, *The Radicalism of the American Revolution* (New York: Alfred A. Knopf, 1992), 234; Pierre Rosanvallon, *The Society of Equals* (Cambridge, MA: Harvard University Press, 2013), 12–21.
5. Alexis de Tocqueville, *Democracy in America,* ed. J. P. Mayer, trans. George Lawrence (New York: Doubleday, 1969), 537–38.
6. John Ashworth, *'Agrarians' and 'Aristocrats': Party Political Ideology in the United States, 1837–1846* (New York: Cambridge University Press, 1987), 66. John Schaar, *Equality: Its Bearing on Justice and Liberty* (Washington, DC: American Political Science Association, 1978), 14. Both writers see the Whig conception through the lens of social class, and both neglect the Whigs' emphasis on uplift and rehabilitation.
7. Richard J. Ellis, "Rival Visions of Equality in American Political Culture," *Review of Politics* 52, no. 2 (1992): 261.
8. Hosea Easton, quoted in James Brewer Stewart, "The Emergence of Racial Modernity and the Rise of the White North, 1790–1840," *Journal of the Early Republic* 18, no. 2 (Spring 1998): 217. Easton made the statement in his pamphlet *A Treatise on the Intellectual Character and Civil and Political Condition of the Colored People of the U States* (Boston, 1837).
9. Hannah Arendt, *The Origins of Totalitarianism* (Cleveland, OH: World Publishing, 1958), 300.
10. Henry Highland Garnet, "Speech Delivered at the Seventh Anniversary of the American Anti-slavery Society," *Colored American,* May 30, 1840. Northern Blacks waged vigorous campaigns for their rights in the decades before the Civil War. See Kate Masur, *Until Justice Be Done: America's First Civil Rights Movement, from the Revolution to Reconstruction* (New York: Norton, 2021).

11. Leonard Bacon, quoted in David Brion Davis, *The Problem of Slavery in the Age of Emancipation* (New York: Alfred A. Knopf, 2014), 157.

12. Judith Shklar characterizes standing as a "mark of civic dignity" and recognition. Judith Shklar, *American Citizenship: The Quest for Inclusion* (Cambridge, MA: Harvard University Press, 1991), 2–3; Lacy K. Ford Jr., "Making the 'White Man's Country' White: Race, Slavery, and State-Building in the Jacksonian South," *Journal of the Early Republic* 19 (Winter 1999): 736–37.

13. Alexander Keyssar, *The Right to Vote: The Contested History of Democracy in the United States* (New York: Basic Books, 2000), tables A-3 and A-4, 348–53; Tocqueville, *Democracy in America,* 252–53. Tocqueville recounts a conversation with a man in Philadelphia who admitted that Blacks didn't often vote because of white threats. He cites this anecdote as an example of the tyranny of the majority. Pennsylvania abolished Black voting rights in 1838.

14. Wilentz, *The Rise of American Democracy,* 403; Paul Goodman, *Of One Blood: Abolitionism and the Origins of Racial Equality* (Berkeley: University of California Press, 2000), 37; Davis, *The Problem of Slavery,* 186–88; Manisha Sinha, *The Slave's Cause: A History of Abolition* (New Haven, CT: Yale University Press, 2016), 165.

15. Andrew Jackson, "Of the Reauthorization of the Bank of the United States," July 10, 1832, American Presidency Project, www.presidency.ucsb.edu/documents/veto-message-the-re-authorization-bank-the-united-states, emphasis in original.

16. Quoted in Joseph L. Blau, *Social Theories of Jacksonian Democracy* (New York: Liberal Arts Press, 1954), 25, emphasis added.

17. Joseph Sieyes, quoted in Rosanvallon, *The Society of Equals,* 12.

18. William Leggett, quoted in Blau, *Social Theories,* 68.

19. Daniel Walker Howe, *The Political Culture of the American Whigs* (Chicago: University of Chicago Press, 1979), 153.

20. Daniel Walker Howe, "The Evangelical Moment and Political Culture in the North during the Second Party System," *Journal of American History* 77, no. 4 (1991): 1225; Richard J. Carwardine, *Evangelicals and Politics in Antebellum America* (Knoxville: University of Tennessee Press, 1997), 106. Channing is quoted in Sam Haselby, *The Origins of American Religious Nationalism* (New York: Oxford University Press, 2015), 204, 200. Channing was typical of New England religious nationalists, as Haselby calls them, who believed their reform program would reconstruct the world.

21. Carwardine, *Evangelicals and Politics,* 5–6, 44; Nathan O. Hatch, *The Democratization of American Christianity* (New Haven, CT: Yale University Press, 1989), 3.

22. Hatch, *The Democratization of American Christianity,* 9–11, 36, 101; Carwardine, *Evangelicals and Politics,* 2; Haselby, *Origins of American Religious Nationalism,* 124. Hatch argues that the causal arrow runs from democratic ideology to religious populism, not the other way around. Haselby, however, thinks that rural Protestantism in early America was a protest movement against the loneliness and isolation of the frontier.

23. Hatch, *The Democratization of American Christianity*, 35. As Hatch notes, religious populists railed against Calvinism and were obsessed with religious oppression as much as Jacksonians feared the monster of a US national bank (171–72).

24. Charles Finney, *Autobiography* (Westwood, NJ, 1908) quoted in Howe, *What God Hath Wrought*, 172.

25. Carwardine, *Evangelicals and Politics*, 15, 20, quote from Finney on p. 17. Hatch, *The Democratization of American Christianity*, 195, 199. However, there was also a strong antipolitical strain among evangelicals.

26. Carwardine, *Evangelicals and Politics*, 122–24, 131–32; Howe, "The Evangelical Moment," 1225; Wilentz, *The Rise of American Democracy*, 349; Daniel Feller, "Politics and Society: Toward a Jacksonian Synthesis," *Journal of the Early Republic* 10 (Summer 1990): 154–55.

27. Louis Hartz, *The Liberal Tradition in America: An Interpretation of American Political Thought since the Revolution* (New York: Harcourt, Brace & World, 1955), chapters 4–5; J. David Greenstone, *The Lincoln Persuasion: Remaking American Liberalism* (Princeton, NJ: Princeton University Press, 1993), 45, 52–53.

28. William Leggett, *Democratic Editorials: Essays in Jacksonian Political Economy*, ed. Lawrence H. White (Indianapolis, IN: Liberty Press, 1984), 4–5.

29. President Andrew Jackson, Fourth Annual Message, December 4, 1832, American Presidency Project, www.presidency.ucsb.edu/people/president/andrew-jackson.

30. The *Globe*, a Democratic newspaper, quoted in Ashworth, *'Agrarians' and 'Aristocrats'*, 29.

31. President Andrew Jackson, Farewell Message, March 4, 1837, American Presidency Project, www.presidency.ucsb.edu/documents/farewell-address-0; Blau, *Social Theories*, 6, 17; Theodore Sedgwick, Jr. ed., *A Collection of the Political Writings of William Leggett* (New York, 1840), quoted in Richard Hofstadter, "William Leggett, Spokesman of Jacksonian Democracy," *Political Science Quarterly* 58, no. 4 (1943): 589. Leggett's conception of economic rights is not to be confused with social rights, a twentieth-century invention.

32. *The Workingman's Manual: A New Theory of Political Economy* (Philadelphia, 1831), quoted in Blau, *Social Theories*, 151–52.

33. Ashworth, *'Agrarians' and 'Aristocrats'*, 20, 25–26.

34. James L. Huston, *Securing the Fruits of Labor: The American Concept of Wealth Distribution, 1765–1900* (Baton Rouge: Louisiana State University Press, 1998), 73; Thomas Piketty, *Capital in the Twenty-First Century* (Cambridge, MA: Harvard University Press, 2014), 150–52, 160–61.

35. Fred S. Rolater, "The American Indian and the Origin of the Second American Party System," *Wisconsin Magazine of History* 76, no. 3 (Spring 1993): 201, 197. Rolater's analysis of Congressional votes showed that Whigs voted against removal 84.5 percent of the time, but Democrats voted in favor of removal 81 percent of the time.

36. Mary Hershberger, "Mobilizing Women, Anticipating Abolition: The Struggle against Indian Removal in the 1830s," *Journal of American History* 86, no. 1 (June 1999): 35–38.

37. Jackson, Fourth Annual Message; Howe, *What God Hath Wrought*, 418–22; Alfred A. Cave, "Abuse of Power: Andrew Jackson and the Indian Removal Act of 1830," *Historian* 65, no. 6 (December 2003): 1338–43. Howe refers to Jackson's policies as "ethnic cleansing" and notes that "White supremacy, resolute and explicit, constituted an essential component of what contemporaries called 'the Democracy'—that is the Democratic Party" (423).

38. Walter Johnson, *River of Dark Dreams: Slavery and Empire in the Cotton Kingdom* (Cambridge, MA: Harvard University Press, 2013), 38.

39. Author's calculations. These estimates are of course approximate, since it is next to impossible to calculate the number of slaves on these lands prior to Indian removal.

40. Daniel Webster, quoted in Ashworth, *'Agrarians' and 'Aristocrats'*, 65; Rosanvallon, *The Society of Equals*, 52. Rosanvallon coined the term "circulation of differences."

41. Daniel Webster, quoted in Ashworth, *'Agrarians' and 'Aristocrats'*, 62.

42. Ashworth, *'Agrarians' and 'Aristocrats'*, 66–68.

43. Alexander H. Stephens, "Address at Emory College," 1852, quoted in Howe, *The Political Culture of the American Whigs*, 29. My analysis of the Whig conception of equality of opportunity is indebted to Daniel Howe's research.

44. Howe, "The Evangelical Moment," 1233.

45. Steven Mintz, *Moralists and Modernizers: America's Pre–Civil War Reformers* (Baltimore: John Hopkins University Press, 1995), 57, 60–71, 82–88; David J. Rothman, *The Discovery of the Asylum: Social Order and Disorder in the New Republic*, 2nd ed. (New York: Routledge, 2002).

46. James W. Trent Jr., *The Manliest Man: Samuel G. Howe and the Contours of Nineteenth-Century American Reform* (Amherst: University of Massachusetts Press, 2012), 56, 61, 81–82.

47. Howe, "The Evangelical Moment," 1222; Fred Hirsch, *Social Limits to Growth* (Cambridge, MA: Harvard University Press, 1978), 141–42; Daniel Bell, *The Cultural Contradictions of Capitalism* (New York: Basic Books, 1996). Hirsch describes the economic function of moral values as a form of public goods that facilitate "collective action and cooperative relationships."

48. Howe, *The Political Culture of the American Whigs*, 36–37; Carwardine, *Evangelicals and Politics*, 100–101; Mustafa Emirbayer, "The Shaping of a Virtuous Citizenry: Educational Reform in Massachusetts, 1830–1860," *Studies in American Political Development* 6, no. 2 (Fall 1992): 391–419; Mintz, *Moralists and Modernizers*, 110.

49. Stewart, "Emergence of Racial Modernity," 182; Alexander Saxton, *The Rise and Fall of the White Republic: Class Politics and Mass Culture in Nineteenth-Century America* (New York: Verso, 1990), 142, 144. The British visitor was Edward Abdy, quoted in Stewart, "Emergence of Racial Modernity," 207. The literature on white racism in the 1830s is extensive; see in particular David Roediger, *The Wages of Whiteness: Race and the Making of the American Working Class* (New York: Verso, 1991) and Rogers M. Smith, *Civic Ideals: Conflicting Visions of Citizenship in U.S. History* (New Haven, CT: Yale University Press, 1998), chapter 8.

50. David Walker, *Appeal to the Colored Citizens of the World* (Boston, MA: David Walker [1829]; Journal of Pan African Studies, 2009), www.jpanafrican.com/ebooks/eBook%20David%20Walker%27s%20Appeal.pdf, 8.

51. Davis, *The Problem of Slavery*, 186, 188; Sinha, *The Slave's Cause*, 205–7. Davis reports that three-quarters of subscribers to the *Liberator* in 1834 were African American, and one-fifth of the first two hundred articles had Black authors. This support was reflected in the editorials of the *Liberator*, where Garrison, Sinha says, "adopted not just the black abolitionist program of anticolonization and citizenship but also its style and rhetoric" (218).

52. Lydia Maria Child, *An Appeal in Favor of That Class of Americans Called Africans* (Boston: Allen and Ticknor, 1833), 208, 209, 211–14.

53. Anti-slavery Convention of American Women, *An Address to Free Colored Americans*, pamphlet (New York: William S. Dorr, 1837), 4, 27, quoted in Goodman, *Of One Blood*, 58.

54. James Brewer Stewart, *Holy Warriors: The Abolitionists and American Slavery* (New York: Hill and Wang, 1976), 43–44; Greenstone, *The Lincoln Persuasion*, 260–61; American Anti-slavery Society, *Prejudice against Color* (New York, n.d.), 7, quoted in Goodman, *Of One Blood*, 58.

55. Amos Phelps, *Lectures on Slavery, and Its Remedy* (Boston, 1834), 155, quoted in Goodman, *Of One Blood*, 107, 110; Walker, *Appeal*, 32.

56. Child, *An Appeal*, 181; Anti-slavery Convention of American Women, *Address*, 6; Davis, *The Problem of Slavery*, 206. Davis writes, "Given these assumptions, one can imagine a 'modern' reformer proposing a massive Freedmen's Bureau rehabilitation program, working to convey equal 'advantages,' to accompany slave emancipation."

57. Rush is quoted in Sinha, *The Slave's Cause*, 113–14; Paul J. Polgar, "'To Raise Them to an Equal Participation': Early National Abolitionism, Gradual Emancipation, and the Promise of African American Citizenship," *Journal of the Early Republic* 31, no. 2 (Summer 2011): 135–37. Ibram X. Kendi, *Stamped from the Beginning: The Definitive History of Racist Ideas in America* (New York: Nation, 2016), 98. Kendi says that Rush was the first person to publicly "commercialize the persuasive, though racist, abolitionist theory that slavery made Black people inferior."

58. Linda K. Kerber, "The Abolitionist Perception of the Indian," *Journal of American History* 62, no. 2 (September 1975): 271–72, 289–90. I am indebted to Paul Frymer for pointing out that rehabilitation was understood to apply to both slaves and Native Americans.

59. Donald Yacovone, "The Transformation of the Black Temperance Movement, 1827–1854: An Interpretation," *Journal of the Early Republic* 8 (Fall 1988): 283; "Characteristics of the People of Color—No. 2," *Colored American*, April 25, 1840. See also Patrick Rael, *Black Identity and Black Protest in the Antebellum North* (Chapel Hill: University of North Carolina Press, 2002), 125–35, 143–50; Eddie S. Glaude, Jr., *Exodus! Religion, Race, and Nation in Early Nineteenth-Century Black America* (Chicago: University of Chicago Press, 2000), 126–34; Sinha, *The Slave's Cause*, 132–42.

60. Quoted in Rael, *Black Identity and Black Protest*, 186.

61. Tunde Adeleke, "Afro-Americans and Moral Suasion: The Debate in the 1830's," *Journal of Negro History* 83, no. 2 (Spring 1998): 132; Rael, *Black Identity and Black Protest*, 173, 175, 202–3; Gunnar Myrdal, *An American Dilemma: The Negro Problem and Modern Democracy* (New York: Harper and Row, 1944), 75. Kendi calls this belief "uplift suasion," and his book is partly dedicated to demolishing its political logic and effect. He is not wrong. See Kendi, *Stamped from the Beginning*, 124–25, 505.

62. Stewart, "Emergence of Racial Modernity," 193; Adam D Simmons, "Ideologies and Programs of the Negro Anti-slavery Movement, 1830–1861" (PhD diss., Northwestern University, 1983), 31–36; Carl E. Prince, "The Great 'Riot Year': Jacksonian Democracy and Patterns of Violence in 1834," *Journal of the Early Republic* 5, no. 1 (Spring 1985): 14; Emma Jones Lapsansky, "'Since They Got Those Separate Churches': Afro-Americans and Racism in Jacksonian Philadelphia," *American Quarterly* 32, no. 1 (Spring 1980): 54–78; Linda K. Kerber, "Abolitionists and Amalgamators: The New York City Race Riots of 1834," *New York History* 48, no. 1 (January 1967): 28–39. Prince's data on riots in 1834 and 1835 reveal that one-third of them were about race and abolition (18–19).

63. Stewart, "Emergence of Racial Modernity," 199.

64. Stewart, "Emergence of Racial Modernity," 204; Lapsansky, "'Since They Got Those Separate Churches,'" 75–77.

65. Lydia Maria Child, quoted in Stewart, "Emergence of Racial Modernity," 197.

66. Walker, *Appeal*, 12.

67. David Ruggles, quoted in Jane H. Pease and William H. Pease, "Black Power: The Debate in 1840," *Phylon* 29, no. 1 (1968): 24.

68. Quoted in Pease and Pease, "Black Power," 24.

69. Wilentz, *The Rise of American Democracy*, 552; Benjamin Quarles, *Black Abolitionists* (New York: Oxford University Press, 1969), 184–85; Reinhard O. Johnson, *The Liberty Party, 1840–1848: Antislavery Third-Party Politics in the United States* (Baton Rouge: Louisiana State University Press, 2009), 245, 251–53; Masur, *Until Justice Be Done*, 194–98. The Liberty Party stated its opposition to racial discrimination in the 1844 platform, resolutions 4, 34–36.

70. Rael, *Black Identity and Black Protest*, 33, 39, 43; Sinha, *The Slave's Cause*, 302.

71. Sinha, *The Slave's Cause*, 299. This statement is an early illustration of Black particularism, the expression of universalism that emerges from "the forcible enclosures of racial stigma." Nikhil Pal Singh, *Black is a Country: Race and the Unfinished Struggle for Democracy* (Cambridge, MA: Harvard University Press, 2004), 44.

72. Glaude, *Exodus!*, 118–19, 124.

73. Quoted in Howard Holman Bell, *A Survey of the Negro Convention Movement, 1830–1861* (New York: Arno, 1969), 127. Bell says that anywhere from 20 to 25 percent of Blacks attending Black conventions in the 1850s embraced emigration and some form of separatism. But these activists also believed in a politics of uplift. Davis, *The Problem of Slavery*, 127–30.

74. Walker, *Appeal,* 23, emphasis in original. Martin Delany to Frederick Douglass, April 15, 1848, in Robert S. Levine, ed., *Martin R. Delany: A Documentary Reader* (Chapel Hill: University of North Carolina Press, 2003), 88; Lewis is quoted in Rael, *Black Identity and Black Protest,* 134.

75. Frederick Douglass, "What to the Slave is the Fourth of July," July 5, 1852, in Philip S. Foner and Yuval Taylor, *Frederick Douglass: Selected Speeches and Writings* (Chicago: Chicago Review Press, 2000), 196.

76. Henry Highland Garnet, speech reprinted in *Colored American,* May 30, 1840; editorial, *Colored American,* March 21, 1840.

77. Foner and Taylor, *Frederick Douglass,* 213–14, 262; Walker, *Appeal,* 23; Martin R. Delany, "Sound the Alarm," *North Star,* January 12, 1849, in Levine, *Martin R. Delany,* 143

78. John W. Blassingame and John R. McKivigan, eds., *The Frederick Douglass Papers, Series One, Speeches, Debates, and Interviews* (New Haven, CT: Yale University Press, 1986), 3: 293. On May 23, 1840, the *Colored American* published a passionate editorial endorsing higher tariffs to protect manufacturing and Henry Clay's American system, which they called "the foundation of our prosperity."

79. Frederick Douglass, "Government and Its Subjects," *North Star,* November 9, 1849, in Foner and Taylor, *Frederick Douglass,* 146.

80. William S. McFeely, *Frederick Douglass* (New York: Norton, 1991), 191. For evidence of abolitionist racism and Douglass's reactions, see pp. 91, 95, 108. See also John Stauffer, "Douglass's Self-Making and the Culture of Abolitionism," in *The Cambridge Companion to Frederick Douglass,* ed. Maurice S. Lee (New York: Cambridge University Press, 2009), 18, 21.

81. Henry Highland Garnet, "An Address to the Slaves of the United States of America," Buffalo, NY, 1843; Henry Highland Garnet, "Self-Help: The Wants of Western New York," *North Star,* January 19, 1849; Glaude, *Exodus!* 145–59. I am indebted to Glaude's interpretation of Garnet's speech. Frederick Douglass, "An Address to the Colored People of the United States," in Foner and Taylor, *Frederick Douglass,* 118–19. Douglass's belief in the need for collective independence is an eloquent statement of the idea of linked fates; see Michael C. Dawson, *Behind the Mule: Race and Class in African-American Politics* (Princeton, NJ: Princeton University Press, 1994).

82. Delany voiced this concern after witnessing a court case in which a Kentucky slave holder sued for damages for slaves he lost. The judge tilted the case to the slaveholder, leaving Delany to comment, "Previous to this decision, colored persons had some slight semblance of liberty, but now every vestige has been wrested from us—each and all of us reduced to the mercy or discretion of any white man in the country, and the colored man in the South with a 'Pass,' as it is termed, may at any moment be arrested as the *property* of another." Levine, *Martin R. Delany,* 114–15. See also Delany, "Political Destiny of the Colored Race on the American Continent," address to the 1854 National Emigration Convention of Colored Men, in Levine, *Martin R. Delany,* 245–79.

83. Free Soil Party Platform, 1848, American Presidency Project, www.presidency.ucsb.edu/documents/free-soil-party-platform-1848; Abraham Lincoln, *Lincoln: Speeches and Writings, 1859–1865* (New York: Library of America, 1989), 90–101.

84. Sumner is quoted in John Ashworth, "Free Labor, Wage Labor, and the Slave Power: Republicanism and the Republican Party in the 1850s," in *The Market Revolution in America: Social, Political, and Religious Expressions, 1800–1880*, ed. Melvyn Stokes and Stephen Conway (Charlottesville: University Press of Virginia, 1996), 138; Eric Foner, "Free Labor and Nineteenth-Century Political Ideology," in Stokes and Conway, *The Market Revolution in America*, 116; Lincoln, *Lincoln: Speeches and Writings, 1859–1865*, 144. Ashworth infers that Sumner is saying that God approves of wage labor, but Sumner's views are those of abolitionists.

85. Foner, "Free Labor and Political Ideology," 105. Evans supported equal rights for whites and Blacks, but his aim was to emancipate the "white laborer, by restoring his natural right to the soil." Helene Sara Zahler, *Eastern Workingmen and National Land Policy, 1829–1862* (New York: Columbia University Press, 1941), 24, 33–34; Jonathan H. Earle, *Jacksonian Antislavery and the Politics of Free Soil, 1824–1854* (Chapel Hill: University of North Carolina Press, 2004), 35, 60–61.

86. Walter Johnson, *The Broken Heart of America: St Louis and the Violent History of the United States* (New York: Basic Books, 2020), 46–47, 117; Richard H. Sewell, "Slavery, Race, and the Free Soil Party, 1848–1854," in *Crusaders and Compromisers: Essays on the Relationship of the Antislavery Struggle to the Antebellum Party System*, ed. Alan M. Kraut (Westport, CT: Greenwood Press, 1983), 102; Paul Frymer, *Building an American Empire: The Era of Territorial and Political Expansion* (Princeton, NJ: Princeton University Press, 2017).

87. Charles Postel, *Equality: An American Dilemma, 1866–1896* (New York: Farrar, Straus, and Giroux, 2017). In describing the post–Civil War movements for equality, Postel does not use the language of antiprivilege egalitarianism, but all three movements reflected this discourse.

88. Author's calculations, based on the number of chapters and members of the American Anti-slavery Society in 1839. Frymer, *Building an American Empire*, chapter 5. Abolitionists, Frymer points out, usually voted in favor of Homestead laws, which opposed slavery (146, 150).

89. Garnet, "Garrit Smith and the Anti-slavery Standard," *North Star*, September 15, 1848; Frederick Douglass, "The Anti-slavery Movement," March 19, 1852, in Foner and Taylor, *Frederick Douglass*, 326–27; Delany, "Sound the Alarm." See also "The Freesoil Party and the Liberty Party," June 24, 1852, *Frederick Douglass Paper*; "Land Reform," April 1, 1852, *Frederick Douglass Paper*.

90. Jonathan A. Glickstein, "'Poverty Is Not Slavery': American Abolitionists and the Competitive Labor Market," in *Antislavery Reconsidered: New Perspectives on the Abolitionists*, ed. Lewis Perry and Michael Fellman (Baton Rouge: Louisiana State University Press, 1979), 198, 209. Beecher is quoted on pp. 205–6. Garrison is quoted in Eric Foner, *Politics and Ideology in the Age of the Civil War* (New York: Oxford University Press, 1980), 71.

91. Lydia Maria Child, *Anti-slavery Catechism* (Newburyport, MA: Charles Whipple, 1839), 18.

92. Child, *An Appeal*, 203–5.

93. Quoted in Jonathan A. Glickstein, *Concepts of Free Labor* (New Haven, CT: Yale University Press, 1991), 85, 88–89; Eric Foner, *Free Soil, Free Labor, Free Men: The Ideology of the Republican Party before the Civil War* (Oxford: Oxford University Press, 1995), 297.

94. Glickstein, *Concepts of Free Labor*, 15, 85; Benjamin D. Weber, "Emancipation in the West Indies and the Freedom to Toil: Manual Labor and Moral Redemption in Transatlantic Antislavery Discourse," *Journal of the Oxford University History Society* 6 (2009): 1–18.

CHAPTER 2. "WHAT SHALL WE DO WITH THE NEGRO?"

1. Charles Lenox Remond, speech at Union Square Church, May 9, 1865 quoted in C. Peter Ripely, *The Black Abolitionist Papers*, vol. 5, *The United States, 1859–1865* (Chapel Hill: University of North Carolina Press, 1992), 322.

2. Douglass, "The Black Man's Future," 498–500. Robert Hamilton, the editor of the *Weekly Anglo-American*, excoriated white teachers who came South after the war: "They have kindness of heart enough to regard the freed people as 'poor unfortunate creatures,' . . . but on the main question of the manhood of the black man, . . . they hold to the opinion of the inferiority of our race." Ripley, *The Black Abolitionist Papers*, 367.

3. Henry Highland Garnet, "Speech from the Colored Citizens of Norfolk, VA, to the People of the United States," June 26, 1865, in Ripley, *The Black Abolitionist Papers*, 300–301; James McCune Smith to Robert Hamilton, August 1864, in Ripley, *The Black Abolitionist Papers*, 337–38, 342.

4. Gerald David Jaynes, *Branches without Roots: Genesis of the Black Working Class in the American South, 1862–1882* (New York: Oxford University Press, 1986), 61–62; James L Roark, *Masters without Slaves: Southern Planters in the Civil War and Reconstruction* (New York: Norton, 1977), 94, 154.

5. Steven Hahn, Steven F. Miller, Susan E. O'Donovan, John C. Rodrigue, and Leslie S. Rowland, eds., *Land and Labor, 1865* (Chapel Hill: University of North Carolina Press, 2008), 89; Samuel Gardner to Samuel Thomas, December 10, 1865, M826, Roll 30; H. H. Alvord to Brevet Brigadier-General Ely S. Parker, September 8, 1865, M869 Roll 34, BRFAL.

6. Carl Schurz, *Report on the States of South Carolina, Georgia, Alabama, Mississippi, and Louisiana*, US Congress, Senate Executive Document No. 2, 39th Cong., 1st Sess. (Washington, DC, 1865) 21, 24, emphasis in original. This was a common view among Union soldiers and Freedmen's Bureau agents. See Samuel Thomas, Senate Executive Document No. 2, 81.

7. James D. Schmidt, "'A Full-Fledged Government of Men': Freedmen's Bureau Labor Policy in South Carolina, 1865–1868," in *The Freedmen's Bureau and Recon-*

struction: Reconsiderations,* ed. Paul A. Cimbala and Randall M. Miller (New York: Fordham University Press, 1999), 223. Jaynes, *Branches without Roots,* makes a similar case for the role of the Freedmen's Bureau.

8. George R. Bentley, *A History of the Freedmen's Bureau* (Philadelphia: American Historical Association, 1955), 49.

9. These data on Freedmen's Bureau agents are drawn from John A. Carpenter's unpublished study of the Freedmen's Bureau. See the appendix for details.

10. John G. Sproat, "Blueprint for Reconstruction," *Journal of Southern History* 23, no. 1 (February 1957): 25–44.

11. James M. McPherson, *The Struggle for Equality: Abolitionists and the Negro in the Civil War and Reconstruction* (Princeton, NJ: Princeton University Press, 1995), 187. See also Oz Frankel, "The Predicament of Racial Knowledge: Government Studies of the Freedmen During the U.S. Civil War," *Social Research* 70, no. 1 (Spring 2003): 45–81; Matthew Furrow, "Samuel Gridley Howe, the Black Population of Canada West, and the Racial Ideology of the 'Blueprint for Radical Reconstruction,'" *Journal of American History* 97, no. 2 (September 2010): 344–70.

12. Heather Cox Richardson, *The Death of Reconstruction: Race, Labor, and Politics in the Post–Civil War North, 1865–1901* (Cambridge, MA: Harvard University Press, 2001), 10, 30–35.

13. Paul D Escott, *What Shall We Do with the Negro?: Lincoln, White Racism, and Civil War America* (Charlottesville: University Press of Virginia, 2009), 73–75.

14. Robert Dale Owen, James McKaye, and Samuel G. Howe, *Final Report of the American Freedmen's Commission to the Secretary of War* (New York: Office of the American Freedmen's Inquiry Commission, 1864), 370, 372, 382.

15. Robert Dale Owen, James McKaye, and Samuel G. Howe, *Preliminary Report to the Secretary of War* (New York: Office of the American Freedmen's Inquiry Commission, 1863), 443–44, 447–48.

16. James S. McKaye to Charles Sumner, January 20, February 5, 1864, Sumner Papers, Harvard University, quoted in Sproat, "Blueprint for Reconstruction," 40–41; James S. McKaye, *The Mastership and Its Fruits: The Emancipated Slave Face to Face with His Old Master; A Supplemental Report to the Hon. Edwin M. Stanton, Secretary of War* (New York: William C. Bryant, 1864), 21.

17. Owen, McKaye, and Howe, *Preliminary Report,* 451; Owen, McKaye, and Howe, *Final Report,* 374.

18. Owen, McKaye, and Howe, *Preliminary Report,* 432–33.

19. Owen, McKaye, and Howe, *Final Report,* 378, 380–82; Owen, McKaye, and Howe, *Preliminary Report,* 449.

20. James E. Yeatman, *A Report on the Condition of the Freedmen in Mississippi* (St. Louis, MO: Western Sanitary Commission, 1864), 16.

21. Banks is quoted in Jaynes, *Branches without Roots,* 14. William W. F. Messner, *Freedmen and the Ideology of Free Labor: Louisiana, 1862–1865* (Lafayette: Center for Louisiana Studies, University of Southwestern Louisiana, 1978), 40–41, 49–50, 57, 59. Messner quotes a Union general who said, "It is possible that there will be less outrage, less loss of life, by freeing these people, if put under strict military

control, than if left free to learn slowly that war has removed the white man who heretofore held them in check, and to yield at last to the temptation in insurrection and massacre" (36).

22. Frederick Douglass, "What the Black Man Wants," speech to the annual meeting of the Massachusetts Anti-slavery Society, Boston, April 1865, in Blassingame and McKivigan, *The Frederick Douglass Papers* (New Haven, CT: Yale University Press, 1991), 158; Wendell Phillips, *National Anti-slavery Standard*, May 14, 1864, quoted in Messner, *Freedmen and the Ideology of Free Labor*, 58.

23. Ann V. Nugent, "The Attitude of the New Orleans Tribune towards the Freedmen's Bureau in Louisiana: 1865–1966," master's thesis, Western Washington State College, 1970), 4–5, 9, 19–20.

24. Charles Sumner, *A Bridge from Slavery to Freedom*, speech in the Senate of the United States, June 13 and 15, 1864 (Washington, DC: H. Polkinhorn & Son, 1864), 2–3. Herman Belz, *A New Birth of Freedom: The Republican Party and Freedmen's Rights, 1861–1866* (Westport, CT: Greenwood, 1976), 71–72.

25. Belz, *A New Birth of Freedom*, 78–82, 98. Wilson is quoted in LaWanda Cox, "The Promise of Land for the Freedmen," in *Freedom, Racism, and Reconstruction: Collected Writings of LaWanda Cox*, ed. Donald G. Nieman (Athens: University of Georgia Press, 1997), 43. *Congressional Globe*, 38th Cong., 1st Sess., 2971–74.

26. See the conference committee report, *"Bureau of Freedmen's Affairs,"* Report No. 9, US House of Representatives, 38th Cong., 2nd Sess, 1865.

27. Cox, "The Promise of Land for the Freedmen," 53–55; Belz, *A New Birth of Freedom*, 106–8. Freedmen's Bureau agents took a dim view of white refugees. Samuel Thomas told Howard they disdained any help in planning for the future and had no problem taking food from the government and not working. Samuel Thomas to O. O. Howard, October 12, 1865, M826 Roll 1, BRFAL.

28. Edward McPherson, *The Political History of the United States of America, during the Great Rebellion* (Washington, DC: Solomons and Chapman, 1876), 149; See also Mark Graber, "The Second Freedmen's Bureau Bill's Constitution," *Texas Law Review* 94 (2016): 1361–1402.

29. See, for example, E. Whittlesey, assistant commissioner, North Carolina, circular no. 2, July 15, 1865; Stuart Eldridge, Mississippi, circular no. 7, July 29, 1865, in US Congress, House of Representatives, House Exec. Doc. No. 70, 39th Cong., 1st Sess., 2–3, 154–155. Messner, *Freedmen and the Ideology of Free Labor*, 69. Michael W. Fitzgerald, "Emancipation and Military Occupation: The Freedmen's Bureau and Social Control in Alabama," in *The Freedmen's Bureau and Reconstruction: Reconsiderations*, ed. Paul A. Cimbala and Randall M. Miller (New York: Fordham University Press, 1999), 49, 54.

30. Gregory Downs, *After Appomattox: Military Occupation and the Ends of War* (Cambridge, MA: Harvard University Press, 2015).

31. H. H. Alvord to Brevet Brigadier General Ely, September 8, 1865, M869, Roll 2, BRFAL. McKaye, *The Mastership and Its Fruits*, 33–34. McKaye believed that reconstruction required a social revolution in the South and the "deliverance of the master population . . . wholly and forever, from their mastership, and from the fatal

delusions and deprivations that are inherent in it" (33). Samuel Thomas to O.O. Howard, October 12, 1865, M826, Roll 1, BRFAL.

32. Downs, *After Appomattox,* 41–51. See appendix for details on the dataset.

33. My estimate of the number of soldiers in the bureau was derived by combining the number of military agents with the number of civilian agents who were former Union officers and enlisted men. This yielded 1,320 military agents and 459 former soldiers, for a total of 1,779, or 78 percent of all agents. True civilians numbered 493, or 22 percent. The total of 2,272 is somewhat less than the universe because of missing cases. See also Donald G. Nieman, *To Set the Law in Motion: The Freedmen's Bureau and the Legal Rights of Blacks, 1865–1868* (Millwood, NY: KTO Press, 1979), 12–13.

34. Paul A. Cimbala, *Under the Guardianship of the Nation: The Freedmen's Bureau and the Reconstruction of Georgia, 1865–1870* (Athens: University of Georgia Press, 1997), 32–33.

35. Susan Eva O'Donovan, *Becoming Free in the Cotton South* (Cambridge, MA: Harvard University Press, 2007), 221–22. Texas is the other state with a significant number of pro-Confederate civilian agents, of whom a Freedmen's Bureau inspector said the bureau "has given the colored people about the same protection that a hungry wolf does a lamb." René Hayden, Anthony E. Kaye, Kate Masur, Steven F. Miller, Susan E. O'Donovan, Leslie S. Rowland, and Stephen A. West, eds., *Land and Labor, 1866–1867* (Chapel Hill: University of North Carolina Press, 2013), 66.

36. E. Allen Richardson, "Architects of a Benevolent Empire: The Relationship between the American Missionary Association and the Freedmen's Bureau in Virginia, 1865–1872," in *The Freedmen's Bureau and Reconstruction,* ed. Paul Cimbala and Randall M. Miller (New York: Fordham University Press, 1999), 120.

37. Owen, McKaye, and Howe, *Final Report,* 370.

38. Amy Dru Stanley, *From Bondage to Contract: Wage Labor, Marriage, and the Market in the Age of Slave Emancipation* (Cambridge: Cambridge University Press, 1998), 2, 18.

39. Captain Richard Hinton to Freedmen's Bureau commissioner for Kentucky, Tennessee, and northern Alabama, July 31, 1865, in Hahn et al., *Land and Labor, 1865,* 632; Thomas to Howard, October 12, 1865, M826, Roll 1, BRFAL.

40. O.O. Howard, circular no. 13, July 28, 1865; circular no. 15, September 12, 1865, documents 99 and 103 in Hahn et al., *Land and Labor, 1865,* 423–25, 431–33. Johnson rewrote Howard's draft of circular no. 15. In effect he unilaterally amended the 1865 Freedmen's Bureau law. On Sherman's Special Order No. 15, see Ira Berlin, Thavolia Glymph, Steven F. Miller, Joseph P. Reiduy, Leslie S. Rowland, and Julie Saville, eds, *The Wartime Genesis of Free Labor: The Lower South,* vol. 3 (New York: Cambridge University Press, 1990), 338–40.

41. Samuel Thomas to O.O. Howard, August 15, 1865; Thomas to Howard, September 14, 1865; Stuart Eldridge to Robert Donaldson, September 11, 1865; M826, Roll 1, BRFAL; Thomas to Howard, September 19, 1865, doc. 104 in Hahn et al., *Land and Labor, 1865,* 433–34. Howard A. White, *The Freedmen's Bureau in Louisiana* (Baton Rouge: Louisiana State University Press, 1970), 47–49.

42. O. O. Howard to Rufus Saxton, October 6, 1865; Shadrack Seabrook to Rufus Saxton, December 8, 1865; James Roy to Lieutenant Colonel W. L. M Burger, December 9, 1865, docs. 107, 112–113 in Hahn et al., *Land and Labor, 1865*, 439, 476–77. Martin Abbott, *The Freedmen's Bureau in South Carolina, 1865–1872* (Chapel Hill: University of North Carolina Press, 1967), 59–60.

43. Committee of Freedmen, October 20 or 21, 1865; O. O. Howard to Henry Bram, October 22, 1865, doc. 108A in Hahn et al., *Land and Labor, 1865*, 440–41, emphasis in original. Edward Magdol, *A Right to the Land: Essays on the Freedmen's Community* (Westport, CT: Greenwood, 1977), 161.

44. Edward Magdol and Edward M Stoeber, "Martin R. Delany Counsels Freedmen, July 23, 1865," *Journal of Negro History* 56, no. 4 (October 1971): 306–7. H. J. Hawkins, *Report of Special Inspection of Port Royal and Area*, August 13, 1865, M869, Roll 2, BRFAL. Hawkins reported that Delany was advising freedmen to avoid signing contracts.

45. Russell Duncan, *Freedom's Shore: Tunis Campbell and the Georgia Freedmen* (Athens: University of Georgia Press, 1986), 24–29; Joseph Reidy, "Aaron A. Bradley: Voice of Black Labor in the Georgia Lowcountry," in *Southern Black Leaders of the Reconstruction Era*, ed. Howard N. Rabinowitz (Urbana: University of Illinois Press, 1982), 281–307; D. E. Sickles to Davis Tillson, December 7, 1865; W. H. Tiffany to D. E. Sickles, December 8, 1865, docs. 111A and 111B in Hahn et al., *Land and Labor, 1865*, 466–67.

46. James Beecher to M. N. Rice, February 6, 1866, doc. 52, emphasis in original; Tillson to O. O. Howard, January 16, 1866, Special Order No. 2, doc. 45 in Hayden et al., *Land and Labor, 1866–1867*, 255, 238; Roy to Burger, December 9, 1865, doc. 113 in Hahn et al., *Land and Labor, 1865*, 478.

47. Steven Hahn, *A Nation under Our Feet: Black Political Struggles in the Rural South from Slavery to the Great Migration* (Cambridge, MA: Harvard University Press, 2003), 135–37; Bayley Wyat, "A Freedman's Speech," December 1865, doc. 85 in Hayden et al., *Land and Labor, 1866–1867*, 336–40; Committee of Freedmen on Edisto Island, South Carolina, to the president, October 28, 1865, doc. 108B in Hahn et al., *Land and Labor, 1865*, 443.

48. Julie Saville, *The Work of Reconstruction: From Slave to Wage Laborer in South Carolina, 1860–1870* (New York: Cambridge University Press, 1994), 40, 42–43, 96; Jaynes, *Branches without Roots*, 282–89. Edward E. Baptist, *The Half Has Never Been Told: Slavery and the Making of American Capitalism* (New York: Basic Books, 2014), 78–83, 85–92, 108. Hahn et al., *Land and Labor, 1865*, 443.

49. Saville, *The Work of Reconstruction*, 48; Duncan, *Freedom's Shore*, 24, 61; Hayden et al., *Land and Labor, 1866–1867*, chapter 9; O'Donovan, *Becoming Free in the Cotton South*, 183–84. Jaynes calls Negro agrarians "born-again Jacobins," *Branches without Roots*, 287.

50. Major General George Hartsuff, General Orders No. 11, in Hahn et al., *Land and Labor, 1865*, 198. Hartsuff was the commander of US forces at Petersburg, Virginia. J. E. Cornelius, report to South Carolina Freedmen's Bureau assistant commissioner, doc. 83 in Hayden et al., *Land and Labor, 1866–1867*, 334. House Exec.

Doc. 70, 4, 25, 58, 135. Davis Tillson enjoined his agents "to exert themselves to convince the freed people that they are utterly mistaken, and that no such distribution [of land] will take place at Christmas, or at any other time, " circular no. 2, October 3, 1865.

51. Quoted in James D. Schmidt, *Free to Work: Labor Law, Emancipation, and Reconstruction, 1815–1880* (Athens: University of Georgia Press, 1998), 109–10.

52. Samuel Thomas, quoted in Steven Joseph Ross, "Freed Soil, Freed Labor, Freed Men: John Eaton and the Davis Bend Experiment," *Journal of Southern History* 44, no. 2 (May 1978): 220.

53. D. G. Fenno, circular no. 20, House Exec. Doc. 70, 25, emphasis in original.

54. Tillson is quoted in Hahn et al., *Land and Labor, 1865*, 688.

55. *Edgefield Advertiser*, quoted in Vernon Burton, "Race and Reconstruction: Edgefield County, South Carolina," *Journal of Social History* 12 (1978): 36; Hahn et al., *Land and Labor, 1865*, 696, 698; Hayden et al., *Land and Labor, 1866–1867*, 914–16.

56. Howard is quoted in Cimbala, *Under the Guardianship of the Nation*, 86. The bureau also believed that the freed people were responsible for funding their schools.

57. Tillson is quoted in Hahn et al., *Land and Labor, 1865*, 684, 733; Ross, "Freed Soil, Freed Labor, Freed Men," 216. Ross says that Eaton believed "the rehabilitation of the freedmen and reconstruction of the south were mutually supportive."

58. Cimbala, *Under the Guardianship of the Nation*, 4, 6; House Exec. Doc. 70, 139. Wager Swayne to O. O. Howard, January 21, 1866, M809, Roll 2, BRFAL. Hahn, *A Nation under Our Feet*, 74. Saxton strongly believed in the cause of the freedmen, and he was one of the most forceful advocates of land redistribution. President Johnson regarded Saxton as a radical and removed him from the bureau. Swayne tended initially to side with planters, but by early 1866 he was a steadfast and vigorous advocate for the freed people. See Fitzgerald, "Emancipation and Military Occupation," 57–60.

59. Eldridge's views coincided with those of his superior, Samuel Thomas, who said, "Slavery has not taught [the freedmen] economy, but, on the contrary, has tended to make them extravagant and thoughtless. " House Exec. Doc. 70, 156–58. Davis Tillson was, if anything, more explicit about the need to change the character of the freedmen. In a circular of November 1, 1865, he wrote of the necessity of "transforming [the freedmen] from characters of liars, thieves, and adulterers, into characters of intelligence, virtue, and piety. " House Exec. Doc. 70, 66.

60. Quoted in Cimbala, *Under the Guardianship of the Nation*, 56–57.

61. Draft letter to the freedmen submitted to Orlando Brown, assistant commissioner for Virginia, in Hahn et al., *Land and Labor, 1865*, 136, 140.

62. Orlando Brown, circular, November 4, 1865, House Exec. Doc. 70, 139, emphasis in original. Jim Downs, *Sick from Freedom: African American Illness and Suffering during the Civil War and Reconstruction* (New York: Oxford University Press, 2012), 55–56, 87–88.

63. Judith N. Shklar, *American Citizenship: The Quest for Inclusion* (Cambridge, MA: Harvard University Press, 1991), 67–68. Greeley is quoted in Jonathan A.

Glickstein, *Concepts of Free Labor in Antebellum America* (New Haven, CT: Yale University Press, 1991), 97. House Exec. Doc. 70, 92–93.

64. O. O. Howard to Captain Charles C. Soule, Orangeburg, SC, June 21, 1865, in Hahn et al., *Land and Labor, 1865*, 221.

65. Hayden et al., *Land and Labor, 1866–1867*, 42.

66. Caryn Cossé Bell, "Une Chimère: The Freedmen's Bureau in Creole New Orleans," quoted in Paul A. Cimbala and Randall M. Miller, eds., *The Freedmen's Bureau and Reconstruction: Reconsiderations,* 141. Samuel Thomas, who tilted toward planter interests, believed that planter and freedmen interests were nearly identical but assumed that it was the freedmen who needed educating on this point. "Just so long as we oppose or treat with passive indifference his mental and moral improvement, so long we direct our influence against ourselves." House Exec. Doc. 70, 66.

67. Quoted in Jaynes, *Branches without Roots,* 115; Steven Hahn et al., *Land and Labor, 1865,* 166.

68. Stuart Eldridge to Captain J. M. Sunderland, September 30, 1867; John Moore to Sunderland, September 30, 1867, M826, Roll 30, BRFAL.

69. J. E. Quinten, report to assistant commissioner for Florida, in Hayden et al., *Land and Labor, 1866–1867,* 123, emphasis added. Garnet Nagel, Report on the Condition of the Freedmen, November 30, 1866, M869, Roll 34, BRFAL; Samuel Gardner to Wager Swayne, August 10, 1865, M809 Roll 18, BRFAL.

70. Report Abbeville District (Anderson, Edgefield counties), October 20, 1866, M869 Roll 34, BRFAL.

71. The data are drawn from the monthly reports of C. W. Buckley, the subassistant commissioner for Montgomery County, Alabama. See M809, Roll 18, BRFAL.

72. Report of George W. Corliss, Freedmen's Bureau officer, to Mississippi assistant commissioner, April 9, 1866, in Hayden et al., *Land and Labor, 1866–1867,* 410. In this vein, see the report of an agent to the Virginia assistant commissioner, who reported that "overseers are often unpopular with the freedmen, even when not very severe." He shrewdly observed that planters simply did not understand the freedmen's character (418).

73. Hahn et al., *Land and Labor, 1865,* 498–99, 533, emphasis in original. The agent quoted was a staunch supporter of the freed people and ridiculed planter complaints in his report.

74. Report from Colleton and Georgetown districts, October 29, 1866, M869, Roll 34, BRFAL.

75. Hayden et al., *Land and Labor, 1866–1867,* 418, emphasis in original.

76. Hahn et al., *Land and Labor, 1865,* 323. H. J. Hawkins, Special Inspection of Port Royal Area, August 13, 1865, M869, Roll 34, BRFAL, ascribed the reluctance to sign contracts to ignorance. Hawkins believed freedmen did not understand that they would be paid a wage.

77. Report of John Moore, October 31, 1867, M826, Roll 30, BRFAL; C. A. de la Mesa, acting subassistant commissioner to Georgia assistant commissioner, July 13, 1866, in Hayden et al., *Land and Labor, 1866–1867,* 616–17.

78. Hayden et al., *Land and Labor, 1866–1867*, 648; Gardner to Swayne, December 2, 1865; R. A. Wilson, Monthly Report, Demopolis, August 31, 1868, M809 Roll 18, BRFAL. Wilson reported, "The financial embarrassment of the planter-princes in the neighborhood are a principal cause [of their unwillingness to pay wages.] It is difficult for them to sustain their present position in society if they deal justly with their colored laborers, who makes the crops on land heavily encumbered."

79. Hahn et al., *Land and Labor, 1865*, 295. Tillson delivered his speech on October 27, 1865. The assistant superintendent for education in Georgia struck the same note in a speech trying to convince white Southerners to support education for the freed people. House Exec. Doc. 70, 66. Cimbala, *Under the Guardianship of the Nation*, 32–33.

80. Karl Polanyi, *The Great Transformation: The Political and Economic Origins of Our Time* (Boston: Beacon Press, 1957), 86–87, 145; Schmidt, "'A Full-Fledged Government of Men'," 224. Schmidt argues that the Freedmen's Bureau "used the power of the state in ways unprecedented in antebellum labor relations and almost without parallel in the twentieth century."

81. Hahn et al., *Land and Labor, 1865*, 382.

82. Schmidt, *Free to Work*, 46, 51.

83. Orlando Brown to O. O. Howard, July 21, 1865; SAC Report, Mobile, Alabama, October 31, 1866, M109, Roll 18, BRFAL; former slaveholder to assistant commissioner for Kentucky, Tennessee and Northern Alabama, September 1865, in Hahn et al., *Land and Labor, 1865*, 622, 638; Jaynes, *Branches without Roots*, 121–23. Jaynes quotes one Freedmen's Bureau agent who reported, "The race of kind human Masters of whom we have heard so much seems to have become extinct and with callous indifference to the condition or sufferings of the free people save where their own interest is concerned seems the principle [*sic*] characteristic of the white population of this district" (121).

84. J. E. Quentin, subassistant commissioner for Madison, Taylor, and Lafayette Counties, Florida, to assistant commissioner for Florida, May 1, 1866, in Hayden et al., *Land and Labor, 1866–1867*, 123. Quentin's report is a powerful denunciation of planters and a plea for federal laws that would protect the freedmen.

85. Jaynes, *Branches without Roots*, 117–19, 122; Roger L. Ransom and Richard Sutch, *One Kind of Freedom: The Economic Consequences of Freedom* (New York: Cambridge University Press, 1977), 44–46.

86. *New Orleans Tribune*, July 16, 1865, quoted in Nugent, "Attitude of the New Orleans Tribune," 49. Wager Swayne likewise advocated abandoning the contract system.

87. Hayden et al., *Land and Labor, 1866–1867*, 106, 125–27. Today these are referred to as noncompete contracts.

88. Samuel Thomas to O. O. Howard, March 13, 1866, M826, Roll 1, BRFAL; O. O. Howard, "Report of the Commissioner of the Bureau of Refugees, Freedmen, and Abandoned Lands," December 1865, United States House of Representatives, House Exec. Doc. No. 11, 39th Cong., 1st Sess., 13; General Alfred H. Terry, commander of the Department of Virginia, to Edwin M. Stanton, secretary of war, June

15, 1865, in Hahn et al., *Land and Labor, 1865*, 339. O. O. Howard, *Autobiography* (New York: Baker & Taylor, 1908), 2: 213–14.

89. House Exec. Doc. 70, 95, 174; Nugent, "Attitude of the New Orleans Tribune," 35.

90. E. A. Koylay, monthly report, January 29, 1866, M869, Roll 34, BRFAL. In his order overturning the Black Codes, General Sickles stipulated that vagrancy laws "shall not be considered applicable to persons who are without employment, if they shall prove that they have been unable to obtain employment, after diligent efforts to do so." As Koylay's reports indicate, agents could interpret this instruction in a variety of ways. Koylay believed that the demand for labor in Orangeburg outstripped supply, and he was willing to enforce vagrancy laws as he saw fit. See Major General D. E. Sickles, General Order No. 1, in Hayden et al., *Land and Labor, 1866–1867*, 81–83.

91. General Absalom Baird to planters of St. Martin, circular no. 29, Senate Exec. Doc. 27, 134–36.

92. Nieman, *To Set the Law in Motion*, chapter 3. Obviously, agents varied considerably in their willingness to enforce vagrancy laws. Ideologically, though, the bureau was committed to using vagrancy laws and policies as tools to enforce work and prevent the dreaded "dependency."

93. William Cohen, *At Freedom's Edge: Black Mobility and the Southern White Quest for Racial Control, 1861–1915* (Baton Rouge: Louisiana State University Press, 1991), 47–49. Thomas was a reluctant supporter of the policy. His views were closer to those of the *New Orleans Tribune*, as he believed the freedmen needed protection from fraud and violence instead of control through labor regulations. If they were protected from violations of their rights, labor supply would adjust to meet demand. Thomas was nothing if not a believer in the efficiency of markets. Thomas to Howard, October 12, 1865, M826, Roll 1, BRFAL.

94. Cohen, *At Freedom's Edge*, 52, 58–59, 72–73, 77. Between 1865 and 1868 the bureau reported having transported almost thirty thousand freedmen to areas with labor shortages. Cohen believes these figures understate the number (59n34). Most of the Bureau's transfers followed the paths of the second passage, from East Coast states such as Virginia and South Carolina to the Mississippi River Valley and, interestingly, southwest Georgia. These were the labor-starved areas of the Deep South.

95. Brevet Brigadier General J. Irvin Gregg, General Orders No. 13, in Hahn et al., *Land and Labor, 1865*, 247; Hayden et al., *Land and Labor, 1866–1867*, 124. In response to a planter's complaints about supporting nonworking members of freedmen's families, Davis Tillson told the planter, "The laws of your own State and the orders of the Bureau require you to provide for your worn out, old, and decrepid slaves until the State makes some other provision to take care of its poor." November 20, 1865, Hahn et al., *Land and Labor, 1865*, 671.

96. O'Donovan, *Becoming Free in the Cotton South*, 183–84, 193, 234; Hayden et al., *Land and Labor, 1866–1867*, 370–71, 556, 607. O'Donovan quotes a Mississippi agent who observed, "The older people are trying to get their families together," and

"Employers will have to contract with the heads of [freed] families." Jacqueline Jones, *Labor of Love, Labor of Sorrow: Black Women, Work and the Family from Slavery to the Present* (New York: Vintage, 1986), 58–59, 65. Jones points out that the status of Black women after the Civil War "cannot be separated from their roles as wives and mothers within a wider setting of kinship obligations."

97. Tillson is quoted in Cohen, *At Freedom's Edge*, 60. Steven Hahn and his coeditors suggest that the bureau was pushing freedmen into "undesirable" employment without dealing with the consequences. Hahn et al., *Land and Labor, 1865*, 612. I think this is an exaggeration, given the bureau's policies on wages, crop liens, and labor mobility.

98. James E. Yeatman to O.O. Howard, July 4, 1865 in Hahn et al., *Land and Labor, 1865*, 361; O.O. Howard, Report of the Commissioner, 12; Stuart Eldridge, General Orders No. 5, July 29, 1865; assistant commissioner for Mississippi, House Exec. Doc. 70, 167, 174. Howard believed agents were setting wages too low due to "a sort of morbid sympathy ... from constant contact with those who really feel that they have lost everything in losing their Confederate money and their slaves. [The agents] do not consider the past dues to the blacks, nor the ability of planters to secure land or crops in payment for labor." O.O. Howard to James Yeatman, July 10, 1865, in Hahn et al., *Land and Labor, 1865*, 360. Wager Swayne to O.O. Howard, August 24, 1865, weekly report, M809, Roll 1, BRFAL.

99. Hayden et al., *Land and Labor, 1866–1867*, 74, 93, quote on 98. Emphasis in original.

100. O.O. Howard, circular no. 11, House Exec. Doc. 70, 185–186; J.B. Kiddo, assistant commissioner of Texas, circular no. 19, August 20, 1866, in Hayden et al., *Land and Labor, 1866–1867*, 168, emphasis in original. James Schmidt describes Kiddo as one of the more conservative agents. Schmidt, *Free to Work*, 127–31.

101. Nieman, *To Set the Law in Motion*, 169. Julie Saville argues that the bureau's policy on liens undermined freedmen's claims because the lien was in effect a wage and already subject to debts for furnishing tenants. But by ensuring that freedmen got paid, liens promoted the well-being of freedmen and their families. Saville, *The Work of Reconstruction*, 120, 135.

102. Eric Foner, *Reconstruction: America's Unfinished Revolution, 1863–1877* (New York: Harper & Row, 1988), 144; William F. Troost, "Accomplishment and Abandonment: A History of the Freedmen's Bureau Schools" (PhD diss., University of California, Irvine, 2007), 86, 96, 104, 111–12, 117. As far as I know, Troost's study is the only quantitative analysis of the effects and location of the Freedmen's Bureau schools.

103. W.E.B. Du Bois, *Black Reconstruction in America, 1960–1880* (New York: Atheneum, 1992), 219.

104. Ransome and Sutch calculate that sharecropping reduced tenants' income by 13.5 percent, a level of exploitation that was lower than slavery but still high. I analyze the tenancy trap in chapter 3. Ransom and Sutch, *One Kind of Freedom*, 167, 169.

CHAPTER 3. SAVING SHARECROPPERS?

1. Franklin D. Roosevelt, rear-platform remarks at Dubuque, IA, October 9, 1936, American Presidency Project, www.presidency.ucsb.edu/documents/rear-platform-remarks-dubuque-iowa; annual message to Congress, January 4, 1935, American Presidency Project, www.presidency.ucsb.edu/documents/annual-message-congress-3.

2. Franklin D. Roosevelt, Jackson Day dinner speech, Washington, DC, January 8, 1936, American Presidency Project, www.presidency.ucsb.edu/documents/jackson-day-dinner-address-washington-dc.

3. Franklin D. Roosevelt, address at Little Rock, Arkansas, June 10, 1936, American Presidency Project, www.presidency.ucsb.edu/documents/address-little-rock-arkansas; acceptance speech for the renomination for the presidency, Philadelphia, PA, June 27, 1936, American Presidency Project, www.presidency.ucsb.edu/acceptance-speech-for-the-renomination-for-the-presidency-philadelphia-pa.

4. Franklin D. Roosevelt, radio address to the Young Democratic Clubs of America, August 24, 1935, American Presidency Project, www.presidency.ucsb.edu/documents/radio-address-the-young-democratic-clubs-america-0; address at the San Diego Exposition, October 2, 1935, American Presidency Project, www.presidency.ucsb.edu/documents/address-san-diego-exposition-san-diego-california; James Holt, "The New Deal and the American Anti-statist Tradition," in *The New Deal: The National Level*, ed. John Braeman, Robert H. Bremner, and David Brody (Columbus: Ohio State University Press, 1975), 27–49.

5. *Hearings before the Committee on Labor, House of Representatives,* 74th Cong. (1935) (statement of Sen. Robert Wagner, D-NY); US National Labor Relations Board, *Legislative History of the National Labor Relations Act, 1935*, vol. 2 (Washington, DC: US Government Printing Office, 1949), 2486; Risa L. Goluboff, *The Lost Promise of Civil Rights* (Cambridge, MA: Harvard University Press, 2007), chapter 5. The national scope of New Deal labor law was greatly circumscribed with the failure to extend unionization into the South. See Michael Goldfield, *The Southern Key: Class, Race, and Radicalism in the 1930s and 1940s* (New York: Oxford University Press, 2022).

6. 74 Cong. Rec. (1935) (statement of Arthur Mitchell), quoted in *A Documentary History of The Negro People in the United States, 1933–1945*, ed. Herbert Aptheker (New York: Citadel, 1974), 180–82; John B. Kirby, *Black Americans in the Roosevelt Era: Liberalism and Race* (Knoxville: University of Tennessee Press, 1980), 32, 55–56, 90.

7. Bunche, "Critique of New Deal Social Planning," 65; John P. Davis, "A Survey of the Problems of the Negro under the New Deal," *Journal of Negro Education* 5, no. 1 (January 1936); Charles S. Johnson, *The Economic Status of Negroes* (Washington, DC: Fisk University Press, 1933); Dona C. Hamilton and Charles V. Hamilton, *The Dual Agenda: Race and Social Welfare Policies of Civil Rights Organizations* (New York: Columbia University Press, 1997), chapter 1.

8. For analysis of the Black Cabinet, see Ralph Bunche, *The Political Status of the Negro in the Age of FDR* (Chicago: University of Chicago Press, 1973), chapter 19; Kirby, *Black Americans,* chapter 6, esp. pp. 114–15.

9. Abram Harris, "Future Plan and Program of the NAACP (Harris Report)," in *Black Protest Thought in the Twentieth Century,* 2nd ed., ed. August Meier, Elliot Rudwick, and Francis I. Brodrick (New York: Bobbs-Merrill, 1971), 180. A. Philip Randolph, "Keynote Address," in Aptheker, *The Negro People,* 215–16; Jonathan Scott Holloway, *Confronting the Veil: Abram Harris Jr., E. Franklin Frazier, and Ralph Bunche, 1919–1941* (Chapel Hill: University of North Carolina Press, 2002), 166–67.

10. W. E. B. Du Bois, "The Negro and Social Reconstruction," in *Against Racism: Unpublished Essays, Papers, and Addresses,* ed. Herbert Aptheker (Amherst: University of Massachusetts Press, 1985), 148–49.

11. W. E. B. Du Bois, "A Negro Nation within the Nation," in *W. E. B. Du Bois: A Reader,* ed. David Levering Lewis (New York: Henry Holt, 1995), 566.

12. Aubrey Williams, "The New Relief Program: Three Great Aims," *New York Times,* April 1, 1934.

13. Statement submitted to the Governor's Commission on Farm Tenancy by the Southern Tenant Farmers Union, Farm Tenancy Committee (FTC), Box 1, Dallas, RG 83, NA, p. 2.

14. David L Carlton and Peter A. Coclanis, eds., *Confronting Southern Poverty in the Great Depression: The Report on Economic Conditions of the South* (New York: St. Martin's Press, 1996), 119–20, tables 1–2; W. E. B. Du Bois, *The Souls of Black Folk* (New York: W. W. Norton, 1999), 78, 85; Daron Acemoglu and James A. Robinson, *Why Nations Fail: The Origins of Power, Prosperity, and Poverty* (New York: Crown Business, 2012), 351–57. Acemoglu and Robinson argue that the South is a prime example of an extractive economy that precluded sustained economic development.

15. Gavin Wright, *Old South, New South: Revolutions in the Southern Economy since the Civil War* (New York: Basic Books, 1986); W. E. B. Du Bois, *Black Reconstruction in America, 1860–1880* (New York: Atheneum, 1992), 703.

16. David Harvey, "The New Imperialism," *Socialist Register* 40 (2004): 73–76.

17. Roosevelt, radio address to Young Democratic Clubs of America, August 24, 1935.

18. W. E B. Du Bois, "Federal Action Programs and Community Action in the South," *Social Forces* 19 (1941): 375–80.

19. Hopkins is quoted in Paul Mertz, *New Deal Policy and Southern Rural Poverty* (Baton Rouge: Louisiana State University Press, 1978), 76; Hopkins to Lawrence Westbrook, an FERA administrator, November 5, 1934, Hopkins Papers, Box 69, FDRL. Pete Daniel, *Breaking the Land: The Transformation of Cotton, Tobacco, and Rice Cultures Since 1880* (Urbana: University of Illinois Press, 1985), 86.

20. Quoted in Jason Manthorne, "As You Sow: Culture, Agriculture, and the New Deal" (PhD diss., University of Georgia, 2013), 189. Manthorne's study of the

Farm Security Administration is the best recent account of the origin and implementation of the agency's understanding of rehabilitation. Unfortunately, it was never published.

21. Charles S. Johnson, Edwin R. Embree, and W. W. Alexander, *The Collapse of Cotton Tenancy* (Chapel Hill: University of North Carolina Press, 1935); Arthur F. Raper, *Preface to Peasantry: A Tale of Two Black Belt Counties* (Chapel Hill: University of North Carolina Press, 1936). Manthorne, "As You Sow," chapters 5 and 6, examines Arthur Raper's views and his role with the Farm Security Administration.

22. Alice O'Connor, *Poverty Knowledge: Social Science, Social Policy, and the Poor in Twentieth-Century U.S. History* (Princeton, NJ: Princeton University Press, 2001), 68–71.

23. Amanda Coleman, "Reform(ulat)ing the Region: Competing Discourses of Region and Regional Change in the Depression-Era U.S. South," (PhD diss., University of Oregon, 2008), 149.

24. Interview with MLB, Sharecropper Oral History Collection of Mary Holmes Junior College, Mississippi State University Library, Special Collections (hereafter MHC Oral Histories). Because verbatim quotes from the interviewees are not permitted, the Special Collections Department of the MSU library granted permission for me to paraphrase statements from the interviews. Individuals are identified by their initials. My thanks to the MSU library staff for their help.

25. Quoted in Harold D. Woodman, "Post–Civil War Southern Agriculture and the Law," *Agricultural History* 53, no. 1 (January 1979): 325. Woodman points out that the changes in lien laws were detrimental to share tenants as well as sharecroppers.

26. The Census Bureau reported that there were 39,073 tenant plantations in 325 Southern counties, 77 percent of which were in Deep South states. See "Plantations in the South," US Bureau of the Census, *The Thirteenth Census (1910)* (Washington, DC: US Government Printing Office, 1913), chapter 12, 880–81.

27. Jay R. Mandle, "The Plantation States as a Sub-region of the Post-bellum South," *Journal of Economic History* 34, no. 3 (September 1974): 732–38; Nan Elizabeth Woodruff, *American Congo: The African American Freedom Struggle in the Delta* (Cambridge, MA: Harvard University Press, 2003).

28. Harold Hoffsommer, *Landlord-Tenant Relations and Relief in Alabama*, Research Bulletin, series 2, no. 9 (Washington, DC: Federal Emergency Relief Administration, 1935).

29. Charles S. Johnson, *Shadow of the Plantation* (Chicago: University of Chicago Press, 1966), 3–4, 19–24, 126–27. Johnson quotes tenants who belie his interpretation (19–20).

30. Johnson, *Shadow of the Plantation*, 127; Raper, *Preface to Peasantry*, 4, 159, 172–73. Raper was aware of the lies and misleading claims of planters. Manthorne argues that he and others simply ignored the exploitation embedded in tenancy in favor of their cultural interpretation. Manthorne, "As You Sow," 241–45.

31. T. Roy Reid to Will Alexander, with attached Constance Daniel report, December 5, 1938, AD-910, Box 394, RG 96, NA, p. 13; Neil R. McMillen, *Dark*

Journey: Black Mississippians in the Age of Jim Crow (Urbana: University of Illinois Press, 1989), 119, 124; Stephen Kantrowitz, *Ben Tillman and the Reconstruction of White Supremacy* (Chapel Hill: University of North Carolina Press, 2000), 15; Woodruff, *American Congo*, 33–37, 79, chapter 4.

32. Allison Davis, Burleigh B Gardner, and Mary R. Gardner, *Deep South: A Social Anthropological Study of Caste and Class* (Chicago: University of Chicago Press, 1941), 331, 356, emphasis in original; Walter Johnson, *River of Dark Dreams: Slavery and Empire in the Cotton Kingdom* (Cambridge, MA: Harvard University Press, 2013), 179–80. Sharecroppers were explicit about how food rationing was used to discipline them. SB said that planters would furnish him and his family with food only every two weeks, and the food was rationed. JB recalled that each member of her family received only so much flour and meat per person, and they had to share food. MHC Oral Histories.

33. Quoted in Theodore Rosengarten, *All God's Dangers: The Life of Nate Shaw* (Chicago: University of Chicago Press, 1974), 107.

34. E. A. Schuler, *Social Status and Farm Tenure: Attitudes and Social Conditions of Corn Belt and Cotton Belt Farmers*, Social Research Report No. 4 (Washington, DC: US Department of Agriculture, Farm Security Administration, 1938), 30, figure 9. Schuler interviewed 2,423 tenants in nine Southern counties and four Corn Belt counties. The survey included counties in four Deep South states—Alabama, Arkansas, Louisiana, and South Carolina.

35. MHC Oral Histories; Schuler, *Social Status and Farm Tenure*, 90, figure 15; Johnson, *Shadow of the Plantation*, 120.

36. Davis, Gardner, and Gardner, *Deep South*, 370; interviews with CA, LC, and AS, MHC Oral Histories. These interviews contain ample evidence of the cheating and violence African American sharecroppers labored under.

37. Davis, Gardner, and Gardner, *Deep South*, 403; McMillen, *Dark Journey*, 138–39, 149–50.

38. T. J. Woofter Jr., *Landlord and Tenant on the Cotton Plantation*, Works Progress Administration, Division of Social Research, Research Monograph 5 (Washington, DC: US Government Printing Office, 1936), 109–10, tables 41, 42; "The Tenancy Problem," Dept of Agriculture, Grey Binder, Box 6, RG 83, NA. Woofter found that tenants had lived on their present farm for an average of 8.2 years.

39. Walter Rowland, oral history, June 1939 Southern History Collection, University of North Carolina (hereafter SHC). Payments under Agricultural Adjustment Programs, Division of Information, AAA, November 10, 1941, Collection Services Branch, National Agricultural Library. Warren Whatley, "Labor for the Picking: The New Deal in the South," *Journal of Economic History* 43 (1983): 914; Daniel, *Breaking the Land*, 95.

40. James D. Ross, *The Rise and Fall of the Southern Tenant Farmers Union in Arkansas* (Knoxville: University of Tennessee Press, 2018), chapters 2–3; Jerold S. Auerbach, "Southern Tenant Farmers: Socialist Critics of the New Deal," *Arkansas Historical Quarterly* 27, no. 2 (Summer 1968): 119; Robin D. G. Kelly, *Hammer and*

Hoe: Alabama Communists during the Great Depression (Chapel Hill: University of North Carolina Press, 1990), chapter 2, 9.

41. The membership data come from a 1937 STFU survey of members and are close to the estimates of historians. Data on county memberships are based on the author's calculations. M. Langley Biegert, "Legacy of Resistance: Uncovering the History of Collective Action by Black Agricultural Workers in Central East Arkansas from the 1860s to the 1930s," *Journal of Social History* 32, no. 1 (Autumn 1998): 88; Coleman, "Reform(ulat)ing the Region," 101; Jason Manthorne, "The View from the Cotton: Reconsidering the Southern Tenant Farmers' Union," *Agricultural History* 84, no. 1 (2010): 25; Woodruff, *American Congo*, 163–64.

42. The data on local Garvey chapters is drawn from Mary G. Rolinson, *Grassroots Garveyism: The Universal Negro Improvement Association in the Rural South, 1920–1927* (Chapel Hill: University of North Carolina Press, 2007). The RA survey and responses are reported in Jack Temple Kirby, *Rural Worlds Lost: The American South, 1920–1960* (Baton Rouge: Louisiana State University Press, 1987), 239–40.

43. Kirby, *Rural Worlds Lost*, 268.

44. Interview with WDS, MHC Oral Histories; Whatley, "Labor for the Picking," 914–16. Whatley calculates that planters received an average AAA benefit payment of $12.72 per acre on land farmed by wage labor, compared to $8.82 for land worked by sharecroppers and $6.43 for share tenants.

45. William C. Holly, Ellen Winston, and T. J. Woofter Jr., *The Plantation South, 1934–1937*, Works Progress Administration, Research Monograph 22 (Washington, DC: US Government Printing Office, 1940), 94–95, tables 21, 23. Hoffsommer, *Landlord-Tenant Relations*, 3, 17.

46. Daniel, *Breaking the Land*, 66, 72, 100; L. C. Gray to Henry Wallace, January 14, 1935, Grey Binder, Box 6, RG 83, NA; Mertz, *New Deal Policy*, 48–67.

47. The decisive evidence on the role of AAA payments in displacing tenants is presented in Briggs Depew, Price V. Fishback, and Paul W. Rhode, "New Deal or No Deal in the Cotton South: The Effect of the AAA on the Agricultural Labor Structure," *Explorations in Economic History* 50 (2013): 466–86. Depew and his colleagues do not explore why so many Black share managers were displaced and why white share managers escaped the initial enclosure. It is possible that many displaced Black share managers ended up working as croppers. This would explain the increase in the number of tenants, however slight, in counties where large numbers of Black share managers were displaced.

48. Nancy Virts, "Change in the Plantation System: American South, 1910–1945," *Explorations in Economic History* 43 (2006): 153–76; Jack Temple Kirby, "The Transformation of Southern Plantations," *Agricultural History* 57 (1983): 257–76. Southern counties contained a mixture of multi-unit and single-unit farms.

49. Mertz, *New Deal Policy*, 118. Russell argued that the money was for landless farmers, mainly tenants, who were not eligible for loans from the Farm Credit Administration. It's a safe assumption that he meant white tenants.

50. Mertz, *New Deal Policy*, 95–102.

51. "The Problem of Farm Tenancy," statement by Secretary Henry A. Wallace, *Hearings on the Bankhead Tenancy Bill*, S.1800, March 5, 1935, 5. See also "The Tenancy Problem," n.d., Grey Binder, Box 6, RG 83, NA.

52. Rexford Tugwell, Diaries, January 23, 1935, FDRL, p. 6; John H. Bankhead to Henry A. Wallace, March 14, 1935, Tenancy, Box 2253, RG 16, NA; Tugwell, Diaries, March 31, 1935. AAA subsidy programs were created to raise the prices of agricultural commodities to parity with the prices of manufactured goods.

53. L. C. Gray to Henry A. Wallace, January 14, 1935, 2–3; Gray to M. L. Wilson, February 18, 1935, Grey Binder, Box 6, RG 83, NA.

54. John P. Davis to Walter White, n.d.; Data on Bankhead Bill, S 2367 (memo); Walter White to Charles Houston, March 22, 1935, NAACP I: C233, Administrative Files, Congressional Action, Bankhead Bill, Library of Congress; NAACP resolution reported in Raymond Wolters, *Negroes and the Great Depression: The Problem of Economic Recovery* (Westport, CT: Greenwood, 1970), 62. Jackson argued that nothing in the legislation provided for adjustments to rent, compensation for improvement to the land, or protections against eviction. Gardner Jackson to Henry A. Wallace and Rexford Tugwell, November 18, 1936, Correspondence on FTC, Box 4, RG 83, NA.

55. F. F. Elliot to Paul Appleby, October 28, 1936, Box 5, RG 83, NA.

56. Jess Gilbert and Steve Brown, "Alternative Land Reform Proposals in the 1930s: The Nashville Agrarians and the Southern Tenant Farmers' Union," *Agricultural History* 55, no. 4 (October 1981): 351–69.

57. Statement submitted to the Governor's Commission on Farm Tenancy by the Southern Tenants Farmers Union, FTC, Box 1 Dallas, RG 83, NA, pp. 3, 19, 25. Supplement to Southern Tenant Farmers' Union Statement on Farm Tenancy, October 10, 1936, FTC, Box 1, Hearings, RG 83, NA pp. 4, 6.

58. Supplement to Southern Tenant Farmers' Union Statement, 19–20.

59. Quotations in Rosengarten, *All God's Dangers,* 108; Ross, *The Rise and Fall of the STFU,* 88.

60. Ross, *The Rise and Fall of the STFU,* 86–87; Manthorne, "The View from the Cotton," 28–29.

61. Quoted in Greta de Jong, *A Different Day: African American Struggles for Justice in Rural Louisiana, 1900–1970* (Chapel Hill: University of North Carolina Press, 2002), 77–79, 109.

62. Schuler, *Social Status and Farm Tenure,* 66, 68, 73. James D. Ross attributes the desire for land ownership to the religious values of tenants. I am skeptical.

63. Mertz, *New Deal Policy,* 149–50.

64. Rexford G. Tugwell, "The Resettlement Idea," *Agricultural History* 33, no. 4 (1959): 160.

65. Tugwell, Diaries, pp. 6, 71.

66. Marie Panor, "The Resettlement Administration: A Study in the Evolution of Major Purposes," (master's thesis, University of Chicago, 1951), 57–58. Panor maintains that without the rural rehabilitation program, Congress would have abolished the RA program in 1936.

67. Roughly 105,200 tenants received an original rural rehabilitation loan in the six Deep South states, about 14.5 percent of all tenants in those states.

68. Oral history interview with Rexford Tugwell, January 21, 1965, Archives of American Art, Smithsonian Institution; Tugwell to Robert Hudgens, Farm Security Administration, January–August 1935, OF 1568, Box 1, FDRL. Robert Nipp, "The Negro in the Rural Resettlement Program: A Comment," *Agricultural History* 45 (1971): 199; Donald Holley, *Uncle Sam's Farmers: The New Communities in the Lower Mississippi Valley* (Urbana: University of Illinois Press, 1975), 186–87; Sidney Baldwin, *Poverty and Politics: The Rise and Decline of the Farm Security Administration* (Chapel Hill: University of North Carolina Press, 1968), 94.

69. L. C. Gray had no illusions about the racist origins of Southern tenancy, though he had a negative view of tenants. He told Wallace, "The tenant system . . . replaced the slavery regime as a means of controlling raw labor power and the social conduct of millions of ignorant and primitive laborers. It was a social order frequently associated with excessive exploitation and considerable economic tyranny." L. C. Gray to Henry A. Wallace, January 14, 1935, Tenancy, Box 2253, RG 16, NA, p. 1.

70. Robert Hudgens, "Rural Problems—The Present Situation in the South," 2, attached to Robert Hudgens to Milo Perkins, March 22, 1937, RR-161, Box 11; Bernard Joy to J. R. Allgyer, assistant director, rural rehabilitation, Alabama, RR-560, Reports Region V, Box 28, RG 96, NA. Olaf F. Larson, *Ten Years of Rural Rehabilitation in the United States* (Washington, DC: Bureau of Agricultural Economics, USDA, 1947), 360, appendix table 7.

71. Johnson, *Shadow of the Plantation*, 208; Manthorne, "As You Sow," chapter 5.

72. Tugwell, quoted in Larson, *Ten Years of Rural Rehabilitation*, 131; Florida FSA administrator quoted in Florida Report, RR 101–103, Box 6, RG 96, NA.

73. Manthorne, "As You Sow," 293, 302–4.

74. Larson, *Ten Years of Rural Rehabilitation*, 131, 134–35, 157. Taylor and Bishop are quoted in Manthorne, "As You Sow," 273, 309.

75. Paul Maris to Joseph L. Dailey, April 3, 1936, RR 560 Reports, Folder Region VI; "RA Does Not Back Debts of Clients," Box 30, RR 503-02, Complaints; Tugwell to Senator Pat Harrison (D-Mississippi), April 7, 1936, RR 503, Folder F, Box 21, RG 96, NA. This policy contradicts Manthorne's argument. His study is unique for its analysis of the cultural model of rehabilitation and his detailed description of the process of supervision. But his failure to examine RA/FSA policies renders his account one-sided.

76. J. R. Butler and H. L. Mitchell to Franklin D. Roosevelt, November 20, 1936; Clyde Johnson to L. C. Gray, January 22, 1937, FTC (Plans) 184–054, Box 7, RG 83. Butler, Mitchell, and Johnson wrote these letters to influence the administration's debate over a new tenant policy to replace the RA.

77. Schuler, *Social Status and Farm Tenure*, 164–68, figure 22, tables 96, 98.

78. Maris to Dailey, April 3, 1936, RR 560, Reports, Region VI, RG 96, NA; Excerpt from regional director's weekly report, January 25, 1937, no. 177, Box 4, RG

83, NA; administrator to T. Roy Reid, December 31, 1936, p. 3, Box 38, Annual Report VI, RG 83, NA.

79. Larson, *Ten Years of Rural Rehabilitation*, 166–67, table 8.

80. Larson, *Ten Years of Rural Rehabilitation*, 171, 174–75. Larson's data show that the median loan amount for croppers was lower than that for tenants or wage labor. Larson provides no explanation. In his 1936 report, Reid said that tenant farmers in Arkansas used 87 percent of their income for food, clothes, and health. Annual Report Region VI, December 31, 1936, 183–04, Box 38 RG 96, NA. Unfortunately, these data are not available by race of tenant or cropper.

81. Julian Brown to Joseph L. Dailey, December 25, 1935, RR 560, Box 28, RG 96, NA; Report of the administrator of the Farm Security Administration, 1939, p. 6; Mertz, *New Deal Policy*, 202; Larson, *Ten Years of Rural Rehabilitation*, 257, 265. Beginning in 1938, FSA policy required a written contract for all loans.

82. Internal FSA memorandum, no author, TP 550–01, E20, n.d. (1937?), Box 43, RG 96, NA.

83. Larson, *Ten Years of Rural Rehabilitation*, 421, appendix table 68. Interview with TB, a sharecropper, MCH Oral Histories.

84. White is quoted in Wolter, *Negroes and the Great Depression*, 61; Carl Taylor to R. B. Atwood, September 16, 1935, RS 169, Box 6, RG 96, NA.

85. Author's calculations based on Larson, *Ten Years of Rural Rehabilitation*, 361–62, appendix tables 8 and 9.

86. The regression analysis is based on expenditure and demographic data drawn from the Deep South New Deal dataset. It includes all 493 counties in Deep South states. The data sources are listed in the appendix. Changes in the number of Black share managers, number of single-unit farms, and cotton acreage are all statistically significant. See table A.1 for specification of the model and details.

87. Carl Taylor to Will Alexander, March 23, 1936, AD-060, Box 7, RG 96, NA; Sarah Boxer, "Whitewashing the Great Depression," *The Atlantic* (December 2020), 102–5. Dorothea Lange was told to take pictures of the "plight of white victims" and to "avoid representing instances of interracial sociality." "The Reminiscences of Will W. Alexander," oral history (New York: Trustees of Columbia University, 1972), 608. Despite his opposition to racial identities, Alexander sought to ensure that Blacks received rehabilitation loans, and as director of the FSA he put Blacks on state committees allocating tenant purchase loans. Kirby, *Black Americans in the Roosevelt Era*, 52.

88. The data are drawn from Richard Sterner, *The Negro's Share: A Study of Income, Consumption, Housing and Public Assistance* (New York: Harper & Brothers, 1943), 299, table 121. Sterner argues that proportionality is a misleading criterion for judging the distribution of loans. He prefers an estimate of low-income farmers and argues that low-income Blacks received 11 percent of loans, compared to whites, who received 22 percent of loans in the four Southern regions. He does not provide data for separate states or any information on how he reached this estimate.

89. De Jong, *A Different Day*, 108. The FSA supervisor for St. Landry Parish told a regional administrator that his office had been "swamped with colored people

wanting loans and stating that they were members of the Farmers Union and were told to apply for loans." Louis Fontenot Jr. to Kate Fulton, February 9, 1937, RR-LA-14, 911–045, Box 393, RG 96, NA.

90. Sterner, *The Negro's Share,* 422, table 71. I analyze the distribution of rehabilitation, tenant purchase loans, and resettlement projects for Black landowners in chapter 4.

91. L. C. Gray, "Disadvantaged Rural Classes," *Journal of Farm Economics* 20, no. 1 (February 1938): 82–83; Daniel, *Breaking the Land,* 243; Manthorne, "As You Sow," 254.

92. Gilbert and Brown, "Alternative Land Reform Proposals," 362.

93. Manthorne, "The View from the Cotton," 34–40.

94. *Hearings, Select Committee of the House Committee on Agriculture to Investigate the Activities of the Farm Security Administration,* House of Representatives, 78th Cong., 1st sess., part 1 (Washington, DC: US Government Printing Office, 1943), 189, 196. Grant McConnell, *The Decline of Agrarian Democracy* (New York: Atheneum, 1969), 104, 106–7.

CHAPTER 4. BLACK ENCLAVES AND THE AFRICAN AMERICAN QUEST FOR LAND

1. Frederick Douglass, *Life and Times of Frederick Douglass* (New York: Library of America, 1994), 932–33.

2. Thavolia Glymph, *Out of the House of Bondage: The Transformation of the Plantation Household* (New York: Cambridge University Press, 2008), 9; Edward Magdol, *A Right to the Land: Essays on the Freedmen's Community* (Westport, CT: Greenwood, 1977), 123, 143. *Proceedings of the National Colored Labor Convention,* Washington, DC, December 1869 (Washington, DC: The New Era, 1870), 30.

3. Jarod Roll, "'The Lazarus of American Farmers': The Politics of Black Agrarianism in the Jim Crow South, 1921–1938," in *Beyond Forty Acres and a Mule,* ed. Debra A. Reid and Evan P. Bennett (Gainesville: University Press of Florida, 2012), 133, 135.

4. Roger L. Ransom and Richard Sutch, *One Kind of Freedom: The Economic Consequences of Freedom* (New York: Cambridge University Press, 1977), 83–85.

5. Loren Schweninger, *Black Property Owners in the South, 1790–1915* (Urbana: University of Illinois Press, 1990), 146; author's calculations based on the 1900 and 1920 US Censuses of Agriculture.

6. Mary G. Rolinson, *Grassroots Garveyism: The Universal Negro Improvement Association in the Rural South, 1920–1927* (Chapel Hill: University of North Carolina Press, 2007); Carter Woodson, *The Rural Negro* (Washington, DC: Association for the Study of Negro Life, 1930), 112, 123–31; Charles S. Aiken, *The Cotton Plantation South since the Civil War* (Baltimore, MD: Johns Hopkins University Press, 1998), 158–60.

7. Peggy G. Hargis, "Beyond the Marginality Thesis: The Acquisition and Loss of Land by African Americans in Georgia, 1880–1930," *Agricultural History* 72, no. 2 (Spring 1998): 246; Robert Higgs, "Accumulation of Property by Southern Blacks before World War I," *American Economic Review* 72, no. 4 (September 1982): 725–37. Higgs's results are not due to an overvaluation of Black property. Andrew Kharl argues that Black property in Georgia was assessed for tax at rates higher than its actual value. This was true for most states in the Jim Crow South but not Georgia, where, according to W. E. B. Du Bois, Black property in the early twentieth century was assessed at $7.1 million but valued at $15 million. Andrew Kharl, *The Black Tax: 150 Years of Theft, Exploitation, and Dispossession in America* (Chicago: University of Chicago Press, 2024), 28; W. E. B. Du Bois, "Georgia Negroes and Their Fifty Millions of Savings," *World's Work* 18 (May 1909): 11551.

8. Author's calculations from 1925 US Census of Agriculture. The mean value of buildings and land for Black landowners in plantation counties was $1,830; for those in nonplantation counties it was $1,174, one-third less. Data for the value of buildings and land by the race of owner are not available from the censuses of agriculture before 1925.

9. Valerie Grim, "African American Landlords in the Rural South, 1870–1950," *Agricultural History* 72, no. 2 (Spring 1998): 407.

10. Elizabeth Rauh Bethel, *Promiseland: A Century of Life in a Negro Community* (Columbia: University of South Carolina Press, 1997), 44–45, 108–10. The marginal economic success of Promised Land farmers was typical for the Piedmont but not necessarily for the Mississippi Delta.

11. Manning Marable, "The Politics of Black Land Tenure: 1877–1915," *Agricultural History* 53, no. 1 (January 1979): 145.

12. Kimberly S. Johnson, "Racial Orders, Congress, and the Agricultural Welfare State, 1865–1940," *Studies in American Political Development,* 25, no. 2 (October 2011): 1–19; Elizabeth Sanders, *Roots of Reform: Farmers, Workers, and the American State, 1877–1917* (Chicago: University of Chicago Press, 1999), chapter 9.

13. Author's calculations from *County Reports of Federal Expenditures, 1933–1939*, report no. 10, vol. 2, (Washington, DC: Office of Government Reports), 1940.

14. *Proceedings of the Southern States Convention of Colored Men,* Columbia, SC, October 1871 (Columbia, SC: Carolina Printing Co., 1871), 25.

15. *Proceedings of the National Colored Labor Convention,* 30.

16. Tunde Adeleke, ed., *Martin R. Delany's Civil War and Reconstruction* (Jackson: University Press of Mississippi, 2020), 52–64.

17. Eric Foner, *Politics and Ideology in the Age of the Civil War* (New York: Oxford University Press, 1980), 139; Michael W. Fitzgerald, *The Union League Movement in the Deep South* (Baton Rouge: Louisiana State University Press, 1989), 117–27.

18. Michael L. Lanza, *Agrarianism and Reconstruction Politics: The Southern Homestead Act* (Baton Rouge: Louisiana State University Press, 1990); Christie Farnham Pope, "Southern Homesteads for Negroes," *Agricultural History* 44, no. 2 (April 1970): 201–12; Rene Hayden, Anthony Kaye, Kate Masur, Steven Miller,

Susan O'Donovan, Leslie Rowland, Stephen West, eds., *Land and Labor, 1866–1867* (Chapel Hill: University of North Carolina Press, 2013), 891–92; Paul W. Gates, "Federal Land Policies in the Southern Public Land States," *Agricultural History* 53, no. 1 (January 1979): 216. Nineteenth-century public land states were those in which a large portion of land was owned by the federal government.

19. Roger L. Ransom, "Reconstructing Reconstruction: Options and Limitations to Federal Policies on Land Distribution in 1866–67," *Civil War History* 51, no. 4 (December 2005): 373–74.

20. *Proceedings of the Constitutional Convention of South Carolina*, January 14–March 17, 1868 (Charleston, SC: Denny A. Perry, 1868), 1: 379–381. Cain was quoting Horace Greeley, editor of the *New-York Tribune*. Richard L. Hume and Jerry B. Gough, *Blacks, Carpetbaggers, and Scalawags: The Constitutional Conventions of Radical Reconstruction* (Baton Rouge: Louisiana State University Press, 2008), 172–73. Hume and Gough report that at the South Carolina convention, the most radical of the state constitutional conventions, Blacks made up 60 percent of delegates.

21. Richard Franklin Bensel, *Yankee Leviathan: The Origins of Central State Authority in America, 1859–1877* (New York: Cambridge University Press, 1990), 349–53.

22. Adeleke, *Martin R. Delany's Civil War*, 48–49. Eric Foner, *Reconstruction: America's Unfinished Revolution, 1863–1877* (New York: Harper & Row, 1988), 236; Frederick Douglass, "What the Black Man Wants," speech, April 1865, in Philip S. Foner, ed., *The Life and Writings of Frederick Douglass* (New York: International Publishers, 1955), 158–59.

23. Orville Vernon Burton, "African American Status and Identity in a Postbellum Community: An Analysis of the Manuscript Census Returns," *Agricultural History* 72, no. 2 (Spring 1998): 223. On the importance of kinship for fostering land ownership, see Bethel, *Promiseland*, 31, 63–65.

24. Carol K. Rothrock Bleser, *The Promised Land: The History of the South Carolina Land Commission, 1869–1890* (Columbia: University of South Carolina Press, 1969), 39, 83, 167.

25. Claude F. Oubre, *Forty Acres and a Mule: The Freedmen's Bureau and Black Land Ownership* (Baton Rouge: Louisiana State University Press, 1978), 28–29; Magdol, *A Right to the Land*, 146; Hayden et al., *Land and Labor, 1866–1867*, 899, doc. 302. Gerald David Jaynes, *Branches without Roots: Genesis of the Black Working Class in the American South, 1862–1882* (New York: Oxford University Press, 1986), 289–93; Duncan, *Freedom's Shore*, 35–37; Steven Hahn, *A Nation under Our Feet: Black Political Struggles in the Rural South from Slavery to the Great Migration* (Cambridge, MA: Harvard University Press, 2003), 457–58.

26. Aiken, *The Cotton Plantation South*, 66–68; J. William Harris, *Deep Souths: Delta, Piedmont, and Sea Island Society in the Age of Segregation* (Baltimore, MD: Johns Hopkins University Press, 2001).

27. W. E. B. Du Bois, "The Negro Farmer," *Bulletin* 8 (Washington, DC: US Bureau of the Census, 1904), 69–98, reprinted in Herbert Aptheker, ed., *Contribu-*

tions by W. E. B. Du Bois in *Government Publications and Proceedings* (Millwood, NY: Kraus-Thomsom, 1980), 291.

28. *Plantations in the South*, Census of the United States, 1910, vol. 5, *Agriculture, 1909 and 1910, General Report and Analysis* (Washington, DC: US Government Printing Office, 1913).

29. Quoted in Neil R. McMillen, *Dark Journey: Black Mississippians in the Age of Jim Crow* (Urbana: University of Illinois Press, 1989), 120.

30. Arthur F. Raper, *Preface to Peasantry: A Tale of Two Black Belt Counties* (Chapel Hill: University of North Carolina Press, 1936), 124; McMillen, *Dark Journey*, 118–19.

31. Robert Zabawa and Sarah T. Warren, "From Company to Community: Agricultural Community Development in Macon County, Alabama, 1881 to the New Deal," *Agricultural History* 72, no. 2 (Spring 1998): 459–86; Marable, "The Politics of Black Land Tenure," 145–46.

32. Michael Rudolph West, *The Education of Booker T. Washington: American Democracy and the Idea of Race Relations* (New York: Columbia University Press, 2006); Harold Cruse, *Rebellion or Revolution* (New York: William Morrow, 1968), chapter 13; Michael C. Dawson, *Black Visions: The Roots of Contemporary African American Political Ideologies* (Chicago: University of Chicago Press, 2001), 281–89.

33. Harold Cruse, *The Crisis of the Negro Intellectual: A Historical Analysis of the Failure of Black Leadership* (New York: Quill, 1984), 20; Robert L. Allen, *Black Awakening in Capitalist America: An Analytic History* (New York: Anchor, 1969), 98–99; August Meier, *Negro Thought in America, 1880–1915* (Ann Arbor: University of Michigan Press, 1963), 101; Karen J. Ferguson, "'Caught in 'No Man's Land.': The Negro Cooperative Demonstration Service and the Ideology of Booker T. Washington, 1900–1918," Agricultural History 72, no. 1 (1998): 33–54. For a revisionist account of Washington, see Desmond Jagmohan, "Booker T. Washington and the Politics of Deception," in *African American Political Thought*, ed. Melvin L. Rogers and Jack Turner (Chicago: University of Chicago Press, 2021), 167–91.

34. Harris, *Deep Souths*, 21–26; Eric Foner, *Nothing but Freedom: Emancipation and Its Legacy* (Baton Rouge: Louisiana State University Press, 1983), 90–96, 107–10.

35. Harris, *Deep Souths*, 26.

36. John C. Willis, *Forgotten Time: The Yazoo-Mississippi Delta after the Civil War* (Charlottesville: University Press of Virginia, 2000), 53, 56–57. I am drawing on Willis's excellent history for this analysis of landowning in the Mississippi Delta.

37. Willis, *Forgotten Time*, 68–69, 128. In 1900 the average age of croppers was 34.3 years, tenants 37.8, and owners 46.

38. Willis, *Forgotten Time*, 166.

39. Louis R. Harlan, *Booker T. Washington: The Wizard of Tuskegee, 1901–1915* (New York: Oxford University Press, 1983), 213–17; Zabawa and Warren, "From Company to Community."

40. Raper, *Preface to Peasantry*, 148.

41. Raper, *Preface to Peasantry*, 129, 132. For a different perspective, see Bethel, *Promiseland*.

42. Marable, "The Politics of Black Land Tenure," 148. Marable provides no evidence for this generalization, but it is a plausible inference from the data.

43. Bethel, *Promiseland*, chapter 1. John Lewis is quoted in Aiken, *The Cotton Plantation South*, 159. Andrew Kharl provides a thorough account of how white officials in Southern towns denied public services to Black neighborhoods. Kharl, *The Black Tax*, chapter 7.

44. Bethel, *Promiseland*, 42–45, 49, table 3.

45. Janet S. Hermann, *The Pursuit of a Dream* (New York: Oxford University Press, 1981), 222.

46. August Meier, "Booker T. Washington and the Town of Mound Bayou," *Phylon* 15, no. 4 (1954): 396–401; Hermann, *Pursuit of a Dream*, 222–25.

47. Robert Higgs concluded that census data on land values were more accurate than tax assessments. See Higgs, "Accumulation of Property by Southern Blacks," 727–28. One difficulty is that the value of white-owned farms is based on both plantation and nonplantation farms. But there is no way around this, since the agricultural censuses do not distinguish between them.

48. Harlan, *Booker T. Washington*, 217; McMillen, *Dark Journey*, 186–90. McMillen concludes that Mound Bayou's "problems "were less the problems of economic scale than of economic separation; its failures, in the last analysis, were the failures of the group economy itself." McMillen is right that Blacks could not build a parallel economy; my point is that their real motivation was establishing a measure of independence and autonomy.

49. Ferguson, "Caught in 'No Man's Land,'" 38.

50. Roll, "'The Lazarus of American Farmers,'" 137; Rolinson, *Grassroots Garveyism*, 28, 30–38; Duncan, *Freedom's Shore*, 21–26, 112–16.

51. Roberts is quoted in Mark R. Schultz, "The Dream Realized? African American Landownership in Central Georgia between Reconstruction and World War Two," *Agricultural History* 72, no. 2 (Spring 1998): 306; Bethel, *Promiseland*, 36.

52. Roll, "'The Lazarus of American Farmers,'" 136–37; Hermann, *Pursuit of a Dream*, 228; "The Lesson of Mound Bayou," *Negro World*, March 30, 1929.

53. Quoted in Bethel, *Promiseland*, 38.

54. Stuart E. Tolnay and E. M. Beck, *A Festival of Violence: An Analysis of Southern Lynchings, 1882–1930* (Urbana: University of Illinois Press, 1995), 154–155. William F. Holmes, "Whitecapping: Agrarian Violence in Mississippi, 1902–1906," *Journal of Southern History* 35, no. 2 (May 1969): 165–85.

55. Roll, "'The Lazarus of American Farmers,'" 134; Rolinson, *Grassroots Garveyism*, 109–13.

56. Roll, "'The Lazarus of American Farmers,'" 142–45; "What to Think about the Government Farm Tenancy Program," Statements of Negro Leaders In Agriculture, Home Economics And Rural Life, Thomas Campbell Papers, Tuskegee Archives, Box 22.

57. Walter Packard to J. O. Walker, April 19, 1937, 505–03, B-3 Project Clients, RG 96, NA. Walker was the resettlement director. Amanda Coleman, "Rehabilitating the Region: The New Deal, Gender, and the Remaking of the Rural South," *Southeastern Geographer* 50, no. 2 (Summer 2010): 200–217.

58. Paul Mertz, *New Deal Policy and Southern Rural Poverty* (Baton Rouge: Louisiana State University Press, 1978), 179, 183–87; Sidney Baldwin, *Poverty and Politics: The Rise and Decline of the Farm Security Administration* (Chapel Hill: University of North Carolina Press, 1968), 195–99, 218. Baldwin quipped that FSA officials administering the tenant purchase program sounded like bankers instead of social workers.

59. Charles Houston to Will Alexander, February 9, 1937, NAACP Administrative Files—part I, Box C-250; Walter White to Harry L. Brown, assistant secretary of agriculture, September 15, 1937, Box C-250, LC.

60. Paul V. Maris to Will Alexander, Reports on TP Program, January 6, 1938; February 1, 1938; March 1, 1938; March 31, 1938, RG 96, NA. The Deep South states received 43 percent of tenant purchase loans.

61. Jonathan D. Rose, *A Primer on Farm Mortgage Debt Relief Programs during the 1930s*, (Washington, DC: Federal Reserve Board, 2013), 2–3.

62. Donald Holley, *Uncle Sam's Farmers: The New Communities in the Lower Mississippi Valley* (Urbana: University of Illinois Press, 1975), 188–89.

63. Quoted in "Farm Family Living Brief," Skyline Farms, RF-AL-16, July 7, 1937, Box 42, RG 96, NA.

64. "Establishment of Community Organizations," January 18, 1936, AD-060, 3. Rexford Tugwell wrote a note at the end of this document: "The President O.K.'d this memo today. But suggested we might exercise mgt. control through the budget." Mileston Farms, Mississippi, MS-56, Box 410, RG 96, NA. Resettlement farms were very different from the cooperative farms the STFU advocated, in which property was collectively owned.

65. Carl Taylor to regional director, Mask, Robert Hudgens, and T. Roy Reid, April 17, 1936, RS 931–84, Box 68, RG 96, NA; Wasserman to C. B. Baldwin, March 26, 1936, RP 931, Box 68, RG 96, NA.

66. "General Information Farm Tenant Purchase Project, 7/8/36," RP 911–041, Box 62, Criteria 1934–36, RG 96, NA. Administrators in Texas accepted only tenants who needed a loan in excess of $600. Both criteria would have excluded sharecroppers and many share tenants. Robert Hudgens to Will Alexander, May 12, 1937, 911–041; Paul Maris to Will Alexander, June 5, 1937, RP 911–041, Box 62, RG 96, NA. Resettlement displaced 5,056 tenants in the four Southern regions; these represented over 60 percent of all tenants displaced by the RA. Most of these tenants were found in the six Deep South states. Walter Packard to J. O. Walker, April 19, 1937, 505–03, Box 30, Project Clients, RG 96, NA.

67. Robert Hudgens to Will Alexander, October 19, 1938, Gee's Bend AL-31, RP-700, Box 83, RG 96, NA; W. F. Rutherford to J. D. Pope, January 19, 1937, Box 469 SC-20, RG 96, NA. An FSA community manager in Georgia told Walter Packard, "As you know it has been rather difficult for me to secure farms for colored

tenants in Georgia." W. H. Thomas to Walter Packard, March 3, 1936, Box 365, RR-GA-25. RG 96, NA. See also Donald Holley, "The Negro in the New Deal Resettlement Program," *Agricultural History* 45 (1971): 179–93.

68. Gee's Bend, RR-AL-31, August 9, 1937, Box 81, RG 96, NA; Prairie Farms History, Box 73, 060, RG 96, NA, p. 1. Prairie Farms was built around Booker T. Washington's efforts to set up Black farmers. See Zabawa and Warren, "From Company to Community."

69. James Byrnes to Carl Taylor, February 26, 1936; Hampton Fulmer to Carl Taylor, November 9, 1935, SC-54/21, Box 468, RG 96, NA.

70. *Macon News* editorial, "Fighting Resettlement Projects," March 24, 1937; Statement of Opponents, March 18, 1937; R. H. Saunders, secretary of Montezuma Kiwanis Club, to Orville Pope, RA, March 18, 1937, GA-27, Box 375, Citizen Attitudes; Sidney Moore to Franklin D. Roosevelt, March 17, 1937, GA-27, Box 374, Local, RG 96, NA. The Kiwanis Club letter supporting the project was signed by local elites: physicians, managers, bankers, auto dealers, the local sheriff, two county commissioners, lawyers, cotton buyers, and landowners.

71. Walter Packard to T. Roy Reid, February 27, 1937, with attachment: Walter Packard to Will Alexander, Plan of Operation, LA-18, AD-930, RG 96, NA.

72. Will Alexander to T. G. Biggs (copy), December 17, 1937, AD-913-01; J. Marion Hamley to Allen Ellender, August 11, 1937, AD-913-01, RG 96, NA. See also Jane Adams and D. Gorton, "This Land Ain't My Land: The Eviction of Sharecroppers by the Farm Security Administration," *Agricultural History* 83, no. 3 (Summer 2009): 323–51.

73. *Pittsburgh Courier*, August 13, 1938; Charles Houston to Will Alexander, June 10, 1938; Thurgood Marshall to Will Alexander, June 16, 1938; Alexander to Houston, June 18, 1938, Newt Mills to T. Roy Reid, July 29, 1938, LA-18, AD-910, Box 394, RG 96, NA.

74. Constance Daniels Report, December 5, 1938, AD-910, Box 394, p. 14; T. Roy Reid to C. B. Baldwin, July 11, 1938, AD-910, Box 394, RG96, NA. Black farmers were present on 76 of 143 occupied farms in Mounds and none of the 160 farms in Transylvania.

75. Mileston Farms was the most expensive community RA project in Mississippi, costing over $831.000, but Black farmers on the project received only an average of $847 in rehabilitation loans, half the state average. It had three cooperative projects building on the work of the NFCF. Theodore Bilbo to T. Roy Reid, November 26, 1938; John L. Webb to Alexander, November 26, 1938, MS-23, Box 410; Will Whittington to T. Roy Reid, September 25, 1936, MS-17, Box 408, RG 96, NA. J. Todd Moye, *Let the People Decide: Black Freedom and White Resistance Movements in Sunflower County, Mississippi, 1945–1986* (Chapel Hill: University of North Carolina Press, 2004), 28, 128.

76. Edward C. Banfield, "Ten Years of the Farm Tenant Purchase Program," *Journal of Farm Economics* 31 (1949): 483. Banfield concluded that the loans went to uneconomical farms, and the "TP program probably could not be justified in the

South, where 70 percent of the loans have been made." Figure 3, p. 138, presents data on the distribution of TP loans.

77. Price V. Fishback, Shawn Kantor, and John Joseph Wallis, "Can the New Deal's Three Rs Be Rehabilitated? A Program-by-Program, County-by-County Analysis," *Explorations in Economic History* 40 (2003): 296, 298.

78. *Report of the Agricultural Committee of the Inter-departmental Group Concerned with the Special Problems of Negroes*, US Department of the Interior, 1934, 13–14. Raper, *Preface to Peasantry*, 233–34. The data for loans include both the federal land banks and the Land Bank Commission, the two entities responsible for making loans. White farmers received an average loan of $2,420, Blacks an average of $1,091.

79. Donnie D. Bellamy, "Henry A. Hunt and Black Agricultural Leadership in the New South," *Journal of Negro History* 60, no. 4 (October 1975): 477.

80. For white owners, variables for FCA loans, percent of acreage planted in cotton, white farmers, and presence of a resettlement project are statistically significant. For Black owners, only rehabilitation loans, percent of acreage in cotton, and Black farmers are significant. See table A.2. The decline in cotton acreage was minuscule after 1938, when cotton prices bottomed out at 8.41 cents per pound. Prices rose to 19 cents per pound by 1943. Robert M. Walsh, "Response of Price in Production of Cotton and Cottonseed," *Journal of Farm Economics* 26, no. 2 (May 1944): 368.

81. Dania V. Francis, Darrick Hamilton, Thomas W. Mitchell, Nathan A. Rosenberg, and Breycew Stucki, "Black Land Loss: 1920–1997," *AEA Papers and Proceedings* 112 (2022): 38–42; Jess Gilbert, Gwen Sharp, and M. Sindy Felin, *The Decline (and Revival?) of Black Farmers and Rural Landowners: A Review of the Research Literature*, working paper, North America series, University of Wisconsin, Land Tenure Center, 2001, 7.

82. United States Commission on Civil Rights, *Equal Opportunity in Farm Programs: An Appraisal of Services Rendered by Agencies of the U.S. Department of Agriculture* (Washington, DC: US Government Printing Office, 1965), 60, 62.

83. Baldwin, *Poverty and Politics*, 402–3; Valerie Grim, "Black Participation in the Farmers Home Administration and Agricultural Stabilization and Conservation Service, 1964–1990," *Agricultural History* 70, no. 2 (Spring 1996): 321–36.

84. United States Commission on Civil Rights, *Equal Opportunity in Farm Programs*, 68–70; Grim, "Black Participation," 322.

85. *Hearings of the Alabama State Advisory Committee to the US Commission on Civil Rights*, Demopolis, Alabama, July 10, 1965, 124–25, 140–48. Grim, "Black Participation," 323. Grim quotes a retired Black cotton farmer who said that Southern whites believed helping "Black farmers and Black folk on the farm would have been a waste of money."

86. Pete Daniel, *Dispossession: Discrimination against African American Farmers in the Age of Civil Rights* (Chapel Hill: University of North Carolina Press, 2013), 226, 230, 232.

87. Lester M. Salamon, "The Time Dimension in Policy Evaluation: The Case of the New Deal Land-Reform Experiments," *Public Policy* 27, no. 2 (Spring 1979): 129–83; Veronica L. Womack, "Black Power in the Alabama Black Belt to the 1970s," in Reid and Bennett, *Beyond Forty Acres and a Mule*, 231–53.

88. Malcolm X argued that all revolutions were about land. He drew a distinction between the "Negro revolution" and a "black revolution." The former was about desegregation and nonviolence; the latter was about land, which was the basis of all independence. In this speech, land was Malcolm X's metaphor for nation building and independence. George Breitman, ed., *Malcolm Speaks: Selected Speeches and Statements* (New York: Grove Press, 1965), 7–9.

CHAPTER 5. THE REVOLUTION STALLED

1. "What the Marchers Really Want," *New York Times Magazine*, August 25, 1963, 8; Whitney M. Young, Jr., "Domestic Marshall Plan," *New York Times Magazine*, October 6, 1963, 129. In his 1893 speech "Self-Made Men," Frederick Douglass asserted, "Should the American people put a schoolhouse in every valley of the South and a church on every hill side and supply the one with teachers and the other with preachers, for a hundred years to come, they would not then have given fair play to the negro." John W. Blassingame and John R. McKivigan, eds., *The Frederick Douglass Papers, Series One, Speeches, Debates, Interviews* (New Haven, CT: Yale University Press, 1992), 5:557.

2. Martin Luther King Jr., *Why We Can't Wait* (New York: Signet Classics, 1964), 3.

3. Dona C. Hamilton and Charles Hamilton, *The Dual Agenda: Race and Social Welfare Policies of Civil Rights Organizations* (New York: Columbia University Press, 1997), 126–27.

4. *Pittsburgh Courier*, August 15, 1964; King is quoted in Thomas F. Jackson, *From Civil Rights to Human Rights: Martin Luther King, Jr., and the Struggle for Economic Justice* (Philadelphia: University of Pennsylvania Press, 2007), 191; Hamilton and Hamilton, *The Dual Agenda*, 133; Thomas Sugrue, *Sweet Land of Liberty: The Forgotten Struggle for Civil Rights in the North* (New York: Random House, 2008), 361–62. *Hearing on H.R. 10440, Economic Opportunity Act of 1964*, 88th Cong., 2nd sess. (1964) (testimony of Whitney Young Jr.).

5. *New York Times*, June 19, 1963. Wirtz is quoted in Hugh Davis Graham, *The Civil Rights Era: Origins and Development of National Policy, 1960–1972* (New York: Oxford University Press, 1990), 102. John F. Kennedy, "Special Message to the Congress on Civil Rights and Job Opportunities," June 19, 1963, American Presidency Project, www.presidency.ucsb.edu/node/236711.

6. "Poverty and Urban Policy," conference transcript of 1973 group discussion of the Kennedy Administration Urban Poverty Programs and Policies, June 16–17, 1973, Brandeis University), 181, JFKL.

7. *Economic Report of the President,* 1964 (Washington, DC: US Government Printing Office, 1964), 73; "Program for a Concerted Assault on Poverty (C.A.P.)," CEA staff memorandum, October 29, 1963, ser. 60.11, Box 11, RG 51, NA.

8. L. J. Duhl to Sargent Shriver, n.d., Box 43, Project Proposal Memos, Shriver Papers, JFKL. Duhl was director of planning at the National Institute of Mental Health.

9. Alice O'Connor, *Poverty Knowledge: Social Science, Social Policy, and the Poor in Twentieth-Century U.S. History* (Princeton, NJ: Princeton University Press, 2001), 117, 121–22. In a memo to Shriver, Harrington argued that draft rejectees were "not simply poor themselves. They were the children of the poor, the hereditary poor, the born poor. If nothing is done they will pass poverty on to their children." Michael Harrington, Paul Jacobs, and Frank Mankiewicz to Shriver, February 6, 1964, Project Memos, Box 43, Shriver Papers, JFKL.

10. Author's interview with Sargent Shriver, Washington, DC, November 14, 1984 (hereafter Shriver interview); Adam Yarmolinsky to Sargent Shriver, February 6, 1964, Poverty Memos, Box 40, Shriver Papers, JFKL.

11. Quoted in Sugrue, *Sweet Land of Liberty,* 361–62. Powell told Robert Penn Warren that the "revolution is interested in schools, housing, jobs. And the Civil Rights Bill will not help them at all." Robert Penn Warren, *Who Speaks for the Negro?* (New Haven, CT: Yale University Press, 2014), 138.

12. *New York Times,* April 1, 1964; Michael K. Brown, *Race, Money, and the American Welfare State* (Ithaca, NY: Cornell University Press, 1999), 224–29; Brandeis University, "Poverty and Urban Policy," 286–87; Jackson, *From Civil Rights to Human Rights,* 193–95, 204, chapter 9. Despite pressure from aides, Shriver, and congressional Democrats, Johnson never approved a public jobs program. For a persuasive explanation, see Anaïs Miodek Bowring, "The Ideological Boundary Condition in Great Society Employment Policy," *Journal of Policy History* 30, no. 4 (2018): 657–94.

13. "Poverty and Urban Policy," 232.

14. "Poverty and Urban Policy," 232, 244, 247–49.

15. 110 Cong. Rec. 13 (July 23, 1964); quoted in Susan Youngblood Ashmore, *Carry It On: The War on Poverty and the Civil Rights Movement in Alabama, 1964–1972* (Athens: University of Georgia Press, 2008), 41; Martha J. Bailey and Nicolas J. Duquette, "How Johnson Fought the War on Poverty: The Economics and Politics of Funding at the Office of Economic Opportunity," *Journal of Economic History* 74, no. 2 (June 2014): 358.

16. Frank R. Parker, *Black Votes Count: Political Empowerment in Mississippi after 1965* (Chapel Hill: University of North Carolina Press, 1990), 67.

17. The best example of this is the Child Development Group of Mississippi (CDGM). See Crystal R. Sanders, *A Chance for Change: Head Start and Mississippi's Black Freedom Struggle* (Chapel Hill: University of North Carolina Press, 2016), 175.

18. Gary Orfield, "Race and the Liberal Agenda: The Loss of the Integrationist Dream, 1965–1974," in *The Politics of Social Policy in the United States,* ed. Margaret

Weir, Ann Shola Orloff, and Theda Skocpol, 313–56 (Princeton, NJ: Princeton University Press, 1988).

19. Stokely Carmichael to Bayard Rustin, August 16, 1966, Bayard Rustin Papers, Reel 13, General Correspondence, LC. Stokely Carmichael, "What We Want," *New York Review of Books,* 22 September 1966; Bayard Rustin, "'Black Power' and Coalition Politics,'" *Commentary,* September 1966. For a cogent explanation of why a Black alliance with labor unions never materialized, see Paul Frymer, *Black and Blue: African Americans, the Labor Movement, and the Decline of the Democratic Party* (Princeton, NJ: Princeton University Press, 2008).

20. Hasan Kwame Jeffries, "SNCC, Black Power, and Independent Political Party Organizing in Alabama, 1964–1966," *Journal of African American History* 91, no. 2 (Spring 2006): 177; William L. Van Deburg, *New Day in Babylon: The Black Power Movement and American Culture, 1965–1975* (Chicago: University of Chicago Press, 1992), 19–27, 112–29. For the statements of Black abolitionists, see pp. 46–48.

21. Sanders, *A Chance for Change.*

22. Martin Luther King Jr., *Where Do We Go From Here? Chaos or Community* (Boston: Beacon Press, 2010), 37, 55. King did agree with SNCC that in Deep South counties where there were no reliable white allies, organizing an independent political party made sense (49–50).

23. Tersh Boasberg to Fred Hayes et al., March 8, 1966, E5, Box 34a, RG 381, NA, p. 2.

24. *The Problem of Starvation in Mississippi,* MCHR Report, n.d. [after April 27, 1967] E1031, Box 79, Miss. General, RG 381, NA, p. 8; author's calculations.

25. Devin Caughey, *The Unsolid South: Mass Politics and National Representation in a One-Party Enclave* (Princeton, NJ: Princeton University Press, 2018), 75, 79, 82–83; Brown, *Race, Money, and the American Welfare State,* 107–10, 132–33, 183–84; Bruce J. Schulman, *From Cottonbelt to Sunbelt: Federal Policy, Economic Development, and the Transformation of the South, 1938–1980* (New York: Oxford University Press, 1991), 140.

26. United States Commission on Civil Rights, *Employment* (Washington, DC: US Government Printing Office, 1961), 84; Judith R. Lave and Lester B. Lave, *The Hospital Construction Act: An Evaluation of the Hill-Burton Program, 1948–1973* (Washington, DC: American Enterprise Institute, 1974), 10–11, 17–19; Sanders, *A Chance for Change,* 68.

27. Minutes of Economic Opportunity Council meeting, February 25, 1966, E1006, Box 2, RG 381, NA.

28. Brown, *Race, Money, and the American Welfare State,* 124–25; Miss. Food Demonstration Project 1966, February 17, 1966, Box 28, E1031, RG 381, NA, p. 5. All of Alabama's food distribution programs were located in white counties in the northern part of the state. Robert Lieberman, *Shifting the Color Line: Race and the American Welfare State* (Cambridge, MA: Harvard University Press, 1998), 136–37. Created during the New Deal, the surplus commodity program was used to buy up surplus food products in order to prop up agricultural commodity prices. This was

the main food distribution program for the poor until Congress created food stamps in 1964.

29. Aaron Henry and Charles Evers to Sargent Shriver and Orville Freeman, February 2, 1966, E1031, Box 28, RG 381, NA, pp. 1–2.

30. Orville Freeman to Kermit Gordon and Walter Heller, January 1964, Ser.60.3a, Box 4, HEW 1962–68, RG 51, NA; "How Title III Will Work," Shriver Papers, Box 64, JFKL; text of H.R. 10440, *Economic Opportunity Act of 1964*, §§ 302, 303, p. 11.

31. Hearings of the Alabama State Advisory Committee to the US Commission on Civil Rights, Demopolis, Alabama, July 10, 1965, 124–25.

32. Sargent Shriver, speech to the Agricultural Stabilization and Conservation Service, May 18, 1967, Shriver Papers, Box 53, JFKL, p. 2.

33. Columbia Law Review Association, "The Federal Agricultural Stabilization Program and the Negro," *Columbia Law Review* 67, no. 6 (June 1967): 1121–36; Pete Daniel, *Dispossession: Discrimination against African American Farmers in the Age of Civil Rights* (Chapel Hill: University of North Carolina Press, 2013), 23, 154.

34. Clayborne Carson, *In Struggle: SNCC and the Black Awakening of the 1960s* (Cambridge, MA: Harvard University Press, 1981), 163, 169.

35. SNCC Vine City Project, *Black Power,* reprint of position paper, US National Student Association, 1966, 2, 6; Carson, *In Struggle,* 191–96; Jeffries, "SNCC, Black Power," 185–86.

36. SNCC Vine City Project, *Black Power,* 4–5; Stokely Carmichael and Charles V. Hamilton, *Black Power: The Politics of Liberation in America* (New York: Vintage Books, 1967), 61. Carmichael and Hamilton wrote, "Our point is that no matter how 'liberal' a white person might be, he cannot ultimately escape the overpowering influence—on himself and on black people—of his whiteness in a racist society." Robert Penn Warren recounts a similar sentiment from a meeting of Mississippi activists who insisted on their independence. Warren, *Who Speaks for the Negro?,* 51, 58. The Black abolitionists who started the convention movement in the 1840s were motivated by similar concerns. See the comments of writer A in *The Colored American,* 47.

37. H. Rap Brown, Report from the Chairman, May 5, 1967, E1005, Box 1, Civil Rights Leaders, RG 381, NA; Carson, *In Struggle,* 163, 169.

38. Charles M. Payne, *I've Got the Light of Freedom: The Organizing Tradition and the Mississippi Freedom Struggle* (Berkeley: University of California Press, 1995), 330, 339; Carson, *In Struggle,* 163–66.

39. Hasan Kwame Jeffries, *Bloody Lowndes: Civil Rights and Black Power in Alabama's Black Belt* (New York: New York University Press, 2009), chapter 2; Ed Terrones et al. to Edgar May, November 11, 1966, E74, Box 29, Acadiana-Neuf, RG 381, NA; Sanders, *A Chance for Change,* 32–33, 78–93, 132–33, 144. Anna Mae King is quoted on p 80.

40. Dudley Morris to Jule Sugarman, June 24, 1965, E 1031, Box 28, RG 381, NA. Sugarman was the associate director of Head Start.

41. Transcript of meeting between OEO and CDGM staff, attached to Frank Sloan to Theodore Berry, November 3, 1966, E1031 Box 28, RG 381, NA. Thelma

Barnes, a former employee of the Delta Ministry, organized Head Start Centers in Washington County, Mississippi. Sanders, *A Chance for Change*, 52.

42. Tom Levin, one of the organizers of CDGM, pointed out, "It is true that the poverty program has distinct 'pork barrel' aspects. The question to be asked will be, who will distribute the pork—the establishment or the poor?" Quoted in John Dittmer, *Local People: The Struggle for Civil Rights in Mississippi* (Champaign-Urbana: University of Illinois Press, 1994), 370; Ashmore, *Carry It On,* 200; LCC-MHR Anti-poverty Application, November 20, 1965, Lowndes Co, E1031, Box 27, Alabama, RG 381, NA, p. 3.

43. Bailey and Duquette, "How Johnson Fought the War on Poverty," 360–61, 366–67; Minutes of meeting of Economic Opportunity Council, July 26, 1967, E1002, Box 4, RG 381, NA.

44. Frank Prial memo to Edgar May and Bob Clampitt, October 11, 1965, E74, Box 1, AL OEO programs, RG 381, NA.

45. Donald C. Mosley and D. C. Williams Jr., *An Analysis and Evaluation of a Community Action Anti-poverty Program in the Mississippi Delta* (Hattiesburg: College of Business and Industry, Mississippi State University, 1967), 31–32; Prial to May and Clampitt, 6.

46. Prial to May and Clampitt, 3–4.

47. Jack Gonzales to Bill Haddad and Samuel Yette, March 30, 1965, E74, Box 23, Alabama, RG 381, NA; Kent B. Germany, *New Orleans after the Promises: Poverty, Citizenship, and the Search for the Great Society* (Athens: University of Georgia Press, 2007), 50–53; Ashmore, *Carry It On,* 105; Tom Heller to Jack Gonzales, RE: CDGM and Black Power, n.d., E1031, RG 381, NA. Miss. Westpoint Mary Holmes Junior College, RG 381, NA. Earl Redwine of the Atlanta Regional Office referred to the Mobile, Alabama, program as a "post-graduate school for crooked politics." Redwine is quoted in Kim Zeitlin to Bill Haddad and Bob Clampitt, July 31. 1965, p. 2. Also see Martha McKay to Bill Haddad, April 15, 1965, E74, Box 1, Alabama OEO Programs, 1964–1965, RG 381, NA.

48. Prial to May and Clampitt, 8ff.

49. Robert Saunders to William Suttle, March 28, 1968, E1005, Box 8, Civil Rights, RG 381, NA.

50. Theodore Berry to Sargent Shriver, August 31, 1966, E1031, Box 27, Lowndes County Alabama, 1966, 3 RG 381, NA. Shriver was opposed to single-purpose agencies, although he funded the CDGM.

51. Sargent Shriver to Lyndon B. Johnson, March 17, 1967, Box 39, Correspondence; OEO Press Release, "OEO Builds Community Action in Mississippi," October 10, 1966, Box 38, CDGM, Shriver Papers, JFKL.

52. Robert Saunders to Maurice Dawkins, June 6, 1967, E1005, Box 8, CR: Robert W. Saunders, RG 381, NA. In 2016 Ronald Collier, the executive director of the Meridian Mississippi Multi-county Community Services Agency, told me that white people in the counties he served still believed that the poverty program was a program for Blacks and not whites. Interview with Ronald Collier, May 16, 2016. White resistance to participating in Great Society programs was widespread. In a

national study of the Concentrated Employment Program in the late 1960s, the Office of Management and Budget discovered that most whites eligible for the program refused to participate in a program with Blacks. Brown, *Race, Money, and the American Welfare State*, 281.

53. Charlotte Lewis to Maurice Dawkins and Larry Horan, October 26, 1967, E128, Box 2, CAA Boards, RG 381, NA.

54. Maurice Dawkins to Sargent Shriver, July 10, 1967, E1005, Box 2, CORE Convention, RG 381, NA; Sargent Shriver to Bill Moyers, August 19, 1965, Moyers Papers, Box 56, "OEO," LBJL. Shriver was given to hyperbole. When the grant to Coahoma County was approved, he told his civil rights chief, Samuel Yette, "This *should* be page one in every negro newspaper." Shriver's handwritten note in Sanford Kravitz to Ted Berry, September 21, 1965, E1031, Box 31, Rural Task Force, RG 381, NA.

55. Harvey Burg to Earl Redwine, OEO Regional Office, August 24, 1965, no. 4, Box 24, Greene County, AL; Tom Levin, "The Pacifist Poor in the War on Poverty," July 13, 1965, E1031, Box 3; Frank Prial, "Keep with Area 11 Programs," October 7, 1965, Box 1, Alabama OEO Programs, RG 381, NA.

56. Tom Heller to Jack Gonzales, 1966, E1031; Burg to Redwine, August 24, 1965; Prial to May and Clampitt.

57. Tersh Boasberg to Sargent Shriver, August 16, 1965, Operation Dixie, Alabama, Box 12, RG 381, NA. Boasberg is quoted in Charles S. Aiken, *The Cotton Plantation South since the Civil War* (Baltimore, MD: Johns Hopkins University Press, 1998), 244.

58. An OEO staff person monitoring the problems in Attapulqus, Georgia (Decatur County), wrote that the county was "70% N, 12 of 26 Bd, 3 of 9 Exec. All exec subj to power structure—we need civ rts groups & independent minority [people]. 2 more exec 4 more board." Note from Steve Lowenstein, November 4, 1965, E4. Box 25, Georgia—CAP, RG 381, NA.

59. Glenn Andrews to Sargent Shriver, July 21, 1966, E4, Box 24; John Cook et al. to Shriver, October 29, 1965, E4, Box 24, Wilcox & Marengo County; Wilcox County SCLC Poverty Committee to Shriver, E4, Box 23, Al CAP, RG 381, NA. John Cook was the president of the Wilcox County Southern Christian Leadership Conference.

60. Handwritten note, February 28, 1965, Box 24, Records Relating to Civil Rights, E4 (Mrs. Lee did not sign the note with her first name); LCCMHR to Sargent Shriver, November 20, 1965, E1031, Box27, Lowndes Co. RG 381, NA. The committee said, "Lowndes County Negroes object to the creation of multi-county area units . . . which on their face and in light of other possible alternatives gerrymander Negro populations, and hence, the percentage of Negroes in any given geographical area of population, so that Negroes are now a minority population-wise in the given area." Principles and Procedures, para. 7, statement attached to LCCMHR to Shriver.

61. "Agenda for Vice President's Meeting on Rural Poverty," Shriver Papers, Box 69, Meetings with the Vice-President, JFKL, p. 2; Theodore Berry to Sargent Shriver, November 12, 1965, E1031, Box 31, Rural Task Force 1966, RG 381, NA. Calculation of the population effects of the change in policy is mine.

62. Counties with a Black population of 40 percent or more constituted 39 percent of all counties in the five Deep South states and 46.5 percent of counties with no CAA. In predominant Black counties the Black population averaged 55.4 percent, and more than half of these counties had a Black population over 50 percent.

63. Gonzales to Haddad and Yette, March 30, 1965, E 74, Box 23, Alabama, RG 381, NA. Ashmore, *Carry It On,* 105–6, 122.

64. Ashmore, *Carry It On,* 269; Perry County Poverty Committee, August 23, 1965, Box 24, no. 4, Greene Co., RG 381, NA.

65. Loren Jenkins to Bob Clampitt, July 12, 1965, E 74, Box 21, Georgia OEO Programs, RG 381, NA. The county unit system was a voting procedure that allocated units to counties. To win an election, candidates had to win a majority of county units. The system favored rural counties.

66. Stephen Tuck, *Beyond Atlanta: The Struggle for Racial Equality in Georgia, 1940–1980* (Athens: University of Georgia Press, 2001), 160. Martha McKay to Edgar May and Bob Clampitt, November 12, 1965, E74 Box 21, Georgia OEO Programs, RG 381, NA. See also Aiken, *The Cotton Plantation South,* 240–41.

67. Germany, *New Orleans after the Promises,* 49–54. Peter Spruance to Edgar May, June 2, 1967, Box 54, Shriver Papers, JFKL. Georgia and Mississippi each lost seven NAACP chapters in the seven years from 1957 to 1964; South Carolina lost seventeen chapters. These data are derived from NAACP annual reports compiled by the Mapping American Social Movements project at the University of Washington, located at depts.washington.edu/moves/NAACP_intro.shtml.

68. Dittmer, *Local People,* 369; Payne, *I've Got the Light of Freedom,* 328; Dudley Morris to Jule Sugarman, June 24, 1965, E1031 Box 3, CDGM, RG 381, NA. Morris pointed out that Mississippi Blacks were enthusiastic about the program, and it was the only OEO agency at the time in which Blacks had a large say in planning and directing the program. In Holmes County, 102 out of 108 staff members were also active members of the MFDP. Kenneth T. Andrews, *Freedom Is a Constant Struggle: The Mississippi Civil Rights Movement and Its Legacy* (Chicago: University of Chicago Press, 2004), 141.

69. Bob Clampitt to Sargent Shriver, June 23, 1965, E1031, Box 3, CDGM, RG 381, NA; "Information for Senator Joseph Clark, Box 38, CDGM, Shriver Papers, JFKL; Engelburg and Jack Gonzales, n.d. [summer 1965], E1031, Box 3, CDGM, RG 381, NA; Sanders, *A Chance for Change,* 109–13.

70. Dittmer, *Local People,* 371; Sanders, *A Chance for Change,* 117–18; Bob Clampitt to Bill Moyers, August 2, 1965, Box 41, WH Correspondence, 1963–65, Shriver papers, JFKL. Nonetheless, many of the people employed by CDGM Head Start centers had been or were affiliated with civil rights organizations.

71. Donald M. Baker to Sargent Shriver, September 27, 1966, Box 38, CDGM, Shriver Papers, JFKL; Sargent Shriver to Archibald Cox, Miss. Food Demonstration Program, March 1966, E1031, Box 28, RG 381, NA. Donald M. Baker, OEO's general consul, concluded after his investigation that CDGM was not qualified to administer the program, as it had violated requirements of the Supplemental Appropriation Act of 1966.

72. John Dean to Sargent Shriver, Miss. Food Demonstration Program, February 24, 1966, Box 28, E1031, RG 381, NA.

73. Robert Moore to Theodore Berry, October 13, 1966, Miss General, E1031, Box 79, RG 381, NA.

74. Theodore Berry to Sargent Shriver, October 4, 1966, Miss. Task Force Weekly Report, Box 18, E1031, 1966, RG 381, NA.

75. Dittmer makes the strongest argument that Shriver caved to Stennis and backed the Loyalist Democrats, but he has no direct evidence and relies mainly on journalistic accounts for his conjectures. Dittmer, *Local People,* 375–78. Sanders makes a stronger case for Stennis's influence on Shriver; Sanders, *A Chance for Change,* 139. Shriver later claimed that he dismantled CDGM because otherwise "the whole war on poverty [would] have been stopped"; quoted in Sanders, *A Chance for Change,* 154. I find Shriver's claim dubious and inconsistent with evidence that he was strongly disposed to disband CDGM.

76. Verbatim transcript of conference between the board of directors of the Child Development Group of Mississippi, their special counsel, Mr. Joseph Rauh, and officials of the Office of Economic Opportunity of Washington, DC, and Atlanta, Georgia, October 24, 1966, 31–35; conference transcript, attached to Frank Sloan to Theodore Berry, November 3, 1966, Mary Holmes Junior College, E1031 Box 28, RG 381, NA, pp. 8–9; Michael L. Kenney to Lear Siegler, June 16, 1966, E1031, Box 28, Mississippi Food Demonstration, RG 381, NA. p. 5. McRee's statement was made at a conference on poverty in Mississippi. Steve Lowenstein to Samuel Yette, February 7, 1966, E1031, Box 28, Mississippi Food Demonstration, RG 381. Kenneth Dean, the executive director of the Mississippi Council on Human Rights, wrote an impassioned letter bluntly telling Shriver that CDGM was the only organization in Mississippi capable of giving Black Mississippians the capacity "to fight the battle of real poverty that is taking shape." Dean to Sargent Shriver, April 13, 1966, E1031, Box 28, RG 381, NA.

77. Kenneth T. Andrews reports that there were sustained or episodic civil rights movements in forty-seven of Mississippi's eighty-two counties; Andrews, *Freedom Is a Constant Struggle,* 8. Twenty-nine counties received grants for CDGM centers. Of these, eighteen were counties with sustained movements, nine had episodic movements, and two had no civil rights movements.

78. In the OEO financial data report, the funds for state economic opportunity offices are listed for the county of the capital city of each state. For example, Alabama EOO funds are reported as part of the Montgomery County CAA. I have separated funds for statewide distribution from the local CAA for each state so that analysis of CAA expenditures is based on only those funds an agency could control.

79. The Mississippi per capita spending rate was influenced by very high spending in Bolivar County, a total of $15.1 million. OEO invested $4.6 million for a hospital and medical center in Mound Bayou, a large one-time expenditure. Eliminating that money reduces the per capita spending rate from $139 to $132 for rural single-county agencies in Mississippi.

80. The mean value of per capita OEO funding in rural single-county CAAs is $77.69. The specification for the model used is given in the appendix. For the dummy variable, I coded single-county agencies as equal to one and multicounty agencies as zero. This estimate is for rural agencies; urban agencies are excluded. The unit of analysis is agency service areas, not counties. The type of agency and the ratio of agricultural to manufacturing jobs are statistically significant.

81. Poverty rates, measured as the percentage of families with an income less than $3,000 in 1960, are almost identical across both types of agencies and those counties with no agency (see table 15). Moreover, poverty rates declined by half between 1960 and 1970, and again there is almost no difference in the percentage of families below the poverty line in the three types of counties. To check whether differences in population could affect the results, I calculated the mean per capita dollars for each grant. The only difference is that FHA loans are not statistically significant.

82. Payne, *I've Got the Light of Freedom*, 347.

83. Tom Heller to Samuel Yette, October 21, 1965, E4, Box 27, Adams, MS, RG 381, NA.

84. My data are drawn from OEO reports and documents for each agency. I have insufficient data for all but two agencies in Georgia and no data for agencies in South Carolina. Three criteria were used to classify agencies: (1) the level of conflict over representation and operation of the agency (a key measure is who initiated the request: white officials or Black civil rights activists); (2) the level of Black mobilization in relevant states and counties; (3) the racial composition of CAA boards, drawn from OEO agency data. These data are available in Records about CAP Grants and Grantees, Grantee Organization Master Files, 1964–1971, NARA, Access to Archival Databases, https://aad.archives.gov.

85. Trip report, June 16–19, 1969, attached to Bo Jones to Frank Carlucci, October 28, 1969, Box 2, Alabama, RG 381, NA; Steve Clapp to Bob Emond, December 5, 1968, E1031, Box 72, RG 381, NA; Composite Report Tri-Co Area 22, March 23, 1970, A3062, Box 14, RG 381, Atlanta Regional Archives, NA.

86. Clapp to Emond, December 5, 1968, E1031 Box 72, RG 381, NA.

87. Kent B. Germany, "Poverty Wars in the Louisiana Delta: White Resistance, Black Power, and the Poorest Place in America," in *The War on Poverty: A New Grass Roots History, 1964–1980*, ed. Annelise Orleck and Lisa Gale Hazirjian (Athens: University of Georgia Press, 2011), 234–35. East Carroll allocated 30 percent of its funding to community services, compared with 43 percent in Evangeline and 52 percent in Grant.

88. Robert Martin to Edgar May, June 20, 1966, Box 1, E74, Alabama OEO Programs, RG 381, NA; Ashmore, *Carry It On*, 164–72.

89. OEO was unsympathetic to Mesher and Bradford's allegations of cooptation. See Robert Martin to Edgar May, June 20, 1966, Box 1, E74, Alabama OEO Programs, 1966, RG 381, NA; Robert Saunders to Samuel Yette, June 24, 1966, Box 24, No. 4, Selma/Dallas County. For Bradford's response, see his letter to Saunders, July 9, 1966, E74, Box 1, Alabama OEO Programs, RG 381, NA. All this was taking place at the same time that OEO was investigating CDGM.

90. McKay to May and Clampitt, November 12, 1965.

91. Michael Coleman to Ed Terrones and Jack Gonzales, February 1, 1966, E74, Box 30 Louisiana OEO, 1966, RG 381.

92. The Acadiana-Neuf Board had reneged on a commitment to appoint people from the Southern Consumers Cooperative; Martha McKay to Bill Haddad and Bob Clampitt, July 30, 1965, E74, Box 29, RG 381, NA.

93. Jack Gonzales to Edgar May, September 29, 1965, E74, Box 29, Acadiana-Neuf; Ivan Scott to Edgar May and Bob Clampitt, November 30, 1965, E74 Box 29. Ed Terrones et al. to Edgar May, November 11, 1966, E74 Box 29, p. 4; Thomas McRae to Edgar May, November 18, 1966, E74, Box 29, RG 381, NA.

94. Andrews, *Freedom Is a Constant Struggle,* 148–50; S.D. Long to Douglas Wynn, March 26, 1966, E74, Box 27, Bolivar County; Frank Sloan et al. (Atlanta Regional Staff) to Ted Berry, April 5, 1966, E74, Box 27, RG 381, NA. On January 25, 1967, OEO awarded Amzie Moore's group two grants totaling $527,077 to continue CDGM Head Start programs. This was in addition to $2 million from prior grants in May 1966. The alternative Head Start program received $1 million.

95. Holmes County was the site of the Mileston resettlement project. It was also the county where the National Federation of Colored Farmers organized its first chapter in the Deep South. Lester M. Salamon interviewed Black farmers who participated in resettlement projects about their involvement in civil rights activity. See Salamon, "The Time Dimension in Policy Evaluation: The Case of the New Deal Land-Reform Experiments," *Public Policy* 27, no. 2 (Spring 1979): 130–31, 171–73.

96. Mississippi Task Force, Community Profiles, Central Mississippi, Inc., September 19, 1966, E1031, Box 79, Miss. General 1969, RG 381, NA, pp. 3–4; Evaluation of CMI, August 12–16, 1968, 3170 MS, Box 3, Atlanta Regional Archives, NA; Andrews, *Freedom is a Constant Struggle,* 146–47.

97. Mississippi Task Force Community Profiles, Pearl River Valley Opportunities, January 27, 1967, E1031, Box 79 RG 381, NA, pp. 1, 4; Report of Forrest-Stone Area Opportunity, Inc, December 10–13, 1968, MS 3124, Box 7, RG 381, Atlanta Regional Archives, NA.

98. Note from Sargent Shriver on Sanford Kravitz to Ted Berry, September 21, 1965, E1031, Box 31, Rural Task Force, RG 381, NA.

99. Mosley and Williams, *Analysis and Evaluation,* 34; Sargent Shriver to Andrew Carr, with attached letter to John Stennis, April 7, 1967, Box 42, Personal Correspondence, Shriver Papers, JFKL. Shriver complimented Carr for writing such a "lengthy and intelligent letter."

100. Germany, *New Orleans after the Promises.*

101. Bob Emond to Sargent Shriver, August 26, 1967, Box 28, E74, Caddo-Bossier Parishes 1967, RG 381, NA.

102. Emond to Shriver, August 26, 1967, E74, Box 28, Caddo-Bossier Parishes 1967, RG 381, NA, pp. 7–8. In a June 1967 report, OEO staff referred to the agency as "one of the more promising in Louisiana with a governing body that is very representative," which meant there were more than a token number of Blacks on the

board. James M. Simons to Edgar May, June 20, 1967, E74, Box 28, RG 381, NA, p. 4.

103. Emond to Shriver, August 26, 1967, p. 3.

104. Mississippi Task Force Community Profiles, Southwest Mississippi Opportunities, E1031, Box 79, RG 381, NA, pp. 1–2.

105. Edwin Marger to Robert Saunders, June 8, 1970, Southwest MS Opportunity Evaluation; Jack Brice and Bill Roth, Evaluation Report of SW Mississippi Opportunities, April 8–10, 1970, Box 13, RG 381, Atlanta. Regional Archives, NA.

106. Sanders, *A Chance for Change*, 181.

107. King, *Where Do We Go From Here?*, 49–50, 55, 64, 144.

CHAPTER 6. WHAT DOES RACIAL JUSTICE REQUIRE?

Epigraph: Armand de la Meuse's speech figured importantly in the thinking of the French revolutionary Gracchus Babeuf, who can be said to have made the first argument for distributive justice as a right.

1. A recent Pew Research Center survey found that 50 percent of white Americans agreed that the legacy of slavery affects Black people today. Eighty-five percent of Black people agreed with the statement, as did 64 percent of Latinos. There were no differences by income. The widest divide on this question turned on partisan identification. Only 29 percent of Republicans agreed, compared to 82 percent of Democrats. Carrie Blazina and Kiana Cox, "Black and White Americans Are Far Apart in Their Views of Reparations for Slavery," Pew Research Center, November 28, 2022, www.pewresearch.org/short-reads/2022/11/28/black-and-white-americans-are-far-apart-in-their-views-of-reparations-for-slavery/.

2. Raj Chetty, D. Grusky, M. Hell, N. Hendren, R. Manduca, and J. Narong, "The Fading American Dream: Trends in Absolute Income Mobility since 1940," *Science* 356 (2017): 398–406; Julia B. Isaacs, *Economic Mobility of Black and White Families* (Washington, DC: Brookings Institution, 2008); Tom Hertz, "Rags, Riches, and Race: The Intergenerational Economic Mobility of Black and White Families in the United States," in *Unequal Chances: Family Background and Economic Success*, ed. Samuel Bowles, Herbert Gintis, and Melissa Osborne Groves (New York: Russell Sage Foundation, 2005), 165–91.

3. Sharon D. Wright Austin, *The Transformation of Plantation Politics: Black Politics, Concentrated Poverty, and Social Capital in the Mississippi Delta* (Albany: State University of New York Press, 2006); Avidit Acharya, Matthew Blackwell, and Maya Sen, *Deep Roots: How Slavery Still Shapes Southern Politics* (Princeton, NJ: Princeton University Press, 2018).

4. Edwin Dorn, *Rules and Racial Equality* (New Haven, CT: Yale University Press, 1979), 115, 139–40, 142. Samuel Bowles and his colleagues show that segregation "prevents the convergence of income distributions following the end of overt discrimination." Samuel Bowles, Glenn Loury, and Rajiv Sethi, "Group Inequality," *Journal of the European Economic Association* 12, no. 1 (2014): 129–52. See also,

Michael Katz, Mark J. Stern, and Jamie J. Fader, "The New African American Inequality," *Journal of American History*, 92, no. 1 (2005): 75–108. They analyze the paradox of inequality or the "coexistence of structural rigidity with individual and group fluidity," an idea that is very similar to Dorn's. The main difference is that Dorn's analysis is theoretical, and Katz, Stern, and Fader's is empirical.

5. Michael K. Brown, Martin Carnoy, Elliott Currie, Troy Duster, David B. Oppenheimer, Marjorie M. Schultz, and David Wellman, *Whitewashing Race: The Myth of a Color-Blind Society*, 2nd ed. (Oakland: University of California Press, 2023), 253–88.

6. Bill Clinton, "Address before a Joint Session of the Congress on the State of the Union," January 24, 1995, quoted in Michael J. Sandel, *The Tyranny of Merit: Can We Find the Common Good?* (New York: Farrar, Straus and Giroux, 2020), 65. Sandel argues that this doctrine begins with President Ronald Reagan, but as I have demonstrated, it goes back to the 1830s. President Barack Obama was prone to voice similar sentiments, but he also articulated a robust conception of equality.

7. Mary McLeod Bethune, "Let the Voices Thunder forth with Power," in *A Documentary History of the Negro People in the United States, 1945–1951*, ed. Herbert Aptheker (New York: Citadel, 1993), 5: 151, emphasis added.

8. *A "Freedom Budget" for All Americans* (New York: A. Philip Randolph Institute, October 1966), 20; Dona C Hamilton and Charles V. Hamilton, *The Dual Agenda: Race and Social Welfare Policies of Civil Rights Organizations* (New York: Columbia University Press, 1997), 147–52.

9. Judith N. Shklar, *American Citizenship: The Quest for Inclusion* (Cambridge, MA: Harvard University Press, 1991), 68.

10. Transcript of a conference on CDGM, October 24, 1966, Atlanta Georgia, attached to Frank Sloan to Theodore Berry, November 3, 1966, Box 28, E1031, Mary Holmes Junior College, RG 381, NA, p. 11.

11. Judith N. Shklar, *The Faces of Injustice* (New Haven, CT: Yale University Press, 1990), 83–84, 108, 119.

12. John H. Schaar, "Equality of Opportunity, and Beyond," in *Legitimacy in the Modern State* (New Brunswick, NJ: Transaction Books, 1981), 198.

13. In 2016 and 2020, the American National Election Survey found that 77 percent of respondents agreed that "society should do whatever is necessary to make sure that everyone has an equal opportunity to succeed," American National Election Survey, https://electionstudies.org/datra-tools/anes-question, variables V162243 and V202260. For a recent debate, see "Is Equal Opportunity Enough?," *Boston Review*, May 2023.

14. Joseph P. Ferrie, "The End of American Exceptionalism? Mobility in the United States Since 1850," *Journal of Economic Perspectives* 19, no. 3 (Summer 2005): 199–215.

15. The technocratic case for luck egalitarianism is elaborated in John E. Roemer, *Equality of Opportunity* (Cambridge, MA: Harvard University Press, 1998). For a trenchant critique of Roemer's conception, see Joseph Fishkin, *Bottlenecks: A New Theory of Equal Opportunity* (New York: Oxford University Press, 2014), 61–64.

16. Sandel, *The Tyranny of Merit*, 19.

17. Fishkin, *Bottlenecks*, 71, 73, 77–78. Both Abraham Lincoln and Lyndon B. Johnson used the metaphor of life as a race to justify their idea of equality of opportunity. I am indebted to Fishkin's powerful and incisive critique of the standard model of equality of opportunity.

18. Fishkin, *Bottlenecks*, 169.

19. Fishkin, *Bottlenecks*, 19. Fishkin's theory of opportunity pluralism is similar to my concept of antiprivilege egalitarianism. Both draw upon Amartya Sen's concept of capability, and both are dedicated to enlarging the possibilities for individual and group autonomy and development. See Fishkin, *Bottlenecks*, 194–95. In the introduction I elaborate on Sen's concept of capability, which underpins my concept of antiprivilege egalitarianism.

20. Pierre Rosanvallon, *The Society of Equals* (Cambridge, MA: Harvard University Press, 2013), 273.

21. Charles Tilly, *Durable Inequality* (Berkeley: University of California Press, 1998); Daria Roithmayr, *Reproducing Racism: How Everyday Choices Lock In White Advantage* (New York: New York University Press, 2014). The Federal Trade Commission has issued a ban on noncompete contracts. J. Edward Morena, "F.T.C. Ban on Worker Noncompete Clauses," *New York Times*, April 23, 2024.

22. The theory of white accumulation and Black disaccumulation is the product of the collective endeavors and contributions of all the coauthors of *Whitewashing Race*. If anyone can take credit for launching us down this path, it is Troy Duster. For a concise summary of the theory, see Brown et al., *Whitewashing Race*, 15–25.

23. Dania V. Francis, Derrick Hamilton, Thomas W. Mitchell, Nathan A. Rosenberg, and Bryce Stucki, "Black Land Loss: 1920–1997," *AEA Papers and Proceedings* 112 (2022): 38–42. The estimate is based on Black landowners in seventeen states.

24. Richard Rothstein, *The Color of Law: A Forgotten History of How Our Government Segregated America* (New York: Liveright, 2017), 48–54; Jessica Trounstine, "The Geography of Inequality: How Land Use Regulation Produces Segregation," *American Political Science Review* 114, no. 2 (2020): 443–55.

SELECT BIBLIOGRAPHY

MANUSCRIPT COLLECTIONS

Franklin D. Roosevelt Library, Hyde Park, NY	FDRL
John F. Kennedy Library—Papers of Sargent Shriver, Boston, MA	JFKL
Library of Congress, Manuscript Division, Washington, DC	LC
Papers of the National Association for the Advancement of Colored People, Library of Congress, Washington, DC NAACP	LC
National Archives, Washington, DC	NA
Records of the Bureau of Refugees, Freedmen, and Abandoned Lands (BRFAL)	RG 105
Records of the Farmers Home Administration	RG 96
Records of the Office of Economic Opportunity	RG 381
Records of the Office of Management and Budget	RG 51
Records of the U.S. Department of Agriculture	RG 83

PUBLISHED SOURCES

Abbott, Martin. *The Freedmen's Bureau in South Carolina, 1865–1872*. Chapel Hill: University of North Carolina Press, 1967.

Andrews, Kenneth T. *Freedom Is a Constant Struggle: The Mississippi Civil Rights Movement and Its Legacy*. Chicago: University of Chicago Press, 2004.

Ashcraft, Richard. "Liberal Political Theory and Working-Class Radicalism in Nineteenth Century England." *Political Theory* 21, no. 2 (1993): 249–72.

Ashmore, Susan Youngblood. *Carry It On: The War on Poverty and the Civil Rights Movement in Alabama, 1964–1972.* Athens: University of Georgia Press, 2008.

Ashworth, John. *'Agrarians' and 'Aristocrats': Party Political Ideology in the United States, 1837–1846.* New York: Cambridge University Press, 1987.

Bailey, Martha J., and Nicolas J. Duquette. "How Johnson Fought the War on Poverty: The Economics and Politics of Funding at the Office of Economic Opportunity." *Journal of Economic History* 74, no. 2 (June 2014): 351–88.

Bell, Howard Holman. *A Survey of the Negro Convention Movement, 1830–1861.* New York: Arno, 1969.

Bethel, Elizabeth Rauh. *Promiseland: A Century of Life in a Negro Community.* Columbia: University of South Carolina Press, 1997.

Blassingame, John W., and John R. McKivigan, eds. *The Frederick Douglass Papers. Speeches, Debates, Interviews.* 5 vols. New Haven, CT: Yale University Press, 1982–1992.

Bleser, Carol K. Rothrock. *The Promised Land: The History of the South Carolina Land Commission, 1869–1890.* Columbia: University of South Carolina Press, 1969.

Brown, Michael K. *Race, Money, and the American Welfare State.* Ithaca, NY: Cornell University Press, 1999.

Brown, Michael K., Martin Carnoy, Elliott Currie, Troy Duster, David Oppenheimer, Marjorie M. Shultz, and David Wellman. *Whitewashing Race: The Myth of a Color-Blind Society.* 2nd ed. Oakland: University of California Press, 2023.

Brown, Michael K., and David T. Wellman. "Embedding the Color Line: The Accumulation of Racial Advantage and the Disaccumulation of Opportunity in Post–Civil Rights America." *Du Bois Review* 2 (2005): 187–207.

Carmichael, Stokely, and Charles V. Hamilton. *Black Power: The Politics of Liberation in America.* New York: Vintage, 1967.

Carson, Clayborne. *In Struggle: SNCC and the Black Awakening of the 1960s.* Cambridge, MA: Harvard University Press, 1981.

Cimbala, Paul A., and Randall M. Miller, eds. *The Freedmen's Bureau and Reconstruction: Reconsiderations.* New York: Fordham University Press, 1999.

———. *Under the Guardianship of the Nation: The Freedmen's Bureau and the Reconstruction of Georgia, 1865–1870.* Athens: University of Georgia Press, 1997.

Cohen, William. *At Freedom's Edge: Black Mobility and the Southern White Quest for Racial Control, 1861–1915.* Baton Rouge: Louisiana State University Press, 1991.

Coleman, Amanda. "Reform(ulat)ing the Region: Competing Discourses of Region and Regional Change in the Depression-Era U.S. South." PhD. diss., University of Oregon, 2008.

Daniel, Pete. *Breaking the Land: The Transformation of Cotton, Tobacco, and Rice Cultures since 1880.* Urbana: University of Illinois Press, 1985.

———. *Dispossession: Discrimination against African American Farmers in the Age of Civil Rights.* Chapel Hill: University of North Carolina Press, 2013.

Darity, William, Jr., and A. Kirsten Mullen. *From Here to Equality: Reparations for Black Americans in the Twenty-First Century.* 2nd. ed. Chapel Hill: University of North Carolina Press, 2022.

Davis, David Brion. *The Problem of Slavery in the Age of Emancipation*. New York: Alfred A. Knopf, 2014.

Dawson, Michael C. *Black Visions: The Roots of Contemporary African American Political Ideologies*. Chicago: University of Chicago Press, 2001.

De Jong, Greta. *A Different Day: African American Struggles for Justice in Rural Louisiana, 1900–1970*. Chapel Hill: University of North Carolina Press, 2002.

Depew, Briggs, Price V. Fishback, and Paul W. Rhode. "New Deal or No Deal in the Cotton South: The Effect of the AAA on the Agricultural Labor Structure." *Explorations in Economic History* 50 (2013): 466–86.

Dittmer, John. *Local People: The Struggle for Civil Rights in Mississippi*. Champaign-Urbana: University of Illinois Press, 1994.

Douglass, Frederick. *Life and Times of Frederick Douglass*. New York: Library of America, 1994.

Downs, Gregory P. *After Appomattox: Military Occupation and the Ends of War*. Cambridge, MA: Harvard University Press, 2015.

Downs, Jim. *Sick from Freedom: African American Illness and Suffering during the Civil War and Reconstruction*. New York: Oxford University Press, 2012.

Du Bois, W. E. B. *The Souls of Black Folk*. New York: Norton, 1999.

———. *Black Reconstruction in America, 1860–1880*. New York: Atheneum, 1992.

Duncan, Russell. *Freedom's Shore: Tunis Campbell and the Georgia Freedmen*. Athens: University of Georgia Press, 1986.

Ellis, Richard J. "Rival Visions of Equality in American Political Culture." *Review of Politics* 52, no. 2 (1992): 253–80.

Fishkin, Joseph. *Bottlenecks: A New Theory of Equal Opportunity*. New York: Oxford University Press, 2014.

Foner, Eric. *Free Soil, Free Labor, Free Men: The Ideology of the Republican Party before the Civil War*. Oxford: Oxford University Press, 1995.

———. *Nothing but Freedom: Emancipation and Its Legacy*. Baton Rouge: Louisiana State University Press, 1983.

———. *Reconstruction: America's Unfinished Revolution, 1863–1877*. New York: Harper & Row, 1988.

Foner, Philip S., and Yuval Taylor. *Frederick Douglass: Selected Speeches and Writings*. Chicago: Chicago Review Press, 2000.

Germany, Kent B. *New Orleans after the Promises: Poverty, Citizenship, and the Search for the Great Society*. Athens: University of Georgia Press, 2007.

Gilbert, Jess, and Steve Brown. "Alternative Land Reform Proposals in the 1930s: The Nashville Agrarians and the Southern Tenant Farmers' Union." *Agricultural History* 55, no. 4 (October 1981): 351–69.

Glaude, Eddie S., Jr. *Exodus! Religion, Race, and Nation in Early Nineteenth-Century Black America*. Chicago: University of Chicago Press, 2000.

Greenstone, J. David. "Against Simplicity: The Cultural Dimensions of the Constitution." *University of Chicago Law Review* 55, no. 2 (Spring 1988): 428–49.

———. *The Lincoln Persuasion: Remaking American Liberalism*. Princeton, NJ: Princeton University Press, 1993.

Grubbs, Donald H. *Cry from the Cotton: The Southern Tenant Farmers' Union and the New Deal.* Chapel Hill: University of North Carolina Press, 1971.

Hahn, Steven. *A Nation under Our Feet: Black Political Struggles in the Rural South from Slavery to the Great Migration.* Cambridge, MA: Harvard University Press, 2003.

Hahn, Steven, Steven F. Miller, Susan E. O'Donovan, John C. Rodrigue, and Leslie S. Rowland, eds. *Land and Labor, 1865.* Chapel Hill: University of North Carolina Press, 2008.

Hamilton, Dona C., and Charles V. Hamilton. *The Dual Agenda: Race and Social Welfare Policies of Civil Rights Organizations.* New York: Columbia University Press, 1997.

Harlan, Louis R. *Booker T. Washington: The Wizard of Tuskegee, 1901–1915.* New York: Oxford University Press, 1983.

Harris, J. William. *Deep Souths: Delta, Piedmont, and Sea Island Society in the Age of Segregation.* Baltimore, MD: Johns Hopkins University Press, 2001.

Hayden, René, Anthony E. Kaye, Kate Masur, Steven F. Miller, Susan E. O'Donovan, Leslie S. Rowland, and Stephen A. West, eds. *Land and Labor, 1866–1867.* Chapel Hill: University of North Carolina Press, 2013.

Hermann, Janet S. *The Pursuit of a Dream.* New York: Oxford University Press, 1981.

Holley, Donald. "The Negro in the New Deal Resettlement Program." *Agricultural History* 45 (1971): 179–93.

Horton, Carol A. *Race and the Making of American Liberalism.* New York: Oxford University Press, 2005.

Howe, Daniel Walker. *The Political Culture of the American Whigs.* Chicago: University of Chicago Press, 1979.

———. *What God Hath Wrought: The Transformation of America, 1815–1848.* New York: Oxford University Press, 2009.

Jackson, Thomas F. *From Civil Rights to Human Rights: Martin Luther King, Jr., and the Struggle for Economic Justice.* Philadelphia: University of Pennsylvania Press, 2007.

Jaynes, Gerald David. *Branches without Roots: Genesis of the Black Working Class in the American South, 1862–1882.* New York: Oxford University Press, 1986.

Jeffries, Hasan Kwame. *Bloody Lowndes: Civil Rights and Black Power in Alabama's Black Belt.* New York: New York University Press, 2009.

Johnson, Charles S. *Shadow of the Plantation.* Chicago: University of Chicago Press, 1966.

Johnson, Kimberly S. "Racial Orders, Congress, and the Agricultural Welfare State, 1865–1940." *Studies in American Political Development,* 25, no. 2 (October 2011): 1–19.

Jones, William P. *The March on Washington: Jobs, Freedom, and the Forgotten History of Civil Rights.* New York: Norton, 2013.

Kahrl, Andrew W. *The Black Tax: 150 Years of Theft, Exploitation, and Dispossession in America.* Chicago: University of Chicago Press, 2024.

Kelly, Robin D. G. *Hammer and Hoe: Alabama Communists during the Great Depression*. Chapel Hill: University of North Carolina Press, 1990.
King, Desmond S., and Rogers M. Smith. *Still a House Divided: Race and Politics in Obama's America*. Princeton, NJ: Princeton University Press, 2011.
King, Martin Luther Jr. *Where Do We Go from Here? Chaos or Community*. Boston: Beacon Press, 2010.
———. *Why We Can't Wait*. New York: Signet Classics, 1964.
Kirby, John B. *Black Americans in the Roosevelt Era: Liberalism and Race*. Knoxville: University of Tennessee Press, 1980.
Lanza, Michael L. *Agrarianism and Reconstruction Politics: The Southern Homestead Act*. Baton Rouge: Louisiana State University Press, 1990.
Larson, Olaf F. *Ten Years of Rural Rehabilitation in the United States*. Washington, DC: US Department of Agriculture, Bureau of Agricultural Economics, 1947.
Lincoln, Abraham. *Lincoln: Speeches and Writings, 1832–1858*. New York: Library of America, 1989.
———. *Speeches and Writings, 1859–1865*. New York: Library of America, 1989.
Magdol, Edward. *A Right to the Land: Essays on the Freedmen's Community*. Westport, CT: Greenwood Press, 1977.
Manthorne, Jason. "As You Sow: Culture, Agriculture, and the New Deal." PhD diss., University of Georgia. 2013.
———. "The View from the Cotton: Reconsidering the Southern Tenant Farmers' Union." *Agricultural History* 84, no. 1 (2010): 20–45.
Marable, Manning. "The Politics of Black Land Tenure: 1877–1915." *Agricultural History* 53, no. 1 (January 1979): 142–52.
McMillen, Neil R. *Dark Journey: Black Mississippians in the Age of Jim Crow*. Urbana: University of Illinois Press, 1989.
Mertz, Paul. *New Deal Policy and Southern Rural Poverty*. Baton Rouge: Louisiana State University Press, 1978.
Nieman, Donald G. *To Set the Law in Motion: The Freedmen's Bureau and the Legal Rights of Blacks, 1865–1868*. Millwood, NY: KTO Press, 1979.
Nugent, Ann V. "The Attitude of the New Orleans Tribune towards the Freedmen's Bureau in Louisiana:, 1865–1966." Master's thesis, Western Washington State College, 1970.
O'Donovan, Susan Eva. *Becoming Free in the Cotton South*. Cambridge, MA: Harvard University Press, 2007.
Oubre, Claude F. *Forty Acres and a Mule: The Freedmen's Bureau and Black Land Ownership*. Baton Rouge: Louisiana State University Press, 1978.
Owen, Robert Dale, James McKaye, and Samuel G. Howe. *Final Report of the American Freedmen's Commission to the Secretary of War*. New York: Office of the American Freedmen's Inquiry Commission, 1864.
———. *Preliminary Report to the Secretary of War*. New York: Office of American Freedmen's Inquiry Commission, 1863.
Payne, Charles M. *I've Got the Light of Freedom: The Organizing Tradition and the Mississippi Freedom Struggle*. Berkeley: University of California Press, 1995.

"Poverty and Urban Policy." Conference transcript of 1973 group discussion of the Kennedy administration urban poverty programs and policies, Brandeis University, June 16–17, 1973. JFKL.

Postel, Charles. *Equality: An American Dilemma, 1866–1896*. New York: Farrar, Straus, and Giroux, 2019.

Ransom, Roger L., and Richard Sutch. *One Kind of Freedom: The Economic Consequences of Freedom*. New York: Cambridge University Press, 1977.

Raper, Arthur F. *Preface to Peasantry: A Tale of Two Black Belt Counties*. Chapel Hill: University of North Carolina Press, 1936.

Reid, Debra, and Evan P. Bennett, eds. *Beyond Forty Acres and a Mule: African American Landowning Families since Reconstruction*. Gainesville: University Press of Florida, 2012.

Ripley, C. Peter. *The Black Abolitionist Papers*, vol. 5, *The United States, 1859–1865*. Chapel Hill: University of North Carolina Press, 1992.

Rolinson, Mary G. *Grassroots Garveyism: The Universal Negro Improvement Association in the Rural South, 1920–1927*. Chapel Hill: University of North Carolina Press, 2007.

Rosanvallon, Pierre. *The Society of Equals*. Cambridge, MA: Harvard University Press, 2013.

Ross, James, D. *The Rise and Fall of the Southern Tenants Farmers Union in Arkansas*. Knoxville: University of Tennessee Press, 2017.

Salamon, Lester M. "The Time Dimension in Policy Evaluation: The Case of the New Deal Land-Reform Experiments." *Public Policy* 27, no. 2 (Spring 1979): 129–83.

Sanders, Crystal R. *A Chance for Change: Head Start and Mississippi's Black Freedom Struggle*. Chapel Hill: University of North Carolina Press, 2016.

Saville, Julie. *The Work of Reconstruction: From Slave to Wage Laborer in South Carolina, 1860–1870*. New York: Cambridge University Press, 1994.

Schaar, John H. *Equality: Its Bearing on Justice and Liberty*. Washington, DC: American Political Science Association, 1978.

———. "Equality of Opportunity, and Beyond." In *Legitimacy in the Modern State*, 193–209. New Brunswick, NJ: Transaction Books, 1981.

Schmidt, James D. *Free to Work: Labor Law, Emancipation, and Reconstruction, 1815–1880*. Athens: University of Georgia Press, 1998.

Schuler, E. A. *Social Status and Farm Tenure: Attitudes and Social Conditions of Corn Belt and Cotton Belt Farmers*. Washington, DC: U.S. Department of Agriculture, Farm Security Administration, 1938.

Sen, Amartya. *The Idea of Justice*. Cambridge, MA: Harvard University Press, 2009.

Shklar, Judith N. *American Citizenship: The Quest for Inclusion*. Cambridge, MA: Harvard University Press, 1991.

———. *The Faces of Injustice*. New Haven, CT: Yale University Press, 1990.

Siegel, Reva. "Discrimination in the Eyes of the Law: How 'Color Blindness' Discourse Disrupts and Rationalizes Social Stratification." In *Prejudicial Appear-*

ances, Robert Post, K. Anthony Appiah, Judith Butler, Thomas C. Grey, and Reve B. Siegel, 99–152. Chapel Hill, NC: Duke University Press, 2001.

———. "The Racial Rhetorics of Colorblind Constitutionalism: The Case of Hopwood v. Texas." In *Race and Representation: Affirmative Action,* edited by Robert Post and Michael Rogin, 29–72. New York: Zone Books, 1998.

———. "Why Equal Protection No Longer Protects: The Evolving Forms of Status-Enforcing State Action." *Stanford Law Review* 49 (1997): 1111–48.

Sinha, Manisha. *The Slave's Cause: A History of Abolition.* New Haven, CT: Yale University Press, 2016.

Smith, Rogers M. *Civic Ideals: Conflicting Visions of Citizenship in U.S. History.* New Haven, CT: Yale University Press, 1998.

Stewart, James Brewer. "The Emergence of Racial Modernity and the Rise of the White North, 1790–1840." *Journal of the Early Republic* 18, no. 2 (Spring 1998): 181–217.

Troost, William F. "Accomplishment and Abandonment: A History of the Freedmen's Bureau Schools." Ph.D. diss., University of California, Irvine, 2007.

United States Commission on Civil Rights. *Employment.* Washington, DC: US Government Printing Office, 1961.

———. *Equal Opportunity in Farm Programs: An Appraisal of Services Rendered by Agencies of the U.S. Department of Agriculture.* Washington, DC: US Government Printing Office, 1965.

Walker, David. *Appeal to the Colored Citizens of the World.* Boston: David Walker, 1829; Journal of Pan African Studies, 2009 (ebook).

Washington, James M., ed. *A Testament of Hope: The Essential Writings of Martin Luther King, Jr.* New York: Harper and Row, 1986.

Wedeen, Lisa. "Conceptualizing Culture: Possibilities for Political Science." *American Political Science Review* 96, no. 4 (December 2002): 713–28.

Willis, John C. *Forgotten Time: The Yazoo-Mississippi Delta after the Civil War.* Charlottesville: University Press of Virginia, 2000.

Woodruff, Nan Elizabeth. *American Congo: The African American Freedom Struggle in the Delta.* Cambridge, MA: Harvard University Press, 2003.

Wright, Gavin. *Sharing the Prize: The Economics of the Civil Rights Revolution in the American South.* Cambridge, MA: Harvard University Press, 2013.

INDEX

AAA. *See* Agricultural Adjustment Administration
abolitionists: anti-abolition riots and, 45–46; Blacks' revolt against paternalism of, 47; breakup into factions, 46; evangelical roots of, 32, 40; and Free Blacks' challenges to discrimination in North, 29; on free labor, 54–55; and hardening of white identity, 41, 46; inflaming of public opinion by, 29; paternalism of, 44; post-Civil War concepts of equality, 3; as postmillennialist Calvinists, 42–43; on Reconstruction, 66; reliance on moral suasion, 43, 45, 46; roots in opposition to Indian removals, 37; second phase of, 29; size of, by 1830s, 29; on slavery and white racism as morally wrong, 42–43; supporters of gradual emancipation, 44; support for Black rehabilitation, 42, 43–44; support for racial equality, 42; white opposition to, 46
abolitionists, Black: and antiprivilege egalitarianism, 50, 234; and Black nationalism, 48; broad reform platform of, 48; call for Black self-determination, 49; challenging of white racism in North, 41; concept of equality of opportunity in, 29–30; ideology of, 48; and Liberty Party, 54; opposition to colonization, 41; and politics of respectability, 49; racial equality as goal of, 41, 48; and rehabilitation, 44–45; setting of terms for larger abolition movement, 41–42; support for land reform, 54; support for uplift, 22, 48; views on Black uplift, 51–52
Address to Free Colored Americans, 42–43
AFDC. *See* Aid to Families with Dependent Children
affirmative action, as antiprivilege egalitarianism, 17
AFIC. *See* American Freedmen's Inquiry Commission
African Americans: relentless insecurity of, 232; views on New Deal, 103–4
agencies created to ensure equal opportunity, 6–7; racial assumptions underlying practices of, 19–20; use of rehabilitation approach to equal opportunity, 19; white backlash against, 19. *See also* Farm Security Administration (FSA); Freedmen's Bureau; Office of Economic Opportunity (OEO)
Agricultural Adjustment Act of 1933, 107; crop subsidy payments to tenants and planters, by region, 133–34, 134*tab*
Agricultural Adjustment Administration (AAA) payments to take land out of production, 116–20; amount spent in South, 146; and enclosure, 117–19; landowners' refusal to pay tenants their share, 116–20, 280n44; landowners' removal of tenants from fallow land, 115, 116; STFU challenges to policies of, 116, 117–18. *See also* New Deal Southern agricultural policy

313

agricultural colleges, Black, 152, 171–72
agricultural loan program, Southern governments channeling of funds from, 191
Agricultural Stabilization and Conservation Service (ASCS), 192
Aid to Families with Dependent Children (AFDC), grants by CAA type, 215, 217*tab*
Alabama Sharecroppers Union (ASCU), 116
Alexander, William, 103–4, 110, 120, 171, 174
American Colonization Society, 28, 45
American Freedmen's Inquiry Commission (AFIC), 62–65, 74
American Missionary Association, 74
American Moral Reform Society, 45, 48
antiprivilege egalitarianism: affirmative action as, 17; associated beliefs, 33–34, 34*tab*; Black abolitionists and, 50, 234; and Black land ownership, 147; and Black power, 187, 229–30; as Blacks' version of equality of opportunity, 11, 18, 22–24; Booker Washington's rejection of, 152; as capabilities approach to justice, 17–18; change from anti- to pro-government view, 14, 16; civil rights movement and, 187; emergence of concept, 26–27; and free labor ideology, 53; in French and American Revolutions, 30; group orientation of, 18; history of, 16; Jacksonian Democrats and, 16, 18, 26–27, 30–31, 34, 34*tab*, 36–37; and land ownership by Blacks after Reconstruction, 147; land redistribution and, 80, 125; New Deal and, 102, 103, 106, 125; and overcoming racial inequality, 241–44; political program of, 16–17; as product of reform liberalism, 13–14; religious influences on, 31–32; and religious populism, 31–32, 259n22; of Roosevelt, 18; as type of equality of opportunity, 16–18; and white supremacy, 18
Anti-slavery Society, 41–42
ASCU. *See* Alabama Sharecroppers Union

Bamberg, Robert, 178–79
Bankhead, John, 120, 121, 136
Bankhead Bill of 1935, 120–21, 122, 125, 135, 140
Bankhead Bill of 1937, 125
Bankhead-Jones Act of 1937, 167
banks, Black-owned: in Black enclaves, 160; and Black land purchases, 152
Barnes, Thelma, 195, 237
Beecher, James, 78, 81
Beecher, Lyman, 31, 55
Belle Ville Farmers Association, 155, 164
Berry, Theodore, 198, 203, 211
Bethune, Mary McLeod, 104, 233
Biden administration, and compensation for Black farmers, 2
Black benevolent societies, 45
Black churches, 45
Black Codes: antienticement provisions in, 92, 93; and efforts to deny land ownership to freed persons, 82; expansion of Freedmen's Bureau's power to counteract, 68; Freedmen's Bureau's weak response to, 93–94; and labor contract system, 89; passage of, 68; purpose of, 10; Sickles' order overturning, 274n90; use to pressure reluctant workers, 92, 93
Black convention movement, 42, 47, 48
Black enclave counties: definition and locations of, 153–54; number and economic status of black-owned farms in, 153–55, 154*tab*, 159; value and size of black-owned farms in, 160–63, 161*tab*
Black enclaves: autonomy as goal of, 163, 164; as bulwark against violence, 159, 165; clustering of Black farms in, 143–44; economic status of farmers in, 160; Garveyism in, 144, 163–64; public services denied to, 159–60; separatism and mutual aid in, 100, 159, 163–65. *See also* plantation Black enclave counties
Black identity, forging of, in response to white identity politics, 41
Black independence: Black Power movement and, 188, 195; civil rights movement and, 186, 187; as collective, 52; as condition for Black success, 51; Douglass on, 57, 58, 62; land ownership as foundation of, 142–43, 145–49; War on Poverty and, 195, 296n42. *See also* Black

nationalism; economic autonomy of Blacks
Black Lives Matter, 1–2, 240
Black nationalism: Black abolitionists and, 48; Black convention movement and, 42; and Black tenant farmer unions, 117; emergence of, 46–47; Garveyism and, 164; and politics of respectability, 48–49; racial equality as goal of, 47–48; radical reform sought by, 47; and rehabilitation, 52
Black Power movement: and ambition for autonomy, 188; and antiprivilege egalitarianism, 187, 229–30; call for Black separatism and solidarity, 193–94; effort to control War on Poverty, 188, 194; rejection of biracial coalition, 187; as response to white betrayal of civil rights revolution, 187; in South, 187–88; and War on Poverty as opportunity to gain autonomy, 195; whites' perception of, 229
Black press, and abolitionism, 41
Boasberg, Tersh, 189, 201
Bond, Julian, 193
Bradford, Ernest, 221–22
Bradley, Aaron, 78, 148, 149
Brown, H. Rap, 194, 200
Brown, Julian, 134–35
Bunche, Ralph J., 101, 104, 106

Cain, Richard, 148–49
Calhoun, John C., 198
Calvinism, and rehabilitation, 31–32
Campbell, Tunis, 78, 80, 142, 149, 155, 164
Carmichael, Stokely, 187–88, 193, 295n36
Carr, Oscar, 225–26
CDGM. *See* Child Development Group of Mississippi
Channing, William Ellery, 31
Child, Lydia Maria: as abolitionist, 37; *Anti-slavery Catechism,* 55; *An Appeal in Favor of That Class of Americans Called Africans,* 42; on Black rehabilitation, 42, 55; on interracial relationships, 46; reliance on moral suasion, 45; on white racism in North, 42
Child Development Group of Mississippi (CDGM): activists' migration to CAAs after closing of, 223, 224, 225, 227–28, 230; Black efforts to boycott successor organizations, 211; Black enthusiasm for, 237, 298n68; effectiveness of, 228; and Head Start, 188, 194, 208, 215, 224, 230; and mobilization of poor Blacks, 195–96, 201, 211, 212; number of centers, 196; OEO defunding of, 199, 202, 208, 209–12, 230, 237, 299n75; OEO funding of, 196; partial restoration of funds, 212; white backlash against, 209–12
Citizens' Crusade against Poverty, 199
civil rights: Black calls for law on, 181; broad meaning of, in 1960s, 180–81
Civil Rights Act of 1866, 58, 68
Civil Rights Act of 1870, 103
Civil Rights Act of 1964, 186, 192, 199
Civil Rights Commission, 177–78
civil rights movement: and ambition for autonomy and self-determination, 187; and antiprivilege egalitarianism, 187; Black landowners as leaders in, 179; call for economic and legal action, 181–82; and ending of Jim Crow, 23–24; gains of, as threatened, 4; militancy in 1960s, 181; need for Southern Black autonomy as basis for progress, 186; stalling of, 24; white backlash against, 232; white suppression of, in Georgia, 207
Civil War. *See* occupation of South
Clay, Henry, 31, 35
Clinton, William J. "Bill," 232–33
Coahoma Opportunities, 225–26
COFO. *See* Council of Federated Organizations
colonization movement: Black opposition to, 29, 41, 45; end of, 58; founding of, 28; and Indian removal, 37; supporters of, 28, 41
color-blind society: and preservation of system of oppression through transformation, 20–21; as white view of equality, 2
Colored American (newspaper), 47, 50
Commission on Interracial Cooperation, 109–10
Committee of Freedmen on Edisto Island, 80

community action agencies (CAAs): Black activist's lack of faith in, 212; Black-controlled, characteristics of, by state, 222–28; Black-controlled, defined, 216; Black controlled, in Mississippi, 212–13; Black demands for control of, 187; Black efforts to control, 230; and Black militants, efforts to prevent involvement of, 200, 202; Black preference for single-county agencies, 202, 229, 238, 297n60; Blacks' anger at capitulations to white pressure on, 202; changes in control of, 216–18, 227; civil rights activists' objection to integration of boards, 200–201; controversy surrounding creation of, in Mississippi, 210–12; dataset sources on, 250–51; Deep South agencies, characteristics and distribution of, 203–5, 204*tab*; delays in creating, in Mississippi, 208; effectiveness of, 228–29; efforts to avoid white backlash against, 199, 296–97n52; establishment of, 193; factors in control of, 218; gerrymandering of service areas for, 203–5, 206, 207; integrated boards as requirement for, 13, 199–200; intended role of, 185; legal requirement for color-blind administration of, 199; number in rural Southern counties, 196; OEO income threshold for establishing, 202–3; OEO staff concerns about Black control of, 201; percentage of Deep South counties receiving aid, 203; single *vs.* multi-county agencies, impact of, 202–5 204*tab*, 207, 213–17, 214*tab*, 217*tab*, 247*tab*; Southern rural Black organizations courting of role in, 194, 195; stalemated (unclear racial control), 216; total expenditures in Deep South, by state, 213–15, 214*tab*; types of control, and resource allocation, 218, 219*tab*; types of control, by race, 216; white-controlled, characteristics by state, 220–21; white-controlled, defined, 216; white controlled, in Alabama, 205–6; white controlled, in Georgia, 206–7; white controlled, in Louisiana, 207–8; white-co-opted, characteristics of, by state, 221–22; white-co-opted, defined, 216; white Southerners' efforts to control, 196–98, 199–200, 201, 202; willingness of Blacks to work on integrated boards of, 201–2

Congress: debate on Freedmen's Bureau, 66, 67; debate on Reconstruction, 65, 66–67; Freedmen's Bill, 67–68

Congress of Industrial Organizations (CIO), 140

Congress of Racial Equality (CORE): and CAAs, 208; call for civil rights law, 181; in Louisiana, 208; opposition to integration, 200; and War on Poverty, 194

Constitutional guarantees of equality, failure to live up to, 2

Conway, Thomas, 69, 93

cooperative tenant farms: Belle Ville Farmers Association and, 164; STFU plan for, 123–24

CORE. *See* Congress of Racial Equality

Cornelius, J. E., 80, 81

Cornish, Samuel, 29, 47

corporations, rise of, and equality of opportunity, 240

Council of Federated Organizations (COFO), 196

critical race theory, pushback against, 2

crop-lien system of farming: benefits of avoiding, 160; as exploitative, 110; New Deal and, 130; planters' control of, 111. *See also* debt peonage

Davis, Allison, 114, 115

Davis, John P., 104, 122, 125

Davis Bend, Mississippi, experiment in farming by freed people, 75, 76, 82

debt peonage: Black entrapment in, after Reconstruction, 22–23; devolution of sharecropping into, 100, 110, 118; Roosevelt administration legal attacks on, 103; sharecropping/tenant farming and, 114–15. *See also* crop-lien system of farming

Delany, Martin: antiprivilege egalitarianism of, 51; and Black nationalism, 164; on Black need for economic opportunity, 29, 49–50; and Douglass, 52; and emigration, 52; as Freedmen's Bureau agent, 77–78, 147; on Free Soil Party, 54; on fugitive slave laws, 264n82; and Liberty Party, 54; on politics of respectability, 49; support for Black emigration, 49, 52

Democratic Review, 30

Department of Agriculture (USDA): ignoring of anti-discrimination laws, 192; New Deal plan to reorganize Southern agriculture, 167; and racist Southern agencies channeling funds from, 191; surplus commodity programs in South, 191, 294–95n28

Dittmer, John, 211, 212

Douglas, Stephen, 53–54

Douglass, Frederick: on American hypocrisy, 50; and antiprivilege egalitarianism, 50–51; on Banks's plan for freed persons' labor, 65; on Black disadvantage, 292n1; on Black independence, 57, 58, 62; on Black need for economic opportunity, 29; and Black uplift, 50–51; break with Garrison, 51; and confiscation of Southern plantations, 148; on equality of opportunity, 181; Fourth of July address, 50; on freed persons' purchase of land, 81–82; on Free Soil Party, 54; and government help for freed Blacks, 58; and politics of respectability, 49; on Reconstruction, 142, 236; "Self-Made Men," 292n1; on self-made men, 51; on white racism, 51

Du Bois, W.E.B.: on Blacks and unions, 105; on equal opportunity standard, 9; on New Deal, 105; on Reconstruction, 98; *The Souls of Black Folk,* 107; on Southern backwardness, 107; on taxation of Black land, 285n7

Duhl, Leonard J., 183–84

economic autonomy of Blacks: Black enclaves and, 163, 164; Black Power movement and, 188; as foundation of equality, in Black view, 4, 9; as goal of civil rights movement, 186, 187; land as requirement for, 9; OEO failure to address, 236; as required for equality, in Black view, 9; War on Poverty as opportunity to gain, 195, 296n42

economic justice: conflict over meaning of, 4; requirements of, as central question in periods of reform, 5

Economic Opportunity Act, 191

Economic Opportunity Council, 196

Eldridge, Stuart, 83–84, 271n59

Eliot, Thomas, 66, 67, 69

Eliot-Sumner House-Senate conference report, 67, 69

Emergency Relief Appropriation Act of 1935, 8

emigration, Black supporters of, 49, 52

equality: Founders' concept of, 26; King on white's unwillingness to pay price of, 1; lack of shared definition between Blacks and whites, 2–3; multiple contested precepts structuring, 3; post-Civil War concepts of, 3; stress on concept, in 1830s, 26; whites' version of, as color-blind society, 2, 3

equality, Blacks' view of: economic autonomy as foundation of, 4, 9; land as requirement for, 10, 17, 22–23; need for redistributive welfare state, 4, 233; rejection of color-blind society, 4

equality of opportunity: agencies created to ensure, 6–8; Black Abolitionists' concept of, 29–30; Blacks' rejection of whites' version of, 9–10, 22; Blacks' version of, as antiprivilege egalitarianism, 11, 18, 22–24; broad reforms needed to achieve in 1960s, 181; damage caused by assumption of, 239; destruction of structural advantages necessary for, 240–44; equality of results as test of, 11–12; as equivalent to liberty, for Roosevelt, 102; failure to address past inequality, 241; failure to consider power and agency, 243; futility of modern attempts at, 240; historical analysis of meaning, methodology for, 12–13; lack of consistent meaning, 11; Lincoln on, 5–6; Lyndon Johnson on, 6, 8; as matter of public policy in Reconstruction, 58; modern supporters of, 232–33; Northern Blacks' antebellum interest in, 29; as

equality of opportunity *(continued)*
originally applied only to whites, 27; origin of concept, 25–27; public support for, 240–41, 303n13; racist beliefs underlying, 13; resentment and unwarranted pride created by, 240; restoration of, as New Deal goal, 101–3; rise of corporations and, 240; Second Great Awakening and, 31–32; tensions between white and Black definitions of, 11. *See also* antiprivilege egalitarianism; rehabilitation
equality of outcome, public rejection of, 241

Farm Bureau, RA/FSA and, 126–27, 140
Farm Credit Administration (FCA): Black adviser to, 176; effect of loans on farm ownership, 176, 246*tab*; loans by, 168; RA's use of funds from, 169; resettlement programs loans, 175–76
Farmers Home Administration (FHA): and Black loss of land, 243; exclusion of Black farmers from programs, 178–79; grants, by CAA type, 215, 217*tab*; as successor to FSA, 23, 177; white Southerners' capture of, 23, 146, 191
farms, Black-owned: in Black enclaves, 100, 153–55, 154*tab*; location as factor in success of, 162. *See also* Black Enclave counties; land ownership by Blacks; Plantation Black Enclave counties; white plantation counties; white tenant counties
Farm Security Act of 1937, 8, 126–27
Farm Security Administration (FSA): and assumption of Black deficiency, 237; attacks on, 140; Black opposition to, 234–35; creation of, 103; effect on Southern Black farmers, 7, 23; effort to regulate tenancy, 238; ensuring equal opportunity as goal of, 6–7; and farmland redistribution plan, 120, 140; FHA as successor to, 23; and financial gains of tenant farmers, 135; integration of Blacks into economy as goal of, 234; and Jim Crow, 236; and land redistribution, failure to implement, 236; limited effect on Black land ownership, 146; mission of, 108; mitigation of tenant farmer exploitation, 134–35; obstacles to dramatic reforms, 140; preservation of old Southern agriculture, 139; rehabilitation policies, 234; replacement by FHA, 177; requirements for planter-tenant contracts, 134–35; and Roosevelt's agricultural revolution, 106; and rural rehabilitation, 108–9; as successor of Resettlement Administration, 7; white opposition to, 234. *See also* Resettlement Administration (RA)
Farm Security Administration/RA loans and grants to farmers: amount spent, 126, 127*tab*; categorization of borrowers, 129; clients' eligibility for crop subsidies, 133–34, 134*tab*; and control of farmers' credit, 131–32; and cultural and racial stereotypes, 128; and cutoff of planter power, 131–33; downplaying of loans to Black farmers, 137, 283n87; economic status of clients, 135–36; eligibility criteria, 135–36; factors in distribution of, 136–37, 245*tab*; financial status or recipients, by race, 138–39; and furnishing of tenants, 131–33, 135; ineffectiveness of, 110; as paternalism, 128; percentage of loans to Black *vs.* white recipients, 135, 137–39, 138*fig*, 283n88; purpose of, 106, 128; as redistributive, 132–33; by region, 126, 127*tab*; rural rehabilitation loans, 126, 169, 175–76, 246*tab,* 290n75; selection of recipients, 136, 283n87; by state and county, 126, 127*tab,* 136; supervision of borrowers' farm operations, 129–30; and supplemental/repeated loans, 131–33, 133*tab*; and sustaining of tenancy, 128–29
FHA. *See* Farmers Home Administration
Finney, Charles, 32–33
First National Black Convention, 45
Fishkin, Joseph, 241, 242, 243, 304n17, 304n19
Floyd, George, 1–2
free Blacks before Civil War: fracturing over direction of abolition movement, 47; as stateless, 27

Freedmen's Bill of 1865, 67, 68–69, 76
Freedmen's Bill of 1866, 78, 147–48
Freedmen's Bureau: abolitionist and Union Army views of free labor implemented by, 69, 74; aid to needy white Southerners, 68; arrival of Union troops in advance of, 70; and assumption of Black deficiency, 236–37; and Black Codes, weak response to, 93–94; Black opposition to, 234–35; broken promises of, 239; concern about freed persons' independent farming, 78; congressional debate on, 66, 67; efforts to regulate labor market, 238; ensuring equal opportunity as goal of, 6–7; failure to dismantle racial hierarchy, 61; and freed persons purchase of land, 81–82; free-labor ideology of, 60–61; goals of, 8; integration of Blacks into economy as goal of, 9, 234; Johnson's opposition to, 8; and land purchases by Black collectives, 150; latitude of action in 1865 statute, 68–69; legislation establishing, 67–68; limited government support of, 62, 68; as military operation, 72; mission of, 58, 60, 61–62, 66; naivety about power issues and conflicts of interest, 237–38; planters' hostility toward, 61; policy on loans to freed persons, 82; policy requiring freed people's purchase of land, 75; powers given to, 8, 68, 74; racial assumptions underlying, 21, 74–75; reauthorization and expanded powers, 68; rehabilitation policies, 21, 60–61, 68–69, 74–75, 234; schools established by, 98; self-support of free persons as policy of, 84–85; and Southern economy, necessity of jump-starting, 59, 65, 82, 83, 94; successes and failures of, 98–100; support for uplift, 22, 75; white opposition to, 234. *See also* labor contracts, Freedmen's Bureau's use of
Freedmen's Bureau, and land redistribution: Bureau's policy on, 82–83, 84; concerns about practicality of, 78–79; equality of opportunity issues in, 81; failure to implement, 236, 241; Johnson's blocking of, 76, 77; number of acres controlled, by state, 76; policy on, 75; rejection of logic underlying, 80–81; supporters within Bureau, 75, 76, 77–78
Freedmen's Bureau staff: demographics of, 62; evangelical influence on, 74; leadership of, 235; military and civilian status, by state, 72–73, 73*tab*; as mostly former military officers, 62, 70–72, 73, 73*tab*, 269n33; number from abolitionist states, 74; number of agents, 70–72; Southern sympathies of some, 73, 269n35
freedom, freed persons' conception of, 79–80
Freedom Budget, 10, 233
freed people: antiprivilege egalitarianism of, 61; conception of freedom, 79–80; demands for land as restitution for slavery, 3, 61, 142; and Freedmen's Bureau labor contracts, 61; and labor contracts, opposition to, 77, 79; preference for cooperative labor, 80; white assumptions about abilities of, 62–63, 64–65; women's withdrawal from labor, 95–96
free labor ideology: abolitionist's support for, 54–55; and antiprivilege egalitarianism, 53; and assumption of Black suitability for manual labor, 56; and Northern whites' assumptions about need for Black rehabilitation, 54, 55–56; Republican Party and, 52–53
free markets, as state-created, 90
Free Soil Party, 52, 53, 54
FSA. *See* Farm Security Administration

Garnet, Henry Highland: on American hypocrisy, 50; on Black emancipation, 27; on Black land ownership, 80; and Black nationalism, 47; call for slave insurrections, 51–52; on land reform, 54; as leader of Black militants, 47; and Liberty Party, 54; on need for Black economic opportunity, 29; and politics of respectability, 49; on Reconstruction, 59; support for Black independence, 51
Garrison, William Lloyd, 15, 29, 37, 41–43, 45, 51, 55. *See also* Anti-slavery Society; *Liberator* (periodical)

Garvey, Marcus, 117
Garveyism: in areas of high anti-Black violence, 165; in Black enclaves, 144, 163–64; platform of, 163–64, 165; as response to economic upheaval of World War I, 165
Glaude, Eddie, Jr., 48–49
Gray, L. C., 118, 121–22, 282n69
Great Society: as critical period of reform, 5; failure to address structural inequalities, 241–42; land reform as Black goal in, 10. *See also* Office of Economic Opportunity (OEO)
Greeley, Horace, 3, 55
Greenstone, J. David, 13–15, 33
Grice, Mary, 201, 206

Harrington, Michael, 184, 293n9
Harris, Abram, 104–5
Harris-Lacewell, Melissa, 253–54n6
Head Start: funding, by state, 214*tab*, 215; integrated programs, as OEO requirement, 199; in Louisiana, 208; in Mississippi, 188, 194, 208–11, 215; white avoidance of, 213, 229; white backlash against, 209–10, 221, 227–28
Heller, Tom, 201, 212, 218
Henry, Aaron, 191, 210, 225–26
Hermann, Janet, 160, 164–65
Higgs, Robert, 285n7, 288n47
Hill-Burton Hospital Construction Act of 1946, 189
Hochschild, Jennifer, 3, 253–54n6
Hoffsommer, Harold, 113, 118
home ownership, racial discrepancies in, as result of past injustice, 242
Homestead Acts: and antiprivilege egalitarianism, 16; and freed persons' purchase of land, 81; restriction to white settlers, 51, 53–54
Hopkins, Harry, 108–9, 121
Hopwood v. Texas (1996), 20–21
Houston, Charles, 167, 173–74
Howard, Oliver Otis: and Black Codes, 94; competence of, 235; evangelical influence on, 74; experiments to increase free people's employment, 94; as Freedmen's Bureau commissioner, 8; on freed persons' purchase of land, 81; and labor contracts, 77; and labor exchanges, 94; naivety about power issues and conflicts of interest, 237; policy on loans to freed persons, 82; and rehabilitation of freed persons, 60; support for land redistribution, 76, 77; and vagrancy laws, 92–93; and wages for freed people, 96–97, 275n98
Howe, Daniel, 31, 38, 39, 40
Howe, Samuel Gridley, 39–40, 62
Hudgens, Robert, 171–72, 172*tab*
Humphrey, Hubert, 182, 183

inequality of outcomes: as accepted by Whigs and Democrats, 38; contemporary public opinion on, 241
injustice: as betrayal, 239; in contracts, 86; as denial of social and economic inequality, 231, 233; of government, 30; as paternalism, 239; to slaves, 50
integration: of Blacks into economy, as Freedmen's Bureau goal, 9, 234; of Blacks into economy, as FSA goal, 234; of Blacks into economy, as OEO goal, 9, 238; of Blacks into economy, as RA goal, 9, 234; of Blacks into economy, as War on Poverty goal, 234; of CAA boards, 13, 199–202; CORE opposition to, 200; of Head Start, as OEO requirement, 199; King on, 229; as Shriver's goal, 198–99, 200, 210, 212, 215, 229, 235, 238; whites' belief in benefits of, 229

Jackson, Andrew: belief in independent farmers as basis of society everywhere, 37; and expropriation of Native American land, 36–37; FDR on, 102; Indian removal policies, 37, 261n37; policies providing support to southern slavery, 37; veto of US Bank charter, 30
Jacksonian age, evangelical culture in, 31–32
Jacksonian Democrats: and antiprivilege egalitarianism, 16, 18, 26–27, 30–31, 34, 34*tab*, 36–37; assumption of similarity in men to guarantee general equality, 36; on class conflict, 39; commitment to

democratic capitalism, 33; commitment to white America, 27; and cultural divide over liberalism, 33; independent-producers as basis of society for, 35; and partisan issues of 1830s, 25; political platform of, 25–26; producer ethic of, 35; resentment of Whig moral reforms, 33; on rights *vs.* privileges, 35–36; shared values with Whigs, 40; on society-created privileges as source of inequality, 34–35; support for equal opportunity but not equal results, 36; views on Whigs, 28–29, 30–31; on white identity, 41

Jim Crow: and Black land ownership, 143; ending of, 23–24; and exclusion of Black farmers from government programs, 177–79; New Deal policies and, 23; as obstacle to War on Poverty, 186, 188–92; welfare state supporting segregation, 190–92; white understanding of restitution for, 3

Job Corps, 183, 184

Johnson, Andrew: opposition to Freedmen's Bureau, 8; and Reconstruction, 60, 68; and return of plantations to owners, 76, 77, 235; self-support of free persons as policy of, 84

Johnson, Charles S., 110, 113, 120

Johnson, Lyndon B., 6, 8, 196

Johnson, Paul, 197, 209, 210

Joint Committee on National Recovery, 104

Julian, George, 75, 147

justice: accounting for beliefs of victims in, 239; capability approach to, 17–18. *See also* racial justice

Kennedy, John F., 182–83

King, Anna Mae, 194–95

King, C. B., 207, 222

King, Martin Luther, Jr.: on Blacks' lack of power, 188; on broad meaning of civil rights, 180–81; call for economic and legal action, 182; and civil rights activism, 186; on equality, 244; on equal opportunity standard, 9–10; on integration and social justice, 229; on lack of shared definition of equality, 2–3, 4; on legal *vs.* full equality, 232; on militancy of civil rights movement in 1960s, 181; and protests in Northern cities, 193; on War on Poverty, 184; *Where Do We Go from Here?*, 1; on white self-delusion about equality, 1, 2; on whites' unwillingness to pay price of genuine equality, 1

Ku Klux Klan: and Head Start, 209, 221, 227–28; as still active in 1960s, 186

labor contracts: Banks's plan for contraband labor and, 65, 66; Black activists' demands regarding, 59, 66; and cash tenants *vs.* share tenants *vs.* sharecroppers, 110–11; freed people's right to make, 58; Garrison on, 55; ineffectiveness of, 22; as metaphor of freedom, 75

labor contracts, Freedmen's Bureau's use of, 7, 8, 21, 60–61, 74, 75; Black Codes and, 92, 93; block on land redistribution and, 77, 78; Bureau's right to supervise, 63, 66, 87–88, 89; and concern about freed persons' independent farming, 78; debate in Congress on, 67, 68; efforts to favor freed people, 98–99; enforcement of, 89, 94–95, 97–98; and equality of opportunity, 83–85; failure to factor in planters' resistance, 99; freed people's delays in signing, 89, 91, 94; freed people's negotiation tactics, 91–92; freed people's opposition to, 77, 79, 88–89; and labor exchanges, 90, 94–95, 274n94; liens on crops to cover wages, 89, 90, 97–98, 238, 275n101; limited effectiveness of, 21, 88, 90–91, 98–99; and literacy education, 98; necessity of regulating labor markets, 90; and planters' financial strain, 89, 273n78; planters' hostility toward, 91; planters' re-creation of slavery conditions through, 86–87, 91; and planters' refusal to support family members, 91, 95, 274n95; planters' strategies for cheating freed persons, 86, 87; quit rights and, 91, 92, 93, 96, 238; as rehabilitation strategy, 83–85, 89–90; setting of wages, 90, 91, labor contracts *(continued)* 95–96, 275n98; supposed balancing of planters' and freed persons' interests, 83–84, 86; and supposed equality before the law, 85–86; types of disputes over, 87–88; vagrancy laws used to pressure reluctant workers, 92–94, 274n90; and wages adequate for family support, 91, 95–96

labor contracts, in New Deal: FSA requirements for, 134–35; tenant farmer unions demands for, 130–31, 134

labor theory of value, 35, 38

land: expropriation for Native Americans, 36–37; low price of, and economic equality, 36; reform of 1840s–50s, restriction to white settlers, 53–54

land cooperatives, Black, 81, 149–50, 164, 223; and Black preference for cooperative work, 80; cooperative tenant farms, 123–24, 164; decline in interest by 1930s, 140; government-sponsored, 76, 78, 170; proposals for, 59, 66, 80, 106, 123–24, 131

landowners, white. losses of land after World War I, 165–66

land ownership by Blacks: after Reconstruction, 146–49; all-Black towns, 160; alternative paths to, 153–59, 154*tab*; and antiprivilege egalitarianism, 147; and appeal of Garveyism, 164; areas of increase after 1880, 149–50, 152, 157; average farm size, by farm region typology, 160–63, 161*tab*; in Black enclaves, 100; and Black labor on Black farms, 144–46; Black-owned banks and, 152; and Black *vs.* white wealth accumulation, 144, 285n7; Booker Washington's plan for, 153; as bulwark against violence, 159; calls for Congress to fund, 148–49; and civil rights activism, 179; and class divide *vs.* whites, 163; collapse of cotton prices after World War I and, 145, 158, 162, 165; collapse of cotton prices in 1890s and, 156–57; decline by late 1960s, 177; dependence on white-controlled banks and infrastructure, 144; disadvantages *vs.* whites, 145; as economic stimulus, 147; and emergence of Black bourgeoisie, 145; estimated value of lost land, 243; and farming success, variation of by region, 150–51; farm value, by farm region typology, 160–63, 161*tab*; as foundation of Black independence, 142–43, 145–49; funding of, in early twentieth century, 152; and futility of rehabilitation-based ideas of equal opportunity, 24; as goal for African Americans, 141; and higher cost of plantation lands, 151; in Jim Crow era, 143, 159, 160, 164; lack of capital and, 147, 148; ladders of opportunity for, 150, 156; land purchases by freed persons, 81–82; and land redistribution, debate on, 147–48; losses of land after World War I, 165–66; meaning to African Americans, 141; and mutual aid, 159; Negro agrarianism and, 100, 149–50, 152; New Deal and, 23, 146, 166; peak in 1945, 177; and racial accumulation and disaccumulation, 243, 304n22; racist exclusion from government programs, 177–79; relations with neighboring whites and, 151–52; renting as path to, 150; as repudiation of rehabilitation, 143; in South, history of, 143–46; in South, number of owners by 1920, 23; South Carolina Land Commission experiment, 150, 155, 159; Southern Homestead Act and, 148; as symbol of equality and freedom, 179; taxation and, 285n7; taxes on white owners and, 156; variation by region, 144, 145–46; white resistance to, 157, 163; white sponsors for, 152; whites willing to sell land, in early twentieth century, 152. *See also* Black enclave counties; Black enclaves; Negro agrarianism; Plantation Black Enclave counties; white plantation counties; white tenant counties

land redistribution: and antiprivilege egalitarianism, 80; Army commanders' opposition to, 76; Army officers' views on, 80; Black support for, in 1930s, 10; concerns about practicality of, 78–79; discussion of, post-Civil War, 147–48;

Douglass's call for, 58; failure in Reconstruction, 142; freed people's belief in justice of, 75, 79–80; as key to Black success, 54, 59; as necessary for Reconstruction success, 80; and Negro agrarianism, 80; New Deal and, 23; opposition to, 149; Republican supporters of, 75; as restitution for slavery, 3, 61, 142, 243; Sherman Reserve experiment in, 76; in South Carolina, 150; supporters in Army, 75; White opposition to, 21; white supporters of, 235. *See also* Freedmen's Bureau, and land redistribution; New Deal Southern agricultural policy, land redistribution plans
Larson, Olaf, 132, 135, 283n80
LCCMHR. *See* Lowndes County Christian Movement for Human Rights
Leggett, William, 31, 34–36
Levin, Tom, 196, 200–201, 296n42
Lewis, John, 159–60
Lewis, John W., 50
liberalism: in America, multiple meanings of, 13; rehabilitation as product of, 13–14
Liberator (periodical), 29, 41, 262n51
Liberty Party, 42, 47, 52, 54, 74
liens laws: to protect wages, Freedmen's Bureau's use of, 89, 90, 97–98, 238, 275n101; whites' rewriting of, after Reconstruction, 111
Lincoln, Abraham, 5–6, 254–55n14
literacy: Black *vs.* white rates in 1930s, 128; Freedmen's Bureau's education programs and, 98
Louisiana Share Croppers Union (LSCU), 130–31, 134, 173
Lowndes County Christian Movement for Human Rights (LCCMHR), 194, 195, 198
Lowndes County Freedom Organization, 187–88
LSCU. *See* Louisiana Share Croppers Union
luck egalitarianism, 240
lynching: Black enclaves as protection from, 165; Garveyism and, 165; plantation South and, 159; threat of, in Jim Crow era, 145

Malcolm X, 9, 179, 292n88
Mann, Horace, 40
Manthorne, Jason, 139, 278n30, 282n69
MAP. *See* Mississippi Action for Progress
Marable, Manning, 145, 159
March for Jobs and Freedom, 180, 181, 182
Marshall, Thurgood, 173–74
McCall, Leslie, 12, 17
MCHR. *See* Mississippi Council on Human Relations
McKaye, James S., 62–63, 268–69n31
McKeithen, John, 197, 207–8, 227
McKinney, E. B., 117, 140
McMillen. Neil R., 288n48
McRee, James, 180, 187, 195, 212
meritocracy, as no longer valid, 240
Mesher, Shirley, 221–22
Messner, William W. F., 267–68n21
MFDP. *See* Mississippi Freedom Democratic Party
Mississippi Action for Progress (MAP), 210–11
Mississippi constitutional convention (1890), 164
Mississippi Council on Human Relations (MCHR), 189
Mississippi Freedom Democratic Party (MFDP), 208–9, 211
Mitchell, Arthur, 103–4, 124
Mitchell, H. L., 116, 140
Montgomery, Isaiah, 151–52, 160, 163, 164
Mound Bayou, Mississippi, 160, 163, 164–65

NAACP. *See* National Association for the Advancement of Colored People
Nashville Agrarians, and New Deal, 123
National Anti-slavery Standard (newspaper), 65
National Association for the Advancement of Colored People (NAACP): and civil rights activism, 230; on corrupt distribution of federal aid in Mississippi, 191; loss of Deep South chapters, 208, 298n67; on New Deal racial discrimination, 104; opposition to Bankhead Bill of 1935, 122, 125; and resettlement programs, 173; and STFU, 105, 117; and War on Poverty, 194

National Committee on Rural Social Planning, 122
National Federation of Colored Farmers (NFCF), 166, 301n95
National Negro Congress, and Bankhead Bill of 1935, 122
National Recovery Administration, 104
National Youth Administration, 103
Native Americans: and Jackson's Indian removal policies, 37; rehabilitation applied to, 44; white expropriation of land from, 36–37
Negro agrarianism: and Black land acquisition, 100, 149–50, 152; disappearance of, 179; as freed people's term for antiprivilege egalitarianism, 22–23, 143; and Garveyism, 164; influence in 1930s, 141; and land redistribution, 80
Negro world (newspaper), 163–64
Neighborhood Youth Corps, 183, 190–91
New Deal: African American views on, 103–4; antiprivilege egalitarianism of, 16, 18, 102, 103, 106; Black Cabinet, 104; Black political influence in, 104; as critical period of reform, 5; dataset sources, 249–50; and Jim Crow, 23; land reform as Black goal in, 10; programs, discrimination in, 104; and racial conflict, plan to eradicate, 103–4; and rehabilitation, 100, 108–9; restoration of equality of opportunity as goal of, 101–3; and right to unions in South, 100; social justice as goal of, 16–17; Southern Democrats and, 189–90; welfare state supporting Southern segregation as legacy of, 188–92
New Deal Southern agricultural policy: and antiprivilege egalitarianism, 125, 140; conflict between enclosure policies and tenant farmer programs, 122; and decline of tenant farmers, by race and type, 118–19, 119*ta*, 280n47; displacement of tenant farmers, 106, 107–8; effect on Southern Black farmers, 23; and entrenchment of planter-merchant class, 107, 108; goals of, 110; increase in farm ownership among Blacks and whites, 166; introduction of capital-intensive agriculture, 108; land redistribution plans, 106, 110, 119, 120–21, 125, 140, 166; opposition to, 106, 123; origins of, 109–10; and paternalistic supervision of tenant farmers, 123; racism-driven stagnation of Southern economy and, 107; and rural rehabilitation, 108–9; similarities to English enclosure act, 107–8; Southern support for, 120, 121; STFU opposition to, 123; transformation of economy, 105–6. *See also* Bankhead Bill of 1935; Farm Credit Administration (FCA); Farm Security Administration (FSA); Resettlement Administration (RA); tenant purchase (TP) program
New Orleans Tribune (newspaper), 65–66, 88, 92, 93, 150
New School Calvinism, 32–33
New York Committee on Vigilance, 47
NFCF. *See* National Federation of Colored Farmers
Nixon, Richard M., 232
North Star (newspaper), 51

occupation of South: calls for military supervision of freed people, 267–68n21; as nearly decade long, 69; number of Union troops and outposts, by state, 69–70, 71*tab*; social upheaval necessary for Black equality, 268–69n31; Union troop deployments in plantation regions, 1865–66, 70, 72*fig*
Odum, Howard, 109–10
Office of Economic Opportunity (OEO): and assumption of Black deficiency, 237; Black cooperation with, 194–95; Black opposition to, 234; broken promises of, 239; ensuring equal opportunity as goal of, 6–7; failure to ensure Black autonomy in program management, 236; faith in cooperation across races, 187; functions of, 8; funding for Northern *vs.* Southern states, 196; integration of Blacks into economy as goal of, 9, 238; investment in rural Southern counties, 195; legal requirements for division of funds, 195–96; as part of War on Pov-

erty, 7–8; per capita funding, by state, 215, 247*tab*; per capita funding, by type of agency, 215, 247*tab*; and preservation of existing power relations, 21–22; pushback from white officials, 10; racist Southern governments channeling funds from, 190–91; rehabilitation policies, 21–22, 234; statutory authority of, 8; stirring of conflict among Black activists in Mississippi, 211, 212; total expenditures in Deep South, by state, 213–15, 214*tab*; white opposition to, 234; white Southerners' efforts to control funding by, 196–97; work-training program, 183. *See also* community action agencies (CAAs)
opportunity hoarding, 242

partisan conflict of 1830s, 25
paternalism, white: Abolition movement and, 44, 47; of Black rehabilitation, 43–44; FSA/RA loans and grants and, 128; injustice inherent in, 239; planters' post-Civil War abandonment of, 91, 95, 273n83, 274n95; in Reconstruction, Black opposition to, 58
Payne, Charles, 194, 209, 212, 216
Perry County Poverty Committee, 206
Philadelphia Working Men's Party, 40
Phillips, Wendell, 65, 74
Pittsburgh Courier (newspaper), 173, 182
plantation Black enclave counties: Black-owned farms, number and economic status, 154*tab*, 155–57, 159; Black-owned farms, value and size, 160–63, 161*tab*; locations of, 155–56
planters: AAA crop subsidy payments to, by region, 133–34, 134*tab*; abandonment of paternalism after Civil War, 91, 95, 273n83, 274n95; control of tenant farmers and sharecroppers, 111; entrenchment of, by New Deal agricultural policy, 107, 108; and FSA requirements for tenant contracts, 134–35; hostility to Freedmen's Bureau, 61; hostility toward freed persons, 69; lack of incentive to replace tenant farmers and sharecroppers, 110; RA/FSA's limits to financial power over tenants, 131–33, 135; Reconstruction-era efforts to retain power over Black labor, 59–60, 69. *See also* labor contracts, Freedmen's Bureau's use of
police: and Black insecurity, 232; reforms, resistance to, 2
poverty, in Deep South states, 189
Powell, Adam Clayton Jr., 184, 293n11
preemption rights, Black settlers and, 50–51
Prial, Frank, 196, 197
procedural equality, 232
Promised Land, South Carolina, 145, 159, 164

quit rights: in labor contracts, Freedmen's Bureau and, 91, 92, 93, 96, 238; vagrancy laws used to undermine, 92–94

RA. *See* Resettlement Administration
race-neutral policies, racist beliefs underlying, 13
racial accumulation and disaccumulation, 242–43, 304n22
racial inequality: and collapse of American economic opportunity, 231; in Deep South today, 231; as distinct from individual success or failure, 231; equality before the law as inadequate remedy for, 232–33; and ongoing racial prejudice, 232; persistence of, 231; rehabilitation as inadequate solution to, 233, 234–39; as result of long history of discrimination, 4; and structural racism, 232
racial inequality, overcoming of, 240–44; antiprivilege egalitarianism and, 241–44; compensation for slavery and discrimination and, 241; destruction of structural advantages and, 240–44; difference principle and, 244; economic equality and, 232–33; equality of opportunity and, 240; multicultural democracy as goal of, 244; public investment necessary for, 243–44; redistribution of housing and land and, 243; removal of bottlenecks to economic opportunity and, 242, 243

racial justice: compensation to Blacks as necessity for, 244; equality of opportunity and, 24; market economies and, 21; scholarship on, 4–5. *See also* economic justice; equality of opportunity; racial inequality, overcoming of

racial mixing: and colonization movement, 41; white fear of, and opposition to abolition, 46

racial order, post-Jim Crow, struggle over, 188

racism: pseudoscientific basis of, 45, 51; as scavenger ideology, 258n52

Randolph, A. Philip: on Black Power movement, 187; on broad meaning of civil rights, 180, 181; and discrimination in the war industries, 140; and Freedom Budget, 233; and labor movement, 105; on need for preferential treatment for Black labor, 182

Raper, Arthur: on Black land purchases, 152; on disintegration of white plantation agriculture, 154*tab*, 158; on exclusion of Blacks from FCA funding, 176; and exploitation of tenant farmers, 278n30; paternalism toward tenant farmers, 113–14, 129; and RA's rural rehabilitation policy, 110; on resettlement programs, 176

Rawls, John, 244

Reagan, Ronald W., 232

Reconstruction: abolitionists' views on, 66; AFIC blueprint for, 62; assumptions about former slaves' abilities, 62–63, 64–65; and Banks's plan for Army-supervised Black labor, 65–66; Black views on needed policies, 58–59, 61, 66; and class conflict, 59; congressional debate on, 65, 66–67; as critical period of reform, 5; dataset sources, 248–49; debate on policies of, 62, 66; Douglass on, 142; Du Bois on, 98; end of, and Blacks' entrapment in debt peonage, 22–23; and equal opportunity as public policy, 58; and land redistribution, AFIC recognition of need for, 63–64, 235; and land redistribution, failure of, 67, 142; land redistribution as Black goal in, 10, 22–23, 235; and linking of race and rehabilitation, 99; and planters' desire to retain power over Black labor, 59–60, 69; planters' hostility toward freed Blacks, 69; proposal for labor associations, 59; and rehabilitation of freed persons, 62–63, 64, 66, 68; sharecropping's emergence following, 99–100; and Southern economy, necessity of jump-starting, 59, 65, 82, 83, 94; and tenant farmer liens on crops, 150; and white paternalism, Black opposition to, 58. *See also* Freedmen's Bureau

redistribution of income, 241

reform liberalism, and antiprivilege egalitarianism, 13–14

reform movements in America, and rehabilitation policies, 15

rehabilitation: abolitionists' support for, 42, 43–44; associated beliefs, 33–34, 34*tab*; and assumption of Black deficiency, 62–65, 236–37, 239; Black abolitionists' support for, 44–45; Black benevolent societies and, 45; Black churches and, 45; and Black nationalism, 52; Black rejection of need for, 143; Blacks' view as betrayal, 238–39; Calvinism and, 31–32; demonstrated ineffectiveness of, 24; as derived from liberal value of positive liberty, 13–14; differences from Black uplift, 49–50; emergence of concept, 26–27; federal government's use of, 19; Freedmen's Bureau and, 21, 60–61, 68–69, 74–75, 83–85, 89–90, 234; FSA and, 234; hierarchy of values inherent in, 15–16; history of, 14–15; ignoring of power struggles and conflicts of interest, 237–39; as inadequate solution to racial inequality, 233, 234–39; and inculcation of white cultural values, 44; Job Corps and, 184; Johnson's War on Poverty and, 183; Kennedy's civil rights programs and, 182; and lack of true equality of opportunity, 239; National Youth Administration and, 103; Native Americans and, 44; as necessary for Black free labor, 55–56; as necessary for equality of opportunity, in whites' view, 11; negation by white anti-Black violence, 45–46; New Deal and, 100, 108–9; paternalism and racist logic of, 43–44; preservation of existing power relations, 21; race-neutral pretense of, 21; racial assumptions underlying, 19–20, 21; Reconstruction and, 62–63, 64, 66, 68, 99; religious influences on, 31–32; as typical approach of government programs, 183; various targets of, 19–20; War on Poverty and, 183–84; Whigs and, 26–27, 31, 34, 34*tab*, 39–40

Reid, T. Roy, 131–32, 137, 174, 283n80

religious populism, and antiprivilege egalitarianism, 31–32, 259n22

reparations: current proposals for, 244; as one avenue for restitution, 241, 244; supporters of, 181

Report on the Economic Conditions of the South (National Emergency Council), 107

Republican Party: and Free labor ideology, 52–53, 55; post-Civil War concepts of equality, 3; and racial equality, 53; and white backlash against civil rights movement, 232

Resettlement Administration (RA): amount of land purchased by, 166; and assumption of Black deficiency, 237; Black opposition to, 234–35; Black tenants' dissatisfaction with, 140; conflict with New Deal enclosure policies, 122; creation of, 8, 108, 120; Farm Security Administration (FSA) as successor of, 7; funding sources for, 169; independence, 126–27; integration of Blacks into economy as goal of, 9, 234; and Jim Crow, 8, 236; leadership of, 235; leading figures in, 110; mission of, 106; as only federal program addressing tenant farmers' needs, 125; powers given to, 8; as predecessor of FSA, 7; as rehabilitation program, 103; and relief for tenant farmers displaced by Roosevelt's Southern enclosure, 121, 136, 139, 166–67; and Roosevelt's land redistribution plan, 120; staff of, 126–27; successes and limitations of, 139–41; survey of tenant farmers, 117; white opposition to, 10, 234. *See also* Farm Security Administration (FSA); Farm Security Administration/RA loans and grants to farmers

Resettlement Administration resettlement programs, 168–77; all-Black projects, 170*tab*, 171–72; amount spent on, 126; Black tenant farmers left behind by, 174; budget for, 169; creation of collective farms, 170; desirability for target locations, 168–69, 172; discrimination in loan availability, 175–76; effect on farm ownership, 176, 246*tab*; FSA loans and, 175–76; greater benefits for whites, 174–77, 175*tab*; hope for self-sufficiency of farms in, 169; and increase in farm ownership, 174–75, 175*tab*; infiltration projects, 169, 172*tab*; number of Black vs. white clients, 172*tab*, 174; number of projects, by race and type, 169, 172*tab*; projects constructing full communities, 169; projects establishing scattered individual farms, 169; RA control of farms in, 170; rehabilitation loans for residents, 169, 175–76, 290n75; selection criteria for tenants, 170–71, 289n66; trial leases offered by, 170; Tugwell's focus on, 125; undermining by New Deal enclosure, 170; white backlash, design of projects to avoid, 171–74, 290n75

responsibility, personal, as replacement for racial justice, 232–33

restitution: freed slaves' demands for land as, 3, 61, 142; public investment in Black communities as one avenue for, 244; racial justice, as point of contention, 5; reparations as one avenue for, 241, 244

riots, anti-abolition, 45–46

Robinson, Joseph, 121, 168

Roll, Jarod, 143, 165

Roosevelt, Eleanor, 103–4

Roosevelt, Franklin D.: on Andrew Jackson, 102; antiprivilege egalitarianism of, 18; groups lobbying for aid to Black tenant farmers, 166; on New Deal goals, 101–3; and *Report on the Economic Conditions of the South*, 107. *See also* New Deal

Rosanvallon, Pierre, 12, 26, 242
Roudanez, Louis C., 65–66
Rowland, Walter, 101, 116
Russell, Richard, 120, 173
Rustin, Bayard, 187, 229

Saunders, Robert, 197, 199
Saville, Julie, 80, 275n101
Saxton, Rufus, 74, 77, 78, 83, 93, 271n58
SCEF. *See* Southern Consumers Education Foundation
Schaar, John, 26–27, 239
Schuler, E. A., 114–15, 124, 131
SCLC. *See* Southern Christian Leadership Conference
Sea Islands, Black land acquisitions on, 61, 77–78, 81, 150, 155
Second Great Awakening, 31–32
Self-Help against Poverty with Everyone (SHAPE), 221–22
Sen, Amartya, 17–18, 241
SHAPE. *See* Self-Help against Poverty with Everyone
sharecropping. *See* tenant farming/sharecropping
Shaw, Nate, 114, 123–24
Sherman, William T., 67, 76
Sherman Reserve, Georgia, 76, 153–55
Shklar, Judith, 2, 85, 234, 239
Shriver, Sargent: ambivalence about community participation in OEO programs, 198; on ASCS, 192; and Black militants, efforts to prevent CAA involvement, 200, 202; and CAAs in Mississippi, 210–12; and CDGM defunding, 209–12, 237; on Coahoma Opportunities CAA, 225–26; as competent manager, 235; faith in cooperation across races, 187; on Great Society programs, 180; and hyperbole, 297n54; integration as goal of, 198–99, 200, 210, 212, 215, 229, 235, 238; naivety about power struggles and conflicts of interest, 237–38; as OEO director, 10; and rehabilitation approach to Black advancement, 183–84
similarity of persons: economic conditions encouraging belief in, 36–37; Jacksonian Democrats on, 30–31, 36; as opposite of privilege, 30–31; Rosanvallon on, 26; unraveling of, under industrial capitalism, 26; Whig's rejection of, 37; white denial of, for African Americans, 27
slavery: public opinion on legacy of, 302n1; slaves' increases in population, 37
Smith, James McCune, 59, 80
Smith-Lever Act of 1914, 146, 163
SNCC. *See* Student Non-violent Coordinating Committee
Social Darwinism, and American liberalism, 13
social equality of Blacks: exclusion from post–Civil War law, 20, 58; Lincoln's opposition to, 6
social justice: King on, 229; as New Deal goal, 16–17
Social Security Act, 102
Soil Conservation Service (SCS), exclusion of Black farmers, 177
South Carolina constitutional convention (1868), 148
South Carolina Land Commission, 150, 155, 159
Southern Christian Leadership Conference (SCLC), 194
Southern Consumers Education Foundation (SCEF), 194, 208, 223
Southern Homestead Act, 148
Southern States Convention, South Carolina, 146–47
Southern Tenant Farmers Union (STFU): appeal to Black farmers, 117; and Bankhead Bill of 1935, 121; benefits to Black farmers from, 141; as biracial union of tenant farmers, 106; Black and white tenant farmers in, 117; and Black nationalism, 117; challenges to AAA policies, 116, 117–18; critique of tenancy, 106; demands for farmer contracts, 130–31, 134; and failure of agrarian reform, 140; flight of members to CIO, 140; and Garvey Chapters, 117; goals of, 106; land reform support, 10, 23, 125, 235; on loans for farmers, 130; opposition to Bankhead Bill of 1935, 122;

opposition to New Deal agriculture plans, 123; support for cooperative land ownership by tenant farmers, 123; survey on tenant farmer preferences, 124; views on Black subordination, 105; whites' refusal to join Black union, 117

statistical models for distribution of FSA loans and grants, 247–48

Stennis, John, 202, 209, 211

Stevens, Thaddeus, 75, 147

STFU. *See* Southern Tenant Farmers Union

Stowe, Harriet Beecher, 50–51

structural racism: previous government policies' failure to address, 241–42; and racial inequality, 232; War on Poverty and, 192; white peoples' recent recognition of, 2

Student Non-violent Coordinating Committee (SNCC): and Black power movement, 187–88; call for civil rights law, 181; on need for Black separatism and solidarity, 193–94; Vine City statement, 193–94; voting right campaign in Georgia, 207; on War on Poverty, 194

Sumner, Charles: and AFIC, 62; and Eliot-Sumner conference report, 67, 69; and Freedmen's Bureau, 67; on free wage labor, 52–53; on guardianship of freed persons, 66; post-Civil War concept of equality, 3; on rehabilitation of freed persons, 66

Supreme Court: and affirmative action, 232; on racial criteria in college admissions, 2, 4

Swayne, Wager, 83, 88, 89, 94, 96, 271n58

systems of oppression, preservation through transformation, 20

Taylor, Carl, 129–30, 135

tenant farming/sharecropping: cash tenants *vs.* share tenants *vs.* sharecroppers, 110–11; and debt peonage, 114–15, 118; decline of, by race and type, under New Deal farm policy, 118–19, 119*tab*, 280n47; devolution into debt peonage, 100, 110; emergence following Reconstruction, 99–100; farmers' dissatisfaction with contracts, 131; farmers' psychological dependence, 113–14; farmers' resistance tactics, 115; landowners' exploitation and control of farmers, 114–15, 279n32; land ownership as goal for most tenant farmers, 124; New Deal debate on aid programs for, 120–24; New Deal ending of, 106, 107–8; and New Deal land redistribution, defeat of, 125; New Deal rural rehabilitation programs and, 108–9; NFCF efforts to organize, 166; paternalistic relationships in, 113–14, 115, 118; as percentage of Southern farmers, by race and state, 111–12, 112*fig*; planters' control of, 111; planters' lack of incentive to replace, 110; sharecropper unions, 116–17; on single-unit tenant farms, by state and race, 119–20, 120*tab*; as slavery in modified form, 282n69; tenant plantation farmers, by race, 112–13; tenants' annual income (1934), 133; white tenant counties, land ownership by Blacks in, 154*tab*, 158–59

tenant purchase (TP) program, 167–68; capture of program by white Southerners, 167; effect of loans on farm ownership, 246*tab*; folding into FHA, 177; renaming as Farm Ownership Program, 177; resettlement program and, 175–76

Thirteenth Amendment, 58, 59, 69, 103

Thomas, Samuel: and Freedmen's Bureau land returns, 76; on Freedmen's Bureau mission, 57; on labor contracts, 83; and labor exchanges, 94, 274n93; on land redistribution, 75; on market protections for freed people, 92; on need for Black rehabilitation, 271n59, 272n66; on oversight of Black farmers, 81, 93; on wages for freed people, 96

Tillson, Davis: belief in benefits of labor contracts, 78–79; hiring of Southerners at Freedmen's Bureau, 73, 90; on labor marker wages, 96; on need for Black rehabilitation, 78, 81, 83, 94, 271n59; on planters' obligation to care for workers, 274n95; on rehabilitation through labor contracts, 83; resistance to land

Tillson, Davis *(continued)*
    redistribution, 78; support for Black land ownership, 81; and wages for freed persons, 96–97; on work as requirement, 93
Tocqueville, Alexis de, 26, 28, 62, 259n13
TP. *See* tenant purchase (TP) program
Tugwell, Rexford: belief in national planning for agriculture, 125–26; competence of, 235; criticism of unsupervised loans to farmers, 121; focus on RA resettlement programs, 125; on purpose of RA loans, 128; and RA authority, 8; and RA/FSA clients' eligibility for crop subsidies, 133; and RA furnishing of farmers, 131–32; and RA staff, 126–27; and resettlement programs, 170, 171; and Southern opposition to RA, 10; on supervision of RA loans, 130
Tuskegee Institute: as agricultural college, 152; Black resettlement community associated with, 171–72; OEO grant to, 213; and Washington's land-buying schemes, 157; Washington's vision for, 153, 163

UNIA. *See* United Negro Improvement Association
unions: Black calls for uniting of Black and white working classes, 104–5; and Black economic opportunity, 104–5; tenant farmers and sharecroppers unions, 116–17. *See also* Alabama Sharecroppers Union (ASCU); Louisiana Share Croppers Union (LSCU); Southern Tenant Farmers Union (STFU)
United Negro Improvement Association (UNIA), 117, 163, 165
unjust privileges, removal to achieve racial equality, 242. *See also* antiprivilege egalitarianism
uplift, for African Americans: abolitionists' support for, 48; American political culture and, 19; Black abolitionists' support for, 22, 48; and Black agency in overcoming discrimination, 48–49; Black views on, 51–52; differences from Whig rehabilitation, 49–50; Freedmen's Bureau and, 22; leaders of antebellum movement, 48; Northern Black reformers' support for, 44–45; as strategy to counter white prejudice, 44–45, 48–49; twenty-first-century controversy over, 48; two different versions of, 48–49; white violence in response to, 45–46. *See also* rehabilitation
Urban League, 104, 105
urban working-class revolts in Northern cities, and white fear, 187
US Bank charter, 30
USDA, 121

vagrancy laws, use to pressure reluctant workers, 92–94, 274n90
Van Buren, Martin, 37
Vance, Rupert, 101, 108, 109–10, 151
voting: in Jim Crow era, 164; as protection for Black rights, 149; replacement of property with skin color as qualification for, 28
Voting Rights Act of 1965, 186

wage labor, opponents of, 53
Wagner, Robert, 103
Wagner Act, 102, 103
Walker, David, 29, 41, 43, 46–47, 49–50
Wallace, George, 196–97, 205–6, 229
Wallace, Henry, 16–17, 118, 121, 133
War on Poverty: anti-discrimination laws' limited effectiveness in South, 192; Black empowerment necessary for success of, 229; Black opposition to, 234–35; Black Power movement's effort to control, 188; Black skepticism about, 194; civil rights leaders' disappointment with, 184; community action program, controversy surrounding, 184–86; failure to include public jobs programs, 184, 293n12; integration of Blacks into economy as goal of, 234; Jim Crow as obstacle to, 186, 188–92; Kennedy's policies as template for, 182–83; leadership of, 235; limited success of, 228–29, 232; naivety about power struggles and conflicts of interest, 237–38; as obstacle to white Southerners' efforts to drive

out Blacks, 196; OEO as part of, 7–8; as opportunity for autonomy, in Blacks' view, 195, 296n42; plans for large redistribution of funds to poor neighborhoods, 185; as program for Blacks run by whites, 213; rehabilitation focus of, 183–84, 186–87; Southern Blacks' interest in, 194; and South's racist culture, 24; and structural racism, 192; white opposition to, 186, 234; white Southerners' blocking of educational and job training programs for Blacks, 198; white Southerners' efforts to control funding from, 196–98. *See also* community action agencies (CAAs)

Washington, Booker T., 152–53, 157, 163

wealth accumulation racial discrepancies, as result of past injustice, 242

Webster, Danial, 38, 240

Weekly Advocate (newspaper), 48

welfare reform of 1996, racist beliefs underlying, 13

welfare state, redistributive, Black calls for, 4, 233

Whigs: belief in values as foundation of free market society, 40; commitment to democratic capitalism, 33; commitment to white America, 27; and cultural divide over liberalism, 33; evangelical social reformers and, 32–33; on fluidity of wealth and status in US, 38–39, 240; on free labor, 55; meritocratic ideology of, 37–38, 240; on necessity of discipline and self-control, 39; and partisan issues of 1830s, 25; political platform of, 25–26, 31; and Protestant ethic, 39; and rehabilitation, 26–27, 31, 34, 34*tab*, 39–40; shared values with Democrats, 40; support for economic diversity, 38; support for remedial institutions, 39–40; views on Jacksonian Democrats, 29; on white identity, 41

Whipper, William, 45, 48

White, Marion Overton, 223

White, Walter, 122, 135, 167

whitecappers, 151–52, 165

white identity: abolition movement and, 41, 46; Jacksonian Democrats on, 41; Whigs on, 41

white nationalism, as view of most whites in 1830s, 27–28

whiteness, overwhelming influence of, 295n36

white plantation counties: Black cash renters in, 158; definition and location of, 157; number and economic status of Black-owned farms in, 154*tab*, 157–58, 159; value and size of Black-owned farms in, 160–63, 161*tab*

white supremacy: Black recognition as root of inequality, 4; as consensus white view by 1840, 41

white tenant counties: definition and location of, 154*tab*, 158–59; number and economic status of Black farms in, 154*tab*, 158–59; value and size of black-owned farms in, 160–63, 161*tab*

Williams, Aubrey, 106, 121

Wilson, Henry, 147, 149

Works Progress Administration (WPA), 100, 169

World War I: and collapse of cotton prices, 145, 158, 162, 165; farmers' loss of lands after, 165–66; Garveyism as response to economic upheaval of, 165

World War II: and cotton prices, 177; and land ownership by Blacks, 177

WPA. *See* Works Progress Administration

Wyat, Bayley, 79, 80

Yeatman, James, 64–65, 96

Young, Whitney Jr., 181, 182

Youth Opportunities Bill, 183

Founded in 1893,
UNIVERSITY OF CALIFORNIA PRESS
publishes bold, progressive books and journals
on topics in the arts, humanities, social sciences,
and natural sciences—with a focus on social
justice issues—that inspire thought and action
among readers worldwide.

The UC PRESS FOUNDATION
raises funds to uphold the press's vital role
as an independent, nonprofit publisher, and
receives philanthropic support from a wide
range of individuals and institutions—and from
committed readers like you. To learn more, visit
ucpress.edu/supportus.

www.ingramcontent.com/pod-product-compliance
Lightning Source LLC
Chambersburg PA
CBHW021336230426
43666CB00006B/309